Marketing Destinations and Venues for Conferences, Conventions and Business Events

Marketing Destinations and Venues for Conferences, Conventions and Business Events introduces students and practitioners to key areas of marketing and promotion that are essential if destinations and venues are to compete successfully in the rapidly expanding global business events sector. It achieves this by looking at issues surrounding business event marketing, strategic planning, destination and venue selling strategies and future challenges.

The second edition has also been updated to include:

- New content on the use of technology by destination marketing organisations and venues. This includes social media, partnership issues, the impact of changes in the global economy and developments in the demand for, and supply of, sustainable meetings locations.
- New case studies on growth areas and emerging markets, for example, Asia, Central and Eastern Europe, Russia and Africa, but also including new material on mature markets for business events.
- A genuinely international focus in terms of content and examples.
- New review and discussion questions and, where appropriate, learning outcomes.
- A new online resource package for students and lecturers, including web and video links, PowerPoint slides and project questions.

Accessible, global and informative, this is essential reading for all current and future business event and conference managers.

Tony Rogers has been involved with the conference and business events sector for over 25 years. He has managed several industry trade associations and now runs his own consultancy specialising in research and destination/venue marketing. He served as a Visiting Fellow at Leeds Beckett University for eight years.

Rob Davidson's main area of expertise is business events. He has written extensively on that theme. As Managing Director of MICE Knowledge, a consultancy specialising in business events research, education and training, he has undertaken research projects for many major organisations including Reed Travel Exhibitions.

Books in the Events Management Series
Edited by Glenn Bowdin, Leeds Beckett University, UK
Donald Getz, University of Calgary, Canada
Conrad Lashley, Nottingham Trent University, UK

1. Management of Event Operations
   *Julia Tum, Philippa Norton and
   J. Nevan Wright*

2. Innovative Marketing Communications:
   Strategies for the Event Industry
   Guy Masterman and Emma H. Wood

3. Events Design and Experience
   Graham Berridge

4. Marketing Destinations and Venues
   for Conferences, Conventions
   and Business Events
   Tony Rogers and Rob Davidson

5. Human Resource Management for Events:
   Managing the Event Workforce
   Lynn Van der Wagen

6. Risk Management for Meetings and Events
   Julia Rutherford Silvers

7. Conferences and Conventions:
   A Global Industry, 2nd Edition
   Tony Rogers

8. Events Feasibility and Development
   William O'Toole

9. Events Management, 3rd Edition
   *Glenn Bowdin, Johnny Allen, William O'Toole,
   Rob Harris and Ian McDonnell*

10. Event Studies, 2nd Edition
    Donald Getz

11. Conferences and Conventions: A Global
    Industry, 3rd Edition
    Tony Rogers

12. Human Resource Management for
    Events: Managing the Event Workforce,
    2nd Edition
    Lynn Van der Wagen and Lauren White

13. Event Studies, 3rd Edition
    Donald Getz and Stephen Page

14. Marketing Destinations and Venues for
    Conferences, Conventions and Business
    Events, 2nd Edition
    Tony Rogers and Rob Davidson

Marketing Destinations and Venues for Conferences, Conventions and Business Events

Second edition

Tony Rogers and Rob Davidson

Routledge
Taylor & Francis Group

LONDON AND NEW YORK

Second edition published 2016
by Routledge
2 Park Square, Milton Park, Abingdon, Oxon OX14 4RN

and by Routledge
711 Third Avenue, New York, NY 10017

Routledge is an imprint of the Taylor & Francis Group, an informa business

© 2016 Tony Rogers and Rob Davidson

First edition published by Butterworth-Heinemann 2006

British Library Cataloguing in Publication Data
A catalogue record for this book is available from the British Library

Library of Congress Cataloging in Publication Data
A catalog record for this book has been requested

ISBN: 978-1-138-85214-3 (hbk)
ISBN: 978-1-138-85215-0 (pbk)
ISBN: 978-1-315-72371-6 (ebk)

Typeset in Iowan Old Style
by Sunrise Setting Ltd, Paignton, UK
Printed and bound in Great Britain by
Ashford Colour Press Ltd, Gosport, Hampshire

- Marketing research   39
- Market segmentation and positioning   41
- Objectives and action plans   47
- The marketing mix   48
- The monitoring and evaluation of marketing plans   49
  - Case Study 2.1   The Rwanda Convention Bureau   50
  - Case Study 2.2   The Seoul MICE Master Plan   56
  - Case Study 2.3   Tourisme Montréal's meetings and conventions blog   59
  - Case Study 2.4   The Detroit Metro Convention and Visitors Bureau Tourism
                      and Convention Sales Marketing Plan   61
- Summary   64
- Review and discussion questions   64
- References   65

3.   **Non-personal marketing communications for destinations and venues: principles and practice**   66

- Chapter overview   66
- Learning outcomes   67
- Introduction   67
- Publications   68
- Websites   72
- Public relations   75
- Advertising   85
  - Case Study 3.1   The Convention Centre Dublin's website   90
  - Case Study 3.2   Kyoto Convention Bureau's PR campaign based on
                      pre-conference meditation   93
  - Case Study 3.3   Atlanta Convention Bureau's I AM ATL campaign   94
- Summary   96
- Review and discussion questions   96
- Bibliography   96

4.   **Personal marketing communications for destinations and venues: principles and practice**   98

- Chapter overview   98
- Learning outcomes   99
- Introduction   99
- Direct marketing   99
- The social media   102
- Exhibiting at trade shows   109
- Workshops and roadshows   115
- Familiarisation trips and educationals   117
- Conference ambassador programmes   121
  - Case Study 4.1   ibtm china and the Hosted Buyer Programme   126
  - Case Study 4.2   The Adelaide Convention Centre workshops   127
  - Case Study 4.3   ibtm world Best Stand Award winners   129
  - Case Study 4.4   The Tourist Office of Spain (Turespaña) virtual trade show
                      for the MICE market   131

Contents

List of figures   *x*
List of tables   *xii*
Foreword   *xiii*
Series Preface   *xiv*
Preface   *xv*

1. The role of marketing and selling in the convention and business events sector   **1**

- Chapter overview   1
- Learning outcomes   2
- Introduction   2
- The history of the conference industry   2
- The products of the conference market   4
- The stakeholders operating in the conference market   4
- The role of marketing in the conference industry   16
- The impacts of the conference industry   21
  - Case Study 1.1   The Gold Coast Convention and Exhibition Centre winning the AMSA National Convention   27
  - Case Study 1.2   The economic significance of meetings for the US economy   28
  - Case Study 1.3   Marketing Moscow as a conference destination   31
- Summary   35
- Review and discussion questions   35
- Bibliography   35

2. Marketing planning for destinations and venues   **37**

- Chapter overview   37
- Learning outcomes   38
- Introduction   38
- The purpose and components of marketing plans   39

- Marketing research   39
- Market segmentation and positioning   41
- Objectives and action plans   47
- The marketing mix   48
- The monitoring and evaluation of marketing plans   49
  - Case Study 2.1   The Rwanda Convention Bureau   50
  - Case Study 2.2   The Seoul MICE Master Plan   56
  - Case Study 2.3   Tourisme Montréal's meetings and conventions blog   59
  - Case Study 2.4   The Detroit Metro Convention and Visitors Bureau Tourism
                     and Convention Sales Marketing Plan   61
- Summary   64
- Review and discussion questions   64
- References   65

3. Non-personal marketing communications for destinations and venues:
    principles and practice   66

- Chapter overview   66
- Learning outcomes   67
- Introduction   67
- Publications   68
- Websites   72
- Public relations   75
- Advertising   85
  - Case Study 3.1   The Convention Centre Dublin's website   90
  - Case Study 3.2   Kyoto Convention Bureau's PR campaign based on
                     pre-conference meditation   93
  - Case Study 3.3   Atlanta Convention Bureau's I AM ATL campaign   94
- Summary   96
- Review and discussion questions   96
- Bibliography   96

4. Personal marketing communications for destinations and venues:
    principles and practice   98

- Chapter overview   98
- Learning outcomes   99
- Introduction   99
- Direct marketing   99
- The social media   102
- Exhibiting at trade shows   109
- Workshops and roadshows   115
- Familiarisation trips and educationals   117
- Conference ambassador programmes   121
  - Case Study 4.1   ibtm china and the Hosted Buyer Programme   126
  - Case Study 4.2   The Adelaide Convention Centre workshops   127
  - Case Study 4.3   ibtm world Best Stand Award winners   129
  - Case Study 4.4   The Tourist Office of Spain (Turespaña) virtual trade show
                     for the MICE market   131

- Case Study 4.5   The York Minster to Westminster showcase   132
- Case Study 4.6   The Great Ambassador Networking Group (GANG)   136
- Summary   138
- Review and discussion questions   139
- Bibliography   139

5. **Sales strategies for destinations and venues: principles and practice**   **141**

- Chapter overview   141
- Learning outcomes   142
- Introduction   142
- The role of personal selling   143
- Sales promotion and yield management   147
- The management of a sales force   150
- Destination and venue selling strategies   153
- Handling enquiries effectively   159
- Submitting professional bids and sales proposals   164
- Managing site inspections and showrounds   167
- Negotiation skills   169
- Business retention   171
- Maximising impact through business extenders   173
  - Case Study 5.1   Singapore's Sales Incentives and Event Support Programmes   174
  - Case Study 5.2   Using a venue representation service: Paje and The Jockey Club   177
  - Case Study 5.3   UniSpace Sunderland's value-added packages   178
  - Case Study 5.4   The International Convention Centre, Birmingham and
                      The Convention Centre Dublin's 'Host Service' and
                      'Client Associate/Client Host' programmes   181
  - Case Study 5.5   Vancouver Convention Centre's Service Excellence Programme   182
- Summary   184
- Review and discussion questions   185
- References   185

6. **The marketing environment for destination marketing organisations**   **186**

- Chapter overview   186
- Learning outcomes   187
- Introduction   187
- Destination marketing or destination management?   188
- Content marketing for destinations   188
- Alignment of destination event bidding strategies with local economy strengths   191
- Subvention and bid support practices   193
- Product development and investment   197
- Sustainability and the environment for destinations   198
  - Case Study 6.1   Destination management in Glasgow, Scotland   201
  - Case Study 6.2   *Germany. Expertise.* brochure   201
  - Case Study 6.3   Sustainable destination best practice: Tampere, Finland   204
- Summary   209
- Review and discussion questions   209
- Bibliography   210

7.   The marketing environment for venues   211

   • Chapter overview   211
   • Learning outcomes   212
   • Introduction   212
   • The growing diversity of conference venues   212
   • Brand alignment as a criterion in selecting venues   214
   • Venues' growing use of technology   215
   • Changing trends in venue design   216
   • Venues and sustainability   219
   • Venue security and accessibility   220
      - Case Study 7.1   SnapEvent   223
      - Case Study 7.2   A technologically advanced venue: the Cleveland
                         Convention Center (USA)   224
      - Case Study 7.3   Venue marketing using social media: Central Hall
                         Westminster, London, UK   225
      - Case Study 7.4   Iconic architecture: the ICE, Kraków, Poland   227
      - Case Study 7.5   A sustainable venue: the Hong Kong Convention
                         and Exhibition Centre   229
   • Summary   230
   • Review and discussion questions   231
   • Bibliography   231

8.   Building effective marketing partnerships   232

   • Chapter overview   232
   • Learning outcomes   233
   • Introduction   233
   • The role of destination marketing organisations in forging partnerships at
     the destination level   233
   • Membership recruitment and retention for destination marketing organisations 237
   • Working with marketing consortia   238
   • Maximising the benefits of membership of trade associations   240
   • Harnessing political support through effective lobbying   242
      - Case Study 8.1   The Three City Alliance   245
      - Case Study 8.2   The IMEX Politicians Forum   247
   • Summary   249
   • Review and discussion questions   250
   • Bibliography   250

9.   Current initiatives in the conferences, conventions and
     business events sector   251

   • Chapter overview   251
   • Learning outcomes   252
   • Introduction   252
   • Research and market intelligence   252
   • Terminology   263
   • Education and training   264

- Quality standards   272
  - Case study 9.1   ICCA's Big Data search tool   276
  - Case Study 9.2   IACC/NYU Certificate in International Conference
                     Centre Management   282
  - Case Study 9.3   Accredited in Meetings quality assurance scheme   283
- Summary   288
- Review and discussion questions   288
- Bibliography   288

Appendix A: The main meetings industry exhibitions   290
Index   292

Figures

1.1   Edinburgh International Conference Centre's sustainability initiatives   25
1.2   Moscow Convention Bureau's stand at a major trade exhibition   32
2.1   Dongdaemun Design Plaza   57
3.1   Digital venue finding services used by UK event organisers   74
3.2   The value of press coverage generated   80
3.3   Average value per month   80
3.4   The position of all press coverage generated   81
3.5   Coverage achieved by type of publication   81
3.6   Guidelines for effective news releases   82
3.7   Personalisation benefits in PR campaigns in standard deviations   84
3.8   First name personalisation in selected industries in standard deviations   84
3.9   Norway's Naked Man advertisement   89
3.10 Previous website access platforms for The CCD website   90
3.11 Pages from The CCD's new website   92
3.12 One of the four images used in the I AM ATL advertising campaign   95
4.1   Twitter's potential for communicating destination and venue marketing messages   107
4.2   Go, inspect, enjoy!   119
4.3   Guidelines for successful destination familiarisation visits   121
4.4   Delegates at the Adelaide Convention Centre Cookery School workshop   128
4.5   The Switzerland Convention and Incentive Bureau winning stand
      team at the ibtm world exhibition 2014   130
4.6   Logo designed for the York Minster to Westminster showcase   134
5.1   Ratings of venue service factors by association buyers   172
5.2   Ratings of venue service factors by corporate buyers   172
5.3   Client hosts and limousine in Dublin   182
6.1   Forms of subvention available   194
6.2   Page illustration from the *Germany. Expertise.* brochure   203
6.3   Tampere and its two lakes   205
6.4   Tampere Hall   208
9.1   Number of international meetings 1963–2012 in the ICCA database
      (5-year aggregated data)   258
9.2   Delegates at the 2013 ECM Summer School in Istanbul   269

9.3   BestCities Client Survey 2014 (a)   275
9.4   BestCities Client Survey 2014 (b)   275
9.5   Big Data's online dashboard   277
9.6   Big Data illustrated search   277
9.7   Search results   278
9.8   Relevant web page where relevant academic is to be found   279
9.9   A view of the information in Microsoft Academic Search   279
9.10   Graphic representation of links between authors   280
9.11   The relative academic strength of local universities   281
9.12   AIM logo   284

Tables

1.1	Characteristics of the different market segments	8
1.2	Number of meetings and participants by meeting type	30
1.3	Number of meetings and participants by host type	30
1.4	Direct spending by commodity	30
1.5	Total economic contributions	31
2.1	Destination brand hierarchy	46
2.2	The marketing mix	49
2.3	Key performance indicators	50
2.4	Rwanda Convention Bureau events calendar	54
2.5	Steps in Rwanda Convention Bureau's strengthening phase	55
3.1	Characteristics of advertising and public relations as promotional tools	87
4.1	Principal market sectors targeted by conference ambassador programmes	123
5.1	The selling orientation–customer orientation scale	145
5.2	Sales promotion techniques	149
5.3	Structures commonly used in organising sales staff	152
5.4	Key factors influencing venue and destination selection	155
5.5	Enquiry support information (Who? What? Where? Why? When? How?)	162
5.6	Singapore MICE Advantage Programme eligibility criteria and benefits	176
7.1	Advantages and disadvantages of using unusual venues	213
7.2	Tools and resources used by meeting planners to compare and select hotel venues	215
7.3	Potential threats faced by venues	221
9.1	Number of meetings per country 2004–13	255
9.2	Number of meetings per city 2004–13	256
9.3	Number of meetings per region 2004–13	257
9.4	Top international meeting countries 2013	258
9.5	Top international meeting cities 2013	258

Foreword

As a global trade association representing conference centres in 21 countries, the International Association of Conference Centres (IACC) is delighted to introduce you to this second edition of *Marketing Destinations and Venues for Conferences, Conventions and Business Events*.

It is clear to us that this book makes an extremely valuable contribution to educating and inspiring the next generation of destination and venue marketing professionals, which aligns it perfectly with one element of IACC's own mission, to provide learning opportunities relevant to the small and medium sized meetings industry. With its well-chosen content, covering all of the major contemporary themes and developments in venue and destination marketing and its rich variety of case studies demonstrating innovative practices from all over the world, this book considerably advances our knowledge of the key elements of the conference industry. *Marketing Destinations and Venues for Conferences, Conventions and Business Events* not only covers the most up-to-date trends in our industry, but also captures the exciting and dynamic nature of the role of marketing a city or a conference centre in today's fast-moving global meetings market.

This book is a welcome addition to the growing body of literature now focusing on our industry and we highly recommend it to you.

Mark Cooper
CEO – International Association of Conference Centres

Series Preface

The events industry, which includes festivals, meetings, conferences, exhibitions, incentives, sports and a range of other events, is rapidly developing and it makes a significant contribution to business and leisure-related tourism. With increased regulation and the growth of government and corporate involvement in events, the environment has become much more complex. Event managers are now required to identify and service a wide range of stakeholders and to balance their needs and objectives. Though mainly operating at national levels, there has been significant growth of academic provision to meet the needs of events and related industries and the organisations that comprise them. The English-speaking nations, together with key northern European countries, have developed programmes of study leading to the award of diploma, undergraduate and postgraduate awards. These courses focus on providing education and training for future event professionals, and cover areas such as event planning and management, marketing, finance, human resource management and operations. Modules in events management are also included in many tourism, leisure, recreation and hospitality qualifications in universities and colleges.

The rapid growth of such courses has meant that there is a vast gap in the available literature on this topic for lecturers, students and professionals alike. To this end, the *Routledge Events Management Series* has been created to meet these needs to create a planned and targeted set of publications in this area.

Aimed at academic and management development in events management and related studies, the *Events Management Series*:

- provides a portfolio of titles which match management development needs through various stages;
- prioritises publication of texts where there are current gaps in the market or where current provision is unsatisfactory;
- develops a portfolio of both practical and stimulating texts;
- provides a basis for theoretical and research underpinning for programmes of study;
- is recognised as being of consistent high quality; and
- will quickly become the series of first choice for both authors and users.

Preface

The first edition of this book, published in 2006, was designed to fill what we perceived as a substantial gap in the provision of literature on the marketing and selling of destinations and venues targeting the conference, convention and business events market. Ten years later, there have still not been many complementary texts published on this fascinating industry. The industry itself has evolved in a number of important areas, for example, in the applications of social media and content marketing and in the emergence of new and highly competitive destinations and venues. In addition, there have been advances in technology and the opportunities for virtual and hybrid events, as well as the myriad of ways in which destinations are focussing their strategic marketing to align their event bidding activity with the core strengths of their local economies, inward investment policies and specialist areas of research.

This new edition, therefore, highlights examples of best practice from around the world in these new areas of marketing while, at the same time, updating and refreshing the material and case studies that expound the more traditional approaches to destination and venue sales and marketing that still have a crucial role to play in this dynamic industry. Our aim once again has been to draw on our complementary interests and backgrounds to produce a book that combines an academic, theoretical approach to the subject with practical, 'hands-on' advice for those with current or future responsibility for marketing destinations and venues in the conference and business events sector.

We have designed the book primarily as an advanced text for undergraduate and postgraduate students. However, we anticipate that, because of the shortage of material of this kind, it will also be of considerable interest to practitioners (e.g. destination marketers operating at a city, regional or national level and sales and marketing staff working in conference and event venues).

Both of us have been privileged to work in the conference, convention and business events industry for many years. In that period, there have been huge changes and developments in the competition for a share of the vast and lucrative market that conferences and conventions represent in a multitude of other ways. Yet, the essence remains the same: the aim of the industry is to bring people together to communicate by sharing information and ideas, to motivate and inspire, to launch new products and disseminate the latest research and to negotiate in order to reach a consensus on the different challenges facing our world. We hope very much that, in this book, we have captured something of the creativity and dynamism of our industry and of the many talented people around the world who are leading this sector and taking it to new heights of professionalism.

The book would not have been possible without the unstinting help, advice and provision of data and material that we have received from literally hundreds of colleagues across the globe. One of the delights of the conference industry, for us both, is this very openness and willingness to share that we have experienced at every turn. To everyone who has helped in any way, we owe an enormous debt of gratitude.

Each chapter follows a similar pattern, with a learning outcome, introduction, main theme, summary, review and discussion questions and references. Extended case studies are presented at the end of most chapters. These give more in-depth illustrations and elaboration of the points made in the body of the chapter.

Rob Davidson and Tony Rogers
May 2015

Chapter **1**

The role of marketing and selling in the convention and business events sector

Chapter overview

This chapter examines how the conference industry has developed through time, reviews the principal stakeholders in the industry and analyses its impacts. It also analyses how marketing as a process has evolved and it highlights the distinguishing characteristics of venue and destination marketing.

This chapter covers:

- The history of the conference industry
- The products of the conference market
- The stakeholders operating in the conference market
- The role of marketing in the conference industry
- The impacts of the conference industry

It includes case studies on:

- The Gold Coast Convention and Exhibition Centre winning the AMSA National Convention
- The economic significance of meetings for the US economy
- Marketing Moscow as a conference destination

On completion of this chapter, you should be able to:

- explain why and how the conference industry developed in the way it did;
- discuss the different products and segments of demand in the conference industry;
- understand the roles of the main stakeholders;
- define how the role of marketing has evolved and its current use by the conference industry; and
- recognise the main positive and negative impacts that are created by the conference sector.

Introduction

> *The human desire to meet and exchange ideas, the basis of conventions and meetings, is as old as humankind.*
>
> *(Weber and Chon, 2002)*

In 1895, Milton Carmichael, a journalist, suggested in *The Detroit Journal* that local business leaders should join forces to promote that city as a meetings destination, as well as to represent Detroit and its many hotels in bidding to win conference business. Two weeks later, the 'Detroit Convention and Businessmen's League' was formed, the world's first conference destination and conference venue marketing organisation. We will never know how Milton Carmichael would have reacted to the fact that, from those humble beginnings in Detroit, during the following century, conference destination and conference venue marketing would have evolved into a major profession, using modern, sophisticated techniques to support and sustain today's multi-billion dollar, global conference industry. Just to take the example of his own country, we can only imagine his response to the knowledge that the US meetings industry contributed over US$115 billion to the GDP in 2012, while directly and indirectly supporting jobs for more than 1.7 million Americans (CIC, 2014).

The history of the conference industry

Although humankind has gathered together to confersince the dawn of civilisation – witnessed still today by the remains of ancient meeting sites such as the Agora of Athens and the Roman Forum – it was not until the latter half of the twentieth century that a specific 'conference industry' was recognised as a commercial activity in its own right. The rapid expansion of this industry on a global scale since the 1950s has been instrumental in creating the need for professionalism in all sectors of the conference industry.

Throughout the centuries, organised gatherings were always an essential element of cultural, political and commercial life; indeed, they contributed significantly to the progress made by society as a whole. The vast majority of such meetings were held locally, in locations such as public spaces, theatres and hotels. Later, the first purpose-built meetings venues, such as the elegant eighteenth century assembly rooms built in many British cities, were constructed.

Spiller (2002) notes that during the late nineteenth and early twentieth centuries, as industrialisation spread through the US and Western Europe, the need for meetings between business leaders and other entrepreneurs materialised, adding to the numbers of those already meeting to discuss and exchange ideas on political, religious, literary, recreational and other varied topics. Advances in transport technology during the same period, combined with rising levels of prosperity for the growing middle-classes and the rise of the professions in many countries, created a more mobile society in which travel to conferences became an increasingly frequent activity for many.

Ford and Peeper (2007) note that the willingness of the American business community to meet and share their knowledge with each other (compared with the European tradition of secrecy in the business and industrial world that prevailed at that time) was a key factor in the growth of demand for conferences in the nineteenth century:

> *Adding to this willingness to share knowledge was the vast amount of knowledge that needed to be shared. The industrial revolution spawned a tremendous growth in the amount of information and that, in conjunction with the huge size of the United States and the growth of its railroad, helped create a meetings and convention business. The growth of the railroad also made it increasingly easy for people to meet with others and to learn about new things. The growth of cities, the creation of larger manufacturing organisations, and the pace of change all made it desirable and necessary for people to get together to talk about new manufacturing techniques, see new products, and talk about the challenges of managing a large number of people spread out over a wide geographic area.*

Lawson (2000:11) suggests several factors that facilitated the rapid expansion of the conference industry in the second half of the twentieth century:

- Expansion of government and quasi-government organisations, together with an increasing need for meetings between the public and private sectors;
- Growth of multinational corporations and pan-national agencies, necessitating more interdepartmental and inter-regional meetings;
- Developments in association interests, co-operatives, professional groups and pressure groups;
- Changes in sales techniques, use of product launches and sales promotion meetings;
- The need to update information and methods through in-company management training, continuing professional development and attendance at ad hoc or scheduled meetings;
- Development of subject specialisation – conferences enabled experts to pass on information.

In response to this surge in demand for conferences, many cities throughout the industrialised world – and, later, in the developing world – recognising the potential economic benefits of hosting conferences, began equipping themselves with purpose-built conference centres, many of them capable of hosting the type of national and international events that can attract several thousand delegates. The idea of a purpose-built conference centre venue was first conceived in the US in the early 1960s and the trend then spread to Europe. For example, London's Wembley Conference Centre, opened in 1977, was one of the first purpose-built conference centres in the UK and in its opening year saw more than 350,000 people visiting 300 events. Growing recognition of the need to market these facilities professionally, as well as the cities in which they were located, was an instrumental element in creating the professions of the destination and venue marketer.

Now, over 100 years after the creation of the world's first convention bureau in Detroit, the conference industry is firmly established and it has become truly international in its scope. In the twenty-first century, this industry comprises the many millions of men and women worldwide who organise business events; who provide the services and facilities that conferences require, from interpretation to audio-visual equipment; and who are responsible for the marketing of venues and destinations. In today's world, it is universally accepted that the most competitive conference destinations and venues are those that understand – and use – the full potential that marketing, as a management function, can offer their organisations.

This book focuses on the marketing techniques used, and the more general knowledge required, by those whose role it is to attract conferences and other business events to the venues and destinations that employ them. These men and women play a vital part in satisfying the apparently unstoppable demand for conferences and other types of business events throughout the modern world. The future expansion of this industry is assured: humans are, above all, a gregarious animal, and there can be no doubt that the need to gather regularly with others who share a common interest is one of the most human of all activities.

The products of the conference market

In marketing, as in many younger disciplines – including the conference industry itself – terms and terminology are still somewhat loose and imprecise.

Even the word 'market' is open to different interpretations. In marketing terms, the term 'market' is used as a collective noun for those customers who buy, or who are likely to buy, a particular product or service. Hence, for example, we can speak about 'the Japanese market for digital cameras', 'the over-60s market for private health care' or 'the trade association market for conferences'. However, in the field of economics, the definition of 'market' is much broader, and it is understood to mean a system encompassing the principal buyers and suppliers of a particular product or service, as well as those intermediaries whose role it is to facilitate the purchasing process between buyers and suppliers.

The stakeholders in the conference market will now be reviewed, but first, it is important to clarify what is meant by the term 'product' as it is applied in this market.

The product

For the sake of convenience, the word 'product' will be used in this book to indicate the services and facilities that are being marketed by a venue or by a destination. In the case of a conference centre, for example, the product is the amalgam of all of the tangible and intangible elements that contribute towards the success of conferences held there: the centre's location, its meetings rooms, audio-visual facilities, catering services, the staff's professional knowledge and their courtesy towards delegates and so on.

In the case of a destination, the composite product that is marketed is also composed of tangible and intangible elements. The tangibles comprise not only all of the meetings venues and accommodation services operating within the destination but also the other suppliers of services, such as local restaurants, shops, tourist attractions and transport operators, all of which may be used by conference organisers and delegates during the event. Important intangibles, for a destination, include its image and its atmosphere, both of which can be crucial factors in determining whether a particular destination is selected for a conference.

Clearly, one key difference between the venue product and the destination product is that those responsible for marketing venues (the marketing department of a particular conference hotel or conference centre, for example) have a high degree of direct control over the product: its quality, appearance, price, etc. But those whose role it is to market destinations (such as convention bureaux) can only indirectly influence most elements of the composite product – which, in reality, is not owned by them.

The stakeholders operating in the conference market

Buyers

For the sake of convenience, the words 'buy' and 'buyers' will be used in this book, even though, in most cases, the product is not actually being bought but 'rented'.

No market can function without buyers, and in the conference market, two separate levels of buyers may be considered. Taken together, both levels constitute the demand side of the conference market. The successful marketing of destinations and venues requires a sound understanding of the specific needs of each of the following types of buyer.

Initiators of demand

In the business events market, demand comes from all of the companies and organisations that make use of conference destinations and venues in return for a fee. These are the originators of the demand for conferences, and they generally initiate such events because they identify some type of need that is best satisfied by bringing together their members, employees or associates in one place for a fixed period. These buyers represent the primary source of demand for the various conference facilities and services offered by suppliers in the conference market.

Therefore, each type of buyer may be regarded as a market segment in its own right, with its particular characteristics and needs. The principal segments are as follows:

CORPORATE BUYERS

The corporate market is generally agreed to be the largest single market segment – estimated by Lawson (2000) to constitute over 65 per cent of all meetings. Companies have a number of important motives for holding meetings and they represent a key market segment. It is certainly the case, however, that, in many instances, company meetings are held on the company's own premises and are organised in-house, bringing no business to the conference industry. However, companies generally understand that there are many compelling reasons for holding off-site meetings. These include:

- lack of capacity in their own premises (few company offices have facilities for large meetings);
- the need to remove staff from their normal working environment (to free them from day-to-day work-related distractions; to help them think more creatively in a different setting);
- the wish to reward or motivate staff by holding the event in an attractive location, usually with leisure elements added;
- the need to keep proceedings confidential, when, for example, sensitive topics are under discussion;
- the need to meet in a 'neutral' place when, for example, two companies are negotiating the terms of a merger between them.

The purpose of most corporations is to make money. They hold meetings to increase their chances of becoming more profitable. Training executives and motivating sales people, for example, are carried out by companies because they believe that these activities will help make the company more profitable. Corporate meetings events may take a number of different forms, including the following:

- *Annual general meetings*: publicly owned companies invite their shareholders (or stockholders) to these events, at which the company's annual results are presented. Shareholders are usually asked to approve the dividend and to endorse a certain number of resolutions, which will determine the company's activities in the year ahead. Every shareholder who wants to take part in the decision-making process of his company has the right to attend such meetings and vote personally.
- *Sales meetings*: a sales meeting is a regular forum used by management to impart information, enthusiasm and team spirit to those selling their products and services 'out in the field'. Sales figures for a particular period are generally reviewed and the achievements of particularly high-performing sales staff may be recognised and praised. The type of information imparted generally concerns the company's

market share, competitors' activities or new legislation that affects the selling process. Such meetings also give those present the opportunity to share their experiences, positive and negative, of selling.

- *Staff training*: it is generally recognised that in order to keep their skills and knowledge up to date, company management and staff must regularly attend training sessions in subjects such as information technology, customer relations skills and employment law.
- *Retreats*: a term used, until very recently, only to signify a temporary withdrawal from everyday life for the purpose of religious contemplation and meditation, the word 'retreat' is now commonplace in corporate language, meaning an off-site, usually residential, board meeting. But such events differ from regular off-site board meetings in a number of ways:
  - Instead of moving quickly through a rigid agenda, board members spend their time at a retreat concentrating on specific long-term issues or thinking more broadly and strategically about the future of their organisation;
  - Retreats are designed to spark creative thought;
  - They can be an effective way to teach new members of staff about a company's goals and values;
  - Retreats often make use of outdoor settings that are conducive to walking and reflecting on what is happening during the event;
  - Time for social interaction is a vital element: teambuilding activities are often requested. Outside facilitators may be used.
- *Product launches*: introducing a new product or service to the market is an important stage in the marketing process. A new car, new perfume, new type of medical insurance . . . whatever the product, companies often use an off-site event as a way of presenting it and explaining its properties and features to those who will be selling it, who may be buying it, and to journalists in the specialist press who may write about it for their readers. Such events are usually short but with high production levels, using special effects, sound and vision, in order to make the maximum impact on the audience.
- *Incentive trips*: it is widely recognised that an extremely effective way of motivating and rewarding staff is by offering them the opportunity to participate in an incentive trip as the prize for exceptional achievement in their work. This exceptional achievement may take the form, for example, of selling more of the company's products than other colleagues sell over a particular period. These trips, often held in exotic and lavish locations, may look like holidays, and indeed, they are designed to be highly enjoyable and memorable; but they are firmly considered business events, as they are, in essence, a management tool, designed to elicit higher levels of performance from the company's employees. When incentive trips are combined with a work element – usually one or more meetings that take place during the trip – such events may be known as 'concentives' – a combination of a conference and an incentive trip.

ASSOCIATION BUYERS

Among the largest and (in terms of days) longest conferences held throughout the world are association events. The countless different associations, clubs, federations and societies that exist throughout the world constitute another major segment of demand for conference services. These are generally non-profit groups, whose members affiliate with one another because they share a common profession, trade or interest in a specific cause. Many of these organisations are trade associations and professional bodies and one of their functions is to help their members maintain the professionalism of the business or industry to which they belong. Associations may draw their members locally, regionally, nationally or internationally – and the geographical spread of their membership will determine the location of their meetings events. For example, the Australian Institute of Architects will almost always hold their annual conference in an

Australian city; the European Association of Archaeologists chooses a city in a European country as the destination for its events and so on.

Almost all associations hold regular meetings for a variety of purposes, but most often these are training/information sessions or the association's annual conference, offering members the opportunity to meet for one or more days in order to discuss matters of importance to their profession or their common cause. Meetings by trade unions would be included in this sector of demand.

One major difference between the corporate market and the association market for conferences is that while, for corporate buyers, conferences and meetings represent a *cost* to the company, for associations, conferences normally represent a *source* of funds. This is because – again, in contrast to the corporate meetings market – they charge their members for attending events. Many associations depend on the income from their annual conference to pay for many of the ongoing costs of running the association – staff salaries, headquarters rental and so on.

GOVERNMENT AND PUBLIC SECTOR BUYERS

Governments at all levels, from local municipalities to the international, intergovernmental scale, as well as public sector bodies, such as those administering national health services, are also an important source of demand for conference facilities and services. The development of effective policies through consultation and negotiation is a key function of political activity and conferences are often used as the medium for carrying out this process, bringing together the various stakeholders concerned by the proposed legislation.

At the international level, many of these conferences are high-profile events, with extensive media coverage – such as the conference of European Union finance ministers held in Riga in 2015; or the conferences sponsored by the United Nations and its agencies – for example, the United Nations Climate Change Conference that was held in Paris in the same year.

Once created, governments' new policies and measures have to be launched, in much the same way that companies' new products and services are launched and this generates regular business for the conference industry. One of the objectives of such events is to attract the attention of the media in order to publicise new government measures. A typical example of such an event was the launch, in June 2014, of the Maltese government's National Literacy Strategy for All in Malta and Gozo (2014 to 2019), which was held in Sliema.

SMERF BUYERS

SMERF is the name given to conferences held in the social, military, educational, religious and fraternal sectors. Often included in the association sector, as not-for-profit organisations, SMERF buyers are increasingly recognised (in North America in particular) as a discrete category of demand for conferences. SMERF meetings occur when groups travel and congregate for a wide range of purposes such as reuniting, discussing issues that are pertinent to their lives or simply to share their common memories, experiences or faith. A sample of SMERF events from around the world demonstrates that there is practically no limit to their variety in terms of size and themes:

- The annual conference of the Lesbian and Gay Christian Movement in the UK
- The Vietnam Veterans 25th Reunion, in Boonville, New York
- The Ninth Annual Teaching and Learning in Higher Education Conference at The University of KwaZulu-Natal in Durban, South Africa
- The 2015 National Barbie Doll Collectors' Convention, with over 1,000 collectors, in Arlington, Virginia

Table 1.1 Characteristics of the different market segments

Corporate	Association	Government	SMERF
The process of deciding where to hold events is relatively straightforward but the actual corporate meeting buyer may be difficult to identify within the initiator's organisation: secretaries, personal assistants, marketing executives, directors of training and many others may book corporate meetings	The process of choosing a destination can be prolonged. A committee is usually involved in the choosing of the destination and the organisers may be volunteers from the association's membership	Considerable variety in terms of length of event and budgets available However, budgets are usually scrutinised, as public money is being used	Price-sensitive, regarding accommodation rates and venue rates but more recession-proof than corporate meetings Held by organisations that are run by volunteers – so the task of identifying them can be challenging
Attendance is usually required of company employees	Attendance is voluntary The annual convention may be booked many years in advance	High security measures are indispensable: these meetings are occasionally accompanied by demonstrations and disruption	Frequently held over weekends and in off-peak periods
Lead times can be short	Events typically last 2–4 days		Often held in second-tier cities, using simple accommodation and facilities
Events typically last 1–2 days			
A higher budget per delegate	A lower budget per delegate, as for some attendees, price is a sensitive issue and they may be paying their own costs		Attended by delegates who bring their partners/families and are likely to extend their trips for leisure purposes
Venues used: hotels, management training centres, unusual venues	Venues used: conference centres, civic and academic venues		
Delegates' partners are rarely invited, except in the case of incentive trips	Delegates' partners frequently attend		

Given the very different characteristics of each of the conference market segments discussed above, it is clear that each segment requires different marketing strategies to be adopted by the destinations and venues targeting its buyers. The key characteristics of these four principal market segments are summarised in Table 1.1.

Delegates

With the notable exception of those attending corporate meetings – for whom participation is usually obligatory – most people who are invited to conferences have the choice between attending and not attending. Delegates, also known as attendees and participants, are therefore the ultimate buyers, or end-consumers, of the conference product. Without the continuing participation of delegates who invest their time – and usually money – in attending business events, the conference industry cannot function, and it is therefore vital that their experience of the conference product is a satisfactory one.

Nevertheless, the experience of the individual delegate is largely dependent on choices made by other stakeholders, notably the initiators of the event and the intermediaries working on their behalf. These are the stakeholders who select the destination, the venue, the accommodation and other key features of the conference product such as the speakers and the social programme. Thus, delegates' level of satisfaction with a conference usually depends on their response to a range of individual elements that have been 'packaged' together for their purchase, over which they have little control.

Most conference buyers and organisers understand the importance of satisfying the end-consumers of their events, and for that reason, post-conference evaluation, using questionnaires for example, is frequently carried out. It is clear that delegates' needs from conferences must be satisfied if they are to return to such events in the future and recommend others to attend. This is an ongoing challenge for the entire conference industry.

The suppliers

Supply-side stakeholders are those who supply the facilities and services that are essential to the effective operation of a conference. For each type of supplier specified below, the marketing function that is the theme of this book is vital to business success. Responsibility for the marketing of these suppliers' services and facilities can range from one person who undertakes all of the marketing tasks discussed in this book, to an entire department managed by a marketing director with specialised staff such as market researchers and sales staff working for him/her.

VENUES

Conferences, at the most basic level, require closed space in which the event can be accommodated, with seats for the delegates. The meeting venues that provide these facilities are, therefore, an essential element of the conference market. Several types of venue have already been mentioned in this chapter. Purpose-built conference centres are the most visible type of venues; indeed, most conferences of several hundred or more delegates are held in such locations. But, in fact, by far the vast majority of meetings are still held in seminar rooms and conference facilities within hotels. These can range from small independent establishments with a single 'function room' to a venue such as the MGM Grand in Las Vegas, one of that city's largest convention hotels, with almost 56,000 square metres of meeting space.

Nevertheless, meetings are increasingly hosted by a growing variety of venues, for many of which conferences are a secondary, but important, commercial activity. These include universities, museums, theatres and cruise ships, as well as a whole range of tourist attractions such as theme parks that offer their facilities for meetings of all kinds. The term 'unusual venues' or 'unique venues' is often used to describe some of the more exotic locations used for meetings events. Product launches and team-building events, in particular, often seek unusual venues to make the events more attractive and memorable. The theme of unusual venues will be explored further in chapter 7.

In the supply of venues, public sector, as well as private sector, operators are important stakeholders. National, state-level, regional and municipal governments throughout the world are involved in the construction and operation of conference facilities; while the private sector, from family-run hotels to multinationals such as Starwood, Marriott International and Accor, are also key players in the provision of meeting space.

Case Study 1.1 gives details of how a major venue worked with a national association to make their events a success.

ACCOMMODATION PROVIDERS

Residential conferences and other business events lasting more than one day require some form of accommodation for delegates, speakers and organisers. In many cases, the venue itself may be equipped to provide the accommodation – as in the case of hotels, residential conference centres, universities and cruise ships, for example.

Nevertheless, when venues without on-site accommodation are used, the conference organiser must ensure that an adequate supply of lodging – of the appropriate standard – is available. In that case, organisers may identify a single 'conference hotel' or may provide delegates with a list of local, approved, hotels or guesthouses that they recommend.

Organisers may book a 'block' of rooms with a particular hotel or hotels, to ensure that their delegates can be accommodated close to the actual conference. By undertaking to fill a substantial number of a hotel's rooms for several days, conference organisers may avail themselves of a valuable negotiating tool with which to discuss rates for the rooms themselves as well as the conference facilities if they are within the same hotel. However, this approach assumes that:

- the organiser is able to determine with some degree of accuracy how many rooms will be required; and
- that delegates will book the rooms in the hotel in which the 'block' has been reserved.

Organisers, as well as providers of accommodation, are becoming increasingly aware that these two conditions cannot be taken for granted. In particular, the phenomenon of delegates 'booking outside the block' (often using the internet to find lower hotel rates) is becoming more prevalent.

OTHER SUPPLIERS

A number of other support services can contribute to the successful operation of conferences.

- *Transport providers* are responsible for carrying delegates to and from the conference destination and for providing transport services within the destination, notably through venue/hotel transfers. Rail and coach operators, taxis and limousines can all be involved in providing these services. For international events, air travel is usually the chosen means of transport for most delegates and this can raise the challenge, for both organisers and transporters, of dealing with groups: determining in advance the size of the group booking and the names of the passengers. For corporate groups, and in particular for incentive events, this information may not become available until the last minute; therefore, some degree of flexibility is required of the airline.
- *Caterers* play a key role in providing delegates with food and beverages (F&B). The quality (and quantity) of F&B is often a talking point between delegates during and after the event and it can be a serious source of delegate dissatisfaction if it falls short of expectations. Conference meals and refreshment breaks serve a number of purposes beyond sustaining the delegates. For example, they provide opportunities for them to network with each other in a more relaxed setting; or they supply the context for entertainment or the participation of celebrity speakers, as in the case of the conference gala dinner, for example.
- *Technical services*, such as the provision of audio-visual equipment and expertise, are vital to the effective functioning of most modern conferences. Sophisticated sound, lighting and data-projection equipment are essential elements of meetings events and these must either be supplied by the venue or, increasingly, leased by the organisers from specialist conference equipment hire companies. Indeed,

the pace of technological progress is now so rapid that many venues and organisers prefer to hire technical equipment and support to ensure that they always have access to the most up-to-date material. Conference video production companies may also be used to film the proceedings, then edit and produce a video that can be used as an effective way of extending the scope of the event.

The range of other suppliers is extensive and they can include the conference interpreters who make international conferences accessible to all, regardless of their linguistic abilities; the companies that hire out interpreting booths; and the florists who decorate the conference stage, the gala dinner tables and who provide 'thank you' bouquets for VIPs and guest speakers.

The intermediaries

While some buyers in the conference market deal directly with suppliers – for example, when a secretary calls a hotel to book a seminar room for a 1-day meeting for managers in his or her company – a vast proportion of all conferences take place with the involvement of some form of intermediary or intermediaries. These are the stakeholders who form a link between buyers and suppliers and the effective functioning of the conference market depends on their specialist skills and knowledge.

It is useful to consider intermediaries in two categories: those working on behalf of suppliers and those working for buyers.

INTERMEDIARIES WORKING ON BEHALF OF SUPPLIERS

DESTINATION MARKETING ORGANISATION

Although most suppliers of facilities and services for the conference industry actively market themselves directly to potential buyers – either individually or through marketing consortia – they usually understand that the success of their own business is partly dependent on the image and reputation of the destination in which it operates. In a highly competitive world, with no shortage of suitable locations for meetings, it is generally easier to attract conferences and other business events to a well-marketed destination. The responsibility for promoting individual destinations to potential buyers lies with the destination marketing organisation (DMO). In general, DMOs are responsible for attracting not only business events but also leisure tourists to the destination; hence the term 'tourism' or 'visitor' is often included in the names of individual DMOs.

There are two categories of DMOs:

- National tourism authorities (NTAs) or national tourism organisations (NTOs), responsible for the management and marketing of tourism at a national level;
- Regional, provincial or state DMOs (regional tourism organisations), responsible for the management and/or marketing of tourism in a sub-national geographic region, sometimes but not always an administrative or local government region such as a county, state or province;
- Local DMOs, responsible for the management and/or marketing of tourism based on a smaller geographic area or city/town.

The structure of these bodies changes from country to country and from city to city. In particular, how DMOs relate to governments and where they find their funding varies considerably. A worldwide survey of DMOs (WTO, 2004) found that, for the 250 DMOs surveyed:

> The simplest status models exist at the NTO and NTA level, where 88 per cent of organisations are either a department of National Government or an agency accountable to National Government. Four of the NTOs/NTAs are not for profit public–private partnerships.

At a regional level the status of organisations is more varied. The majority are accountable to regional, provincial or state government, either as an agency or in fewer cases (18 per cent) as a department of local government. However, 37 per cent have private sector involvement (21 per cent within a public–private partnership), which is much higher at the regional level than the national level.

39 per cent of City DMOs have regional, provincial or local government accountability, and the percentage of public private partnerships (33 per cent) and profit driven companies (6 per cent) is highest in this sector.

At all levels, DMOs may have a dual function of promoting their destinations to the leisure market, as well as the market for conferences and other business events. The proportion of DMO resources devoted to attracting conferences varies considerably from destination to destination. However, it is extremely rare for any destination to ignore the conference market entirely.

CONVENTION AND VISITOR BUREAUX

The use of the term convention and visitor bureau that originated in the US is becoming widespread throughout the world. In this book, the term convention bureau will be used to refer to the type of not-for-profit DMO that is responsible for stimulating interest in the destination in order to persuade conference buyers to hold their events there or so that intermediaries may recommend them to their clients. (It should be pointed out, however, that those responsible for marketing their destination for conferences might work in tandem with colleagues whose role it is to market the same destination for leisure: holidays, short-breaks, day-trips, etc.)

As well as being responsible for promoting a favourable image of their destination, convention bureaux can also serve as the focus to unify the marketing efforts of the various suppliers operating in the area they cover and provide a shared sense of direction and unity to a range of individual marketing programmes.

With this function in mind, Harrill (2005) describes convention bureaux as 'umbrella' marketing or promotional agencies, under which the extensive collection of businesses that promote their own products and services stand. This is often referred to as a 'consolidated' approach to marketing, the principle being that consolidated efforts provide greater strength and unity, and therefore, enhanced results; while segmented, fragmented individual marketing programmes yield less impact and success.

The convention bureau function may be undertaken at any geographic level: a country, a region within a country, or a specific town or city. Although, as stated at the beginning of this chapter, the original convention bureau concept was created in the US at the end of the nineteenth century, the first *national* convention bureaux were founded in Europe many years later. The German Convention Bureau, established in 1973, and the Finland Convention Bureau, established in 1974, were, for example, two of the first national convention bureaux in Europe.

However, the vast majority of convention bureaux operate at the level of the individual city or town, operating on behalf of the suppliers there, to attract conference business to that locality, thus filling the meetings venues, bringing guests to hotels and attracting clients for local restaurants, shops and the other service providers as discussed. It is difficult to estimate the number of convention bureaux that exist around the world and their numbers are constantly growing as more and more cities market themselves as new conference destinations. Nevertheless, the trade body Destination Marketing Association International (previously known as the International Association of Convention and Visitor Bureaus) counts over 600 convention bureaux in its membership.

In some cases, individual convention bureaux join forces to market a particular region that is considered to be recognised as a single destination for the purposes of tourism and conferences. For example, the

French Riviera Convention Bureau operates in concert with the convention bureaux of Antibes, Cannes and Nice to promote the Côte d'Azur as a conference destination.

Whatever the geographical scope of their responsibilities, convention bureaux derive their funding from one or more of the following sources:

- Public sector contributions
- Hotel (or lodging) transient occupancy taxes
- Membership fees (from members, such as venues, accommodation providers, transport operators, etc.)
- Contributions from members participating in joint commercial activities
- Commission charged to venue members in return for conference business placed with them, by the convention bureau

Most published surveys on this issue primarily reflect the situation of convention bureaux in the US, which has by far the largest numbers of bureaux in the world. However, there are fundamental differences between continents with regard to how convention bureau operations are financed.

A major source of public income of US-based bureaux is the local transient or hotel tax, a tax that can be imposed upon visitors, with one of its specific objectives being to fund the marketing of the destination to future visitors. Revenue collected in this way either can go directly to the relevant convention bureau or can be included in the funding provided to it by local authorities. Such hotel room taxes have been used since the 1950s to fund both the construction and operation of conference centres as well as the activities of convention bureaux in the US. Nevertheless, while the concept of being funded by a tax dedicated to subsidise the costs of destination marketing may be attractive for some convention bureaux, the system of collecting transient occupancy taxes has not been widely adopted outside the US. Koutoulas (2005) suggests one reason for this:

> *It would be quite challenging to persuade local tourism associations that the benefits of introducing a tax outweigh any costs such as becoming a more expensive destination. Even when stakeholders and legislators agree with its introduction, it would be challenging to establish an efficient mechanism to enforce and collect the tax.*

Alternative sources of funding are therefore likely to remain imperative for most convention bureaux operating outside the US for the foreseeable future. In most countries, convention bureau funding comes from two sources: public sector grants and fees paid by the members of the convention bureau, who are generally the local suppliers who stand to gain in terms of additional business if the destination successfully markets itself as a city or region or country in which to hold conferences.

The marketing activities on which convention bureaux spend their funding are a major theme of this book, and will be considered in detail in later chapters. Case Study 1.3 describes the role of Moscow Convention Bureau in developing and marketing Moscow as an international business events destination.

Intermediaries working on behalf of buyers

Although some associations and companies use their own staff to organise events, most buyers rely on the expertise and experience of a range of professional intermediaries. This is particularly the case when the conference to be organised is large and complex, when it demands technical knowledge or when it is to be held far from the company's or association's office – notably overseas.

In these cases, buyers are able to draw on the specialist skills and knowledge of a range of intermediaries who can work on their behalf.

PROFESSIONAL CONFERENCE ORGANISERS (INDEPENDENT MEETINGS PLANNERS)

Professional conference organisers (PCOs) are independent, specialist meetings planners who work on a consultancy basis, being temporarily hired by associations and companies to organise a specific event or series of events. In return for a fee, they can offer a very comprehensive range of services, including:

- Venue selection, booking and liaison
- Reservation and management of delegate accommodation
- Event marketing, including the design of conference programmes and promotional materials, PR and media co-ordination, presentations to organising committees and boards
- Conference programme planning, speaker selection and briefing
- Provision of an administrative secretariat, handling delegate registrations, recruitment and briefing of conference staff
- Co-ordinating of delegates' travel arrangements
- Organising of exhibitions, including sales and marketing functions
- Advising on and co-ordinating audio-visual services and the production of the event, including the provision of multilingual interpretation and translation services
- Arranging social events, tour programmes and technical visits
- Arranging security cover and advising on health and safety issues
- Recording, transcribing and producing the proceedings of meetings for publication, arranging poster sessions and processing of abstracts
- Preparation of budgets, managing event income and expenditure, generating revenue through sponsorship, exhibitions and satellite meetings and handling VAT and insurance issues
- Preparation of contracts with venues and other suppliers

VENUE-FINDING SERVICES

Venue finding services (VFSs) provide a much more limited service, yet one that is extremely valuable to any buyer who simply needs a few suggestions of where their meeting could be held. They therefore save their clients (most commonly, companies) time and effort by finding them suitable venues for their events.

VFSs generally begin by asking their client specific questions regarding their requirements for the event being planned: its date, location, the number of delegates and the budget for the event. Using these criteria, they then undertake the necessary research and produce a number of options for venues that match the client's requirements, with a quotation for each venue short-listed by them. The VFS may also set up viewing appointments for their client.

In the majority of cases, this service is provided free to the client, as the VFS gets commission from the venue booked. Many conference venues obtain the major part of their business from VFSs, who can be a valuable source of repeat business for them.

ASSOCIATION MANAGEMENT COMPANIES

Managing an association involves undertaking a considerable number of tasks: attracting and maintaining members, financial management, public relations and lobbying on behalf of members, providing educational and training opportunities for members, publishing the annual report and association newsletters and organising the annual conference and other events. Traditionally, these activities have been undertaken either by volunteer staff drawn from the association's own membership or, in the case of large associations, by full-time salaried staff based in the headquarters.

However, in the past few decades, many associations have become aware of the limitations of both of these models of association management. On the one hand, volunteer staff appear to have less and less time available for association-related duties – and, in some cases, lack the experience and expertise necessary to carry out their tasks effectively. On the other hand, maintaining full-time staff and office facilities can result in a major investment in overheads for associations.

As the need for the effective and professional management of associations has become increasingly recognised, many of them have turned to an alternative concept of association management – the association management company (AMC).

AMCs are staffed by skilled professionals whose goal is to provide management expertise and specialised administrative services to trade associations and professional societies in an efficient, cost-effective manner. Based on the concept of shared resources, an AMC provides volunteer organisations with the expertise they need when they need it, usually assigning specific executives and administrators to conduct each client association's day-to-day operations.

An AMC also provides a centralised office that serves as the client association's headquarters, and the overhead costs for these offices are shared by all of the AMC's client associations and societies. In this way, the need for individual associations to make major capital investment in their own headquarters and staff is obviated.

One of the key tasks undertaken by AMCs on behalf of their association clients is the organising of their annual conference and other events for members. In this respect, AMCs must employ staff with similar professional expertise and experience to that required by PCOs. AMCs are growing in importance as intermediaries between association buyers of conferences and those who supply the facilities and services that make such events possible.

DESTINATION MANAGEMENT COMPANIES

Most organisers of large, complex conferences could not do their jobs effectively without using the skills and knowledge of a destination management company (DMC) – particularly when the conference is being held in a destination with which the organiser is unfamiliar. Previously known as 'ground handlers', these intermediaries are agencies that are based at the destination in which the event takes place and their valuable contribution to the conference planning process derives from their in-depth knowledge of the destination. This includes their familiarity with local suppliers of conference-related services and their knowledge of the language and customs of the destination. DMCs act, therefore, on behalf of PCOs, AMCs and other event planners as the prime local contractor for logistical services. They can provide assistance with a range of services, including:

- Creative proposals for special events within the meeting
- Transport services, such as transfers
- Pre- and post-conference tours
- VIP amenities and transportation
- Shuttle services
- Entertainment, such as after-dinner speakers
- On-site registration services
- Accommodation services

CONFERENCE PRODUCTION COMPANIES

For high-profile events requiring advanced specialist technical facilities and expertise, conference organisers often use the services of conference production companies. These intermediaries are valuable sources of the ideas and inspiration necessary to making meetings memorable – particularly important in the case of events such as product launches, awards ceremonies and other motivational events.

Creativity and technical knowledge are the qualities that production companies bring to the successful operation of conferences and they are particularly valued for the services they provide in the fields of:

- Design and printing of conference materials
- Lighting, sound, projection, stage/set design
- Script writing
- Video production
- Web-streaming

It is clear from the above list of professionals that an extensive range of specialist knowledge and skills is available to buyers of conference and other business events. However, three important points arise from the preceding description of intermediaries' roles:

- The roles of these intermediaries are not always as clearly delineated and differentiated as outlined above. As will be seen in chapter 9, terminology in the conference sector is still far from precise and this is nowhere more evident than in the titles used by the different intermediaries. In most countries, all of these professions are unregulated, and this fact, coupled with a lack of clear demarcations for most conference-related occupations, means that there is considerable scope for agencies to offer their clients services that go beyond their specific field of expertise. For example, many venue finding services, destination management companies and conference production companies will readily offer to undertake tasks more commonly associated with a PCO, such as managing the budget for the conference and dealing with matters such as protocol and insurance.
- In many cases, two or more of these intermediaries are working together to make the conference a success. In particular, PCOs need to draw upon the expertise of DMCs and conference production companies for certain events. In those cases, the PCO becomes a subcontractor, assigning certain aspects of the event planning and production process to other agencies.
- Although some buyers may go directly to venues and other suppliers, this is the exception rather than the rule. The planning of most conferences involves the participation of one or more intermediary working on behalf of the buyer. As a consequence, suppliers very often have to market to, and negotiate with, a range of intermediaries as well as the actual buyers of the event. The next section examines the particular challenges of marketing in the conference sector.

The role of marketing in the conference industry

It is clear from the preceding section that the effective functioning of the conference, convention and business events market depends on the interaction of two factors – demand and supply, where the demand-side stakeholders are represented by the buyers of conferences and the supply-side stakeholders are those offering the facilities and services required for the successful operation of such events.

If the conference market is the process of interaction between these buyers and sellers, then what is marketing itself? The Chartered Institute of Marketing gives a broad definition as follows:

> *Marketing is the management process responsible for identifying, anticipating and satisfying customer requirements profitably.*

A number of key points may be developed out of this definition.

Marketing is considered a process (not just a particular marketing technique or series of techniques) that is concerned with satisfying customer (buyer) needs. This particular philosophy – based on the belief that those suppliers who anticipate customers' needs and respond to them first and/or best will be those that succeed – is often referred to as the 'marketing orientation' that characterises the approach taken by most modern suppliers of products and services.

However, the conference industry, in common with many other sectors of the economy, has evolved through at least two earlier marketing stages before adopting a marketing orientation. That evolution, related to the changing supply and demand relationships and the competitive conditions prevailing during earlier stages of capitalism, is summarised below.

Production orientation

This level is characterised by a shortage of supply, when suppliers' priority is to produce maximum volumes by increasing output. Such an approach only works effectively when a business operates in very high growth markets when goods and services sell easily, in other words, a sellers' market. It is generally accepted that, for Europe and the US, the production orientation was the dominant manufacturing business philosophy from the beginning of capitalism until the mid-1950s, during which time there was a shortage of manufactured goods relative to demand.

For the conference industry in Europe, this era lasted longer as the demand for conference venues and other services continued to exceed supply into the 1980s.

Sales orientation

A sales orientation tends to be used when supply out-paces demand, leading to a buyers' market, in which there may be a downward pressure on prices. In these market conditions, businesses concentrate on persuading customers to buy the available stock, using selling, pricing and promotion strategies. However, little attention is paid to customers' needs and wants. Economists trace the beginning of the sales orientation era for the manufacturing sector to the mid-1950s, by which time supply was starting to outpace demand in many industries. This arose because of converting industrial plant from wartime production to the production of consumer goods at the end of the Second World War.

Nevertheless, it may be argued that the supply of conference facilities and services did not exceed demand until the beginning of the 1990s, when a global recession coincided with the first conflict in the Gulf. These events dealt a severe blow to venues of all types, when they found themselves with an enormous amount of spare capacity at the same time as buyers were negotiating from a position of power not previously witnessed in the conference market.

Marketing orientation

In the twenty-first century, the marketing orientation strongly prevails in most sectors of the economy in most parts of the world – including the worldwide conference industry. This is an approach that allows the wants and needs of customers and potential customers to drive all of an organisation's strategic decisions, so that its entire culture is systematically committed to creating customer value. This is also an approach that requires the full support of the entire organisation – not only its marketing department. The customer is the focus of marketing orientation. This means that suppliers now place much more importance on understanding customer needs and working with customers to fulfil those needs, which is a huge shift in business emphasis.

The rationale behind adopting a marketing orientation is that the more an organisation understands and meets the real needs of its consumers, the more likely it is to have satisfied customers who bring it repeat business and/or recommend the organisation's products and services to others. In this way, this process can entail the fostering of long-term relationships with customers. In order to determine customer wants and needs, the organisation usually needs to conduct market research, which, if carried out correctly, may provide the company with a sustainable competitive advantage.

Recognising the way in which marketing had evolved, the American Marketing Association in 2013 announced a new definition of marketing:

> *Marketing is the activity, set of institutions, and processes for creating, communicating, delivering, and exchanging offerings that have value for customers, clients, partners, and society at large.*

It is clear from this definition that the responsibilities of those involved in marketing activities and processes have a broad responsibility to a number of stakeholders, extending beyond their customers and partners. This concept of marketers having a wider responsibility to society at large is well aligned with the modern-day expectations of DMOs.

It has been stated earlier in this chapter that convention bureaux work on behalf of the suppliers in the city or region or country. However, as bodies in receipt of public funding, they also have a wider responsibility to the host community – those who live and work in the territory covered by the convention bureau – as well as to the natural environment of the destination. All members of the host community, therefore, may be regarded as important stakeholders whose general well-being should be taken into account by the organisation that is responsible for the marketing of the place where they are located.

When a convention bureau, a venue, or indeed any organisation, accepts this wider responsibility to the welfare of the community and to the protection of the natural environment and takes these into account in its approach to its marketing, it may be said that it is adopting a *societal marketing orientation*, a fourth level in the hierarchy of the evolution of marketing approaches. Kotler *et al.* define this concept as 'the idea that an organisation should determine the needs, wants and interests of target markets and deliver the desired satisfactions more effectively and efficiently than competitors in a way that maintains or improves the consumer's and society's well-being' (Kotler *et al.*, 2003:882).

Clearly, for organisations adopting a societal marketing orientation, the marketing orientation, as described above, is maintained; but a new, broader, responsibility to stakeholders is introduced at this fourth level. Pike (2004:13) elaborates on this definition of societal marketing and emphasises its relevance to the tourism (and, by association, the conference) sector. He states that the societal marketing approach adheres to a marketing orientation,

> *but [is] operationalised in a way that also considers the well-being of society and the environment. DMOs, as representatives of a host community and natural environment as well as commercial tourism services, have such a wider societal obligation.*

However, even when the societal marketing orientation is, explicitly or implicitly, adopted by a convention bureau or by an individual venue in its programme of promotional activities, there is no guarantee that all stakeholders at the destination will benefit from the positive impacts that the conference industry can bring to a destination; and neither is this approach to marketing a way of ensuring that all stakeholders will be protected from the negative impacts that can be created by conference activity.

These positive and negative impacts are the subject of the final section of this chapter. However, in order to complete the analysis of marketing as it applies to the promotion of destinations and venues, it is important to develop the theme of marketing as it applies to the conference industry.

Business-to-business marketing

There are a number of fundamental differences between the approach of those marketing destinations and venues to conference buyers and that of those who are marketing chocolate bars to the general public. These differences derive from the fact that the former are engaged in business-to-business (B2B) marketing, while the latter are active in the field of business-to-consumer (B2C) marketing.

Business-to-business marketing used to be called 'industrial marketing' when it primarily focused on transactions of products produced by companies for other companies (raw materials, machine tools and so on). In the past few decades, the term 'industrial marketing' has given way to the term 'business-to-business marketing', and its meaning has grown to encompass the activity of 'building mutually value-generating relationships (including both products and services) between organisations' (Lilien and Grewal, 2012). Many of the distinctions between these two approaches arise from the contrasts in the buying behaviour of organisations as opposed to that of individuals.

Mackay and Wilmshurst (2012) highlight two of the key differences between the customers in B2B markets and those in B2C markets. According to them, the B2B market is characterised by:

1. A rather more rational, deliberative and scientific approach to buying (although some 'industrial consumables' (stationery, etc.) are sometimes bought with very little thought; and expensive consumer purchases (cars, houses, etc.) may sometimes be approached very scientifically).
2. A more complex decision-making unit (although in some domestic purchases, the whole family may be involved).

In the B2B market, the decision to purchase is typically a multi-step process that involves more than one person. This is certainly typical of the association meetings market, where a conference committee within the association may be created to choose the destination for a forthcoming event such as the association's annual conference. There may be a 'call for proposals', inviting destinations to bid to host the conference, with the interested convention bureaux preparing detailed documentation (in tandem with the suppliers in the destination) to compete to win the bid. This complex and often-lengthy procedure may be contrasted with the decision-making process in the corporate market, when the decision may be made by one person, with little or no consultation with his or her colleagues. Nevertheless, given the cost of booking venues even for small corporate meetings and the scrutiny of all corporate spending, such decisions increasingly are made jointly, with the involvement of companies' purchasing or procurement departments.

One consequence of the particular features of the B2B market is that the personal sales force of any convention bureau or venue may carry a much greater weight of responsibility for winning meetings business than other promotional techniques such as advertising, which, by way of contrast, is a vitally important tool in the realm of B2C marketing. Companies and organisations operating in a B2B market, such as that for meetings destinations and venues, usually place a greater focus on relationship building and communication through marketing activities, producing leads that are fostered during the sales cycle. This building of 'mutually value-generating relationships' is a major objective of customer relationship management.

Customer relationship management

A central tenet of the marketing orientation is customer relationship management (CRM). This is the term used for the 'set of techniques, designed to help build up-close and favourable contacts with an organisation's key customers . . . over a long time period' (Holloway, 2004:114). This set of techniques is particularly appropriate to the marketing of destinations and venues in a B2B environment.

A key objective of CRM is to create loyal customers. According to Canning (2004), CRM is a philosophy that should mobilise an entire organisation toward serving the customer better in order to create loyal, satisfied customers who may purchase more, cost less to sell to and who will refer other customers to the company. A further reason for companies seeking to create loyal customers is given by Pike: 'The rationale for stimulating relationships with customers is that these will be more profitable over time than one-off sales transactions, since the cost of reaching a continuous stream of new customers will far outweigh the cost of keeping in touch with existing customers' (Pike, 2004:127).

The different degrees of relationships that suppliers can develop with their customers are illustrated in Kotler's scheme of the five levels of relationships that can be formed with, for example, a hotel's clients who have booked a room for a meetings event:

1. Basic. The company sells the product but does not follow up in any way.
2. Reactive. The company sells the product and encourages the customer to call whenever he or she has any questions or problems.
3. Accountable. The company's representative phones the customer a short time after the booking, to check with the customer and answer questions. During and after the event, the salesperson solicits from the customer any product improvement suggestions and any specific disappointments. This information helps the company to improve its offering continuously.
4. Proactive. The salesperson or others in the company phone the customer from time to time with suggestions about improvements that have been made or creative suggestions for future events.
5. Partnership. The company works continuously with the customer and with other customers to discover ways to deliver better value.

(Kotler et al., 2003:391)

Effective CRM, therefore, offers the possibility of organisations entering into a relationship with their buyers that is closer to an ongoing partnership than simply a transactional connection.

CRM has been enabled by advances in ICT, which allow organisations to identify and manage large numbers of customers. Key to effective CRM is the gathering and analysis of customer data to create accurate, up-to-date customer profiles, which can be used to inform customer interaction and enhance the relationship. Data warehousing and data mining enable companies to learn from customer data through, for example, tracking the buying patterns of their clients. The use of ICT, therefore, has enabled suppliers to manage vast amounts of data quickly and accurately and to use the results to make intelligent decisions about their products, sales strategies and competitive advantage.

For conference destinations and venues, a CRM approach to marketing is being increasingly used as a means of strengthening the links between themselves and their actual or potential customers.

It is clear that, for destinations and venues, loyal customers represent a potential source of considerable profit because of the opportunity they bring for repeat purchases. Hotels in particular understand that their success in the corporate meetings market depends in part on nurturing quality relationships with key customers in that segment.

It is also clear that communication is the key to the success of customer relationship management, laying the foundation for customer satisfaction and business growth. Chapters 3 and 4 will examine the range of communications channels through which destinations and venues communicate with their customers and potential customers.

However, in order to complete our overview of the conference industry, this chapter ends with a review of the impacts of that industry on the wider environment within which it operates.

The impacts of the conference industry

All industries and all human activities have impacts, which can be positive or negative. These impacts may be seen primarily in changes to the state of the economy, to the natural and built environment and to people's quality of life and the culture of society in the widest sense.

For each impact, a number of different stakeholders may be affected, positively or negatively. In the final section of this chapter, the principal impacts of the conference industry are reviewed.

Economic impacts

One of the primary motivations for a community developing any industry are the economic benefits expected to result from that industry. It is generally accepted that the conference sector is a high-yield, year-round market, and it is the possibility of reaping substantial economic gains that represents the main motivating factor that has spurred so many destinations proactively to pursue the conference market. However, as well as economic benefits, there may be also considerable costs incurred by any community targeting this sector.

Many commentators have acknowledged that a continuing problem for conference destinations is that of *quantifying* the benefits and costs associated with this market. For example, Dwyer (2002:21) points out that:

> *little hard data are available upon which to estimate the precise magnitude of these effects. This is unfortunate because decisions about resource allocation by both private and public sector stakeholders greatly depend on accurate information regarding potential gains.*

Nevertheless, a number of government statistical agencies, tourist boards, convention bureaux and industry associations are engaged in the attempt to estimate the economic impacts of the conferences that are held within the territories they cover. One such attempt to quantify the economic contribution of the conference industry is undertaken on an annual basis by the Convention Industry Council in the USA (see Case Study 1.2).

The main economic impacts are reviewed below.

Positive economic impacts

Inbound earnings

Smith (1990:68) quotes a US city mayor who extols the economic benefits of the conference industry as follows:

> *When we have a convention in town, it is as if an airplane flew overhead dropping dollar bills on everyone.*

When these conference dollar bills are spent by visitors to the city, this means that 'new' spending is coming into local businesses such as shops, restaurants, entertainment centres and taxis. Furthermore, when a proportion of the delegates originate from abroad, their spending represents a boost in foreign exchange earnings for the destination.

A single conference can make a substantial impact on the local economy of the destination. For example, in 2014, Gen.Con (www.gencon.com) the 'the original, longest-running, best-attended gaming convention in the world' attracted over 56,000 people to the Indiana Convention Centre and had an economic impact of more than US$50 million.

CONTRIBUTION TO GOVERNMENT REVENUES

Conference-related spending results in benefits, not only for individual companies, but also for local and national governments. Government revenues from the conference sector can be categorised as either direct or indirect contributions. *Direct* contributions are generated by taxes on incomes from employment in the conference industry, taxes on the profits of businesses operating in this sector and by direct levies on conference delegates such as airport departure taxes. *Indirect* contributions are those originated from taxes and duties levied on goods and services supplied to delegates, such as VAT (value added tax) charged on the champagne consumed at a conference reception.

EMPLOYMENT GENERATION

A wide range of employment is created by a thriving conference industry. As a service-sector, this industry is one of the most labour-intensive industries and it is responsible for sustaining a significant proportion of the jobs found in the hotel and transport sectors, for example, as well as the specialist conference-related professions represented by all of the suppliers and intermediaries discussed earlier in this chapter. Although conference-related employment is often amalgamated, in statistical analyses, with the jobs generated by tourism and leisure, it tends to demonstrate slightly different patterns to those sectors, notably in its less seasonal nature.

STIMULATION OF INVESTMENT

The development of a conference industry can induce national and local governments to make infrastructure improvements, such as better water and sewage systems, roads, electricity supply, telephone and public transport networks, all of which can improve the quality of life for residents as well as facilitate the expansion of the conference industry at the destination. Other industries may also be attracted by the improved infrastructure, leading to the type of inward investment so desired by many economies.

Negative economic impacts

While the positive economic impacts of conferences are generally visible – and increasingly proclaimed by the conference industry itself, there can also be significant hidden costs to developing and operating a conference industry, which can also have a number of unfavourable economic effects on the host community.

INFRASTRUCTURE COSTS

The development of the infrastructure necessary for the operating of a significant conference industry can cost national and local governments (and, by extension, taxpayers) a great deal of money and can require a substantial outlay of funds long before the first conference arrives in the destination. In order to equip the destination to receive large numbers of delegates, governments may have to improve airports, roads and other elements of the infrastructure. They may also have to provide tax breaks, investment incentives and other financial advantages to conference centre and hotel developers, for example.

This type of government spending may bring with it a significant 'opportunity cost', as public resources spent on subsidised infrastructure or tax breaks can reduce government investment in critical areas such as education and health.

PROMOTIONAL COSTS

In a competitive world, destinations vie with one another to attract conferences and other business events. Promotion is generally undertaken by the types of DMOs discussed earlier in this chapter. A destination promoting itself to conference buyers and intermediaries may do so in tandem with its promotion of itself as a leisure destination or it may create a separate entity. Either way, the vast majority of countries and cities around the world have some form of tourism organisation or convention bureau that undertakes this task.

The costs of establishing and maintaining such organisations can be a considerable drain on the public resources of some countries, particularly when, as is often the case, offices must be maintained in key overseas markets. The Netherlands Board of Tourism and Conventions, for example, promotes that country as a conference destination through its offices in London, New York, Paris, Brussels, Stockholm, Milan, Madrid, Cologne and Tokyo. For any developing country, supporting such a network of offices in foreign cities would be a significant financial burden, and yet many do exactly that, in their efforts to attract conferences to their cities.

Leakage

Developed nations are often better able to profit from being a conference destination than less developed ones. One of the reasons for this is the developed nations' ability to retain a high proportion of the expenditure arising from the conferences that take place within their territory.

Dwyer (2002) emphasises the importance of recognising that not all conference-related expenditure is retained within the destination hosting the conference. 'Leakage' is the term given to income that is lost to the host destination because it 'leaks out' to other regions or to other countries. This can take several forms. For example, a significant amount of the economic benefits arising from the spending of delegates attending international conferences can go to foreign airlines and to international hotel chains based outside the host nation, when delegates use these instead of locally owned accommodation and the national airline of the host country. Similarly, nations that need to import goods from other countries, in order to service their conference sector also experience leakage of the economic benefits. For example, a country that needs to import building materials and hotel equipment and furnishings in order to build a conference facility is automatically losing some of the gains accruing from its conference industry.

Large, developed nations with advanced and varied economic sectors suffer least from leakage, as they are able to produce most of what is required to establish and maintain a viable conference industry. The consequence is that while the least developed countries may have the most urgent need for the income, employment and rise in the general standard of living that can be generated by the conference industry, they are often the destinations that are least able to realise these benefits.

Environmental impacts

The quality of the environment, both natural and man-made, is important to the successful functioning of the conference and business events industry. Delegates expect a clean, attractive locality, and this is particularly true when there is a motivational element to the conference, as in the case of an incentivised meeting. However, the conference industry's relationship with the environment is complex, bringing both positive and negative impacts.

Positive environmental impacts

At the most basic level, towns and cities hosting conferences need to ensure that the physical environment is maintained in a clean, tidy and healthy condition, in just the same way that certain standards of housekeeping are required when receiving guests in one's home.

Knowing that delegates expect conference localities that are at least as clean and attractive as they find in their home towns, no conference planner would knowingly choose to hold an event in a destination in which the environment was despoiled and polluted.

Beyond creating the need for municipalities to maintain the quality of their built and natural environment, the conference industry also has the potential to create beneficial effects on the environment of destinations by contributing to environmental enhancement and conservation. For example, many urban regeneration programmes throughout the world have been based on the construction of new conference centres in neglected and often derelict areas. The Edinburgh International Conference Centre, for instance, which opened in 1995, was the showpiece of the regeneration of that city's Exchange Business District, a previously run-down area of Edinburgh, now entirely revitalised with the iconic EICC as its flagship development. Similarly, the Hilton San Diego Convention Center Hotel, located across from the San Diego Convention Center, is built on the site of the former Campbell Shipyard, which fell into disuse and extreme contamination before being cleared for hotel development, as part of its regeneration programme.

The conference industry has also contributed in no small measure to urban conservation initiatives, notably through the re-conversion into conference centres of buildings that might otherwise have been demolished. From private mansions to palaces and factories, countless examples of architecturally valuable buildings have been saved by their conversion into conference facilities. Ottawa's Government Conference Centre is an outstanding example of this type of conservation, being converted from that city's former Union Train Station, which was designed in the Beaux-Arts style with a former monumental waiting room that was copied from the great thermal baths of Rome.

Negative environmental impacts

On first impressions, the conference industry would appear to be one that makes very little negative impact on the environment. After all, it has no factory smokestacks, releases no chemicals into the water and soil, and only uses, for its functioning, machines such as computers and photocopiers that account for a relatively modest proportion of energy consumption.

Nevertheless, on closer examination it becomes clear that the conference industry can indeed have a number of adverse environmental effects. Some of these impacts are linked with the construction of the infrastructure necessary for the hosting of events, and there are examples throughout the world, from Niagara Falls Convention Center in New York State to the Spanish city of San Sebastian's Kursaal Conference Centre, of venues that have been controversial in their design or in their location, or both.

Conferences may also be criticised at times for their use of natural resources, notably paper. For example, the paper required in order to present each of 500 delegates with a conference pack of information (the conference programme, list of delegates, print-offs of presenters' notes, etc.) can represent a substantial use of natural resources, even though memory sticks are increasingly being used for the distribution of such information. Aware of the potential for this, and other forms of wastage, some venues have taken the initiative of offering advice to conference planners on how to minimise this (see Figure 1.1).

However, the most damaging impact made by the conference industry on the natural environment is now widely believed to be the energy use and the emissions associated with travel to meetings, in particular to international events. Most travel to international conferences uses air transport and the negative environmental impacts from movements in the upper atmosphere are considerably greater than for movements at ground level. Globalisation of the economy has greatly increased the volume of travel to international corporate events and this situation has been mirrored in the growth of international and regional associations whose annual events also contribute significantly to the amount of air travel mobility around the globe.

Høyer and Nœss (2001:467) have expressed their concern over this issue in unambiguous terms:

> *The increase in travel to international meetings forms one of the environmentally most worrying changes in the mobility of post-industrial society. It is a paradox that the consequences for global environmental problems arising from the use of local transport have gradually been put*

The EICC website emphasizes the venue's green credentials:

Consider the environment…

We understand that event organisers are increasingly concerned with environmental issues associated with the events industry. This is why we are proud to have created Plan-it green™; our sustainable events programme comprising committed stakeholders throughout the EICC.

Greening the conference and events sector has become a moral challenge worldwide, requiring leadership, vision and above all, commitment by each one of us.

At the EICC we have already put in place the following initiatives which each of our operations teams have made a commitment to pursuing:

- Establishment of a property specific "green team", to adopt and implement earth-friendly practices in our businesses and to become better stewards of the natural resources that we utilise.
- Sourcing and purchasing environmentally sensitive products and services locally, whenever possible.
- Purchasing organic fresh and sustainable foods locally grown, whenever possible.
- Creating partnerships with other organisations that have demonstrated a commitment to preserving the environment.
- Leading our associates to apply eco-friendly practices in their daily operations.
- Energy efficient lighting, heating and cooling systems, as well as water-saving devices.
- Implementing tools that allow us to continually measure the progress of our environmental operations.

We're not here to tell you how green your next event should be, that's up to you, but if you're as serious as we are about environmental sustainability, then we can help you. We can offer advice and support through every stage of the planning process to support your own objectives.

Figure 1.1 Edinburgh International Conference Centre's sustainability initiatives

Source: www.eicc.co.uk.

> *higher on the environmental agenda, while there is virtually no focus on the long job-related journeys. For the individual conference participant, one such trip usually represents an amount of transportation larger than the total mobility for all other purposes during a whole year.*

While it is certainly true that the volume of travel for leisure purposes, such as holidays and visits to friends and relatives, far exceeds business- and conference-related travel, this fact by no means absolves the international conference industry from being a major contributor to the growing threat to the state of the global climate.

As an indication of how public concern over the impact of conference-related travel on global warming has increased, a growing number of conferences are declaring themselves 'climate-neutral' and compensating for the carbon dioxide emissions resulting from the travel of their delegates to the conference destination. For example, the International Conference on Greenhouse Gas Technologies (GHGT-10) that was held in Amsterdam in 2014 aimed for climate neutrality by buying carbon credits from the Gold Standard (www.goldstandard.org), which not only ensured that the carbon credits were real and verifiable but also that they made measurable contributions to sustainable development worldwide.

Reconciling the demand for air travel to international conferences with the need to conserve energy use and prevent the further deterioration of the global climate will undoubtedly continue to be one of the major challenges facing the conference industry in the years ahead.

Social and cultural impacts

By definition, most conferences involve the influx of groups of people from other localities to the destination where the event is held. During the conference, therefore, two populations may come into contact with each other: the 'host' population (the local residents) and the 'guests' (the delegates themselves).

In many cases, the delegates may be indistinguishable from the local people in terms of their physical appearance, manner of dress and visible level of prosperity, as well as their beliefs and general level of education. In that case, the social and cultural impacts can be minimal. However, when, as is often the case, a considerable gulf exists between the different ways of life of host and guest, this can lead to the possibility of both positive and negative effects on both sides.

Positive social and cultural impacts

The rich literature on the social and cultural impacts of tourism demonstrates that many benefits can arise from the encounter of two different populations and the conference industry offers many of the same advantages. The open and equal interaction between 'hosts' and 'guests' can generate a useful exchange of ideas and greater mutual understanding. Exposure to different traditions can be a progressive and liberating experience when, for example, the inhabitants of developing countries see female delegates interacting on an equal basis with their male colleagues.

Moreover, the very nature of most conferences, at which ideas are presented and discussed by those in attendance, lends itself to the sharing of views and the production of new intellectual capital. These are among the most important yet intangible benefits of this industry, which ought never to be taken for granted.

Negative social and cultural impacts

Nevertheless, the negative impacts of the influx of large groups of people into host communities are also well documented.

These problems tend to be most exacerbated when there is a marked contrast in the standard of living between host and guest. It must be remembered that many conferences and other business events take place in destinations where a significant proportion of the local population is living in relative poverty in close proximity to the luxury hotels and palatial conference centres that provide the accommodation and venues for such events.

Local people may easily come to perceive delegates to be privileged incomers who throw their own deprivation and hardship into sharp focus. This is particularly true when the group of delegates is large and visible. Incentive groups are especially vulnerable to being observed in this way. Davidson and Cope (2003:183) note that:

> In the case of travel for conference or trade fair attendance, visitors spend most of their time indoors, engaging in activities that are related to their work. By comparison, the lavishly funded and occasionally frivolous activities indulged in by incentive travel award-winners run the risk of contrasting severely with the lifestyles and values of those living in some of the destinations chosen for incentive trips.

Sharp inequalities between the host and the temporary guest populations can produce a climate in which crime and exploitation can thrive, for the duration of the event. In unfamiliar surroundings, delegates can be the victims of such crime, suffering at the hands of pickpockets, muggers and fraudsters, for example. They can also exploit their own superior financial status over local people and the relative anonymity that being in a new destination for a few days offers. An example of this particular negative impact of conferences was highlighted by Wadhwani (2015), writing in *The Tennessean* about how major conferences can intensify the problem of sex trafficking in the destinations in which they are held. This was expected to be one result of Nashville's hosting of the annual convention of the National Rifle Association, with over 70,000 attendees, overwhelmingly male.

The Gold Coast Convention and Exhibition Centre

The AUD $167 million Gold Coast Convention and Exhibition Centre (GCCEC, http://www.gccec.com.au) opened on 29 June 2004, providing Australia's Gold Coast with its first and Queensland with its third convention centre. Located in the heart of the Gold Coast, the GCCEC features a Main Arena, Exhibition Halls and Meeting Rooms catering for ten to 6,000 people. It is Australia's largest regional convention centre, capable of handling corporate and association conferences and meetings, national and international incentives, banquets, exhibitions, concerts, sporting and special events. The venue features a 6,000-seat arena divisible into three spaces, 6,000 square metres of exhibition space divisible into four halls and 22 meeting rooms of varying size.

The Australian Medical Students Association Convention

In 2013, the GCCEC was the venue chosen by the Australian Medical Students Association (AMSA) for its 54th Annual AMSA National Convention, with 1,400 attendees. The event lasted 7 days in all, from 7–13 July. The intensive 4-day academic programme, featuring high profile and inspirational keynote speakers and an impressive social programme complete with a lavish gala dinner was the highlight of the year for many of the students from 20 medical schools across Australia and New Zealand.

As the main representative body for Australian medical students, the key mandate of the AMSA is to connect, inform and represent 17,000 medical students. Providing a platform for advocacy, the world's largest student-run convention celebrates advances in knowledge and technology including the major shifts in how the medical profession teaches and practises medicine. The 2013 Convention enabled delegates to explore broad topics including mental health, medical training and refugee health in addition to practical workshops including the basics of suturing, venipuncture and laparoscopy.

The AMSA event continued its successful tradition of combining the academic programme, leading speakers and social calendar with an exciting off-site programme, consisting that year of visits to Warner Bros. Movie World, Outback Spectacular, field trips including a summit climb of the Southern Hemisphere's tallest building the Q1 and a sports day where the Guinness World Record (529) for most participants spooning together to create an oval shape was successfully broken when 1,100 students took part in the feat.

Matching the venue to the client's needs

In seeking a conference destination, the client (AMSA) wanted a venue and location that would complement an interchanging educational programme and satisfy delegates' wishes for an active and varied social programme. Many of the delegates had just completed half-yearly exams and a quick transition into the annual Convention was taken into consideration.

The GCCEC was up against competing venues and locations including Canberra. Ultimately, a variety of decisive factors, including the central location of the venue (close proximity to 3,000 accommodation rooms catering to various student budgets), entertainment and the ability to provide a complete experience for delegates not only in terms of space but overall ambiance, audio-visual capabilities and helpful staff, encompassed just some of the key selling points.

Attracting 1,400 delegates and more than 5,000 room nights booked at hotels and apartments situated within walking distance of the GCCEC, the conference made a significant impact on the local economy. While the Convention was situated in-house at the Centre for most of the time, there were daily social evening offsite events, field trips and a charity brunch in addition to other dining options and entertainment. In addition, many delegates took the opportunity to extend their stay and explore the destination more fully.

Logistics and challenges

The AMSA Convention used approximately 7,800 square metres of event space. The ability of the GCCEC to provide a dynamic space flexible enough to cater for the smallest and most complex production requirements, including tight room turnaround for various activities, was a vital factor in winning this event. The Arena provided a flexible staging area for main plenary sessions, lectures, week-long debating series and competitions. Other requirements for space were a trade show featuring 20 exhibition booths, an advanced surgical skills unit bus (virtual medical procedures), a room for live music and interactive games and a 'chillout lounge' where delegates could relax and interact. Furthermore, eight breakout areas originally set for lecture-style sessions required fast room turnaround for the afternoon workshop programme and they had to be quickly modified for debating, yoga, dance area and laparoscopy. All the foyer space throughout the venue was used for an 'amazing race' style activity complete with mental and physical challenges for 75 teams.

Client testimonial

Immediately after the Convention, Patrick Tunney, Deputy Convenor of the Australian Medical Students Association, gave the following testimonial, which still appears on the GCCEC website:

> The Gold Coast Convention and Exhibition Centre was the perfect place for this year's 54th Annual AMSA National Convention. The facilities of the venue were well-suited to our needs and were flexible in meeting these needs. The staff were incredibly helpful in bringing our ideas to life, and worked to ensure that the entire event ran as smoothly as possible. The food available at the GCCEC was top-notch. Overall our Convention was a major highlight of our delegates' year, in a large part thanks to the amazing facilities and service provided by the Gold Coast Convention and Exhibition Centre.

CASE STUDY 1.2   The economic significance of meetings for the US economy

In 2013, the consultants PricewaterhouseCoopers LLP undertook a research project on behalf of the Convention Industry Council (CIC) to measure the economic significance of meetings to the US economy. The project was an interim update to a study prepared by the consultants on behalf of CIC for the calendar year 2009, to reflect meetings activity in the US during 2012.

The 2009 Study involved a comprehensive primary and secondary research effort to quantify the size and economic significance of the US meetings industry, including more than 6,000 surveys of meeting organisers, meeting venue managers, DMOs, meeting delegates and exhibitors. The study found that nearly 1.8 million meetings took place in the US during calendar year 2009, which involved an estimated 205 million participants and generated more than US$263 billion in direct spending and US$907 billion in total industry output.

The surveys and interviews conducted as part of the 2009 study were not updated as part of the interim update approach. Nevertheless, examples of secondary sources considered in the interim update included the following:

- *Government sources*: Bureau of Economic Analysis, Office of Travel and Tourism Industries, Census Bureau, Bureau of Labor Statistics and others;
- *Industry sources*: PCMA Meetings Market Survey, CEIR Exhibition Industry Index, U.S. Travel Association Domestic Travel Report, MPI Business Barometer, ICCA International Association Meetings Market, Business Travel News' Corporate Travel Index, GBTA BTI Outlook, Smith Travel Research and others;
- *Proprietary sources*: PwC Convention Center Report, PwC Hospitality Directions, previous PwC studies involving the meetings industry and other such sources.

For purposes of the 2009 study and the 2012 interim update, a 'meeting' refers to a gathering of ten or more participants for a minimum of 4 hours in a contracted venue. Meetings include conventions, conferences, congresses, trade shows and exhibitions, incentive events, corporate/business meetings and other meetings that meet the aforementioned criteria. Excluded from the definition of meetings are social and recreation activities, certain educational and political activities and gatherings for sales of goods/services such as consumer shows. The following extract from the findings of the study demonstrates the significance of meetings for the US economy.

Meetings volume

More than 1.8 million meetings were estimated to have been held in the US during calendar year 2012 and they involved an estimated 225 million participants. The majority of meeting participants were generated by corporate/business meetings (50 per cent), followed by conventions/conferences/congresses (27 per cent) and trade shows (12 per cent). See Table 1.2.

In terms of host types, the majority of meetings and meeting participants in 2012 were hosted by corporations (55 and 49 per cent, respectively). Association/membership organisations hosted the second largest share of meeting participants (26 per cent), followed by non-government, not-for-profit organisations (23 per cent). See Table 1.3.

Direct spending

Direct spending is defined as spending within the US economy from purchases of goods and services attributable to meetings activity. Total direct spending associated with US meetings activity in 2012 was estimated at over US$280 billion. Approximately US$130 billion or 46 per cent of the direct spending in the meetings industry was on travel and tourism commodities such as lodging, food service and transportation. The majority of direct spending, however, was not travel-related, with US$150 billion or 54 per cent involving meeting planning and production costs, venue rental and other non-travel and tourism commodities that fall outside the Travel and Tourism Satellite Account.

Total economic significance

Direct spending, as shown in Table 1.4, reflects the spending in those industries that comprise the meetings industry. *Indirect spending* is attributable to the suppliers to the meetings industry,

Table 1.2 Number of meetings and participants by meeting type

Meeting type	Meetings	Participants	Participants (%)
Corporate/business meetings	1,298,300	113,337,000	50
Conventions/conferences/congresses	273,700	60,960,000	27
Trade shows	10,900	26,768,000	12
Incentive meetings	67,700	9,172,000	4
Other meetings	182,600	14,710,000	7
Total	1,833,200	224,947,000	100

Table 1.3 Number of meetings and participants by host type

Host type	Meetings	Participants	Participants (%)
Corporate	1,017,000	109,571,000	49
Association/membership	315,400	59,495,000	26
Non-government, not-for-profit	432,100	51,572,000	23
Government	68,600	4,308,000	2
Total	1,833,200	224,947,000	100

Table 1.4 Direct spending by commodity

Commodities	Direct spending (in millions – $)	Per cent
Travel and tourism commodities		
Accommodation	39,315	14
Food and beverage	29,832	11
Air transportation	23,761	8
Retail	8,235	3
Gasoline	7,498	3
Recreation and entertainment	7,034	3
Car rental	6,258	2
Travel services and other tourism commodities	3,707	1
Other transportation	2,369	1
Urban transit	1,577	1
Rail and water transportation	600	<1
Subtotal	130,186	46
Meetings and other commodities		
Meeting planning and production	106,658	38
Venue rental	10,363	4
Other meetings – related commodities	33,195	12
Subtotal	150,216	54
Total direct spending	280,402	100

Commodities include both goods and services.

and the *induced spending* arises from spending by the employees of the meetings industry and its suppliers. Together, direct, indirect and induced spending contributions comprise the total contribution of meetings activity to the US economy (see Table 1.5).

Table 1.5 Total economic contributions

Economic contributions	Industry output (in millions – $)	Contribution to GDP (in millions – $)	Employment	Labour income (in millions – $)
Direct effects	280,403	115,615	1,787,000	66,892
Indirect effects	276,267	156,889	2,080,000	99,139
Induced effects	213,706	121,280	1,440,000	68,608
Total economic contributions	770,375	393,784	5,307,000	234,639

Economic Significance Study (www.economicsignificancestudy.org).

CASE STUDY 1.3   Marketing Moscow as a conference destination

Many people would be surprised to hear that a city as geopolitically and culturally important as Moscow should have waited so long before creating its own convention bureau. But as this assessment by Andrey Danilov, Communications Manager of the Moscow Convention Bureau, shows, the organisation is making up for lost time.

Moscow as an events destination

With 12 major exhibition and convention centres and 30 congress hotels, offering a total of over 40,000 square metres of congress space and 560,000 square metres of exhibition space, Moscow's plentiful supply of venues constitutes the basis of its business events infrastructure. In the past few years, the city has hosted over 50 major association meetings, including the 21st World Petroleum Congress (WPC), the 12th International Conference on Nanostructured Materials (NANO 2014), the 40th Scientific Assembly of the Committee on Space Research (COSPAR) and the sixth Global Entrepreneurship Congress (GEC 2014). Moscow will also host the FIFA World Cup in 2018, which will give the city the opportunity to demonstrate its mega-events hosting skills to the world.

The Moscow Convention Bureau

The Moscow Convention Bureau (MCB; http://en.moscowcvb.ru/index.php) was set up by the Government of Moscow in August 2013 with the purpose of providing assistance and guidance to convention organisers willing to consider Moscow as the next meetings destination. The MCB is a non-commercial organisation and all of its services are provided free of charge. It is entirely supported by public funds.

The MCB's main objectives are:

- Raising the status of Moscow as a major business, science and industry centre
- Development of a 'one-stop shop' for international meeting planners

- Development of the convention and exhibition industries in the Russian capital
- Increasing the input of the convention and exhibition industries to the social and economic development of the city

In the first 2 years of its existence, the MCB won seven bids for hosting international association meetings. The World Conference of the International Association of Science Parks (IASP), the European Academy of Allergy and Clinical Immunology Summer School, the World Congress on Controversies in Obstetrics Gynecology & Infertility (COGI), the Biennial Congress of the Eurasian Colorectal Technology Association and the International Federation for Heat Treatment and Surface Engineering Congress.

Raising Moscow's profile as a business events destination

One of the MCB's core activities is presenting Moscow to the global conference community at important international exhibitions for the meetings industry (Figure 1.2), including IMEX and ibtm world – a total of ten events per year. The MCB is a member of ICCA and European Cities Marketing. To date, the Bureau has made direct contacts with over 1,000 association executives, leaders of academic communities and high-ranking meetings industry professionals.

The MCB was the first convention bureau in Russia not only to take steps in the way of promoting its city as a highly prospective meeting destination, but also to actively participate in bid procedures for attracting major international events. The MCB thereby set a precedent for all similar organisations in Russia. Many of the Bureau's marketing activities are founded on the 'seeing is believing' principle and these are designed to convince key stakeholders by giving them a direct experience of the city and its attractions for meeting planners and delegates. Thus, familiarisation trips, site visits and press-tours are offered on a regular basis, giving foreign guests detailed insights into Moscow's major meetings venues and tourist facilities, showing them the most spectacular vistas of the capital and suggesting original ideas for social programmes as well as ways to entertain business visitors.

Figure 1.2 Moscow Convention Bureau's stand at a major trade exhibition

Managing the business events product in Moscow

As well as informing international audiences of Moscow's immense potential as a meeting destination, industrial centre and scientific hub, the MCB focuses on the development of the city's burgeoning meetings industry. Among MCB's current goals is collecting and sharing objective and independent data on the players of the local convention market. To date, an extensive database of venues and convention service providers compiled by the MCB is available online and is being used as a reliable reference by meeting planners. The Bureau uses these resources to offer tailor-made, comprehensive solutions for international and local events of all shapes and sizes.

Another task undertaken by the Bureau is the audit and accreditation of the local meetings industry players. The accreditation procedure comprises two stages: the analysis of application papers provided followed by a site inspection visit by the Bureau's specialists. Successful applicants then receive the status of accredited partner, which is valid for 2 years. The audit and accreditation procedures ensure that the information and advice provided by the MCB to international meeting planners is solid and well grounded, which goes a long way in giving the city a high level of credibility.

At the same time, the MCB, realising the importance of compiling reliable figures on Moscow as a convention and exhibition centre, collects and publishes statistics on more than 560 conventions and 215 exhibitions running in the Russian capital annually. Not only are quantitative and qualitative data analysed, but a thorough research of the impact of major events on Moscow's economy is given a high priority. The MCB considers statistics as an important factor in ensuring that both the state authorities and the businesses make unbiased and well-considered decisions.

Promoting Moscow's industrial and scientific potential

In terms of local expertise, Moscow is reinventing itself as one of world's leading centres for high technology and innovation. With its very own silicon valley, dozens of technological clusters, some of Russia's most skilled researchers and substantial investment both from the Federal Government and insightful multinational companies, Moscow is on the fast track to becoming one of the hi-tech centres of Europe, specialising in fields such as IT, nanotechnology, microelectronics, robotics, space research and biomedical technology. Given how the high technology industries are booming in the Russian capital, the MCB is on a mission to promote the city's technological potential alongside its attraction as a meeting destination. By highlighting the innovative and highly competitive products made in Moscow and providing other forms of marketing support to the city's leading technoparks, the Bureau is helping to build the image of Moscow as a major hi-tech capital.

The MCB has also established close contacts with the city's academic community and maintains working relationships with over 100 potential local hosts, drawn from the Russian scientific elite. The Bureau supports these potential local hosts in their networking with their international colleagues and promotion of Moscow as a centre of competence in their respective fields. The MCB also co-operates with numerous industrial associations in Moscow, one of the most recent partnership agreements being signed between the MCB and the Russian Chemists Union.

The MCB is open to bidding for all types of international events, but there remains a tight focus on those having the highest potential for the development of the city's key industries and those most beneficial to the city's scientific and business communities. An example of just such an event was the sixth Global Entrepreneurship Congress held in Moscow in March 2014 that drew several thousand delegates from 153 countries, including government leaders, entrepreneurs, researchers, policymakers and investors.

Reaching out to the local meetings industry

The Bureau caters for the needs of the local convention and exhibition industries by organising a series of seminars, workshops and round tables for educational and matchmaking purposes, bringing together the key players from both industries and their prospective collaborators from a variety of fields. The list of events organised by the MCB includes a series of TECHWEEK 'Modern Technology for the Event Industry' webinars, the first ever International Association of Professional Congress Organisers' (IAPCO) seminar in Russia as well as a variety of smaller but highly appreciated events.

Another important project in the portfolio of the MCB is the educational programme 'Organisation of an International Meeting in Theory and Practice' for university and college students. A unique and pioneering project in Russia, the course is based on global best practice, while retaining a focus on the specific aspects of the Russian meetings industry. The programme, developed by the MCB, is currently running in several major business events-oriented educational institutions, which have the potential to supply the local meetings and exhibitions industries with young, able professionals who are willing to contribute to establishing Moscow as one of world's most prominent convention capitals. In 2015, the programme produced 49 up-and-coming young convention professionals.

All the above functions are distributed between the MCB's four departments, each with its distinct area of responsibility: International Marketing, Industry Development, Special Projects and Marketing and Analytics.

MCB services for international meeting planners

The Bureau's primary aim is to provide insights to those meeting planners interested in considering new destinations and ready to see the immense range of opportunities that Moscow has to offer. Using their detailed knowledge of the city's suppliers, the staff of the MCB offer international meeting planners assistance in sourcing suitable venues, accommodation, travel support, catering, transport services and entertainment options for their events. The Bureau also acts as a trusted intermediary in all negotiations with the local service suppliers, as well as a government relations consultant, media partner and, most importantly, an invaluable source of advice for international meeting planners.

MCB faces the music

Entering the field of destination marketing from zero is not easy, especially in the highly competitive environment that characterises the international meeting destinations market. From the very start, the MCB had to prove that Moscow could stand tall alongside other European capital cities, such as Vienna, Barcelona, Berlin, London and Paris, all of which are well established as international conference destinations. The mission was, and still is, to help meeting planners discover the unique 'vibe' of the Russian capital. But, on the positive side, working for a young organisation such as the MCB offers considerable scope for innovation, initiative and creative input. Though charged with a mission made even more challenging by the difficult economic environment that Russia experienced not long after the inception of the MCB, the Bureau was not daunted in the task to build a bridge of scientific, business and cultural collaboration between Moscow and the rest of the world.

SUMMARY

This chapter has introduced the conference industry in all its complexity. It has been shown to be a relatively young area of economic activity, involving a complex and broad range of stakeholders, some of whom – such as transport operators – depend only partly on conference business for their income. The extraordinary diversity of demand for conferences and meetings is matched by a wide range of suppliers providing facilities and services for the hosting and organising of these events. In many cases, a DMO takes responsibility for promoting the destination as a whole and bringing together suppliers with buyers.

In the conference industry, business-to-business marketing is dominant, and this brings a number of challenges that are not generally encountered in business-to-consumer marketing, notably a longer and more complex decision-making process on the part of buyers. Marketing techniques themselves change over time and the prevailing approach to marketing goods and services focuses on the well-being of consumers and of society as a whole, not only on suppliers and their shareholders.

Customer relationship management, which makes use of advances in information technology, is of central importance in marketing conference destinations and venues. The conference industry, like all sectors, has a range of negative as well as positive impacts on the economy, the environment and on the lives of those working and living at the destinations where such events take place. Those responsible for the marketing of destinations and venues are increasingly taking into account all of these impacts, in order to create a truly successful conference industry that is managed in such a way that the needs of all stakeholders are satisfied to the greatest extent possible.

REVIEW AND DISCUSSION QUESTIONS

- Visit the website of an international association conference that is being held in your country this year, by entering into a search engine the words 'international association conference' followed by the year. Based on your reading of the website, list as many different stakeholders as you can, for that particular conference, categorising them by the categories: buyers, suppliers and intermediaries. From your reading of this chapter, are there any other groups of people who might be considered as stakeholders for that conference?
- For the capital city of the country you live in, use the internet to find an example of each of the following types of conferences that have been held there this year or last year: a corporate conference, a national association conference, an international association conference, a governmental conference and a SMERF event.
- Visit the website of the DMO or convention bureau that has the responsibility of marketing your city (or a large city close to where you live) as a conference destination. How is that website different from the website that markets the same city as a leisure tourism destination?
- For the conference that you found for Question 1, above, make a list of its possible impacts, both positive and negative. Who are the people who stand to benefit in some way from the conference and how might they benefit? What could be the negative consequences of the conference for the host destination?

BIBLIOGRAPHY

Boone, L. E. and D. L. Kurtz (1998) *Contemporary Marketing Wired*, Oak Brook: Dryden Press.
Canning, L. (2004) 'Relationship marketing: dialogue and networks in the e-commerce era', *European Journal of Marketing*, 38(8): 1031–2.
CIC (2005) *The 2004 Economic Impact Study*, Convention Industry Council.
CIC (2014) *2012 Economic Significance Study*, Convention Industry Council.

Davidson, R. and B. Cope (2003) *Business Travel: conferences, incentive travel, exhibitions, corporate hospitality and corporate travel*, Upper Saddle River: FT Prentice Hall/Pearson Education.

Dwyer, L. (2002) 'Economic contribution of convention tourism: conceptual and empirical issues', in K. Weber and K. Chon (eds.), *Convention Tourism: International Research and Industry Perspectives*, Binghamton: The Haworth Hospitality Press, pp. 21–36.

Ford, R. C. and W. C. Peeper (2007) 'The past as prologue: Predicting the future of the convention and visitor bureau industry on the basis of its history', *Tourism Management*, 28(4): 1104–14.

Gehrisch, M. (2004) *Emerging Meeting & Business Travel Trends for 2004*, Washington, DC: DMAI.

Harrill, R. (2005) *Fundamentals of Destination Management and Marketing*, Educational Institute of the American Hotel and Motel Association.

Holloway, J. C. (2004) *Marketing for Tourism*, Upper Saddle River: Prentice Hall.

Høyer, K. G. and P. Nœss (2001) 'Conference tourism: a problem for the environment, as well as for research?' *Journal of Sustainable Tourism*, 9, 6.

Kotler, P., J. Bowen and J. Makens (2003) *Marketing for Hospitality and Tourism*, Upper Saddle River: Prentice Hall.

Koutoulas, D. (2005) *Benchmark Survey of Convention & Visitors Bureaux*, Koutoulas Consulting.

Lawson, F. (2000) *Congress, Convention and Exhibition Facilities: Planning, Design and Management*, New York: Architectural Press.

Lilien, G. L. and R. Grewal (2012) *Handbook of Business-to-Business Marketing*, Cheltenham: Edward Elgar.

Mackay, A. and J. Wilmshurst (2012). *Fundamentals and Practice of Marketing*, London: Routledge.

Pike, S. (2004) *Destination Marketing Organisations*, Oxford: Elsevier.

Smith, G. V. (1990) 'The growth of conferences and incentives', in M. Quest (ed.), *Horwath Book of Tourism*, London: Macmillan.

Spiller, J. (2002) 'History of convention tourism', in K. Weber and K. Chon (eds.), *Convention Tourism: International Research and Industry Perspectives*, Binghamton: The Haworth Hospitality Press, pp. 3–20.

Wadhwani, A. (2015) 'Big conventions can draw sex trafficking', *The Tennessean*, 12 April.

Weber, K. and K. Chon (eds.) (2002) *Convention Tourism: International Research and Industry Perspectives*, Binghamton: The Haworth Hospitality Press.

WTO (2004) *Survey of Destination Management Organisations Report*, Madrid: World Tourism Organization.

Chapter **2**

Marketing planning for destinations and venues

Chapter overview

This chapter examines the importance, for destinations and venues, of systematically planning their marketing strategies. It then demonstrates the key role played by any organisation's marketing plan in helping it devise, execute and monitor successful marketing programmes.

The chapter covers:

- The purpose and components of marketing plans
- Marketing research
- Market segmentation and positioning
- Objectives and action plans
- The marketing mix
- The monitoring and evaluation of marketing plans

It includes case studies on:

- The Rwanda Convention Bureau
- The Seoul MICE Master Plan
- Tourisme Montréal's meetings and conventions blog
- The Detroit Metro Convention and Visitors Bureau Tourism and Convention Sales Marketing Plan

On completion of this chapter, you should be able to:

- appreciate the advantages offered by effective marketing planning;
- understand the use of marketing research in the planning process;
- understand the role of, and techniques used in, segmentation and positioning;
- discuss how branding may be applied to the marketing of a destination or venue;
- appreciate the use of the marketing mix; and
- understand the techniques that may be used to evaluate and monitor a marketing plan.

Introduction

There can be no doubt that the success of any destination or venue depends on effective planning. All studies of managerial functions highlight the fact that planning is a key responsibility of management. Stevens *et al.* (2013:8) define planning as:

> *A managerial activity that involves analysing the environment, setting objectives, deciding on specific actions needed to reach the objectives, and providing feedback on results.*

The same authors emphasise that this process should be distinguished from the plan itself, which is a written document containing the results of the planning process: 'The plan is a written statement of what is to be done and how it is to be done. Planning is a continuous process that both precedes and follows other functions. Plans are made and executed, and then results are used to make new plans as the process continues' (ibid.:8).

It is, therefore, essential that marketing managers devote sufficient time and energy to planning for the future and the tangible manifestation of that planning process is the destination or venue's marketing plan.

An organisation's marketing plan is a vital element of its corporate strategic plan or business plan. It is the fundamental tool that enables it to devise, execute and monitor successful marketing programmes. Gartrell (1994) describes marketing plans as a kind of 'navigational chart' for organisations; and, to continue with the nautical metaphor, it is clear that any convention bureau or conference centre, for example, attempting to market its facilities and services without a formal plan would risk going seriously adrift and being obliged to rely on a series of ad-hoc decisions and extemporised reactions to external events.

Middleton (2001:194) emphasises that the marketing strategy planning process 'is essentially proactive in the sense that it defines and wills the future shape of the organisation as well as responding to changing industry patterns, technology, market conditions and perceived consumer needs'. A marketing plan, then, helps managers develop a clear direction for a set of complex, interrelated, activities to be carried out over the course of a specified period – usually 1 year.

There are further advantages offered by effective marketing planning. Kotler *et al.* (2003) list the purposes of a marketing plan as follows. It:

- Provides a road map for all marketing activities . . . for the next year
- Ensures that marketing activities are in agreement with the corporate strategic plan
- Forces marketing managers to review and think through objectively all steps in the marketing process
- Assists in the budgeting process to match resources with marketing objectives
- Creates a process to match actual against expected results

The purpose and components of marketing plans

An effective marketing plan is a working document that ultimately enables the destination or venue to instigate practical strategies in the form of a series of action plans. However, prior to the formulating of those strategies, a number of key steps must be taken.

The devising of marketing plans is a common theme of the marketing literature and authors generally agree that the process includes following several interdependent steps in a logical progression. Although there is little agreement as to the number of actual components in the marketing planning process, or the terminology used for each one, several elements are almost universally recognised as being indispensable:

1. The conducting of marketing research;
2. The selecting of target segments and the positioning of the organisation;
3. The establishing of objectives and action plans (what is to be done, when, and by whom);
4. The monitoring and evaluation of the marketing plan.

The rest of this chapter will explore each of these elements in turn.

Marketing research

The planning process generally begins with the organisation undertaking some form of research in order to evaluate its current and possible future position in the market. Commonly described as a *situation analysis* or *SWOT analysis*, this initial step involves a systematic assessment of the product (destination or venue) itself, as well as of the external market environment.

The product

This element of the marketing plan involves the destination or venue undertaking a detailed review of where and how it stands in the marketplace, its market share and its relation to its competitors. It is clear that, in order to be effective, such a review must be frank and comprehensive, and must be, in part, based on the organisation's own internal, 'micromarket' information: sales figures, client profiles, post-event evaluations, studies of advertising/promotional effectiveness and so on.

A rigorous review of both the strengths and the weaknesses of the product, in the widest sense, is a key part of this process. In chapter 1, the interdependence of destinations and venues was emphasised. Accordingly, therefore, any venue's situation analysis must include a review of the destination's particular strengths and weaknesses, as well as its own – and vice versa.

Similarly, a 'competitor analysis' – a frank and full appraisal of the capabilities and limitations of competing venues or destinations – is indispensable at this point in the process. Sincere competitor analysis requires a recognition on the part of the destination or venue that true competitive advantages are limited to those factors that are recognised by meetings buyers and planners and they influence their purchasing decisions. A competitor analysis, properly conducted, can offer the following advantages:

- It can uncover the destination or venue's unique selling propositions (USPs)
- It can highlight areas in which products and services leave room for improvement
- It can help in establishing where the destination or venue can best place and price itself within the market
- It can assist sales teams when they are pitching for business

The external market environment

All organisations operate within an external market environment over which they have little or no control. That environment constitutes the range of external forces that affect an organisation but over which the organisation has little or no control. These forces are often encapsulated in the acronym PEST (the political, economic, social and technological environment) or, when legal and environmental factors are also incorporated, PESTLE.

Marketers, therefore, need to undertake research in order to become fully aware of the principal environmental factors likely to affect their particular destination or venue. This can put them in a position to make the most of positive trends (opportunities) and to identify actual and potential obstacles to success (threats). This aspect of situation analysis is sometimes known as environmental forecasting.

Some of the opportunities and threats will inevitably be created as a result of the activities and business performance of the destination or venue's direct and indirect competitors. For example, if a conference hotel's closest rival in the same city plans to expand or refurbish its meeting facilities, this represents a potential threat that the hotel must take into account in its marketing plan. Conversely, any conference destination affected adversely as a result of, for instance, repeated strikes by the local workforce or the national airline, would present business opportunities to its competitor destinations that should be reflected in their marketing plans.

However, for all organisations, the main element in their assessment of the external market environment will be a comprehensive PEST or PESTLE analysis of all of those issues and trends that could have an impact on their future operation in general – and, in particular, on the level of demand for the facilities and services that the organisation offers. For any destination or venue, therefore, this analysis will comprise a careful consideration of the types of political, economic, social, technological, environmental and legal trends that are reviewed in other chapters of this book. For example, new legislation limiting how much pharmaceutical companies may spend on sponsoring medical conferences; or a significant change in currency exchange rates; or new advances in the quality of teleconferencing technology; or new transport links. A broad analysis of all of these types of factors is a vital step for any organisation systematically appraising its present position and identifying significant opportunities and threats.

Generally, the following questions should be addressed:

- What have been the major trends of the past year or two?
- What are the expected trends in the next year or two?
- What have been/will be the impacts of these trends on our destination or venue?
- What have been/will be the impacts of these trends on our competing destinations or venues?
- How should we change our marketing approaches in order to adapt to these trends?

Research into this aspect of situation analysis is generally undertaken using whatever relevant 'macromarket information' is available to destinations and venues. This may take the form of 'big picture' research reports or surveys produced by national tourist organisations, industry associations, consultants, academics or the meetings and incentive industry press. The annual ibtm world TrendsWatch report on changes affecting the worldwide meetings industry is an example of research that is commissioned and published by the organisers (Reed Travel Exhibitions) of the major meetings industry trade show, ibtm world (www.ibtmworld.com). Such macromarket information can comprise reports on general trends in conference demand and supply, economic forecasts or the type of performance tables produced by the International Congress and Convention Association (ICCA) or the Union of International Associations (UIA) for example.

Market segmentation and positioning

Once an organisation has conducted research to evaluate its marketing position, it can begin the next stage of its marketing plan: selecting its target segments and positioning the organisation.

Segmentation

It is generally agreed that interest in market segmentation – or segmentation analysis – has been growing in importance over the past few decades, as its contribution to improving the effectiveness of destination and venue marketing has increasingly been recognised.

Kotler *et al*. (2003) define market segmentation as the sub-dividing of a market into homogeneous sub-sets of customers, where any sub-set may conceivably be selected as a market target to be reached with a distinct marketing mix. In other words, market segments are composed of customers who are alike in some way or another and who may appear in the marketing plan as discrete targets for specific mixes of marketing activities undertaken by the destination or venue.

Fifield (1998:130) notes that 'such a breaking up of . . . marketing into a number of different mixes is obviously much more costly in terms of marketing investment and control, but the argument goes that with a more relevant mix you would improve your penetration of a given market segment and the increased volume would pay off the additional costs incurred'.

A vital element of any marketing plan, therefore, is the analysis of available market segments and the selection of the most appropriate segments for targeting. The list of available segments will include segments currently targeted by the destination or venue, as well as newly recognised market segments. It follows that the task of selecting the most appropriate segments will inevitably require careful consideration of the information gleaned from the situation analysis stage of the marketing plan, as effective market segmentation presupposes an accurate understanding of where and how the organisation stands in the marketplace and of the principal forces shaping the market environment – some of which may generate new segments or exclude existing segments.

A well-conducted situation analysis is, therefore, a destination or venue's key to becoming aware of the market segments that are available, and understanding their own ability to satisfy those particular segments' specific demands.

There are a number of different possible bases for segmenting the market for conferences, conventions and business events.

- By geographical zones: for example, a conference venue may choose to target primarily regional and national events – such as the annual conferences of professional associations, and/or the business events of companies based in the region in which the venue is located;
- By industry sector: Vienna, for instance, specialises in attracting medical congresses to its many meetings venues;
- By price sensitivity: for example, given the ability of most UK university venues to offer genuinely competitive rates, they generally target market segments seeking value-for-money, such as youth groups or the SMERF market (social, military, educational, religious and fraternal groups);
- By purpose of visit: the island of Mauritius, for example, with its image of luxury and exclusivity, targets, primarily, the incentive travel and incentivised meetings market.

Nevertheless, whatever the basis or bases used for segmenting any market, segments are usually characterised by three principal components. According to McDonald and Dunbar (2004):

1. The first component of a market segment is the list of needs that the individuals in that segment regard as important to them when selecting which competing offer to buy.

2. The second component of a market segment is the profiling attributes of its decision-makers. An understanding of who is to be found in each of the chosen segments is necessary so that there is some way of communicating with, and reaching, them and to enable successful targeting of segment-specific offers

3. The third and final component of a market segment is its size in terms of volume and/or value.

However, commentators are generally agreed that, in practice, segments are not created by marketers but, rather, *identified*, by them. This is put most succinctly by Fifield (1998:132), who states that:

> *Probably the most powerful aspect of . . . segmentation is that it forces the marketer to understand a fundamental truth about market segmentation, and that is that it is not the organisation or the marketer who actually segments the marketplace; it is the marketplace which segments itself. People fit themselves into market segments. Our job is not to divide the marketplace – our job is to identify how the market divides itself up and then to package and present our marketing mix accordingly.*

Positioning

Following the identification and selection of their target segments, the next task for venues and destinations is to influence the ways in which their products are perceived by those segments. This is the process known as product positioning, or simply positioning – establishing a product's *position* in the minds of the targeted customers.

In a market characterised by an abundant over-supply of products that are broadly similar in many ways, the potential buyer's perception of particular venues and destinations plays a vital role in the decision-making process. Holloway's (2004:77) observations on the importance of perception as a factor in leisure tourism decisions may be equally applied to the conference sector:

> *For those who have not actually visited a destination, perception is reality. Thus, building a distinct, positive and appealing image in the marketplace is critical. The image should not, however, be created through illusions. A product's image must be grounded in its unique and appealing attributes and developed through an intentional and systematic product positioning approach.*

Middleton (2001:199) also stresses the importance of image, summarising the important role of product positioning as follows: 'positioning underpins product/market growth through creating and sustaining a long-term favourable image or perception among prospective customers and other key stakeholders'.

It is clear, therefore, that in order to increase their chances of succeeding in attracting business from their target market or markets, venues and destinations must, first, establish a clear position for themselves and then effectively communicate this to buyers. Such products should be clearly positioned in relation to the actual and potential needs of the target market. Essential to this process, then, is the identifying of the product's benefits and demonstrating to the target markets how their needs are satisfied by these benefits. Once again, this information should have been gleaned from the situation analysis stage of the marketing plan.

Holloway (2004) outlines four different approaches that may be used in devising a positioning strategy:

1. Positioning by *product benefits*: showing how a product/service feature will produce benefit/value for customers. Marriott, for example, have positioned their Courtyard properties as a product catering for the business market and they use the slogan: 'Courtyard by Marriott: the hotel designed by business travellers'.

2. Positioning by *price and quality*: this strategy is generally easier to accomplish and more effective at the extreme ends of the pricing scale – high-priced luxury and low-priced economy products. The annual Luxury Travel Market trade show held in Cannes features a number of exhibitors representing meeting venues that are clearly positioned at the top quality end of the market – chateaux and palaces, for instance, which offer opulent meetings facilities – at considerable cost.

3. Positioning relative to a *product class*: this approach involves emphasising a particular class of products to which the venue or destination belongs. This may take the form of either *likening* the product to others in the same class (as in the case of Edinburgh, for example, positioning itself as a member of the BestCities consortium; or *disassociating* a product from others, in order to give it an enhanced position (as in the case of Mexico positioning itself as the only South American country to offer 0 per cent VAT on conferences and exhibitions organised in their country by foreign companies).

4. Positioning relative to a *competitor*: sometimes known as 'head-on positioning', this positioning strategy takes direct aim at the product's own direct or indirect competition and draws them into the advertising campaign. For example, Eurostar has effectively positioned itself in the business travel market by favourably comparing its own services with those of the airlines flying to those destinations served by the Eurostar trains.

It is useful to make the distinction here between positioning and re-positioning. In the sense that, by definition, a new product has no pre-existing image in the minds of buyers, an image must be created for it, in order to determine how it is perceived. Establishing a position for a new venue or destination is made somewhat easier by the fact that there are no pre-existing negative images to be counteracted.

The need for repositioning – changing the current position of an existing image – can arise due to different sets of circumstances, including the arrival of a new competitor. Most often, however, the need for repositioning derives from a change in the way the venue or destination relates to the market. For example, due to a lack of maintenance and product enhancement, conference venues in some UK seaside resorts have not been able to continue to satisfy the rising expectations of planners and delegates, and have, as a result, had to reposition themselves as centres for popular entertainment.

In a further example of how a product has been repositioned in response to changes in demand, Gartrell (1994) notes that many larger convention and visitor bureaux in the US have attempted to redefine their destinations as small meeting or corporate meeting sites as a result of market pressures (the rise in importance of small and medium-sized events), even though they have been traditionally known as major convention cities.

It is clear that even in the case of established venues and destinations, it is vital to constantly assess the validity of their image and decide to either maintain it or change it through a repositioning strategy.

Once the desired position has been established, the *positioning statement* may be written. Holloway (2004) describes a positioning statement as a document that is created for use within the organisation – a concise theme/statement that is woven through all marketing communications. In essence, it is an internal document that helps the firm direct its marketing efforts by communicating a consistent viewpoint and a *unified* goal that can be shared by all members of the organisation.

A marketing *slogan*, on the other hand, is an external marketing tool – often a phrase generated from the positioning statement that is designed to capture the attention of the target market and reinforce a product's image. It should indicate how the product is different from the others by highlighting the venue or destination's *USP* and use words that produce a very distinctive image ('biggest, fastest, least expensive'. . .).

A slogan, then, may be seen as a proposition that helps to identify and position a venue or destination in the minds of prospective users, and differentiate it from all others. Such labels abound in both leisure tourism ('I love New York') and business events (the Polish city of Wroclaw has as its slogan 'The Meeting

Place'). In the context of tourist destinations, Middleton (2001) considers the use of such slogans, noting that in order to be successful, they must:

- be based on genuine product values and attributes that can be delivered and that visitors recognise as authentic, not fake;
- be readily understood by customers;
- involve at least the leading players in the commercial sector;
- be incorporated into the promotional efforts of a country's regions and resorts;
- be sustained over several years (to overcome communication inertia, etc.);
- be systematically exploited in a range of sales-promotion and customer-servicing techniques designed to reach visitors on arrival at the destination, as well as prospective visitors in countries of origin.

Branding

Increasingly, the concept of branding is being linked with the positioning of all types of products, including venues and destinations.

The brand concept is best considered as simply a set of associations that is linked to a particular destination, venue or chain of venues, which resides in buyers' memories and helps them understand:

- What the brand is;
- Why it is potentially relevant to them; and
- How it differs from other, competitor, brands.

Brand associations spring from various marketing actions undertaken by the supplier of the product, including advertising and general media communications, as well as certain product characteristics (including the name and the logo or slogan). Information about the brands from the press, opinion leaders and word of mouth also affects the nature of these associations.

Essentially, then, a brand is a collection of perceptions in the mind of the potential buyer. 'It is the psychological, emotional, and (one hopes) motivational link between the customer and the product' (Harrill 2005:32).

Long before attempts were made to brand destinations and venues, the concept was applied to consumer goods, where the need for branding arose because of increasing global competition and the increasing difficulty for consumers to differentiate what were effectively very similar products in very crowded markets. The impact of branding today can be witnessed in the market for mineral water, for example, where branding is extensively used in order to distinguish near-identical products from others in the range.

But to what extent can the branding concept be usefully applied to the marketing of venues and destinations?

In terms of venues, since the early 1990s, many hotel chains have branded their meetings spaces product, to assist in the differentiation of their meetings facilities and services from their competitors' and to build customer loyalty. Branding was introduced in part to guarantee buyers that they would receive the same quality-assured level of service whichever hotel in the chain was used. From the point of view of the buyer, one of the major advantages of branding was the security of knowing that their meeting would be planned and would take place according to a number of assured, written standards. Such standards may, for example, state how promptly the initial enquiry would be dealt with, exactly how the hotel would assist on the day of the event, how the meetings room would be set up, how the bill would be calculated and how soon after the event it would be sent to the client (Davidson and Cope, 2003). The branding of hotel meetings facilities continues to be used as an effective way of marketing meetings packages, providing clients with confidence and reassurance when making their crucial venue selection decisions.

Some examples of hotels' meetings product brands:

- For example, Hilton Worldwide's branded product is 'Meetings Simplified™', specifically targeting meetings of up to 25 delegates. The package is promoted as 'making booking your next meeting easier than ever – at an all-inclusive price' and is available at 'over 180 hotels throughout Europe, the Middle East and Africa' (as at June 2014). The package includes:
  - Room hire
  - Free Wi-Fi
  - Two-course lunch
  - Two servings of tea/coffee
  - LCD projector and screen
  - Flipchart
  - Stationery
  - 24-hour cancellation

For further details visit: www.hiltonworldwide.com/simple.

- Mercure Hotels launched (Summer 2014) its 'Meet with Mercure' brand – www.meetwithmercure.com
- The Kempinski Group of luxury hotels announced (August 2014) the development of a level of standards that will remain consistent across the brand. The 'Kempinski Group & Event Signature Standards' focus on consistency in response time (to enquiries), site inspections, and incentives that can include anything from free rooms for meeting planners to free Wi-Fi to free telephone use. Kristina Mees, Kempinski's corporate director of group sales, commented ('International Meetings Review, August 18, 2014):

  > It's a commitment from our side that all groups and events have certain standards when they are held in a Kempinski hotel.

It may be convincingly argued that hotel chains' use of branding initiatives such as this has brought them a considerable measure of *brand equity* in the form of the four major assets described by Aaker's (1991) model of consumer-based brand equity, as explored in Pike (2004):

Brand loyalty – repeat and referral custom, arising from the desire for a reduced risk of an unsatisfactory experience.

Brand awareness – the foundation of all sales activity. Awareness represents the strength of the brand's presence in the mind of the target. There is general agreement that planners' familiarity with hotels' meetings facilities brands has increased through repeated exposure and strong associations.

Perceived quality – there is little point in branding any product that is of poor or variable quality.

Brand associations – A brand association is anything 'linked' in memory to a brand. These associations are a combination of *functional* and *affective* attributes, of which some will represent key buying criteria. 'What is most critical is that brand associations are strong, favorable and unique, in that order' (Keller, 2003, quoted in Pike, 2004).

Nevertheless, while meetings facilities may be similar to consumer goods, regarding the way in which branding may be applied to them, the application of branding principles to destinations is a much more complex matter. Pike and Page (2014) offer the following challenges facing destination marketing organisations (DMOs) attempting to harness the benefits of branding:

- Success is most likely when the range of differentiated features emphasised is limited to one or a few features or benefits, and yet a destination usually comprises a diverse and eclectic range of features that must somehow be summarised into a short, single minded proposition.

- The market interests of the diverse and eclectic stakeholders found in any destination are not homogeneous.
- The politics of DMO decision-making can make the best theories unworkable in practice.
- Destination marketers have no control over the actual delivery of the brand promise.
- The ultimate aim of branding is to stimulate brand loyalty, and yet DMOs rarely come into contact with visitors to enable meaningful post-visit engagement to stimulate repeat visitation.

Pike (2004) nevertheless argues that, despite these challenges, promoting product features alone is not sufficient to differentiate against any destination's competitors, and therefore, branding is required. Consequently, he claims, the fundamental challenge for DMOs is to develop and promote a brand identity that encapsulates the essence or spirit of a destination.

He admits that the processes of brand development, implementation and management are more complex for destination marketers than for those marketing individual venues, as the former exert no control over the actual delivery of the brand promise. He adds a further factor that contributes to the complexity of establishing a coherent destination brand – the existence of a 'destination brand hierarchy', comprising several 'brand' levels, as shown in Table 2.1.

It is clear that, assuming that destinations can be branded, one aspect of the complexity of this process would be the need to ensure that the brands of all levels of the hierarchy were compatible – and that a destination's business events brand was compatible with its leisure tourism brand. Harrill (2005) also emphasises the need for destination brands to be supported by different levels in the hierarchy, noting that for a branding exercise to prove successful, it must also enjoy the proactive participation of the destination's constituents (at sub-country levels) in their own marketing communications delivery systems.

Despite these challenges, however, branding has become a key pillar in destination marketing and it is widely believed by advocates of destination branding that the future of destination marketing will be a battle of the brands, as 'it is likely that most destinations will become increasingly substitutable, if not already so, and therefore commodities rather than brands' (Pike 2004:69). They believe that the brand may be the one thing that makes a difference to consumers' thinking about competing destinations all offering features of a similar quality, and that, consequently, branding ought to be at the very heart of marketing strategy, with the purpose of all destination marketing activity being to enhance the value of the brand.

Academic commentators have followed – and, in some cases, have led – the growing trend towards destination branding. Pike and Page (2014) note that while the topic of destination image has been popular in the academic literature since the 1970s, destination branding did not emerge as a field until the late 1990s. Since then, academic interest in the topic has increased exponentially, with branding becoming one of the fastest growing topics in the destination marketing literature.

Table 2.1 Destination brand hierarchy

Level	Entity
1	Country brand
2	Country business events brand
3	State business events brands
4	Regional brands
5	Local community brands
6	Individual suppliers' business brands

Adapted from Pike (2004).

The clamour of the destination branders is deafening, therefore, and dissenting voices are few and far between. Nevertheless, one, Holcomb (1999), is quoted by Pike: 'packaging and promoting the city to tourists can destroy its soul. The city is commodified, its form and spirit remade to conform to market demand, not residents' dreams'.

Objectives and action plans

After the situation analysis has been completed and used to segment the market and position the product, a venue or destination may proceed to the stage of programme planning, which begins with establishing clear, prioritised objectives. It is only at this stage (of deciding the marketing objectives) that the active part of the marketing planning process begins, as these objectives then help the marketer to devise a set of the most effective marketing strategies based on the marketing mix. In addition, a list is created of action plans designed and implemented for each specific market segment, in order to meet the objectives set. This essential stage in marketing planning is indeed the key to the entire marketing process.

Objectives

Marketing planning requires the venue or destination to establish both short-term and long-term objectives. Typical objectives that might be set could include, for example, achieving a certain level of sales growth within a given period of time or increasing market share by a certain percentage with a certain period. For each established marketing objective, a separate mix of marketing communications activities must be planned.

It is generally agreed that, in order to be effective, objectives should demonstrate certain key characteristics. According to Kotler *et al*. (2003), for example, they should be:

- Quantitative (expressed in monetary terms or some other unit of measurement, such as occupancy rate, number of conferences hosted, etc.);
- Time-specific (1 year, 6 months . . . or, in the case of the Seoul Master Plan featured later in this chapter as a case study: 6 years);
- Profit/margin specific (such as an average margin of 22 per cent).

Action plans

The action plan outlines the designated marketing activities required to achieve each specific objective. This usually takes the form of a comprehensive calendar that lists all the major marketing activities month by month for the period of a year. The implementation of these activities is the *action* phase of the marketing plan. For that reason, *timelines* must be clearly stated to show what must be done by which date in the marketing calendar. The action calendar will take into account fixed dates, such as the dates of major trade shows and the start and finish dates for major promotional campaigns, as well as dates for already arranged familiarisation trips and sales trips.

The issue of the resources required to implement the action plan should also be dealt with and recorded in this section of the marketing plan. This involves both staff and money. Those members of staff assigned to lead on various activities in the action plan should also be named, so that there are clear lines of responsibility in the implementation process. And, crucially, the budget required for each activity should be specified in detail.

However, the principal consideration at this stage of the marketing plan is the question of precisely what is to be offered to each market segment – and how – in order to most effectively meet the stated objectives and to yield the maximum return on the destination or venue's investment in its marketing endeavours.

The combination of all the tools available to the marketer to plan and implement the marketing strategy and meet the marketing objectives is known as the marketing mix.

The marketing mix

The concept of the marketing mix lies at the heart of all marketing planning. The different variables that constitute the marketing mix are traditionally known as the four Ps: product, place (or process of delivery), price and promotion. For any venue or destination, these are the *controllable* elements of the marketing plan – which clearly distinguishes them from those factors that the organisation *cannot* control, such as the PEST elements in the market environments and the actions of competitors.

The marketing mix selected for each particular target segment forms the foundation of the marketing plan's strategy.

- *Product* is what a venue or destination offers for sale in order to satisfy customer needs. This will include all of the tangible elements (the AV equipment, seating, conference food, etc.) as well as the intangibles (such as the manner in which delegates are received, or the atmosphere of the destination).
- *Place* is generally taken to describe those distribution channels the venue or destination uses to make its product available and accessible to prospective customers. These might include trade shows as well as websites through which planners can access information.
- *Price* is the amount charged for services provided – and is therefore a more important consideration for venues than for convention bureaux (CVBs). Indeed Pike (2004) identifies price as an aspect of the marketing mix that is problematic for DMOs, which generally have little or no control over the price of their destination's products.
- *Promotion* includes all of the marketing communications techniques that may be used in order to reach the selected market segments.

In recent years, attempts have been made to enhance this quartet by the addition of three or four extra Ps. For example, Holloway (2004) suggests adding 'People' (the destination's inhabitants) as well as 'Physical evidence' (all of the cues present at the destination, based on sight, sound, etc.).

Burke and Resnick (2000) indicate that some travel marketing experts have added four extra Ps – physical environment, purchasing process, packaging and participation. They feel that these additional Ps are necessary to describe the process involved in marketing travel services. A convincing case may be made for applying the same eight Ps to the variables that a venue or destination can control when trying to attain its goal of successfully marketing its facilities and services.

An illustration may be given, such as a case of a hotel with conference facilities (see Table 2.2).

Establishing the appropriate marketing mix for each segment may be seen as the culmination of all of the preceding stages in the marketing planning process. A venue or destination, having decided whom it wishes to reach, what it is selling, how much it must charge in order to make a profit and through which channels it will reach its audience, must then devise a means of communicating its message to its audience. These marketing communications techniques are the focus of the next three chapters of this book.

By recording the marketing mix in an annual marketing action plan, an organisation is committing itself in writing to a particular marketing strategy for the 12 months ahead. This does not mean, however, that no element of the mix can be changed during that period. Changing circumstances in the market environment can produce new opportunities (such as a competitor venue struck by some unforeseen crisis) or threats (a currency devaluation in a country that is a major inbound market, for example). There is, therefore, a

Table 2.2 The marketing mix

The Ps	Definition	Example
Product	What a company is offering for sale	A hotel's conference rooms
Place/process of delivery	Channels of distribution and delivery	A hotel booking agency
Price	The amount of money paid for a product, based by seller on certain factors	A €100 day-delegate rate
Promotion	Activities that stimulate interest in a product	Advertising in a trade magazine
Physical environment	The environment in which the sale takes place	Website, trade workshop
	The environment in which the product is produced and consumed	
Purchasing process	Motivations and information search	Selecting a conference destination
Packaging	Bringing together of complementary products	Providing pre- and post-conference tours and/or partners' programmes
Participation	The transaction or experience	Buyer, intermediary and seller interaction

Adapted from Burke and Resnick (2000).

need to avoid absolute rigidity in the marketing plan, without allowing so much flexibility that the plan no longer fulfils its role as a navigational chart.

In any case, while some elements of the marketing mix clearly may be changed at very short notice (promotion, price) others take much longer to alter (product, channels of distribution).

The monitoring and evaluation of marketing plans

All marketing plans and their results must be subject to monitoring and evaluation in order to determine how effective the destination or venue is, in attaining the goals and objectives stated in the plan.

The following comments from Morrison (2013:271) on DMOs' accountability equally well apply to venues:

> *Measuring effectiveness is about measuring results and . . . DMO accountability includes project-ing results and then measuring [them]. The projected results should be based upon specific plans that the DMO has prepared, e.g. the marketing plan . . . and need to be justified by research that the DMO has conducted.*

One term commonly used to describe the type of measurements that companies can use to evaluate their degree of success in using a marketing plan is key performance indicators (KPIs). KPIs form an important part of the information required to determine and explain how any company or organisation progresses towards its business and marketing goals. They are a form of *quantifiable* marketing metrics that, in the context of destination and venue marketing, help DMO and venue marketing managers monitor the effec-tiveness of each marketing activity included in their marketing plan.

Against what kind of quantifiable KPIs can a marketing plan's results be assessed?

Table 2.3 Key performance indicators

KPI description	Target	Achievement
Convention bureau		
Convention bid wins (including BCEC led bid wins)	38	45
Economic value of bid wins	$44M	$49.9M
Request for proposal sent to convention members	265	247
Target business events that are aligned with investment attraction, Qld Gov and BCC	25%	75%
Membership number and value of convention members	125/$220,000	151/$212,000

Adapted from Brisbane Marketing (2011).

Gartrell (1994) suggests the following, measurable, criteria, most of which may be applied to venues as well as destinations:

- Room-nights booked
- Total delegate attendance
- Distribution of delegate attendance (local, state, regional, national, international)
- Total conventions booked
- Distribution of booked business (local, etc.)
- Types of bookings (convention, exhibitions, trade shows, special events, small meetings)
- Business booked by facilities (convention centre, arenas, hotels)
- Business booked through various marketing techniques (trade shows, direct mail, direct sales, advertising, etc.)
- Number of leads generated
- Conversion rate
- Housing reservations
- Total economic impact of convention business
- Amount of local taxes generated

An example of actual KPIs is shown in Table 2.3. These are the KPIs of the convention bureau-related marketing activities of Brisbane Marketing, the economic development agency of that city, as included in their annual report. Targets from their marketing plan are compared with actual achievements.

It is clear that, whatever the criteria used, it is only by evaluating the performance of each element in the marketing mix that a venue or destination will be in a position to answer the crucial question of the extent to which it is getting an adequate return on the often costly investment it is making in its marketing activities.

CASE STUDY 2.1   The Rwanda Convention Bureau

Rwanda: the remarkable country

Rwanda is located in east/central Africa, bordered by the Democratic Republic of Congo, Uganda, Burundi and Tanzania. Previously a French colony, this young African country is now experiencing strong economic growth [8 per cent average year-on-year growth in gross domestic product

(GDP)] and a stable inflation rate. Rwanda has a population of 11.5 million with a variety of languages, including Kinyarwanda, French, English and Kiswahili. The country covers an area of more than 26,000 square kilometres and has a temperate climate with average temperatures of 24 to 27 degrees centigrade. Its capital city is Kigali.

Rwanda is politically stable with well-functioning institutions and rule of law and zero tolerance of corruption. It is an increasingly attractive destination for foreign investment, with a market and customs union across east Africa offering a potential market of 125 million people.

The country is also a potential major tourism destination, featuring:

- 4,000 hectares of bamboo forest
- 1,000-plus hills and volcanos, the highest volcano soaring to over 4,000 metres and tea and coffee plantations
- 700 bird species and seven important birding areas
- 14 species of primates including one-third of the world's remaining endangered mountain gorilla population
- A rich culture including music and dance and growing contemporary art and craft industries
- 227 kilometres of the breath-taking Congo Nile trail

Rwanda as a conference and business events destination

Rwanda has recently successfully hosted a number of high-level large conferences such as the Transform Africa Summit in 2013 (2,000 delegates) and the Africa Development Bank General Assembly in 2014 (2,800 delegates).

Rwanda's capital city is preparing to unveil the US$300 million Kigali Convention Centre (KCC), due to open in mid-2016. Positioned on a hilltop in the heart of Kigali near the parliament, the development is set to become one of the most recognised modern structures in Africa. Encompassing a translucent dome, a multi-functional hall with a maximum capacity of 2,600, the KCC will help position Rwanda as the leading business events or MICE destination in East Africa.

In tandem with the KCC, a number of international 5-star hotel brands are currently under development (e.g. Radisson Blu, Marriott, Park Inn, Sheraton, Kempinski) with over 600 bedrooms coming on to the market.

Just 10 minutes from the city centre, the Kigali International Airport has recently been upgraded and is now able to handle 1,500,000 passengers annually, triple its previous capacity.

Rwanda's other key assets and benefits for the business events sector include:

- An excellent infrastructure and telecommunications capabilities
- Easy air access and a streamlined visa process
- High levels of safety and little traffic congestion
- An exceptionally clean country
- An array of iconic tourism attractions in close proximity
- Ranked second in Africa in terms of 'Ease in Doing Business' (World Bank 2013)

Conference topics of particular relevance to meetings hosted in Rwanda include:

- Conservation, biodiversity and sustainability
- Unity, justice and reconciliation

- Women's rights and gender issues
- Urban management
- Health and HIV
- Poverty reduction
- Good governance
- Development of biogenic medicine
- East African market economy
- Security issues

In 2013, Rwanda was ranked 21st among African countries in ICCA's ranking of international conference destinations. At a global level, Rwanda occupied 141st place.

Formation of the Rwanda Convention Bureau

The conference and business events or MICE sector has been identified by the Rwanda Development Board as providing a clear and long-term opportunity to diversify and grow Rwanda's export strategy. In 2013, the decision was taken to establish a national convention bureau for Rwanda and it was envisaged that this would serve as the focal point for the co-ordination of all MICE industry activities, respond to business leads, generate event bids and track conversion rates, all leading to the achievement of Rwanda's Economic Development Poverty Reduction Strategy II (EDPRS) goals.

The Business Tourism Company (headed up by Rick Taylor) was appointed to implement Rwanda's National MICE Strategy for the period November 2013 to November 2014. The key objective of the MICE Project was to grow the business tourism sector in Rwanda with the focus on providing technical expertise in establishing a Convention Bureau, thus contributing to the achievement of EDPRS II objectives.

Project implementation was planned with a phased approach as follows:

- Phase 1: *development phase* – November 2013 to March 2014. This foundation stage of the project encompassed the review, drafting and approval of key documents and strategies. The *National MICE Strategy* was adopted by Cabinet; the Rwanda Convention Bureau (RCB) was established and acting MICE Division Manager was appointed.

- Phase 2: *implementation phase* – April to November 2014. RCB was launched both nationally and internationally; a professional MICE brand identity was developed; collateral was produced and a sales strategy activated.

- Phase 3: *strengthening phase* – 2015. To ensure a sustainable Rwanda Convention Bureau, investment in staffing resources for the Bureau was planned for activation during 2015. The Business Tourism Company's contract was to be renewed and included appropriate mentoring of key Bureau staff.

The RCB is responsible for building the country's business and events brand and aims to position Rwanda in the top 20 African meeting destinations by 2015–16, in the top 15 by 2018–19 and in the top 10 by 2019–20 (based on ICCA Africa rankings). Under the strapline 'Meet in Remarkable Rwanda', the RCB was launched nationally in May 2014 to stakeholders in the country, with a formal international launch taking place at the IMEX exhibition in Frankfurt, also in May 2014.

Specific functions of the RCB include:

- Promoting private sector MICE-related investment opportunities
- Strengthening the domestic economic circle (value chain) thereby
  - developing local business networks and supporting small and medium-sized enterprises (SMEs);
  - growing private sector participation and capabilities; and
  - decentralising MICE tourism receipts to regional and district levels
- Developing human resources and building capacity, driving job creation across all industries.

The Convention Bureau is the central co-ordination body for MICE in the destination. It serves to create linkages between the demand and supply sides of the sector and to promote Rwanda as a viable national, regional and international meetings destination. It is envisaged that it will play a leading role in meeting ambitious targets to deliver MICE receipts of US$207 million by 2017.

RCB marketing activity

The broad objectives of the RCB marketing strategy are to brand and market Rwanda as a preferred MICE destination working with key institutions (e.g. RwandAir, tour operators, industry stakeholders) and to position Rwanda as a regional MICE hub.

Specific objectives include:

- Increasing visitors' and delegates' length of stay and the value of their spend in the destination – *Get Around, Dine Around* and *Shop Around* marketing collateral has been produced
- Marketing Rwanda as a MICE destination to build awareness – leaflets, advertisements and video have been produced and a website has been launched. Achieving PR and editorial exposure using international MICE media to the value of US$15,000 had been achieved by November 2014.

RCB sales activity: functions and achievements

The objectives are to:

- Increase MICE sales and accelerate new tourism revenue growth
- Sales activity: participate at specific global MICE trade shows, for instance, IMEX Frankfurt, ibtm world, Meetings Africa and ibtm Africa
- RCB to join leading global MICE associations, for sales and database development – membership of ICCA has been finalised
- Represent the Government when making official bids for events – a MICE 'Bid Book' has been compiled for use when tendering to attract major events
- A cost/benefit analysis for all MICE bids will be undertaken by RCB to help to drive an ROI (return on investment) mind-set
- Identify/support events with potential to grow MICE benefits – local events have been identified for support and mentoring has commenced
- Originate and maintain a calendar of events – aiming to drive event management into the private sector. Table 2.4 shows a calendar of confirmed events as at July 2014

Table 2.4 Rwanda Convention Bureau events calendar

Confirmed Events (as at July 2014)	Month/year	Potential foreign delegates
World Export Development Forum (WEDF) for Africa/Women Vendor Exhibition and Forum (WVEF)	16–17 September 2014	500
East Africa Business Summit (EABS)	23–25 October 2014	1,000
African Leadership Network Annual Gathering	5–8 November 2014	300–400
East African Law Society Summit	13–14 November 2014	300–500
Tenth International Conference Kangaroo Mother Care	17–19 November 2014	500
Innovation Africa Summit	18–20 November 2014	150
CISA Ninth Edition: International Sport Convention in Africa 2015 (Rwanda National Olympics and Sports Committee)	11–15 March 2015	400 4 days
Mining conference	March 2015	400
Rotary District Annual Conference	April/May 2015	500
African Nations Championship (CHAN 2016)	January/February 2016	
Africa Society of Blood Transfusion	May 2016	800

Challenges faced

Delays in the construction of the Kigali Convention Centre (it was originally scheduled to open in 2014) and of some of the major hotels have called into question the RCB's ability to deliver on the MICE Strategy targets.

As at November 2014, there was an encouragingly busy schedule of MICE events generated by a number of government ministries. However, these did entail some levels of government sponsorship. It was felt to be important for Rwanda to adopt international best practice guidelines in hosting events and generating private sponsorship for the full economic benefits of the MICE sector to be achieved.

Other issues to be addressed as at November 2014 included:

• The appointment of full-time dedicated staff to RCB, together with the implementation of capacity building;

• Capacity building within the private sector needed to be facilitated, for instance, Professional Conference and Event Organiser capacity building workshops and accreditation programme;

• A focus on the implementation of a V×V×LOS×GS×S strategy was essential, for instance, volume×value×length of stay×geographical spread×seasonality.

Strengthening phase: the way forward 2015

A number of important tasks were identified by the consultant for implementation during 2015 – the strengthening phase of the RCB/MICE strategy project and forming the basis of RCB's business plan. These are listed in Table 2.5:

Table 2.5 Steps in Rwanda Convention Bureau's strengthening phase

Strategy implementation	
Rwanda Convention Bureau Steering Committee	Formalise, activate, inform and convene Committee
Cost/benefit strategy	Rollout the discipline to both public and private sectors
Market research activation	Activate first dedicated MICE delegate expenditure survey
Geographical spread strategy	Strategic plan to develop key MICE destinations (Gisenyi, Huye, Musanze, Akagera)
Product development strategy	Leverage destination strengths to initiate and attract MICE products: meetings/incentive packages/exhibitions
	Identify MICE investment opportunities
Marketing activation	
Advertising and public relations	Awareness building via advertising and editorial coverage in selected MICE media
Collateral	Ongoing development of RCB MICE collateral
Familiarisation trips – buyers/media	Identify and host key MICE journalists and buyers
Market representation	Establish market representation in key source markets
MICE awards	Participate in global programmes (ICCA, M&IT, Site) to build destination credentials and awareness
Sales activation	
Bidding strategy	Concretise bidding activation via stakeholder connectivity and ICCA database
Develop CRM strategy	Employ research data to drive repeat visits by delegates as leisure tourists
MICE trade shows and roadshows	Leverage international MICE trade shows to position Rwanda/generate sales leads
	Together with market representative – conduct appropriate roadshows
Site inspections	Hosting of confirmed client site inspection visits
Stakeholder engagement	
Capacity building	Quarterly stakeholder planning meetings
	Targeted training workshops
Establish Rwanda Association of Professional Conference Organisers (RAPCO)	RAPCO – to build destination credentials
	Accreditation programme via RCB training and linkages with international associations
Ambassador campaign	Identify Rwanda corporates, universities, NGOs and associations to source MICE business opportunities
	Assist with bidding

Looking ahead, Rick Taylor of The Business Tourism Company has commented:

> At the core of Rwanda government planning is the Economic Development Poverty Reduction Strategy, which aims for Rwanda to be the first middle class country in Africa. This means that, by 2020, everyone will have a job. By establishing a pro-business, pro-investment financial context, Rwanda will use business events to attract inward investment and talent.

Further information: www.rwandaconventionbureau.rw and www.thebusinesstourismcompany.com.

CASE STUDY 2.2   The Seoul MICE Master Plan

Seoul, capital of South Korea, is already a very successful conference, meetings and incentive, or MICE, destination. Ranked in the top five convention cities, according to the 2013 International Meetings Statistics Report by the Union of International Associations (UIA) and ninth in the 2013 Country and City Rankings statistics report compiled by the International Congress and Convention Association (ICCA), both released in 2014, the city is served by an award-winning international airport, used by tens of thousands of international delegates every year.

Value of the MICE market in Korea

According to research data released by the Korea Tourism Organisation (KTO) in 2011, the expenditure of business visitors in Seoul for meetings-related activities (US$2,585 per business visitor) was 1.8 times that of the general tourist (US$1,410). In 2013, the rate increased to 1.9 times: US$3,088 per event participant and US$1,610 per general visitor.

Induced expenditure generated by the Korean meetings industry amounted to 28 trillion KRW in 2011 and, in 2012, this increased to 36.7 trillion KRW, according to the MICE industry statistical report released by KTO.

In terms of job creation rates, the Korean meetings industry exceeds manufacturing industry by a factor of two and the IT industry by a factor of five.

Seoul's MICE Master Plan

Seoul has focused its endeavours on the production of a Master Plan that, in broad terms, aims to treble the city's business events capacity by 2020 and propel it into the world's top three convention cities by 2018. Specifically, Seoul aims to increase the number of international events hosted from 253 to 350, the number of participants from 0.5 million to 1.0 million and the spending per delegate from US$3,088 to US$4,500.

Seventeen meetings involving 69 industry experts and professionals were held during 2013 to formulate the Master Plan, which includes five main policy objectives and ten core business goals. The Plan is an excellent illustration of long-term planning and investment strategies for the MICE or business events sector. The remainder of this case study provides more detail on the content of the Master Plan, based on its executive summary.

The vision statement and aim of the plan are:

Vision statement: To develop Seoul as a leading global brand.

Aim: To increase MICE visitors and their expenditure and to attain world top three convention city status.

The five policy objectives cover: infrastructure expansion; strategy to attract meetings; plans to increase MICE visitor spending; the nurturing of MICE domestic events; and strengthening of the MICE industry.

Infrastructure expansion

The aim is that Seoul's MICE infrastructure should be three times larger than the 2013 MICE facilities by 2020. This expansion will be achieved in three phases:

Phase 1: scheduled for completion in 2018, Phase 1 will see the development of Seoul's central district, with the addition of Dongdaemun Design Plaza (DDP) and the convention centre near Seoul Station. DDP opened its doors on 21 March 2014. DDP features five facilities with 15 function spaces including an international conference hall, a learning centre, a design museum, an exhibition hall and a history and culture park. Figure 2.1 shows DDP.

Phase 2: scheduled for completion in 2020, phase 2 will see the creation of Seoul's largest MICE multi-complex in the Yeongdong area, home to the Coex convention and exhibition centre, with an additional 88,700m^2 of space. Running all the way to the Jamsil Sports Complex, the multi-complex will also contain additional accommodation, shopping and other facilities for cultural and entertainment events. As part of the redevelopment, the district's sporting facilities – which previously hosted the 1988 Summer Olympics – will be upgraded, as will the land along the Hangang River. This massive undertaking has been made possible through agreements reached with Coex and other stakeholders such as the Korean Electric Power Corporation.

Phase 3 will see the redevelopment of Seoul's Magok district, close to Gimpo International Airport, as an all-embracing convention district.

Figure 2.1 Dongdaemun Design Plaza

Strategy to attract meetings

Marketing activity to generate new and increased numbers of meetings to Seoul will combine research with collaborative partnerships as well as other initiatives. They include:

- Expanding research capabilities by utilising Big Data Search as a tool for international conferences from the ICCA database. Initial research has shown that there are potentially 276 conferences with 500 or more participants that have not yet been held in Korea.

- Forming liaisons with global enterprises and corporations by working with their local regional offices to attract events. The number of global companies represented in Seoul is 7,903.

- Devising a joint marketing plan to work with KTO and the Korea Trade-Investment Promotion Agency (KOTRA) to collaborate further. This will involve, inter alia, co-operation with the respective regional offices to share information and undertake joint promotional events. Both organisations have a global reach.

- Active participation in international MICE exhibitions/trade shows, including IT&CM, ibtm china, IT&CMA, ITB Asia, AIME, IMEX Frankfurt, IMEX America, ibtm arabia and ibtm world.

- Identifying and expanding the inventory of unique facilities/venues that can be promoted and thus help to provide Seoul with its USP. It is also about ensuring the quality of the venues being represented.

Plans to increase MICE visitor spending

All destinations seek to maximise the economic impact and benefit of the business events staged. Seoul will aim to achieve this through the following:

- Develop and provide customised MICE tourism products and services:
  - By facilitating industry-related site inspections and tours for trade and corporate meeting participants
  - For incentive planners: develop options for themed activities and team building programmes
  - For officials and event organisers from governmental organisations and/or non-governmental organisations: co-ordinate Seoul Metropolitan Government policy information and related tours

- Create MICE-customisable tours and promotional systems, thus adding tourism benefits to business events and extending the stay of business visitors:
  - Provide tour programme information to the event organiser
  - Operate the specialist support centre for MICE visitors within Coex Convention and Exhibition Centre
  - Manage the website for MICE specialist tours and develop mobile web applications
  - Recruit and train Korean cultural heritage commentators and guides

Seoul Convention Bureau information on customisable tours can be accessed at http://miceseoul. com/tool-kits/.

- Produce a MICE card for MICE visitors:
  - Provide an all-in-one MICE card that can be used by delegates/attendees for public transportation and convenience stores
  - Sell the cards to the event organiser (for business-to-business types of MICE events)

Nurture domestic MICE events

- Foster Hallyu*-related business and incorporate Hallyu into MICE events: convention, trade show, cultural events, etc.

  Hallyu (or 'Korean Wave') covers a broad range of attractions. Korean fashion, cosmetics, pop music, and television have all become popular items in Asia, often generating further interest in Seoul as a result.

- Develop domestic MICE events into global events – identify domestic exhibitions and conventions that have the potential to grow into global events:
  - Use a competition to select three domestic events and support them for three years

Strengthening Seoul's MICE industry

- Train MICE professionals – connect education and industry; establish stability in the supply and demand of events sector employees:
  - Work together with MICE sector associations in operating education and training sessions, internships, and recruitment
- Raise awareness of the MICE industry in the local community:
  - Organise programmes such as the international forum, MICE planning competition, etc. Seoul MICE Week 2014 was the pilot programme that was launched in December 2014 to promote the MICE industry to local residents
- Expand and strengthen MICE organisations
  - Expand and strengthen Seoul Convention Bureau
  - Set up an advisory committee, MICE research support centre and MICE ambassadors
  - Expand and invigorate the Seoul MICE Alliance (SMA), a partnership between government agencies and private-sector organisations formed in 2008 to enhance the city's global business events competitiveness. In 2014, membership increased from 143 to 170.

Seoul Convention Bureau information on SMA: http://miceseoul.com/sma/. For further information on Seoul as a convention and business events or MICE destination, visit www.miceseoul.com.

CASE STUDY 2.3   Tourisme Montréal's meetings and conventions blog

DMOs are diversifying their brand communications in order to create more content to distribute more frequently across their spectrum of digital channels. Tourisme Montréal (www.tourisme-montreal.org) is leading the trend in North America with multiple targeted websites, special events and collaborative partnerships with content providers and travel suppliers.

Tourisme Montréal has been moving toward a more content-oriented approach in all its marketing strategies to its various publics. This began with a shift toward social media and blogs for the leisure (consumer tourist) market in 2009 and it has been evolving ever since. The DMO's blogging initiatives were introduced as part of a conscious change to align marketing and communication efforts around travel behaviours rather than traveller types, required by the rapid fragmentation of traditional consumer travel patterns.

According to Emmanuelle Legault, Vice-President of Marketing at Tourisme Montréal:

> *We don't talk about segments of travellers first anymore we talk more about niches and their motivations to travel. And then within those niches, we look at the segment that would be interested in them, where there's a good fit within the city and what we have to offer.*

The DMO was the first of its kind to launch an official destination blog as a supplement to its website in 2009. Tourisme Montréal's leisure travel blog was aimed at ten niche markets: cutting-edge, nightlife, gay life, gastronomy, fashion, family, outdoors, attractions, arts and culture and festivals and events. Millennial/generation Y demand for more experiential travel played a role in conceptualising those themes and the blog's overall design and direction.

Later, Tourisme Montréal was the first in the industry to launch a dedicated meetings/conventions blog to attract more of that lucrative market.

Lynn Habel, Editor-in-chief of Tourisme Montréal, describes the initiative as follows:

> *We began applying this approach for the meetings and conventions market in 2013 with the creation of the Meetings à la Montréal blog, which provided us with a more agile platform for timely content that didn't really have a 'home' on the website. The idea was to have a platform that would act as a hub for content that we could then distribute and make available to our target audiences via social media (Twitter, Facebook, Pinterest, LinkedIn, Google+) and through newsletters and other direct marketing channels.*

Our original objectives were to:

- *Build awareness for Montréal as a creative, innovative and appealing destination for meetings and conventions;*
- *Position Tourisme Montréal as a thought-leader in the industry and as a source of practical help and inspiration;*
- *Generate visibility for Montréal and our partners and build engagement with our target audiences.*

> *The first year (2013) was about building the foundations: creating the bank of content, trying different topics and approaches to see what resonated best with our clienteles. In the second year, we applied the learnings acquired through data analytics and social media metrics and began to adapt the content accordingly. We looked at the most-read articles, the most-shared articles, the articles that generated the most time on site and where the content was most retweeted or commented upon on LinkedIn. One key learning was that 'how-tos' and inspirational/idea posts worked better than more obviously 'branded' content. We also learned that it was very difficult to break through the 'noise' on social media platforms without some kind of paid promotion. By adding Facebook ads (even though we do not have a Facebook page dedicated solely to the meetings and conventions market), sponsored tweets and LinkedIn ads, we generated significantly more views for the blog.*

> *Because of the nature of the market and the way in which groups choose destinations for their meetings – long lead times (usually several years for large groups), predetermined rotation patterns and a host of other factors – it is difficult to point to a concrete cause-and-effect relationship between a piece of content and a booking. However, there is one anecdote that demonstrates the potential of the blog in supporting sales efforts:*

> *We had been bidding for several years to win a major annual meeting of an international association. In the interim, we had succeeded in booking one of their smaller regional*

meetings. We posted a profile about the meeting on the blog. The meeting planner enjoyed the post and shared it on their social platforms. The article turned out to be an excellent showcase for the association and the planner received several new membership requests. Impressed by this result and Tourisme Montréal's role in facilitating these contacts, Montréal was then short-listed for the major international meeting we originally sought to host. While there were many more factors involved, of course, the blog and its role in helping the planner achieve some of the organisation's goals for acquiring new members, clearly generated goodwill toward Montréal and Tourisme Montréal's sales team.

The topics covered are a mix of industry tips and trends, profiles of Montréal partners and key economic sectors of activity, profiles of hotels and venues, as well as case studies and photo essays of meetings hosted in Montréal.

Evaluation of the meetings and conventions blog

According to Legault, the meetings and convention blog's principal value is the ability to communicate directly with corporate and association planners who are notoriously busy and sometimes reluctant to take calls from DMOs. Established planners are approached by an endless stream of travel suppliers because of their significant purchasing power. Tourisme Montréal, however, identified an opportunity for utilising a blog to target younger planners. She continued:

We were surprised. We found that a lot of Millennials who are trying to break into the meetings market, use the social media and read blogs rather than read advertorials. So that's why we decided that we should start a new blog and try to bring added value to our customers, by bringing them to our content, which then gives us a chance to engage with them. The investment is starting to pay off, and now planners are reaching out to Tourisme Montréal's convention services staff. What we're seeing is a lot more time spent on the blog and a lot more comments than we used to get, which shows that we're starting to engage with the planners. The fact that we took an approach that's more content-oriented, and provides more added-value to them, allows us to always be in the top of their minds. And then when they do have a question, they are contacting us to get more information.

In terms of statistics, Tourisme Montréal has seen a steady increase in readership and social sharing throughout 2014.

CASE STUDY 2.4   The Detroit Metro Convention and Visitors Bureau Tourism and Convention Sales Marketing Plan

Each year the Detroit Metro Convention & Visitors Bureau (DMCVB) publishes its Tourism and Convention Sales Marketing Plan, which includes its departmental objectives and strategies.

In that part of the 2015 Tourism and Convention Sales Marketing Plan focusing on the conventions and meetings segment, these objectives were listed, followed by the strategies designed to achieve the objectives.

Objectives

- Increase the number of multiple hotel conventions Downtown by 50 per cent over a 5-year period

- Increase the awareness of metro Detroit as the 'comeback city' and prime destination for meetings, in order to increase total number of visitors and economic impact to the region
- Implement marketing initiatives designed to showcase the assets of metro Detroit suburbs, with emphasis on cultural attractions/museums, automotive and family-friendly experiences
- Leverage partnerships with third party planners and key customers to secure marketing sponsorships and ad placements to further expose the destination to potential meetings customers
- Create awareness and interest in the revitalised Cobo Center in order to increase bookings
- Highlight the Suburban Collection Showplace and hotels as prime locations for meetings and conventions
- Support marketing efforts of incoming conventions into the region to ensure successful meetings and increase the awareness of the destination to new customers such as the American Society of Association Executives (ASAE), Evangelical Lutheran Church in America (ELCU) and National Baptist Convention, USA, Inc.
- Increase the number of single hotel leads to meet growing inventory throughout the region

Strategies

Sales

- Work with core hotel groups to determine priority accounts
- Grow business from companies and associations that have booked smaller programmes
- Have DMCVB sales managers in Washington, DC and Chicago promote Detroit to customers
- Attend meetings on a local, state, regional and national basis with key industry organisations
- Attend trade shows and conduct monthly sales trips
- Work with third parties to grow awareness and business
- Grow local support to help generate interest and bring national events to metro Detroit
- Determine accounts best suited for Cobo Center and Suburban Collection Showplace
- Work on multi-year agreements for state association groups that would utilise Cobo Center or Suburban Collection Showplace
- Determine accounts that have met in Grand Rapids, Lansing and Traverse City
- Establish Michigan Customer Advisory Board (CAB)
- Determine accounts that have met in cities that are our competitors, to determine their interest in metro Detroit
- Continue to host family reunion planning seminar in the fall
- Solicit Canadian tour operators

Advertising

- Continue to evolve the 'America's Great Comeback City' advertising campaign to focus on new development in the region and completion of Cobo Center expansion
- Develop sales collateral piece in third quarter that highlights regional assets

- Secure prime advertising positions in leading meetings and conventions publications. Publications include *Associations Now, Convene, The Meeting Professional, Meetings & Conventions* and *Successful Meetings*
- Promote Cobo Center and Suburban Collection Showplace as well as other key meeting venues in prominent convention trade publications
- Execute partnership elements with Cvent and ASAE
- Integrate ASAE messaging into creative executions geared to association markets
- Implement search engine marketing and additional digital displays (banners) beyond sponsorship packages
- Support print with targeted online ad network digital media buy
- Provide marketing materials and advertise in key trade publications to assist in securing tour groups or family reunions into metro Detroit

Interactive

- Retain social media consultant throughout 2015 for execution of meeting planner and ASAE social media plans
- Publish meetings content that generates 30,000 sessions in 2015 to meetdetroit.com and visitdetroit.com
- Produce quarterly sales e-newsletter for sales database
- Explore social sites of key upcoming meetings booked by sales to populate with destination information and monitor comments
- Continue development and refinement of email marketing messages
- Continue to encourage web visitors to opt-in to database and receive email welcome series
- Support sales team efforts through interactive marketing elements
- Implement online media strategy including improved search engine optimisation (SEO), Google advertising and key social media elements to drive Detroit and suburban room nights

Public Relations

- Work with Detroit Regional Convention Facility (Cobo) Authority to execute a schedule of press releases and events to keep media up to date on Cobo expansion progress
- Host a familiarisation tour for trade media during the North American International Auto Show (NAIAS) to showcase the new Cobo
- Target key trade publications for feature articles about Detroit that leverage advertising partnerships for value added editorial
- Visit New York and Chicago-based trade editors to provide Detroit update post-bankruptcy
- Attend International Pow Wow (IPW) Media Marketplace to reach international trade media with metro Detroit updates
- Engage local media as advisory committee for ASAE to galvanise the hospitality community and create ambassadors during large conventions
- Host a progressive media reception/tour during ASAE

- Pitch stories on attractions and events that include Sea Life Michigan Aquarium, Detroit Zoo Penguin Conservation Center, new limited property hotels in Dearborn, Royal Oak and Troy and new Virgin Atlantic direct flight between London and Detroit
- Distribute quarterly tip sheets highlighting attractions and events to key leisure and trade publications
- Partner with metro Detroit attractions and hotel properties on media events, as warranted

Print and Digital Publishing

- Produce up to 400,000 copies of *Visit Detroit* magazine (200,000 two times per year). Primary distribution is metro Detroit hotels, visitors and convention delegates, meeting planners and reunion attendees. Include four pages of dedicated content on each county, including high-quality photography, specific editorial on things to do, dine and stay and seasonal events
- Provide listing of events by county in each *Visit Detroit* magazine edition
- Produce and launch new 'Show It and Save' discount programme targeted for convention delegates
- Update meeting planners guide and online press kit with photos and descriptions of metro Detroit hotels and meeting venues
- Develop sales collateral piece in third quarter that highlights regional assets
- Produce quarterly sales e-newsletter for customers in database to promote metro Detroit meeting facilities

SUMMARY

The tangible manifestation of any destination or venue's marketing planning process is its marketing plan. It is this document that helps managers develop and maintain a clear direction for the set of complex, interrelated marketing activities they undertake on behalf of their destination or venue.

A well-constructed marketing plan based on sound research should culminate in the production of an appropriate marketing mix for each segment to be targeted. In this respect, devising an effective marketing plan is one of the marketing manager's most important tasks.

The following two chapters will explore the theories underlying the various marketing communications techniques that are elements of the marketing planning strategies used by destinations and venues. They will also examine the practical applications of those techniques, highlighting examples of best practice.

REVIEW AND DISCUSSION QUESTIONS

- Read the Objectives of the DMCVB Tourism and Convention Sales Marketing Plan on pages 61–62. To what extent do they demonstrate the key characteristics of Objectives as described by Kotler *et al.* on page 47?
- Not all businesses have a Marketing Plan. In your opinion, what could be the main reasons for that?
- Conduct online research to identify a conference centre that posts a calendar of events on its website (a list of forthcoming conferences to be held there). From the conference titles and initiators, what evidence is there that the venue is targeting one or more specific segments of the meetings market? The market could be segmented by geographical zones, industry sector, price sensitivity or purpose of visit, for example.

REFERENCES

Aaker, D. A. (1991) *Managing brand equity*, New York: Free Press.

Brisbane Marketing (2011) *Annual Report 2010–2011*, Brisbane: Brisbane Marketing.

Burke, J. and B. Resnick (2000) *Marketing and Selling the Travel Product*, Independence: Delmar Thomson Learning.

Davidson, R. and B. Cope (2003) *Business Travel: Conferences, Incentive Travel, Exhibitions, Corporate Hospitality and Corporate Travel*, Upper Saddle River: Pearson Education.

Fifield, P. (1998) *Marketing Strategy*, Oxford: Butterworth-Heinemann.

Gartrell, R. (1994) *Destination Marketing for Convention and Visitor Bureaus*, Dubuque: Kendall Hunt Publishing.

Harrill, R. (2005) *Fundamentals of Destination Management and Marketing*, Educational Institute of the American Hotel and Motel Association.

Holcomb, B. (1999) 'Marketing cities for tourism', in D. R. Judd and S. S. Fainstein (eds.), *The Tourist City*, Newhaven: Yale University Press, pp. 54–70.

Holloway, J. C. (2004) *Marketing for Tourism*, Upper Saddle River: Prentice Hall.

Kotler, P., J. Bowen and J. Makens (2003) *Marketing for Hospitality and Tourism*, Upper Saddle River: Prentice Hall.

McDonald, M. and I. Dunbar (2004) *Market Segmentation: How To Do It, How To Profit From It*, Oxford: Elsevier Butterworth-Heinemann.

Middleton, V. (2001) *Marketing in Travel and Tourism*, Oxford: Butterworth-Heinemann.

Morrison, A. M. (2013) *Marketing and Managing Tourism Destinations*, London: Routledge.

Pike, S. (2004) *Destination Marketing Organisations*, Oxford: Elsevier.

Pike, S. and S. Page (2014) 'Destination marketing organizations and destination marketing: a narrative analysis of the literature', *Tourism Management*, 41: 1–26.

Stevens, R. E., D. L. Loudon, B. Wren and P. Mansfield (2013) *Marketing Planning Guide*, 3rd edn, London: Routledge.

World Bank (2013) *Doing Business 2013: Smarter Regulations for Small and Medium-Size Enterprises*, Washington, DC: World Bank Group.

Chapter **3**

Non-personal marketing communications for destinations and venues

Principles and practice

Chapter overview

This chapter examines the various non-personal marketing communications techniques that may be employed by conference destinations and venues as techniques of promotion, one of the four elements of the marketing mix described in chapter 2. It focuses on how organisations communicate with their customers, potential customers and other key stakeholders through the use of publications, websites, public relations and advertising. In each case, following an analysis of the principles underlying each technique, best practice in the use of these tools is explored.

This chapter covers:

- Publications
- Websites
- Public relations
- Advertising

It includes case studies on:

- The Convention Centre Dublin's website
- Kyoto Convention Bureau's PR campaign based on pre-conference meditation
- Atlanta Convention Bureau's I AM ATL campaign

On completion of this chapter, you should be able to:

- understand the respective benefits of outsourcing marketing communications functions and handling them in-house;
- understand the uses of publications and best practice in their applications to destination and venue marketing;
- understand the uses of websites in marketing and best practice in their applications to destination and venue marketing;
- understand the types and uses of public relations and best practice in their applications to destination and venue marketing; and
- understand the principles of advertising and best practice in the use of advertising.

Introduction

As is the case for marketers in any industry, those responsible for marketing venues and destinations have to focus much of their energy and creativity on developing and distributing positive promotional messages about their products. This is in order to inform business event organisers about their facilities and services and generate their interest in order to enable sales of their products to be achieved.

The words and images included in those promotional messages have a vital and major role to play in the marketing of destinations and venues. They may form the first contact or communication between destinations/venues and their target audiences – conference and business event organisers. Marketers use promotional messages in the attempt to control the image that their potential buyers have of their products.

Of course, there are many other 'uncontrolled' messages that may be received by potential buyers – messages that are beyond the control of marketers. These include the information conveyed by visitors to the destination or venue after their visit has taken place or the words and pictures used by radio, television or newspaper journalists reporting on an incident or news story in a particular location – one which may be totally unrelated to its use as a conference destination or venue but which nonetheless creates an impression of the destination/venue among their listeners or readers.

This chapter will explore how marketing communications use words and images creatively to paint a picture of a destination or venue in the minds of potential buyers, helping them to visualise what the location is going to be like and to feel positively about it as a possible site for their business events. In this chapter, we will be looking primarily at non-personal communication channels – promotional activity that targets a wide audience, also known as above-the-line marketing communications. Chapter 4 will then look at personal communication channels that operate on more of a one-to-one, or 'below the line', basis with potential clients.

However, before examining the use of non-personal communication channels by venue and destination marketers, it will be useful to make the general point that, as many venues and destination marketing organisations (DMOs) are small or medium-sized enterprises, many of them choose to outsource their marketing communications to a specialist marketing agency or consultancy, rather than trying to maintain this specific expertise in-house. Such consultancies can operate on a 'full-service' basis (i.e. covering generic marketing planning and marketing mix strategies as outlined in chapter 2, as well as design, public relations and advertising services) or focus specifically on generic marketing planning and then sub-contract design, public relations, etc. to other specialist companies. See later in this chapter for a discussion of the use of PR agencies.

The benefits of outsourcing these marketing functions can include:

- bringing external expertise and experience combined with an objective view of a venue's or destination's strengths and weaknesses;
- providing new ideas and fresh perspectives together with new contacts and opportunities;
- the contract can be for a limited period of time (for example, 2 to 3 years), allowing renewal at the end of this period or the option to contract a different agency; and
- staffing costs/overheads are not incurred as the function is outsourced.

Such benefits need to be compared with the benefits of managing marketing activities in-house, which include:

- staff having a full understanding of, and immersion in, the venue's or destination's strategic planning, objectives and overall culture;
- retaining direct control of the marketing activities and developing a sense of 'ownership' of the marketing planning, and a pride in successful outcomes; and
- being able to build and train the marketing team and retain their services, providing continuity and stability to the marketing activity.

Nevertheless, whether a venue or destination's marketing activities are handled in-house or outsourced, it is essential that its managers have a sound understanding of the various marketing techniques that are available and best practice in their use. This is the theme of this chapter and the next.

Publications

The use of publications in marketing

Promotional brochures, destination planning manuals and newsletters are all examples of key marketing and promotional tools used by destinations and venues. In the context of destination marketing, Gartrell (1994:92) notes that 'publications serve as the primary marketing and communications tool for bureaus', and the same might be said in the case of venues.

Also known as 'collateral', publications play a vital role in transmitting the destination or venue's image to the market. A key objective of most destination and venue publications is the maintaining of positive communications with stakeholders. These stakeholders may include actual and potential clients but their distribution will certainly be much wider than that particular group. A convention bureau's Annual Report, for example, may serve as an important communications tool and it should therefore reflect the image that the destination wishes to transmit. Some of the most frequently used publications will now be considered.

Paper-based or digital?

In this increasingly digital age, is there still a need for destinations and venues to produce hard copies of their publications? While it is undeniably the case that more and more resources are being committed to digital communications media, there still appears to be a need and a role for printed guides. They have not yet been completely replaced by USBs, DVDs and websites, although the popularity of tablet computers has no doubt hastened their demise. The particular advantages of digital technology include:

- Storage capacity: huge amounts of information can be stored on diminutive devices
- Continuous updating: data can be updated easily and continuously, ensuring that clients only receive current information

- Moving images: moving images, with sound, can present engaging perspectives of the destination and venue, including virtual tours and show-rounds
- Presentation tool: digital guides can be used for presentations, enabling conference organisers and meeting planners to give an audio-visual presentation about a particular destination or venue to their senior management team or to a selection committee
- Lower distribution costs: guides can be distributed electronically at zero cost. Where they need to be mailed to clients (as a USB or DVD, for example), postage costs should be less than those for printed guides
- Benefits to the environment with lower or zero use of paper and the minimal negative impacts generated by the distribution of the digital guide

Aileen Crawford, Head of Conventions for Glasgow City Marketing Bureau, outlines Glasgow's policy on printed and digital guides and describes the city's innovative, client-centred approach:

> *We do not produce a brochure guide at all – we have gone fully digital as far as venue information provision for clients is concerned. The link below allows clients to create a venue brochure from scratch, for the client by the client. The client can search on type of venue, location and meeting room size and layout, or by support service, and from there the client can export their favoured choices into a PDF: http://conventions.peoplemakeglasgow.com/organising-a-conference/find-a-venue-or-service/*
>
> *The benefits of moving away from providing a printed brochure are many: from the reduction of cost to the positive environmental impact; and the bespoke nature of our service that allows clients to create their own listings which they can access at any time, from anywhere. Going online ensures that we offer real-time information, easily updated and current.*

Davidson (2004:9) predicted that the use of the internet for marketing purposes for venues and destinations would become ever more ingenious and creative. Meetings planners' use of that medium would continue to expand, particularly for the purpose of researching venues: 'More and more event planners will be logging on to the Internet, rather than opening the filing cabinet full of brochures and venue guides. Access to destination and venue information via nearly instantaneous technology has already reduced response times dramatically, as elements of the site-selection process that used to take days or even weeks can now be measured in minutes or hours'.

Paradoxically, however, it could just be that the profusion of digital communications may, in some cases, give the printed guide a competitive edge – its relative novelty gives it a value and helps to distinguish it from the constantly growing number of digital communications received by meeting planners, an increasing proportion of which seem to go unopened. As a visit to any meetings industry exhibition will confirm, there is still a demand for paper-based publications such as brochures and catalogues, an abundance of which are to be found on the exhibition stands and in the hands of visitors. Destinations and venues will continue to weigh up the pros and cons of print versus digital media, aware that there may still be a level of demand for print media from the more traditional sectors of the market place.

Destination guides

Many destinations produce a factual guide for use by conference and event organisers, updated on an annual basis or sometimes less frequently. The destination guide provides an overview of the destination and its attractions, including information on transport connections and the communications infrastructure, key suppliers (such as audio-visual companies, coach operators, professional conference organisers), together with detailed information on each of the conference and event venues represented in the guide.

Newsletters

One of the most commonly used publications for broad communication is the newsletter. Gartrell recognised the importance of this form of publication, noting that they: 'can serve not only as information tools but as sources for business leads. A newsletter may also carry stories on the bureau's marketing activities, information on what is happening among bureau members, and dates and descriptions of forthcoming meetings and educational forums'. (Gartrell, 1994:92).

Newsletters have long been a popular marketing medium for destinations and venues. Their combination of attractive photos/illustrations and short, snappy news items has proved to be an effective CRM vehicle, strengthening the relationship between destination/venue and client through the provision of a regular flow of information. Although the production costs can, to some extent, be controlled by limiting the size of the newsletter (six to eight pages would typically be a maximum length), newsletters can prove to be fairly expensive to produce, as budgets need to cover copy-writing, professional photography, design and typesetting, printing and mailing/distribution costs.

In this digital era, however, the printed newsletter has, largely, been replaced by the e-newsletter. This latter is much less expensive to produce and to circulate and it can include significantly more information, if required. E-newsletters are usually distributed as a PDF attachment to an e-mail or as an email with links to the pages of a website, each page containing a different article. The latter option allows the recipient to view an index or summary of the e-newsletter articles and click on those of particular interest in order to read the full article.

The e-newsletter of Vienna Convention Bureau, for example, is a good example of a newsletter embedded in an email. It has the following features:

- It is distributed four times a year to 15,000 client contacts on the bureau's database and each newsletter is personalised to the recipient (i.e. Dear Mr. . .)
- Each news item has a short title, one or two sentences of text, a colour image, and a 'read more' link to additional information
- The newsletters typically contain five to ten items of information, allowing recipients to look through them quickly and identify items of particular interest to them

Examples of past newsletters can be viewed on the Vienna Convention Bureau website: http://www.vienna.convention.at/Home/Newsletter.aspx.

Visit Manchester produces three separate bi-monthly e-newsletters for (i) agencies; (ii) general business tourism contacts; and (iii) conference ambassadors. The agents' e-newsletter, for example, contains short news items accompanied by a graphic image and a link to more detailed information. It is quick and easy to scan and includes 'News in brief', which are simply headings with an in-built link to further information. The newsletter contains 'Tweets we like' plus options to unsubscribe, view as a webpage and forward to a colleague. Past newsletters are accessible at http://communicatoremail.com/F/gMTmJnEXWd4EQFrvQn-QHZ/.

A variation on the theme of e-newsletters are e-shots, typically a short email covering just one item of news. The QEII conference centre in London regularly uses e-shots with its client database to maintain contact and convey items of topical interest or, simply, just to develop its relationship with its clients (e.g. 'Pop in for a mince pie and a cuppa', distributed in early December 2014). The e-shots have an image or images and a few sentences of snappy text and contact details.

Best practice in the use of publications

Authors agree that in general it is essential for publications to be designed, where possible, on a tailor-made basis. McCabe *et al.*, for example, emphasise that collateral materials should be developed for the specific market segment targeted. 'The production of a single brochure to satisfy all possible customer needs is not effective. . .Collateral material should highlight and promote the benefits of the product that are important to the specific customer segment' (McCabe *et al.*, 2000:180).

A useful example of this approach is seen in the example of Convention Edinburgh, who publish three separate newsletters for (i) corporates; (ii) conference ambassadors; and (iii) their members. The corporate newsletter is entitled 'Corporate Matters' and combines a clickable 'Table of Contents' with narrative text interspersed with images and covers, inter alia, new infrastructure developments, familiarisation visits and B2B events, information on the city's delegate reward card scheme, special offers from Edinburgh venues and suppliers, testimonials from clients and details of awards and accolades. Copies of the ambassadors' newsletter can be accessed on Convention Edinburgh's website: http://www.conventionedinburgh.com/ ambassadorprogramme/newsletter.

Reader surveys should be carried out from time to time to obtain feedback on the usefulness and readability of any newsletter and there should be an evaluation process to monitor how successful the newsletter has been in meeting the objectives set for it. Such objectives may include changing perceptions of a venue/destination, creating a higher profile or generating specific business leads and enquiries.

For the specific case of destination guides, whether in paper or electronic form, in order to achieve their maximum effectiveness, they should:

- use high quality photography;
- have two-level maps showing (i) the destination's location within the country and/or region and (ii) the location of each of the venues within the destination;
- include a comprehensive index;
- include a see-at-a-glance summary of the rooms and capacities for all of the venues listed to enable conference organisers to determine quickly which venues could potentially accommodate a particular event;
- contain some information in other languages if designed for international use.

Liverpool Convention Bureau's 2014–15 guide was the winner of the 2014 Meetings Industry Marketing Awards 'best brochure' category. The 67-page publication contains eight, clearly tabulated and easy-to-navigate sections:

- About Liverpool
- Venues
- Accommodation
- Food and Drink
- Suppliers
- Travel
- Venue Index
- Maps

All of the venue and accommodation entries are supported by good quality, colour images, the 'About Liverpool' section contains testimonials from high profile clients and there are three maps showing the location of Liverpool within the UK, the Liverpool city region and Liverpool city centre with places of interest marked. For more information: www.liverpoolconventionbureau.com

Similarly, venue brochures should include:

- Detailed maps and location information – again best practice would suggest that at least two maps should be included: one showing the location of the venue within a particular town/city/region and one showing its detailed position and access within a locality (with names of adjacent roads, details of any one-way traffic systems operating, proximity to railway station, etc.).
- Photographs of the venue showing at least one external shot, plus a number of internal shots to illustrate meeting rooms, bedrooms, restaurant(s), leisure facilities and so forth. Such photographs are always much more effective with people in them, rather than being unpopulated as is so often the case!
- Detailed technical information on each of the meeting and conference rooms: capacities for different seating layouts, room dimensions including ceiling height, air conditioning, whether the room has natural light and details of any dedicated audio-visual facilities built into the room.
- An internal layout plan. This is a particularly useful feature because it illustrates the location of the various meeting rooms within the venue – this assists conference organisers to select the rooms most appropriate to their needs and it gives them the chance to minimise time wasted when delegates have to move between different meeting rooms (for syndicate sessions, for example, or to visit a concurrent exhibition).
- Details of the venue's Wi-Fi capabilities and whether it is free of charge.

If they are available in print form, destination and venue guides should ideally be produced in A4 (or quarto) format, enabling conference organisers to store reference copies easily in standard filing cabinets. Occasionally, venues and destinations, driven by the creative flair of design companies, publish guides of a different size and, while this is not a problem if they are smaller than A4, it can cause problems if the guides are larger than that, because they will not fit into a filing cabinet and, as a result, may be disposed of rather than kept for reference.

It is also possible that distribution costs will be higher because special envelopes may be needed and postage/mailing costs greater. Distribution costs need to be incorporated into the overall marketing budget. Will the guide be distributed principally by post and, if so, will the circulation be national or international? Alternatively, will substantial quantities be given to recipients, for example, when visiting the destination or venue, or be handed out from an exhibition stand, thus incurring minimal or zero distribution costs?

The production of any type of publication in hard copies poses a dilemma over the quantities to produce, as well as the methods of distribution. Destination and venue marketers have to estimate accurately the print-run for any particular item of collateral. If they under-estimate the quantities required, additional printing or production can be relatively expensive, making the net cost per brochure higher than it need have been had they printed the correct, larger quantity in the first place. Conversely, producing too many copies can also waste money if it should prove impossible to put all of the brochures and guides to good use. The solution chosen by many destinations and venues is to print on demand or to produce USBs on demand, although the unit costs are likely to be somewhat higher than when printing a bulk supply.

Websites

The use of destination and venue websites in marketing

Almost every destination and venue active in the conference and conventions sector has its own website, although in the case of chain hotel venues this may be as part of the group's website rather than as a dedicated venue site. As already mentioned, websites have the benefit of continuous updating, a major advantage over printed guides, one of whose inherent weaknesses is that, once published, the data they contain cannot be altered. Many guides and directories are partly out of date even as they are published and they may be very inaccurate indeed, once they have been in circulation for a year or more.

Websites can also be accessed 24 hours a day, 7 days a week from anywhere in the world. Distribution costs are minimal, although there are some promotional costs through registration with search engines and the need to inform clients of the website's content and, of course, its address. Creative venues and destinations have made use of the full capacity of websites, harnessing their power to show images and movies of, for example, short interviews with satisfied clients. In addition, many offer online accommodation booking services for use by event organisers or by their delegates/attendees.

The importance of websites for the purposes of marketing cannot be overestimated. In the context of venue promotion, Davidson and Hyde (2014:33) state that:

> *Within the past decade, there has been a major and rapid move to online tools, in terms of the methods that meeting planners use when seeking and evaluating potential venues for their events. Online is where new prospects tend to go first, if they are conducting a general search for a venue. As a response to this trend, many venues no longer use printed brochures, but, instead, seek to maximise the effectiveness of their online presence, notably through their websites and the use of e-brochures. The website has become the main shop-front for most venues. Effectively-designed websites can generate enquires and build venues' leads databases.*

The power of websites as marketing tools received a major boost with the advent, in the twenty-first century, of Web 2.0. The term Web 2.0 describes a combination of concepts, trends and technologies that focuses on user collaboration, sharing of user-generated content and social networking. Web 2.0 applications allow users to interact and collaborate with each other as creators of user-generated information in a virtual community, in contrast to traditional Web sites where people are limited to the passive viewing of content. Examples of Web 2.0 features include social networking platforms, blogs, wikis and video sharing.

Companies and organisations of all kinds have integrated Web 2.0 tools into their websites. Websites which were, prior to the advent of Web 2.0, often little more than on-screen versions of printed brochures, have become much more interactive and dynamic in their design. Regularly updated blogs, for example, are used to drive traffic to venues' and destinations' websites; links are displayed that lead the website visitor to click through to the venue or destination's Facebook or LinkedIn pages; tools such as Twitter are used in order to introduce an element of dialogue into webpages formerly characterised by their one-way modus operandi.

A study by Davidson and Keup (2014) into the uses being made of Web 2.0 tools by European convention bureaux in their marketing communications programmes found that YouTube, followed by Facebook, LinkedIn and Twitter were the applications most commonly used in this context, with blogs, Flickr and Slideshare featured to a lesser extent. In terms of matching specific Web 2.0 tools to specific marketing objectives, the study found ample evidence that convention bureau marketing managers were familiar with the particular strengths of each tool. Recognition of the distinct powers of Facebook and Twitter was evident. For example, Facebook and Twitter's power as instant, simple two-way communication forums would explain why, between them, they accounted for 72 per cent of the convention bureaux' use of Web 2.0 for the purpose of stimulating dialogue about their destinations.

Conversely, LinkedIn, which offers detailed biographies of registered users, was found to be the single Web 2.0 tool most frequently used by convention bureaux to accomplish their objective of profiling clients for sales purposes. In connection with the objective of convention bureaux of creating awareness and enhancing brand reputation, YouTube emerged as the leading Web 2.0 tool, reflecting that application's proven effectiveness in connecting the emotions of consumers to individual brands.

In chapter 4, the use of the social media in venue and destination marketing is explored in more detail.

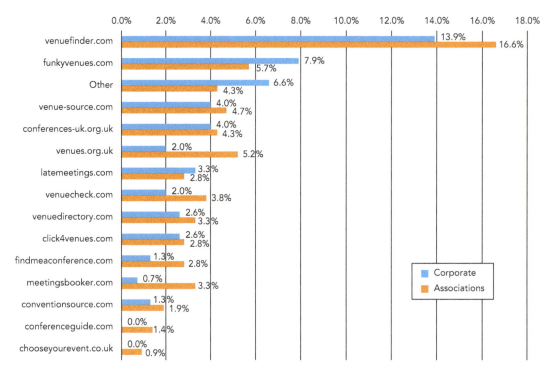

Figure 3.1 Digital venue finding services used by UK event organisers

Source: 'British Meetings and Events Industry Survey 2014/15' – www.meetpie.com/bmeis. Copyright: CAT Publications – reproduced with permission.

Third-party websites and printed directories

As well as producing their own guides, many venues also promote themselves through other printed directories and third-party websites. This is because they know that meeting planners often go directly to these third-party sources to conduct their venue searches.

One of the leading internet-based venue finding enquiry systems, covering venues in most regions of the world, is that operated by Cvent (www.cvent.com). Cvent offers destination 'landing pages', which then lead into descriptions of individual venues and suppliers within those destinations.

Figure 3.1, taken from the 'British Meetings and Events Industry Survey 2014/15', reveals the main digital venue finding services used by UK-based conference organisers and meeting planners. Sites such as these allow meeting planners to enter their own venue search criteria online and details of venues that match are supplied to them within a matter of seconds. Meeting planners can then look at detailed information on the venues, including images, and may also be able to undertake a 'virtual' tour of the venue. There is also the facility to send a specific enquiry ('Request for Proposal' or 'RFP') to the venues they have shortlisted.

Factors influencing the selection of the most appropriate digital venue finding service are likely to include:

- The range, depth and accuracy of the information provided
- The user-friendliness of the search tool(s)
- Does it provide destination-level descriptions and data as well as venue profiles?
- The costs to access: some are free of charge, some charge a fee or subscription

Best practice in the use of destination and venue websites

Successful websites for destinations and venues are likely to have features such as:

- be quick-loading and have easy navigability;
- be visually attractive and make use of the full screen;
- excellent maps and travel directions;
- virtual tours;
- testimonials from satisfied clients such as conference organisers;
- case studies of business events held in the destination or venue;
- regular blogs;
- downloadable information on venue layouts and capacities;
- content weighting – a clear hierarchy of headings should be used to ensure that the most important content appears closer to the top of each page – this is also a useful way of ensuring accurate search engine indexing;
- an appropriate choice of domain name; and
- some/all information in other languages, dependent upon the relative importance of specific overseas markets.

A useful feature of some meeting venue websites is what might be termed an interactive meeting room planner that allows the event organiser to choose a theme and/or type of event and then arrange the tables, chairs and stage in the room to create a preferred layout. This layout can then be downloaded by the venue to enable a personalised meeting area to be set up prior to the organiser's arrival at the venue. An example of this feature can be seen on the website of the Hilton Birmingham Metropole hotel (www.hilton.com/birmingham – see the Meetings and Events section). A similar 3D room planning tool is available on the Austria Center Vienna's website (www.acv.at).

Rogers (2013) provides best practice ideas for developing and optimising a winning website. Case Study 3.1 features the award-winning website of The Convention Centre Dublin (The CCD), detailing how and why the website was redesigned and re-launched in 2014 in response to The CCD's research among its clients.

Public relations

The use of public relations in marketing

In venues and destinations' arsenal of marketing techniques, public relations (PR) is perhaps the most underestimated method of creating and maintaining a positive image. Yet, effectively used, PR can assist in developing a strong, positive image of a successful conference destination or venue.

Holloway (2004:339) describes PR as 'a series of communications techniques designed to create and maintain favourable relations between an organisation and its publics'; while according to the Chartered Institute of Public Relations, PR is about reputation – the result of what you do, what you say and what others say about you. 'Public relations is the discipline which looks after reputation, with the aim of earning understanding and support and influencing opinion and behaviour. It is the planned and sustained effort to establish and maintain goodwill and mutual understanding between an organisation and its publics'.

Middleton underlines the similar objectives of both advertising and PR, noting that both are 'primary means of manipulating demand and influencing buyer behaviour. Simply stated, they enable businesses to reach people . . . And to communicate to them messages intended to influence their purchasing behaviour' (Middleton, 2001:237).

Nevertheless, most authors emphasise the contrasts between PR and advertising, rather than the similarities shared by the two communications tools. One important difference between them is that the range of target audiences for PR is generally much wider than for advertising. It can include local residents, local and central government politicians, existing and potential buyers, employees, the media, shareholders, suppliers, investors, professional/trade associations and pressure groups.

Robert Wynne, in his contribution to the forbes.com website entitled 'The Real Difference between PR and Advertising', contrasts advertising with public relations as follows:

> *Advertising is paid media, public relations is earned media. This means you convince reporters or editors to write a positive story about you or your client, your candidate, brand or issue. It appears in the editorial section of the magazine, newspaper, TV station or website, rather than the 'paid media' section where advertising messages appear. So your story has more credibility because it was independently verified by a trusted third party, rather than purchased.*

He quotes from Michael Levine, a well-known publicist and author of the book, Guerrilla P.R.: 'The idea is the believability of an article versus an advertisement. Depending on how you measure and monitor, an article is between ten times and 100 times more valuable than an advertisement'.

Furthermore, the rapid growth in the volume of advertising 'noise' that consumers are exposed to means that many are increasingly immune to the persuasiveness of the claims made in advertisements. This has created an opportunity for the role of PR which, when properly used, can generate a greater level of credibility than advertising. The other frequently mentioned advantages of PR are that it has the benefit of giving 'free' media exposure; it is perceived as independent and it is also measurable.

In the context of destination marketing, Pike (2004:144) contends that the use of public relations is 'a concerted effort by the DMO to develop favourable impressions of the destination. This involves both the generation of positive publicity by the DMO as well as the stimulation of positive relations between internal and external stakeholders. He adds that 'The cost-effectiveness of PR initiatives is usually not lost on DMOs, particularly given the limited resources of most'.

What are the principal techniques that conference destinations and venues can use in their PR campaigns? Holloway (2004) and Kotler *et al*. (2003) agree on the five main activities associated with the role of PR:

- *Press relations*. Placing newsworthy items of information into the news media, to generate favourable publicity or to diminish the impact of unfavourable publicity.
- *Product publicity*. Implementing tactics to draw attention to particular products: new or renovated hotels, special events, etc.
- *Corporate publicity*. Generating a favourable image for the organisation itself, both internally and externally.
- *Lobbying*. Dealing with legislators and government officials to promote a cause or defeat a particular piece of legislation.
- *Counselling*. Advising management about public issues, particularly with respect to any sensitive issues with which the organisation may be associated. In this respect, the PR department has a research and monitoring function.

Holloway (2004), Kotler et al. (2003)

Two of these techniques will now be examined in further detail.

Press relations

As stated at the beginning of this chapter, it is clear that much of the publicity, both positive and negative, about destinations and venues that appears in the media is beyond the influence or control of these suppliers. Nevertheless, positive editorial coverage is essential for the image of destinations in particular – more essential than extensive advertising, according to many commentators. That is why positive relations with the press are an essential element of destination and venue marketing.

Gartrell (1994) acknowledges the importance of advertising, but maintains that it is positive *editorial coverage* that can most effectively extend and create the image of a destination in a way that advertising cannot. From another perspective, McCabe *et al.* emphasise the power of PR in correcting negative images of destinations: 'Negative destination images or publicity in the general consumer media ... must be addressed. Such negative publicity can rarely be overcome simply by advertising. Responses and 'good news stories' must be channelled through the same media that the negative stories appeared in, in order to begin an effective campaign to overcome the bad publicity' (McCabe *et al.*, 2000:182).

The challenge of achieving positive editorial coverage has been intensified by the ways in which the world of journalism has changed in recent years. Staff numbers on most magazines and newspapers have been drastically reduced, yet output has significantly increased. A journalist previously responsible for, say, weekly or monthly news reports, may now also be tasked with daily or even twice-daily digital news updates. This is good news for PR insofar as demand for stories is high, but journalists now spend very little time assessing a news release for possible inclusion. Many of the rules that were once 'set in stone' for news (or press or media) release writing are no longer appropriate. For instance, very few journalists now have time to read a generically written release and decide if there is an angle in it to suit their particular audience. If the angle is not immediately clear, the release is deleted immediately. A release about the opening or refurbishment of a conference venue, for example, should be tailored to describe the venue's potential use by meeting planners and their delegates if it is to be published in a magazine or on a website targeting event organisers. If, on the other hand, the release is to be used mainly in the local community to demonstrate the addition of new, quality infrastructure for a particular destination, its content and key story line will be different and it will need to be structured to meet this different target audience.

Similarly, there is no appetite now for releases that are written over a couple of pages, developing the message to a great conclusion or announcement. Most journalists need the story to hook them in the first couple of lines, and increasing numbers admit that they only assess the subject line before deciding whether to open or delete. Best practice in the writing of press releases will be explored later in this chapter.

Lobbying

Another key role of PR is the lobbying of governments, especially (but not exclusively) for convention bureaux and venues wholly or partly funded from public sector finances. Gartrell (1994:93) emphasises the importance of effective governmental relations for convention bureaux. 'This broad arena encompasses more than just monitoring legislative issues and bills. It also means developing rapport and working with those elected officials with whom the bureau comes in contact on almost a daily basis. Those elected officials will have control over the contractual arrangements for public funds. It is imperative that the bureau maintains a positive relationship with such officials, to nurture their understanding of the bureau and its mission'.

In this respect, a number of convention bureaux have one or more members of staff whose responsibility it is to oversee the political activities of the bureau.

For example, the Louisville Convention and Visitors Bureau has established a Public Affairs Committee, which has the following roles: 'Develop and guide the LCVB with regard to legislative matters and remain current with the political issues (State & Local) that may directly or indirectly influence the growth and development of the Bureau' (http://www.lcvb.info/about-us/public-affairs-committee).

Best practice in the use of public relations in marketing

Working in partnership with the media is essential in the context of venue and destination marketing. Organisations' communications staff must liaise with the trade press to stimulate the publication of articles on the destination or the venue; they can host press trips for individual journalists or groups of journalists and they can produce a media kit that provides basic information about their services and facilities.

It is generally regarded as good practice for organisations to maintain a PR resource library in order to be able to respond quickly and effectively to the media's requests for material such as photographs, statistics and video footage. A number of destinations and venues have used the power of the internet to develop their own online media centres, where journalists can download press releases, photographs, brochures and newsletters. An example of this facility is the online media centre created for Newcastle-Gateshead, two adjoining northern English cities that are jointly promoting themselves in the leisure and business events markets. The NewcastleGateshead Initiative PR team describe themselves and their activities as follows:

> *The NewcastleGateshead Initiative PR team provides a 24hr media service for journalists, businesses and industry professionals seeking up-to-date and factual information about the destination.*
>
> *We boast a wealth of knowledge and expertise to support journalists, from business editors to feature writers, broadcasters to bloggers. So whether it's events listings, interviewees, feature ideas, support with media visits, facts and figures, great photography or simply a good old fashioned news story, the NewcastleGateshead Initiative PR team should be your first port of call.*
>
> *We're a talented team (Chartered Institute of Public Relations 'Gold' winners for outstanding in-house team at PRide Awards North East) with experience in tourism, events and business PR, we are dedicated to delivering a quick and professional service. (http://www.newcastlegateshead. net/media/home).*

Nevertheless, while many destinations and venues choose to handle their PR functions in-house, others opt to use the services of a PR agency.

Factors to consider when choosing a PR agency are likely to include:

- Their understanding and knowledge of the venue or destination, with an indication that they have carried out some initial research
- Their awareness and experience of the business events sector
- Their existing client base and whether it includes any potential competitor venues or destinations
- How they plan to handle the client destination/venue's account and what level of staff seniority will be attached to it
- How personable is the client account manager? Is he/she someone that is pleasant to work with?
- The range of services that can be offered and the prices to be charged
- The provision of positive testimonials from other satisfied clients.

But whether PR is handled in-house or outsourced, PR activities have to be properly planned, with the PR Plan dovetailing into an overall venue or destination Marketing Plan (see chapter 2), ensuring as well that all appropriate marketing activities are supported by PR. The PR element of the Marketing Plan should include sections such as the following:

Objectives – (such as):

- To communicate a specific piece of news
- To raise the profile of the destination or venue
- To raise the profile of the destination or venue team

Identifying the customer and, therefore, the target audience:

- Corporate event organisers
- Association convention organisers
- Agencies or intermediaries
- Government or public sector bodies

Identifying possible PR vehicles to use. These could include:

Events

- Industry exhibitions
- Specific exhibitions aimed at a certain market (for example personal assistants/secretaries)
- Association-linked events
- Press events/launches

Media

- Conference and events industry press
- Vertical press (telecommunications, pharmaceutical, financial services, etc.)
- Job title specific press (e.g. PAs, training managers)
- General business press
- Local press
- Local Chamber of Commerce publications
- National press
- TV and radio

Awards

- Industry awards
- Job title specific awards (e.g. sales team/PAs)
- National business awards

Speaker platforms

- Industry conferences or exhibitions
- Destination-organised events.

As part of the exercise of evaluating the Marketing Plan as a whole, it is essential to monitor the quality and quantity of the PR being achieved on behalf of the destination or venue, and to measure the returns on the investment (ROI) being made in the PR activities. Figures 3.2 to 3.5 illustrate how PR results can be measured, both in terms of the circulation achieved by a piece of news, an article/feature or a photo and in terms of its value in financial terms. They relate to PR activity by UK-based Friday's Media Group on behalf of a global client, part of whose business entails conference organising.

Figure 3.2 shows:

- The actual value of press coverage generated each month during the period
- The value of press coverage totalled £312,985 and averaged at £31,298.50 per month
- Average coverage has risen across the period, both in terms of presence (i.e. coverage) and value per month

Figure 3.3 shows:

- The overall value per month of coverage achieved (blue line) and the average value per cutting (yellow line)
- The average value of coverage rose consistently, indicating a rising trend of presence and coverage
- As the volume of coverage has grown, the average value per cutting has been maintained indicating delivery of PR value
- The value of the cuttings has also risen, demonstrating the exposure achieved in key high value titles

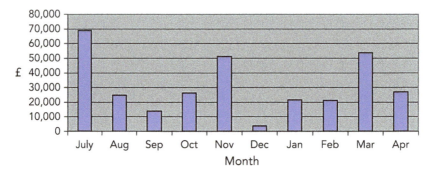

Figure 3.2 The value of press coverage generated

Source: Friday's Media Group.

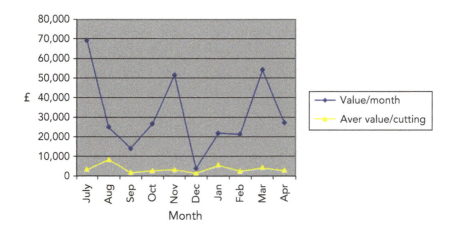

Figure 3.3 Average value per month

Source: Friday's Media Group.

Figure 3.4 shows:

- The position of all the coverage generated during the period
- It reflects page prominence, ranging from a mention in the heading of the page to a mention in the body copy and whether the mention is of the company/event name or a quoted individual
- During this period, the client achieved prominence with the name being mentioned in the heading of the article in 39 per cent of the cuttings, a named quotation in 51 per cent and mention in the first paragraph in 52 per cent of the articles
- In 21 per cent of the articles the company was mentioned in the headline and had a named quotation

Figure 3.5 shows:

- Where the coverage was achieved by type of publication

Best practice in specific types of PR activities will now be reviewed.

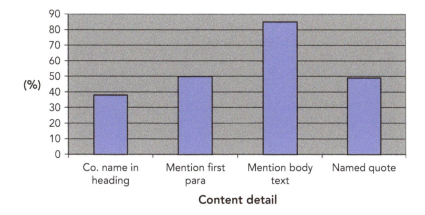

Figure 3.4. The position of all press coverage generated

Source: Friday's Media Group.

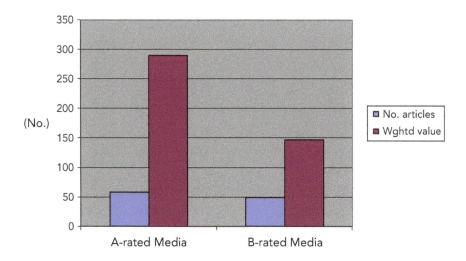

Figure 3.5 Coverage achieved by type of publication

Source: Friday's Media Group.

Press releases are more likely to be used by media editors if they follow proven principles and tips:

- Make the story newsworthy – editors are looking for original news (e.g. focusing on 'the first. . .', 'the best. . .', 'the biggest. . .' etc.).
- Aim to create a word picture: rather than simply saying 'the new exhibition space is x square metres', use a description such as 'the new space can hold x London buses' or 'can fit in y football pitches (or Olympic-size swimming pools)'.
- Use a catchy headline – one that summarises the story being promoted. Busy editors will ignore a release if the headline does not grab their attention! However, they should not be silly. Puns are fun, but should be left to the sub-editors. The content should be clear from the headline.
- Summarise the release in the first paragraph, this will help an editor to judge whether they want further details from which to develop a story – this can come in the body of the release but the opening paragraph must engage their interest.
- Remember the 'five Ws': Who is involved? What is happening? When is it happening? Why is it happening? Where is it happening?
- Product releases should incorporate information on key features, the benefits to the user, price, availability and a general description, as well as contact details to provide further information.
- Use short sentences and paragraphs. Avoid slang, jargon, opinion and boasts – stick to the facts. Ensure that any statement made can be justified. A press release is not like sales literature. It should be factual and written as a news story would appear in a magazine or newspaper.
- Include a quote if possible, preferably from a key person in the organisation – or better still a testimonial from a client.
- Avoid elaborate fonts and colours – it is the content that is important.
- When providing images electronically, ensure that they are around 1–2 MB, are scanned at 300dpi (the standard resolution for most publications) and can be read by PC and Mac. Change file names to something relevant to the story and make it clear which caption refers to which file.
- Finally – only issue a press release if there is something newsworthy to say!

Figure 3.6 Guidelines for effective news releases

Source: Friday's Media Group.

News releases

One of the simplest ways of communicating a news story is by a news (or press/media) release. This must be well written and contain interesting, newsworthy and topical information. Such characteristics will significantly enhance the chances of the release being used and thus gaining exposure.

News releases remain one of the most effective ways of promoting a destination or venue but the reality is that the majority of press releases are simply deleted. Adherence to the guidelines set out in Figure 3.6, compiled by specialist UK PR agency Friday's Media Group (www.fridays-group.com) will increase the likelihood of a release being used.

In an article entitled 'The Anatomy of a press release' (*Conference News* magazine, January 2015), Philip Cooke makes some useful additional points:

- Expect to be scanned: magazines are not read like novels, but scanned for material that might be of interest to the reader. In Western cultures, this process starts at the top and goes down and across the page. Both the human eye and the search engine scanner will first 'read' and evaluate the headline or subject line, then the first paragraph.
- 'Man Bites Dog!': this is not just a way of attracting the reader's attention, it is how to construct the headline that will work. It attracts attention as the 'subject – active verb – object' structure puts the target audience's or client's name at the start of the 'is this of interest to me?' evaluation process.

- Sleep on it: if there is no-one to second or third-read it, always sleep on it.
- One at a time: do not send out the release via the blind cc box. Instead, build a database of individually named editorial contacts and send it out one at a time.

With most news releases now being delivered digitally, via email to journalists and (increasingly) bloggers, a fundamental challenge is getting the email opened and read by the recipient. Clearly, a compelling subject line that can excite the recipient's interest is worth spending time on, but there are other factors to be taken into consideration.

Email distribution platform Mailchimp looked at how much of a difference a single word can make in a campaign's open rate [an email's open rate is a measure used by marketers to indicate how many people 'view' (or 'open')] in the commercial electronic mail they distribute. It is most commonly expressed as a percentage and calculated by dividing the number of email messages opened by the total number of email messages sent out (excluding those that bounced), for instance, whether or not the release was actually opened rather than deleted or ignored by recipients (http://blog.mailchimp.com/subject-line-data-choose-your-words-wisely/). They studied approximately 24 billion delivered emails with subject lines composed of approximately 22,000 distinct words, looking at subject lines both in general and within specific industries.

Results for comparable word groups

Choosing the right words can result in higher open rates without altering the bottom line of the message. To interpret these results, it is important to know that a standard deviation is a standardised measurement of how much something deviates from the average value. One standard deviation for a user who tends to see large swings in open rates will be a higher percentage than it will be for someone with consistent open rates. This means that choosing words wisely will have a larger impact on open rates for people with a higher standard deviation, while users with very consistent open rates can expect to see smaller changes.

Personalisation works

The impact that including recipient names in campaign subjects or bodies has on open rates has been debated before but the consensus is that it is positive. The Mailchimp analysis found that personalisation does indeed increase open rates. One of the most interesting findings is that, though the use of both first and last names in a subject is less common, it has the largest positive impact on open rates. Figure 3.7 illustrates the benefits of including recipient names in campaigns.

Mailchimp's analysis also showed that first name personalisation is used much more frequently than last or full names and so they decided to see how the impact varied by industry. They focused on industries where the impact was significant, and found that there are several industries where use of the first name has a large positive impact. The most surprising finding, however, is that first name personalisation has a *negative* impact on open rates for the legal industry. Figure 3.8 shows the relative effectiveness of first name personalisation by selected industry.

Features

The editorial content of most conference industry magazines can be split into four areas: news, comment/opinion columns, topical articles and issue/destination/venue-led features. While a press/media release will work to gain coverage in the news pages, opportunities to obtain exposure in the other three sections should not be ignored. Such exposure may be achieved by:

- Being alert to journalists' needs. More than ever, writers plan features and other content on a just-in-time basis and specialist PRs will maintain a dialogue so that they are always 'in the know'

- The provision of appropriate 'comment' from the destination or venue into existing special features and reports
- Venues and, particularly, destinations could also 'pitch' to magazine editors suggesting ideas for special reports that would include the destination or elements of the destination
- Another approach could be through the promotion of the personalities behind the destination or venue as 'thought leaders' and industry 'gurus'
- Another source of ideas will come from case studies of successful events held. These should be researched and written up and the issues unearthed could form the basis of features and comment columns

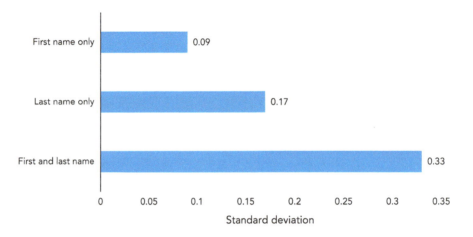

Figure 3.7 Personalisation benefits in PR campaigns in standard deviations

Source: Mailchimp http://blog.mailchimp.com/subject-line-data-choose-your-words-wisely/.

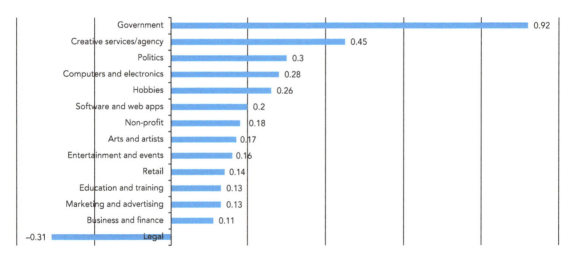

Figure 3.8 First name personalisation in selected industries in standard deviations

Source: Mailchimp http://blog.mailchimp.com/subject-line-data-choose-your-words-wisely/.

Press packs

It can be useful to compile a press pack about the destination or venue for use with journalists. It should not be difficult to build up a digital dossier that can be personalised to a particular journalist's needs. The dossier could contain:

- The venue brochure or destination guide
- Maps and images of the destination with appropriate permissions and copyright details so that they can be reproduced to illustrate articles
- Details of major events staged successfully, ideally including testimonials from satisfied clients
- Details of major future events confirmed
- Copies of recent media releases issued
- Factsheet(s) and statistical material
- Contact details for key players in the destination or venue, including PR agency contact details where appropriate

Advertising

The use of advertising in marketing

Advertising is defined by Hackley and Hackley (2014) as paid-for promotional messages from an identifiable source, transmitted via a communications medium. Those messages may be transmitted through a variety of channels such as television, radio, newspapers, magazines, direct mail, outdoor displays and, increasingly in the modern world, through the internet in the form of online advertising.

In defining the uses of advertising, Percy and Rosenbaum-Elliott (2012:4) suggest that 'in a very real sense, advertising is meant to turn us towards a product or service by providing information or creating a positive feeling – something that goes well beyond simply calling our attention to it. Advertising is an indirect way of turning a potential customer towards the advertised product or service by providing information that is designed to create a favourable impression. This . . . then helps place the consumer on the path towards seeking out the product or service advertised'.

Ultimately, of course, the ultimate function of advertising is to help produce sales, but, as suggested by Lavidge and Steiner (2000:137) '. . .all advertising is not, should not, and cannot be designed to produce immediate purchases on the part of all who are exposed to it. Immediate sales results (even if measurable) are, at best, an incomplete criterion of advertising effectiveness'.

In other words, the effects of advertising on consumers are long-term, and should be measured with that in mind. Lavidge and Steiner (2000) contend that advertising may be thought of as a force that must move people up a series of seven steps:

1. Near the bottom of the steps stand potential purchasers who are completely unaware of the existence of the product or service in question.
2. Closer to purchasing, but still a long way from the cash register, are those who are merely aware of its existence.
3. Up a step are prospects who know what the product has to offer.
4. Still closer to purchasing are those who have favourable attitudes towards the product – those who like the product.
5. Those whose favourable attitudes have developed to the point of preference over all other possibilities are up still another step.

6. Even closer to purchasing are consumers who couple preference with a desire to buy and the conviction that the purchase would be wise.

7. Finally, of course, is the step that translates this attitude into an actual purchase.

However, as the authors point out, the various steps are not necessarily equidistant. In some instances, the distance from awareness to preference may be very slight, while the distance from preference to purchase is extremely large. In other cases, a potential purchaser may move up several steps simultaneously. In the case of conference destinations, for example, a meeting planner may be instantly seduced by an advertisement that shows the beauty and excitement of an exotic country and extols its many advantages as a place in which to hold a business event. Nevertheless, many years may pass, due to rotation factors in the destination selection process for instance, before the planner finally opts to hold a conference in the destination advertised.

In order to explain the process by which different buyers move up through the seven steps outlined above, Lavidge and Steiner (2000:13) offer the following hypothesis:

> *The greater the psychological and/or economic commitment involved in the purchase of a particular product, the longer it will take to bring consumers up these steps, and the more important the individual steps will be. Contrariwise, the less serious the commitment, the more likely it is that some consumers will go almost 'immediately' to the top of the steps. An impulse purchase might be consummated with no previous awareness, knowledge, liking or conviction with respect to the product. On the other hand, an industrial good or an important consumer product ordinarily will not be purchased in such a manner.*

It is therefore the role of advertising to inform and persuade potential buyers – and occasionally simply to remind them that a particular product is still on the market. One of the basic choices to be made, as regards advertising a company's products, is which media channels may be most productive

In the previous section on Public Relations, a number of comparisons were made, which contrasted advertising with PR. We return to this theme in this final section of the chapter, with a summary of the differences between PR and advertising, highlighting the particular characteristics of both as promotional tools (see Table 3.1).

Advertising is typically far more expensive than PR. It is expensive to originate and media costs are high, but the message, choice of media, positioning and timing are totally within the control of the destination/venue.

However, one characteristic that both advertising and PR have in common is that these activities are often carried out by specialist agencies. The duties of an advertising agency working on behalf of a client may include:

- Assisting in setting clear and measurable objectives for the advertising campaign: for example, is the campaign mainly concerned with creating an awareness of the destination/venue, changing perceptions, creating a pre-disposition to visit or to book or to generate actual responses in the form of business enquiries?
- Producing designs for an advertisement or a series of advertisements
- Advising on where these should be placed (in magazines, business newspapers, or on websites, for example)
- Helping to monitor response rates to advertising campaigns

The agency will normally do this work based on a brief from the destination/venue, finalised in the form of a contract that also includes details of fees and expenses to be paid. An example of an advertising campaign produced by an agency on behalf of a convention bureau is given in Case Study 3.3 in this chapter.

Table 3.1 Characteristics of advertising and public relations as promotional tools

Advertising	Public relations
Paid	Earned
Builds exposure	Builds trust
Audience is sceptical	Media gives third-party validation
Guaranteed placement	No guarantee, must persuade media
Complete creative control	Media controls final version
Adverts are mostly visual	PR uses language
More expensive	Less expensive
'Buy this product'	'This is important'

Best practice in the use of advertising

Planning an advertising strategy

Advertising has to be planned strategically, carried out over a period of time as a 'campaign', and integrated with the overall sales and marketing plan for a destination or venue. Planning how advertising will be used within a company's media strategy should include a consideration of the following points suggested by Mamoon (2014):

- Determine who your present and potential buyers are. Demographic and geographic data are necessary here. List your buyers' predispositions toward and against your products or services. When do they use them and why? What do they like and dislike about them?

- Define your business as local, regional, or national in distribution. Then list all available media for your distribution definition.

- Set your budget. If you are selling more than one product, establish the advertising allocation for each one. The amount of money you have to spend frequently helps determine which media you choose, as there may be some media you can afford and others you cannot.

- Evaluate past and present advertising. What media have you used? How much was spent? How effective were you in maintaining and increasing market share? Do a definitive study of your copy, headlines, and layouts and try to determine what worked and what did not.

- Collect competitors' print media ads. Do a comparison contrast with your own ads for media used, image conveyed, selling points, number of items featured, positioning, copy and layout techniques, size and so on. Gather what data you can about your competitors' use of other media.

Choosing the most appropriate media

The decision of which media can be used most effectively for advertising should involve consideration of three factors: *reach*, *frequency* and *continuity*. The size of the advertising budgets available to most destinations and venues dictates that they cannot aspire towards using media in such a way that their campaigns are characterised by all three of these factors. Therefore, careful trade-offs are necessary in deciding which of these factors will most effectively bring in meetings business.

Emphasising the *reach* factor means companies choosing the media that will carry their advertisement to the largest number of different people (even though, of course, there can be no guarantee that all of or even most of those people will respond to or even see the advertisement). Nevertheless, as Mamoon (2014) points out, as the advertising costs of most media are computed on the basis of how much circulation they provide the advertiser, emphasising reach as a factor can be costly. A useful benchmarking technique for comparing different media in terms of reach is to establish a cost-per-thousand for the exposure a message is receiving. Cost-per-thousand (CPM) is a simple equation:

$$\frac{\text{Amount of money spent}}{\text{people reached (thousands)}} = \text{CPM}$$

This computation can be used for each of the media under consideration as prices and numbers of people reached are available from every medium.

As most research shows that reaching an audience only once with a marketing message is usually not enough to convince them to buy, the *frequency* factor should also be considered. Frequency refers to the number of times a potential consumer is exposed to a message over a given period. For example, a venue may choose to advertise in a monthly meetings industry magazine every month over the period of a year. This kind of repetition aids retention and boosts the chances of the advertisement being noticed.

Continuity, the third factor, emphasises the length of time that a campaign, or series of messages, runs. In order to achieve considerable levels of continuity, companies may choose to run the same ads in the same trade publications for six, 12, or even 24 months before rewrite or redesign.

In deciding upon where, with what frequency and for how long advertisements should be placed, destinations and venues should take the above factors into account and determine the best balance for their specific objectives. For example, it would be a mistake for a venue with a small advertising budget to aim for a broad target – say, for example, by placing a one-off advert in the pages of national newspapers in countries representing its key source markets. In this case, it would be more effective to reduce the reach objective and aim for a smaller audience – with sufficient frequency to be effective. This may mean advertising in fewer markets or advertising only in media that reach a precisely defined group of people, such as a meetings industry trade magazine.

The need for creativity

But in an over-communicated society, what is the key to breaking through the 'clutter' and getting advertisements noticed? Morgan and Pritchard (2013) emphasise the importance of creativity in this process, and suggest a number of factors that can contribute to the success of an advertising campaign:

- Producing a tightly defined, research-based, advertising brief
- Precisely targeting the audience
- Harnessing creative energy
- Being interesting, surprising and relevant
- Inventing indelible imagery
- Perfect timing
- Having a consistent approach
- Appearing effortless – good adverts provide the audience with intense experiences, delivered with a maximum of cool

Elaborating on the first point above, the need for clients to produce an effective brief for their advertising agency, the authors argue that organisations should consider the following questions and incorporate the answers into the advertising briefs that they give their agencies:

- What should the advertising achieve?
- How does the advertiser want to influence customers?

- Does the advertiser want to raise their awareness?
- Does the advertiser want to change their perceptions?
- Who is the brand competing against?
- How does the brand compare with its competitors?
- How can it be truly differentiated from the rest?

Nevertheless, creativity, to return to Morgan and Pritchard's central point, is clearly a prerequisite of success in marketing campaigns.

In his blog for *Entrepreneur*, Williams (2015) reviewed the results of a Wharton School of Business (University of Pennsylvania) study that investigated the correlation between the amount of money invested in advertising by firms and the results gained. One of the key findings was that there is no direct correlation between dollars invested and results gained. Rather, according to the study, results from advertising are inextricably linked to the message:

> *Ads that speak to the heart of the customer and touch a nerve are the ones that turn little companies into big companies. But few people know how to write such an ad. Most business owners approach advertising with the goal of merely getting their name out. But there is no evidence to suggest this will help you in the slightest. The Wharton study indicates that everything hinges on the message you attach to your name. Is your message predictable and, consequently, boring? Is it believable? Is it relevant to the perceived need of the reader/listener/viewer? Tempt a dog with a bowl of rice, and he'll ignore you. Put a steak in the bowl, and you'll have his undivided attention. Your prospective customers are no different. What have you been putting in their bowls?*

An outstanding example of an imaginative, surprising advertisement is the one featuring the 'Naked Man', created to raise the profile of Norway as a meetings destination. Bearing the slogan, 'Norway. . .for Natural Reasons', the campaign depicted the rear view of a naked man (see Figure 3.9) enjoying the

Figure 3.9 Norway's Naked Man advertisement

Source: Nordic Life/Terje Rakke.

elements. The campaign certainly proved popular, with a survey showing 84 per cent of polled meeting planners registered a positive approach to the 'Norway. . .for Natural Reasons' brand. It is estimated that the 3-year €1 million marketing campaign helped attract incoming international visitors worth €93.6m for the local economy. In 2009, the Norway Convention Bureau won the ICCA Best Marketing Award for the campaign.

CASE STUDY 3.1   The Convention Centre Dublin's website

Research and objectives

The Convention Centre Dublin (CCD) launched its first website 3 months prior to the Centre opening in September 2010. Whilst it received very positive reviews and won a gold award at the Meeting Industry Marketing Awards (MIMAs) in 2011, by 2013, it was 3 years old and The CCD felt it could be updated and refreshed.

With this in mind, the venue critically assessed its website across all platforms and found that visitors accessing theccd.ie from tablet and mobile devices had increased by over 100 per cent since 2011. As the original website was developed with desktop users in mind, it was, therefore, not fully optimised for use with mobile and tablet devices. This meant that users viewing the site on smaller screens had to zoom in and move around each page to access information, resulting in a poorer user experience relative to viewing it on a desktop. Figure 3.10 reveals web analytics on the original website.

Following this insight, The CCD carried out a Needs Analysis, which looked at industry trends and consumer behaviours in internet usage and website design. It found that the use of smartphones and tablets to access the internet was set to overtake desktop users in the near future and that the vast majority of internet users were moving between devices to accomplish a single goal. It also found that more and more websites were moving towards fully responsive designs, which automatically adjust the display based on the size of the user's screen for better user experience and easier navigation.

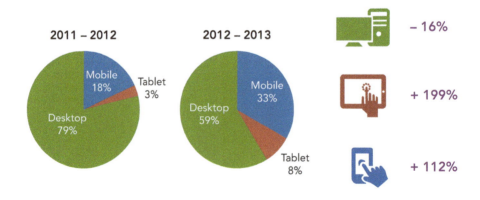

Figure 3.10 Previous website access platforms for The CCD website

Source: The Convention Centre Dublin.

The venue decided a responsive design would make sure that the same information and services would be available to users irrespective of the device they were using, ensuring continuity of a customer's brand experience at every step of their journey. Nick Waight, CEO of The CCD, said:

> We decided to move to a responsive design as we want our clients and delegates to get the best possible experience of The CCD, and this includes the virtual impression they get before they even set foot in the building. It was also important, therefore, that the new site not only acted as an information portal, but also as a vehicle to reflect our brand and culture, so visitors not only get a sense of what we do, but who we are.

The venue's primary objectives in building a new responsive website were as follows:

- To ensure that all visitors receive the optimal user experience of theccd.ie, regardless of whether they are viewing it on a desktop, tablet or mobile
- To incorporate a new look and feel that captured The CCD's brand values and culture
- To improve the user experience for all of the venue's key audiences (clients, exhibitors and delegates), by examining what information they were looking for and how best to communicate this to them
- To improve visitor engagement and interaction levels by updating and sharing relevant content
- To showcase Dublin and promote it as an international conference destination
- To increase website traffic by improving SEO (search engine optimisation) performance
- To generate revenue by adding an interactive map-based 'visiting' section with third party advertising opportunities. Elaine Phillips, Head of Marketing and Communications for The CCD, said:

> Our aim was not only to create a very visual, progressive design, but also to ensure the new site benefits all of theccd.ie's different users. So an event organiser on their laptop overseas, or a conference delegate in the venue on their mobile, can find the information they're searching for on our website quicker and easier.

Design and development

The CCD worked with Irish web design agency Strata3 to develop a clean, contemporary website that focused on imagery and typography, with easy access to information and a clear navigation. The venue also wrote new content for the site, incorporating custom meta-details and keywords to ensure it was fully optimised for search engines.

A host of new, user-friendly features and functionality have also been added to the new site, not only to help showcase the venue but also Dublin as a destination. To help facilitate the event planning process for clients, the new site includes a mobile-friendly Google 360 degree tour of the building, as well as downloadable floorplan factsheets for every room. The inclusion of more images and photo galleries lets organisers see how the venue's 'blank canvas' rooms and halls are brought to life to stage world-class events.

In addition, The CCD redeveloped its original 'Destination Dublin' section of the website that is focused towards event delegates. Now titled 'Visiting', this section features an interactive map, where visitors can get a sense of how compact and accessible the city of Dublin is. To help them plan their stay and get the most out of Ireland's lively capital city, visitors can use this map to explore the various facilities and attractions, including many restaurants, bars and hotels that lie near the venue. As The CCD hosts over 250,000 delegate days a year, the new map also gives local businesses the opportunity to promote their services directly to this audience.

Results and feedback

Metrics following the site's launch in July 2014 indicate that the new site is performing beyond the KPIs set out at the start of the project, namely to increase engagement (pages per session) and the percentage of new sessions, as well as reducing bounce-rates and increasing inbound sales enquiries.

The multi-award winning venue is one of only a handful of convention centres in the world that have adopted this forward-thinking approach to website design. By focusing on increasing simplicity, improving content structures, refining navigational flows and adding 'swipe and tap' functionality, the new site has been streamlined and de-cluttered, and feedback from the industry has been extremely positive. Anna Taylor of Touch Associations comments:

> The CCD's website doesn't just sell the great facilities at The CCD but the whole city of Dublin, which is a major factor in clients choosing a destination. It offers lots of useful features that help to get a sense of the venue including a room search function, floor plans and capacity charts, as well as an interactive tour. These features, combined with great imagery, help event organisers visualise how an event will work at a venue and are great assets for a venue website to have.

Following on from the positive feedback that theccd.ie has received post-launch, the venue is planning to add a number of further features to the new site. These plans include translating key pages of content into six additional languages, creating a careers portal that facilitates job application uploads and digitalising its customer feedback survey to make it easier and quicker for clients to complete. Figure 3.11 illustrates pages from the new website.

For further information visit: www.theccd.ie

Figure 3.11 Pages from The CCD's new website

Source: The Convention Centre Dublin.

CASE STUDY 3.2   Kyoto Convention Bureau's PR campaign based on pre-conference meditation

In 2011, the following story was widely reported in the international meetings industry press and in many other publications unrelated to the meetings industry itself:

> *A recent study in Kyoto, Japan, found there is a significant improvement in learning outcomes if meeting participants undertake at least 10 minutes of meditation before a meeting. Imagine if every meeting in the world was 12.5 per cent more efficient, what an effect that would have on the event, conference and meeting industry.*

Highlights of the Research identified:

- *Average improvement of 12.5 per cent across all tasks*
- *Largest improvement for single task 117 per cent*
- *Largest individual improvement 21 per cent (across all tasks)*
- *Smallest individual improvement 2 per cent*

> *Reverend Matsuyama, a Zen Buddhist priest, who conducted the meditation session comments: 'It is a simple principle, if your tea cup is already filled; there is no point in pouring more tea in it. People who come to attend seminars and meetings are often under pressure and tired either because of long journeys or work based stress. If they are to take on board new information they must first make room for it. Simple meditation exercises can make all the difference – enter the meeting in a calm state of mind, take a few deep breaths. The difference is profound and it can also have a brilliant effect in bringing out a lot of positive energy in you'.*

> *Research was undertaken in spring 2011 by the Kyoto Convention and Visitors Bureau based on the assumption that a short meditation at the start of a meeting helps clear the mind and allows the participants to take in more of the taught material than if meditation is not practiced.*

> *As part of the research, a group of people (20 individuals), taking part in a regular event, undertook five separate exercises on two separate occasions (12 days apart). These included memory, language, comprehension and listening tests. Before the first session there was no preparation, before the second session there was a 10-minute mediation exercise. Yoshiaki Matsui from Kyoto Convention and Visitors Bureau, the organisation behind the research said: 'The findings of the survey are simply astonishing. Japan has traditionally been known for meditation and we are very happy to have some of the finest schools of meditation and teachers here. We are taking the results of the research very seriously and making a concerted effort to include them in future events and meetings'.*

> *Yoshiaki continues: 'The event industry calendar here is steadying after the recent turmoil across the country. However, this has nonetheless made the introduction of these sessions slower than we hoped. Despite these challenges, we are so convinced by the research that we are starting a campaign to persuade organisers around the world to take up the use of meditation. Above all these simple 5–10 minute meditation exercises are not meant to take time away from people's work – but to help them be more successful at their jobs'.*

Several years later, Yoshiaki Matsui, who is cited in the story above, elaborated upon the rationale behind the campaign and gave insights into the impacts it had.

Simply, the motivation for the research was a conversation between Reverend Matsuyama, who led the meditation, Adam Baggs of Soaring Worldwide (a UK-based strategic communications agency), and myself. We just realised that this was something that Japan could add to meetings globally, which is not location-specific. Basically if there is someone in the meeting that can lead meditation, then meditation can add value to meetings. It also happened to be potentially positive PR for Kyoto, which it turned out to be – it was most certainly the best coverage we got for any media-relations project in terms of numbers of articles generated and feedback in terms of direct enquiries. It went well beyond our target of meeting professionals into fields of study and interest for wider society.

The success of the campaign led Yoshiaki Matsui to offer the following testimonial on Soaring Worldwide's own website (www.soaringww.com):

Soaring Worldwide has taken the Kyoto Convention and Visitors Bureau on a communications journey, understanding our desires, promoting us and improving our reputation across a variety of target markets. They understand both our commercial and cultural needs, combining them with international requirements in a way domestic agencies have been unable to achieve. This has led to a positive, long term relationship as well as the achievement of our marketing targets.

Yoshiaki Matsui, Deputy Director Conventions, Conventions and Conference Planning Division, Department of Conventions and Tourism, Kyoto Convention and Visitors Bureau, Kyoto, Japan.

CASE STUDY 3.3   Atlanta Convention Bureau's I AM ATL campaign

Aimed at meeting planners and launched in 2012, the US$1.1 million I AM ATL (I am Atlanta) campaign for the Atlanta Convention and Visitors Bureau (ACVB) included four concepts that ran in print and digital industry trade publications, targeting the large and mid-sized meetings market. Each advertisement incorporated an actual member of Atlanta's hospitality industry who delivered key messages about the city's walkability, accessibility, dining and collaborative hospitality community.

The marketing agency that developed the I AM ATL campaign for the ACVB was USDM (www. usdm.net). The agency describes the campaign as follows:

Atlanta Convention & Visitors Bureau's main goal for the I AM ATL Campaign was to drive large and mid-size meetings to the city in order to generate economic impact. In Atlanta, the people are the city's biggest advocates and will bend over backwards for meeting planners, attendees, exhibitors and visitors. They are very proud of their city and want everyone to have a great experience. But, if you're a meeting planner, you may not even consider Atlanta due to misperceptions on things to do for attendees. So, we developed a new campaign and a detailed messaging strategy for the four key promotional pillars of Walkability, Accessibility, Dining and Collaboration, which highlight Atlanta's strengths and challenge these misperceptions. Pillar extensions included nightlife and things to do. Actual industry personalities were selected to illustrate the key messaging pillars, welcoming meeting planners to experience the destination, people and customer service which make Atlanta.

With an August tradeshow deadline looming, in 90 days we conceived, wrote, designed, cast and shot four ads for the campaign. We also designed, developed and launched the microsite, display ads, emails, a 20 feet by 20 feet exhibit, graphics and screen savers for show kiosks and promo wraps for show dailies. Three more ads followed. Ads continue running in target print pubs and their online assets including email sponsorships and pay-per-click (PPC). Digital impressions through January are over 23.8 million. Email open rates average 32 per cent. Banners and PPC average 0.27 per cent click-through rate. Print ad circulation is over 79.7 million to date. By November, traffic spiked 1,578 per cent over October to 10,308 visitors. December spiked once again to 28,351, or 175 per cent over November. With 56,000 page views since launch, the small but mighty meeting planner market is taking notice via desktop and mobile. The buzz is even better. ACVB reports an 8 per cent increase in leads in the 6 months after the campaign launch, compared to the 7 months before launch.

The I AM ATL campaign received recognition from the advertising industry itself when it won the Web Marketing Association 2013 Internet Advertising Competition Award for Best Travel Integrated Ad Campaign. An image from the advertising campaign is shown in Figure 3.12.

Figure 3.12 One of the four images used in the I AM ATL advertising campaign

Source: ACVB.

SUMMARY

Non-personal marketing communications are an essential component in the promotion of a conference destination or venue. While the mix of communications tools will vary (i.e. whether to put the emphasis on an advertising campaign or PR activity or web-based promotions, for example), both from venue to venue and from destination to destination, but also from time to time (what may be most appropriate one year may be less so the following year), it is indisputable that the effective use of such communications is fundamental to the future success of other marketing and sales activities. They lay the foundations, namely an awareness of, and a positive interest in, a destination or venue on the part of clients, upon which further promotional activity can be undertaken and ensure that such activity has a greater chance of being successful.

The next chapter will examine the range of personal marketing communications techniques that are available to destinations and venues.

REVIEW AND DISCUSSION QUESTIONS

- Compare and contrast hard copy newsletters and e-newsletters. What are their respective advantages and disadvantages:

  1. from a venue/destination (i.e. as publisher or producer of the newsletter) perspective?
  2. from a recipient (i.e. conference organiser/buyer) perspective?

- Undertake critical evaluations of press releases issued by (i) a venue or venue consortium or (ii) a business events destination. Use the best practice guidelines for press releases in this chapter as the benchmark for your evaluations. Press releases may be found on the websites of venues and convention bureaux, often under the heading of 'Media'.

- Scrutinise the pages of the meetings industry press to identify examples of advertisements for venues and destinations, and assess their quality, using the factors listed by Morgan and Pritchard earlier in this chapter. Many meetings industry magazines are available online in digital form. For example: www.cimmagazine.com, www.citmagazine.com and www.convene-digital.org.

BIBLIOGRAPHY

BI Intelligence in conjunction with Edison Research (2014), *Social Network Popularity by Age Group*, published online at https://intelligence.businessinsider.com/ (accessed 28 July 2015).

Davidson, R. (2004) *EIBTM 5-Year Trends Report: Technology and Transport*, Richmond: Reed Travel Exhibitions.

Davidson, R. and A. Hyde (2014) *Winning Meetings and Events for your Venue*, Oxford: Goodfellow Publishers.

Davidson, R. and M. Keup (2014) 'The use of Web 2.0 as a marketing tool by European convention bureaux', *Scandinavian Journal of Hospitality and Tourism*, 14(3): 234–54.

Gartrell, R. B. (1994) *Destination Marketing for Convention and Visitor Bureaux*, Dubuque: Kendall Hunt Publishing.

Hackley, C. and R. A. Hackley (2014) *Advertising and Promotion*, London: Sage.

Holloway, J. C. (2004) *Marketing for Tourism*, Upper Saddle River: Prentice Hall.

Kotler, P., J. Bowen and J. Makens (2003) *Marketing for Hospitality and Tourism*, Upper Saddle River: Prentice Hall.

Lavidge, R. J. and G. A. Steiner (2000) 'A model for predictive measurements of advertising effectiveness', *Advertising & Society Review*, 1(1): 137–43.

Leventhal, B. (2015) 'All models are wrong but some are useful: the use of predictive analytics in direct marketing', *Quality Technology and Quantitative Management*, 12(1): 93–104.

Mamoon, Z. (2014) 'Choosing advertising media', *Journal of Research in Marketing*, 2(2): 143–50.

McCabe, V., B. Poole, P. Weeks and N. Leiper (2000) *The Business and Management of Conventions*, Chichester: Wiley.

McCann, R. (2014), 'US and UK customers will switch more than US$60 billion', *Journal of the International Customer Management Institute.*

Middleton, V. (2001) *Marketing in Travel and Tourism*, Oxford: Butterworth-Heinemann.

Morgan, N. and A. Pritchard (2013) *Advertising in Tourism and Leisure*, London: Routledge.

Percy, L. and R. Rosenbaum-Elliott (2012) *Strategic Advertising Management*, Oxford: Oxford University Press.

Pike, S. (2004) *Destination Marketing Organisations*, Oxford: Elsevier.

Rogers, T. (2013) *Conferences and Conventions: A Global Industry*, 3rd edn, London: Routledge.

Williams, R. H. (2015) *Selecting the most effective advertising media*, published online at http://www.entrepreneur.com/article/64738 (accessed 28 July 2015).

Wynne, R. (2014) *Selecting the most effective advertising media*, published online at http://www.forbes.com/sites/robertwynne/2014/07/08/the-real-difference-between-pr-and-advertising-credibility/2/ (accessed 28 July 2015).

Chapter **4**

Personal marketing communications for destinations and venues

Principles and practice

Chapter overview

This chapter looks at the principles and best practices associated with the dissemination of personal marketing communications messages about destinations and venues, concentrating on ways in which such communications are carried out primarily on a one-to-one basis with clients. What distinguishes these tools from those investigated in chapter 3 is that while non-personal tools such as advertising do not aim to start a dialogue with customers, most of the marketing communications techniques explored in this chapter are much more interactive and delivered on a one-to-one basis.

This chapter covers:

- Direct marketing
- The social media
- Exhibiting at trade shows
- Workshops and roadshows
- Familiarisation trips and educationals
- Conference ambassador programmes

It includes case studies on:

- ibtm china and the Hosted Buyer Programme
- The Adelaide Convention Centre workshops
- ibtm world Best Stand Award winners

- The Tourist Office of Spain (Turespaña) virtual trade show for the MICE market
- The York Minster to Westminster showcase
- The Great Ambassador Networking Group (GANG)

On completion of this chapter, you should be able to understand the theories and principles underlying the use of the following marketing tools and techniques by business events destinations and venues. In addition, in practical terms, you should be able to:

- understand the strengths and purposes of direct marketing;
- appreciate the key principles and best practice in the applications of social media marketing for business event destinations and venues;
- identify the core strategies for successful participation in trade exhibitions;
- distinguish between exhibitions, workshops and roadshows and understand the benefits and opportunities which each provides;
- understand the role of familiarisation trips in the marketing communications process;
- explain the purpose, operation and development of conference ambassador programmes.

Introduction

It is perhaps not surprising that, in the business events industry, events themselves can be used as a major tool in marketing communications. The events can range in size from industry exhibitions attracting thousands of visitors and exhibiting companies, through workshops and roadshows for tens or perhaps a few hundred people, to quite intimate events such as familiarisation trips for just a handful of event organisers. In all cases, they are forms of face-to-face marketing which involve personal interaction with potential customers. Their focus is on below-the-line marketing activity, generating one-to-one encounters with the aim of establishing and building productive relationships with individual clients.

Conference ambassador programmes, on the other hand, seek to recruit and work with stakeholders in a particular community to act as the destination's representatives or communicators, in effect to become the medium through whom marketing messages and event bids can be channelled. This chapter explores how such channels of face-to-face communication between stakeholders in the meetings industry can be used to optimum effect. But it begins by analysing how the power of direct marketing can be harnessed for venue and destination marketing.

Direct marketing

The use of direct marketing

Closely linked with CRM, as described in chapter 1, is the marketing tool known as direct marketing. Direct marketing is the opposite of so-called 'mass marketing' and it is characterised by all marketing through which people are addressed directly and personally. Today, direct marketing is varied. It includes targeting new and existing customers using personalised forms of address through a variety of different channels including direct mail and e-mails, as well as phone calls and telemarketing. The Direct Marketing Association defines direct marketing as: 'direct communication with an individual or institutional customer, meant to generate a reply, in the form of an order (direct order), an information request (sale preparation) and/or the visit to a store or another place to buy a certain product or service (traffic creation)'.

Leventhal (2015) elaborates upon this definition, noting that direct marketing works by identifying groups of people who will be the best recipients for marketing messages. For example, some of the groups and messages could be:

- Non-customers who are most likely to be interested in the company's products and services – direct marketing can be used to offer these people a trial
- Existing customers who are most likely to purchase additional products – direct marketing can be used to communicate cross-sell or up-sell promotions
- Existing customers who may be thinking of switching to a competitor's product – direct mail can be used to make these people a retention offer

Each of these activities could form the basis for a separate direct marketing campaign, designed to recruit new customers, generate increased sales or reduce attrition (respectively).

For all such types of direct marketing activities, the essential tool is a professional CRM system. In the late twentieth century and continuing into the present century, the progress made in ICT, in particular the internet, has radically changed direct marketing. It has provided organisations with a fast, effective and convenient means of maintaining regular contact with their customers. It has also facilitated the creation of sophisticated databases to manage customer relations.

The development and use of customer profile databases lies at the heart of effective direct marketing. For meeting industry suppliers, Rogers (2003:105) describes the range of data that destinations and venues typically record for each customer or potential customer: 'full contact details (client name, job title, company name and address, telephone and fax numbers and e-mail address, as a minimum) . . . then . . . a profile of the client's buying requirements (e.g. kinds of conferences organised, types of venues used, sizes of events, locations considered)'.

When these customer profile databases have been established, a number of direct marketing methods may then be employed to enable organisations to maintain contact with actual or potential clients:

The methods most commonly used by destinations and venues are:

- *Direct response media advertising*. The placing of advertisements in, for example, the trade/professional press, inviting readers to respond by post, using coupons or to call direct-response telephone numbers.
- *Direct mail*. Mail-shots sent to previous customers or in response to enquiries/returned coupons from advertising. This may take the form of a joint mailing between relevant partners, such as convention bureaux, conference centres and airlines serving the destination.
- *E-mail*. An electronic form of direct marketing, this form of communication is frequently used, for example, in the weeks leading up to trade shows, to encourage visitors to come to the destination's or venue's stand at the event. Clearly, one problem of this technique is the issue of buyers already receiving too many e-mails, meaning that many are simply deleted, unread.
- *Telemarketing*. The use of the telephone to reach customers or potential customers. In the consumer market, this method may be used via a call-centre. But business-to-business use of call centres is rarer than in the business-to-consumer situation, as is the 'cold call'. In the field of destination and venue marketing, telemarketing campaigns are more often operated using lists of previous enquirers.

Although these four methods have been listed as discrete techniques, they are often used jointly, for maximum impact. Kotler *et al.* (2003) describe the technique known as Integrated Direct Marketing, which comprises a multi-vehicle, multi-stage campaign:

Paid ad with a response channel	→	Direct mail mechanism	→	Outbound telemarketing	→	Face-to-face sales call

In the above example, the paid advertisement creates product awareness and stimulates enquiries. The company then sends direct mail to those who enquire. Within 48 to 72 hours, following mail receipt, the company telephones, seeking an order. Some prospects will place an order and others might request a face-to-face sales call (Kotler *et al.*, 2003:656). Kotler *et al.* claim that whereas a direct mail piece on its own may only generate a 2 per cent response rate, it is possible to generate responses of 12 per cent or more using integrated direct marketing.

It is clear that direct marketing is, therefore, a tool for conference destinations and venues. It offers them opportunities for developing a strong relationship with their customers through dialogue, with the aim of generating responses from them and turning them into loyal clients.

Best practice in the use of direct marketing

The tips given below are adapted from an article entitled 'The Secrets of Effective Direct Mail' which can be accessed at http://www.secondopinionmarketing.co.uk/articles/communicationandpromotions/secret.aspx.

Planning is a crucial component of any direct marketing activity. There need to be clear, quantifiable objectives for a direct mail campaign. How many responses are expected and what should be done if this target is not achieved? How will responses be followed up? Will respondents be sent more information, or an appointment be made to visit them, or can actual sales be made directly by telephone?

When undertaking direct mail campaigns, it is important to understand how old the CRM data to be used is, as well as its reliability. Databases of customers and prospects may have been used for previous marketing campaigns but the lists are only good if they have been kept up-to-date.

It is possible to buy or rent lists from commercial suppliers but spending money in this way needs to be based on an understanding of the quality of what is being bought, ensuring that the list source is a reputable one.

The importance of having an accurate list should never be underestimated. This means checking names (including spelling), job titles, address and postcode/zip code details, email address, telephone number(s), and in some cases, the contact's degree or level of purchasing responsibility.

Understanding your prospects

What do your prospective customers think, feel, and want at the moment? What do you want them to think, feel and want as a result of your mailing? Not all mailings will require a response – you may simply be looking for a change of perception or a better understanding of your venue, destination or service.

Getting the content right

Be very clear about what you want to communicate in your message. Only clear, simple messages will be understood. Avoid long words, long or complex sentences and any jargon that the recipient may not understand.

What is the single-minded proposition that you seek to convey? And, given that most direct mail is looking for a response, be very clear in your 'call to action' – what do you want the reader to do next?

The overall structure of the letter or email is very important – remember that many people will not read beyond the subject line and opening sentence and so their attention must be grabbed immediately.

Keep the opening paragraph brief and state the reason for writing. The body of the letter or email can give a bit more detail, such as brief details about the product or service and the benefits the recipient will gain from using it. It may help to include a short example, case study or testimonial.

Also think about options such as a special offer, discounts and rewards. Use trigger words such as 'save', 'free' or 'complimentary', 'special' and 'offer', but do not overdo these and only use if they are true.

Closing the letter or email is important too. What do you want the reader to do next? Is it absolutely clear? It may be useful to ask a colleague to read the draft text and what he or she would do if they were to receive it.

It is worth remembering that, according to many direct-mail gurus:

- 40 per cent of a piece's impact comes from sending it to the right list in the first place
- 40 per cent comes from the value of the offer
- 20 per cent comes from the design or writing of the piece.

VisitYork4Meetings, the conference destination marketing organisation (DMO) for the City of York (England), used a direct marketing campaign in 2015 to implement a perception study of York as a meetings destination among a targeted group of professional conference organisers (PCOs) and event management agencies. A well-researched and cleaned list of such intermediary buyers was used, with 250 contacts receiving personalised emails inviting them to take part in the research study (a small incentive was offered to those responding in the form of complimentary entrance tickets to major tourist attractions in York). A second follow-up email was sent to those who had not responded within 3 weeks of the original email. The result was a response rate of more than 50 or at least 20 per cent, well above the normal rate for direct marketing activity.

The social media

When the first edition of this book was published, in 2006, social media was not a familiar term and certainly not one in use in the lexicon of the conference and business events industry. In the years since, social media has become a mainstream form of everyday communication across the globe, affecting many aspects of people's lives. It has also become an integral part of conference venue and destination marketing activity and we begin this chapter by exploring the practical uses of social media marketing by destinations and venues in securing, increasing and retaining their conference and meetings business.

Social media networking is a major part of the lives of countless millions, probably billions, of people around the world and there is exponential growth in the use of the various social media. For example, in 2013, only 3 per cent of respondents aged 12 and older said that they used Snapchat, but only 12 months later, 13 per cent said they were users. A report from BI Intelligence compiled with Edison Research, 'Social Network Popularity By Age Group', indicated that:

- 43 per cent of 12 to 24 year olds said they use Snapchat and more than half of the survey's respondents in the same age group said that they have an Instagram account
- Only 36 per cent of teenagers and young adults said that they ever use Twitter, seven percentage points fewer than those using Snapchat
- Twitter takes the lead over Snapchat when looking at all respondents aged 12 and older
- Having an account on Instagram was still more common across all age groups, at 19 per cent, than using Twitter, at 16 per cent
- Facebook still matters. It is by far the most popular social network, with 80 per cent of respondents aged between 12 and 24 and 58 per cent of all age groups saying that they have a personal profile on this social network.

But how can this global phenomenon be used by business event destinations and venues to enhance their marketing and generate increased levels of business? The following section examines this key question.

The use of social media in marketing

In order to achieve the ultimate goal of marketing – winning new customers and keeping existing customers – marketers use various tools to transmit messages about their products. The methods employed by marketing professionals have evolved over time to incorporate an array of technical innovations, including the opportunities offered by the internet and, more recently, social media and other applications of Web 2.0.

The term Web 2.0 is attributed to Tim O'Reilly and Dale Dougherty (O'Reilly, 2005) and it has been described by the former as a set of principles and practices that include looking at the world wide web as a 'platform' with the aim of 'harnessing collective intelligence'. Elaborating upon that definition, Kennedy *et al.* (2007) refer to Web 2.0 as a loose collection of 'second generation' web-based technologies and services, many of which are designed to facilitate collaboration and sharing between users. It is precisely the power of these technologies to enable the instant sharing of information in many forms that has led to the use of Web 2.0 applications in general, and social media in particular, becoming so prevalent in modern life. The general public have been enthusiastic adopters of these applications, increasingly integrating them into their daily lives to communicate and interact with each other, as well as – crucially in a marketing context – to inform themselves about products and services prior to making actual purchases.

From the marketer's perspective, Web 2.0 has provided organisations and companies with a broad range of new tools and strategies for communicating with their customers and marketers are increasingly capitalising on these developments by actively engaging in the use of Web 2.0 applications as part of their overall marketing strategies. Constantinides and Fountain (2008) suggested how Web 2.0 can be used as a means of reaching customers and online opinion leaders such as bloggers and podcasters to inform them about their products, services and new market offers.

- Advertise in well-selected blogs and popular search engines
- Actively listen-in to what people are saying about the firm and its products in blogs, podcasts, forums and online communities
- Launch corporate blogs and podcasts, encouraging customers to interact and express their feelings, suggestions or remarks about the company and its products

Nevertheless, it is in the use of social media for marketing purposes, be it business-to-consumer (B2C) or business-to-business (B2B), that Web 2.0 has made its greatest impact in the world of commerce. Companies in practically all sectors of the economy have now significantly penetrated the online social networking scene, offering direct links from their corporate websites to platforms such as Facebook and Twitter, and using these tools to promote their brands and support the creation of brand communities (Kaplan and Haenlein 2010). Firms now make extensive use of social media in order to build direct relationships with customers, increase traffic to their websites, identify new business opportunities, create communities, distribute content, collect feedback from customers and generally support their brand (Breslauer and Smith 2009).

However, while social media clearly offer companies a wide range of marketing advantages, there is widespread acknowledgement among commentators that the use of these tools in marketing has heralded the advent of a new marketing communications paradigm. This is in stark contrast to the traditional marketing dynamic of using unilateral and one-to-many channels such as print, radio, television, and more recently, the internet, to broadcast carefully controlled messages of persuasion with limited opportunities for reciprocity (Berthon *et al.*, 2008).

The use of social media technologies has radically altered this dynamic by enabling an elevated degree of two-way dialogue between the marketers and their customers, as well as providing a mechanism for customers to communicate freely among themselves (Motameni and Nordstrom, 2014). One consequence of this consumer-to-consumer communication made possible through social media and identified by authors such as Li and Bernoff (2008), is that there has been a significant shift in the power relationship between customers and companies, whereby rather than companies controlling customers' attitudes, customers themselves are guiding the dialogue by using new media to communicate among themselves about products and companies – often critically. This use of social media has created new and significant challenges for marketers.

A further challenge for marketers using these tools comes in the form of social media metrics. As with every marketing tool, social media need to be evaluated for their effectiveness in achieving marketing objectives. In an era of increasing transparency and accountability and static or decreasing marketing budgets, the development of an effective system of metrics is paramount for marketers, who are under constant pressure to show results for their spending. Michaelidou *et al.* (2011) argue that traditional marketing metrics are based on a linear form of communication and they do not suit the interactivity of Web 2.0 tools. Consequently, the measurement of the effectiveness of such networks poses problems for marketing managers, who need to be able to demonstrate evidence of the return on investment from their spending on each marketing method.

We will return to the issue of social media metrics in the following section, which examines best practice in the use of these tools in marketing in general and by business events venues and destinations in particular.

Best practice in the use of social media in marketing

The social media most commonly used by venues and destinations in their marketing have been described as the 'big four': Twitter, LinkedIn, Facebook and YouTube were found by Davidson (2011) to be the four main Web 2.0 channels being used to market UK conference centres. The survey of European convention bureaux undertaken by Davidson and Keup (2014) found that for these DMOs, Twitter, LinkedIn, Facebook and YouTube were also the Web 2.0 tools most widely used in their marketing efforts.

Clearly, there is a growing trend towards incorporating using these tools, and others, into the marketing mix of venues and convention bureaux. But in the rush to adopt social media, many companies and organisations have been disappointed with the results. What are the features of the effective use of these tools? Rogers (2013:147) summarises a successful social media strategy as including the following actions:

- *Define your objectives/goals* – why do you think you should be on social media? What do you want to say? What do you expect to achieve? Defining goals is one of the fundamental steps in implementing a social media strategy.

- *Define your target audience* – who do you want to reach? Where are they? Understanding your target audience and how they use social media is key.

- *Use the right tools* – today people have many ways to discover, share and tell others what they think. Analyse your options and choose the most effective and appropriate way to communicate with your audience.

- *Value your content* – obsolete, outdated conversation has no place on your Facebook page or Twitter account. What you say is as important as when you say it. Conversation must be alive, current and up-to-date. You must be prepared to add value.

- *Measure your results* – whichever social media tools you adapt, it is important to monitor their effectiveness against pre-defined goals and adapt your activity accordingly. There is no 'one size fits all' solution to social media analytics but in order to manage it you have to measure it.

A report entitled 'Social Media Marketing for Global Destinations in the Meetings and Conventions Industry', published by Marketing Challenges International (MCIntl) in September 2013, highlights the current use of social media by destinations and also identifies a range of best practice. The report states that the most commonly used social media in the travel industry include networking platforms such as Facebook, Twitter, LinkedIn and Google+. Video and photo platforms such as YouTube and Flickr are also widely popular. Some convention bureaux are also experimenting with newer platforms such as Instagram, Vine, Pinterest and Foursquare, as highlighted by Davidson and Keup (2014). MCIntl suggests that important to any social media marketing campaign are management systems and analytic tools, which can help to measure a campaign's reach and effectiveness.

In the meetings and conventions industry, according to the same source, social media marketing has two main purposes:

> *First, to promote the destination* (and this could apply equally to the 'venue') *to potential new clients, and second, to help meeting planners with delegate boosting. Destinations have found creative ways to utilise all social media platforms available for both content delivery and networking.* (The report cites examples of destinations such as Barcelona, Berlin and Switzerland maintaining separate Twitter accounts for the conventions market, while others such as Vienna and Malaysia have launched mobile apps specifically for meeting planners.)

The report recommends that, when implementing social media marketing, convention bureaux should consider three key strategies:

> *First, using social media as a simple, cost-effective way to promote the destination's brand; second, building professional networks to meeting planners and other decision-makers by making connections on platforms such as LinkedIn, Facebook, and Twitter; and lastly, using social media to provide value-added services for meeting planners to help delegate boosting, including building special content guides or offering 'social concierge' services to meeting attendees/delegates. Destinations can also leverage social media marketing as a convention service to win bids.*

Although many companies maintain a LinkedIn presence, not all account holders fully capitalise on the tools available via the platform. Organisations such as the Sydney Convention and Exhibition Centre and Tourism Australia use their LinkedIn company profiles actively to broadcast business news that is targeted to professionals in the industry. This is a contrast to their respective Facebook pages, where the updates are lighter and geared towards event-goers and travellers. Other organisations such as ExCeL London and the Abu Dhabi National Exhibitions Company (ADNEC) have used the LinkedIn group feature to maintain special networking groups to build connections with meeting and convention organisers.

Newer platforms such as Pinterest and foursquare are much less used, although convention bureaux are finding unique ways of incorporating them into their social media efforts. For example, the DMOs Visit Berlin and MySwitzerland have created Pinterest accounts to depict the visual vibe of a city – offering up fun and engaging pinboards on topics such as 'Berlinicious' and 'Swiss vintage'.

MCIntl found that, in the North American meetings market, convention bureaux are inventing unique ways to use social media as a service for meeting planners. For example, the Phoenix and Seattle convention bureaux provide a 'social concierge' during conventions:

> *Using a specially created hashtag for the conference, CVBs (convention and visitor bureaux) can tweet directly to attendees/delegates to answer questions about the destination and notify them of local events, deals, and restaurants and entertainment. The Chicago CVB now works with its convention clients to develop interactive gaming challenges with SCVNGR (pronounced*

'scavenger'), a mobile app in which users can visit places, complete challenges, and earn points. Visit Orlando now offers its potential clients the services of its convention marketing executive, who works directly with planners on developing social media campaigns for their events.

Offering social media marketing as part of convention services has also given some destinations an edge over others in winning events. In a bid presentation for the World Congress on Disaster and Emergency Medicine, the Toronto Convention and Visitors Association included the use of Twitter as a way of exchanging information before, during and after the meeting. As the association was trying to increase its student delegation, Toronto's use of social media in the bid stood out and the destination ultimately won the bid.

From the examples given above, it is clear that Twitter offers destinations and venues considerable potential in terms of communicating their marketing messages. What gives this particular tool its power? Figure 4.1, provided by Richard McCann of Friday's Media Group in a personal communication to the authors, shows some of the possible explanations.

In terms of best practice in the use of Twitter in the specific context of venue/destination marketing, a good tweet should look to encompass at least some of the following features:

- Aim to be amusing from time to time and informative all of the time
- Passing on (or retweeting – known as RT) interesting points made by others will often lead to reciprocation
- Links are good: for example, if a venue has had news published about its expansion, instead of writing 'We are expanding our facilities by adding . . .' write '£2 million investment in venue reports Conference and Incentive Travel magazine, see full story here > (link)
- Include a picture: people like them and they are far more likely to read and pass on
- Once the tweet has been drafted, aim to add or turn keywords into hashtags to help people searching
- And, if it is important that specific people read the tweet (a magazine editor, for example), add them and they will receive a notification.

The MCIntl report suggests that social media is an easy and inexpensive way to build a destination's brand. It recommends that convention bureaux and DMOs capitalise on the content being generated by the leisure tourism sector (e.g. on culture, history, nightlife, cuisine) by integrating it into their own web presence.

Some additional useful advice for DMOs comes from some of the European convention bureaux that responded to the survey carried out by Davidson and Keup (2014: 251):

- Do not start (using social media) without integration in a marketing plan and budget. Set goals: what do I want to achieve? Plan this in your work schedule on fixed days/hours and keep it up.
- It is all about *content*. What are you going to tell me that I have not heard before? And are you just going to tell me or are you going to let me be part of the conversation too?
- Social media marketing simply lives by the idea of collaboration between information providers and the relevant interest groups. So if you do not have relevant information to provide over a new communications channel, then do not start one.

The MCIntl report echoes the first point above, stressing that convention bureaux should remember that success in social media marketing requires clear objectives and adequate time and resources. Destinations should have a good understanding of the market as well as trends in technology so that they can find the most creative and cost-effective ways of reaching their target audiences. It should be remembered that many of the report's findings and recommendations are as relevant to venue marketers as they are to destination marketers.

- *It's a form of distribution*

  It is an effective way of spreading ideas, information and content. Do not be distracted by the 'apparent' 140-character limit - many marketers and PRs use links to take the reader to more! It is instantaneous. Its reach can be immensely far and wide.

- *It's where SOME things happen first*

  Not all things. News organisations still break lots of news. But, increasingly, news happens first on Twitter. The chances are that regular Twitter users will have checked out many rumours of breaking news on Twitter first. As more people join, the better it will get.

- *It's a search engine*

  Many people still don't understand that Twitter is, in some respects, as good as or better than Google. Google is limited to using algorithms to search for information in hidden corners of the Web. Twitter goes one stage further - harnessing the mass capabilities of human intelligence to the power of millions in order to find information that is new, valuable, relevant or entertaining.

- *It's an aggregation tool*

  If Twitter is set to search out information on any subject, it will often bring the most topical information there is. In other words, it is not simply the Twitter user who is searching. In fact, users can relax and let other people go out searching and gathering on their behalf.

- *It's a form of marketing*

  The white paper has been written, the article has been published or a new blog post has been added. Now Twitter can let everyone know it is there, so that they come to the site. The community of followers is alerted. In marketing speak, it drives traffic and it drives engagement. If they like what they read, they will tell others about it. If they really like it, it will, as they say, 'go viral'.

- *It can be a series of common conversations*

  As well as reading what has been written and spreading the word, people can respond. They can agree or disagree or denounce it. They can blog elsewhere and link to it. (Tweets can be linked to a person's LinkedIn profile so that one updates the other.) With Twitter, an instant reaction is achievable from scores, or hundreds or thousands of people in real time.

- *It's diverse*

  Traditional media allowed a few voices in. Twitter allows anyone.

- *It's a level playing field that changes notions of authority*

  Instead of waiting to receive the 'expert' opinions of others, Twitter shifts the balance to so-called 'peer to peer' authority. A recognised 'name' may initially attract followers in reasonable numbers. But if they have nothing interesting to say, they will talk into an empty room. The energy in Twitter gathers around people who are interesting, even though they may be 'unknown'. They may speak to a small audience, but they may well be republished numerous times and the exponential pace of those re-transmissions can, in time, dwarf the audience of the so-called big names.

- *It creates communities*

  Communities form themselves around particular issues, people, events, artefacts, cultures, ideas, subjects or geographies.

- *It is an agent of change*

  Twitter is having an increasing effect on people in authority. Companies are already learning to respect, even fear, the power of collaborative media. Twitter is not so good at complexity – though it can link to complexity. It does not, of itself, verify facts. It can be distracting, indiscriminate and overwhelming. But it is certain that the motivating idea behind these forms of open media is not going away and it would be a serious communications mistake to be blind to their capabilities.

Figure 4.1 Twitter's potential for communicating destination and venue marketing messages

Source: Friday's Media Group.

An exemplar of social media marketing success, the Austin Convention and Visitors Bureau (ACVB) in Texas, USA, maintains a well-designed website that serves as a hub for both the leisure and meetings markets. From the site (www.austintexas.org/meet), meeting planners can access all of Austin's social media platforms (Facebook, Twitter, YouTube, Flickr, Pinterest and foursquare), as well as download the official Austin Visitors Guide app. The site also features a 'Social Media Lounge' that feeds all social media content into the site. Visit Austin provides content to visitors about the city's offerings, including food, music, events, nightlife and more.

Additionally, ACVB curates content targeted specifically to meeting planners and event attendees. ACVB's expertise in social media has also allowed them to provide free social media marketing to their clients, giving even more value to their convention services. For the Biomedical Engineering Society's (BMES) annual meeting, ACVB and Sparkloft Media, its social media agency, worked to build a following for BMES members and suppliers by posting updates on Facebook and Twitter about the conference. During the conference, the team uploaded content, videos and photos from the conference using a designated hashtag. A customised map of Austin was also created for BMES's Facebook followers to help delegates find shopping, entertainment and restaurants. Photos and videos were posted to the society's Flickr and YouTube accounts.

Social media management and measurement

Numerous tools exist to help companies and organisations manage and analyse social media data. Many of the individual social media platforms have their own analytics programmes, but for companies running multi-platform social media marketing campaigns, additional third-party tools may prove to be useful. Some examples of these are given below.

Hootsuite, a social media management system, allows businesses collaboratively to execute campaigns across multiple social networks from one secure, web-based dashboard. It also helps to streamline team workflow with scheduling and assignment tools and to reach audiences with geo-targeting functionality

Klout tracks influencers based on the ability of a company or user to drive action. Klout uses data from social media networks to measure 'True Reach' (how many people one influences), 'Amplification' (how much one influences the network) and 'Network Impact' (the influence of one's network). Companies and brands can partner with Klout to offer 'perks' to top influencers

Platforms such as *Simply Measured* and *Radian 6* offer comprehensive metrics on a company's social media efforts as a whole. Various analytic metrics include level of engagement (i.e. number of likes, tweets, etc.) to measure brand awareness; level of sentiment (i.e. positive versus negative posts) to measure brand favourability or intent to purchase; and level of virality (i.e. reposts, retweets) to measure brand reach. Although these are typically paid services, some analytic platforms, such as Simply Measured, offer free reports. Another useful new tool is *Buffer*, which is similar to Hootsuite in allowing users to schedule posts ahead of time to social media accounts and track their successes (reach, clicks, etc.).

Analytics are a very valuable tool to measure engagement when using social media as a value-added service for meetings planners and delegates/attendees. It can be useful to measure how much the delegates/attendees have used the social media tools available to them, for example, how many people asked the concierge questions? How many created their own content (photos)? How big was the reach of the posts beyond the conference delegates/attendees?

When it comes to using social media for building professional networks, success can be measured by the engagement of the groups. The same tools can measure how many people are in a group, how active the group is (how many posts) and how engaged the group is (direct engagement with group posts, such as likes or retweets).

For more information on the MCIntl report visit www.mcintl.com or email Michel Couturier at mc@mcintl.com.

There is no doubt that social media marketing has now secured its position as an essential marketing tool for destinations and venues. However, many destinations and venues are still at the exploratory stage regarding how best to use this tool to greatest effect. There is clearly an important educational role here for the meetings industry associations, whose members need to gain a better understanding of how to use social media in their marketing. One example of associations' responses to this issue is the *Guide to Social Media* published by the International Association of Conference Centres (IACC, 2012).

It will be interesting to see how this marketing tool has evolved by the time that the third edition of this book is published!

Exhibiting at trade shows

The use of trade shows in marketing

Trade shows (also sometimes called trade fairs or exhibitions) are business events at which companies and organisations in a specific industry (the exhibitors) showcase and demonstrate their products and services to an invited audience (the visitors). Generally, trade shows are not open to the public and can only be attended by company representatives and members of the press.

Trade exhibitions are a well-established marketing medium, whose origins are to be found many centuries ago. According to Gopalakrishna and Lilien (2012), trade shows have long been used as a forum for promoting sales of a variety of products, dating back to medieval times when artisans and villagers exhibited their wares at local fairs. Those fairs were a convenient way for local producers to gain access to large numbers of potential buyers who came to attend the events from neighbouring towns and villages.

In the twenty-first century, trade shows continue to occupy a prominent position within the B2B communications mix and the basic distinguishing principle remains unchanged: trade shows are differentiated from personal selling, the dominant element in the B2B marketing mix, by the fact that they bring current and prospective customers to the seller rather than vice-versa.

Gopalakrishna and Lilien (2012: 227) explain how the three key stakeholders in any trade show must be satisfied, for that trade show to come about and be successful:

> *The show managers, who organise and manage the event, transact with exhibitors for the sale of floor space and to provide other fee-based show services. They want exhibitors to have a successful experience, such that they will return to exhibit again at a future show. Exhibitors will return to a show only if the attendees they were able to attract to their booth were of good quality and the interactions led eventually to successful outcomes. Similarly, attendees will want to return only if they felt that they had a cost-effective experience that enabled them to find products/ solutions from alternative suppliers.*

It is clear that trade shows play a vital role in the marketing mix, offering a wide range of benefits to the companies and organisations that use them. They do more than just sell: they offer exhibitors the opportunity to build product branding and strengthen existing customer relationships. They can produce high quality leads, educate exhibitors and attendees through seminar programmes, generate media coverage and are often used to launch new products in the media spotlight.

Nevertheless, despite the fact that exhibitions are widely accepted as extremely effective tools for marketing, they also present a number of challenges for the participating exhibitors and visitors. Principal among these is the significant investment required, in terms of staff time and expenditure on travel, accommodation and sustenance and pre-event marketing.

Nevertheless, the future of exhibitions as a key element of a company's marketing mix seems assured. At a 2011 meeting of the Exhibition and Event Association of Australia, the forty industry leaders present explored the impact of new technologies on the exhibition sector and how this would affect the evolution of the industry up to 2020. Despite technology innovations and the explosion of social media, the delegates unanimously agreed that exhibitions would remain relevant as the only marketing channel to offer a flexible face-to-face buying experience. However, they also concluded that exhibitions would need to deliver an outstanding experience for their stakeholders and utilising technology and personal portable devices to complement the show's offering would be a key success driver.

Dedicated trade shows for the business events sector have existed for several decades. They exist at different geographical levels, from regional to global. A listing of the most relevant trade shows for the conference industry is given in appendix A.

Business events trade shows bring together under one roof the whole range of key industry players that were described in chapter 1. The list of exhibitor categories on the ibtm world website (http://www.ibtmworld.com) demonstrates the diversity of suppliers of business events facilities and services that hire stand space at the trade show.

- Airlines and cruise lines
- Attractions and entertainment
- Business travel suppliers
- Conference and meeting venues
- Convention and visitor bureaux
- Destination management services
- Event support services
- Hotels, resorts and spas
- Incentive destinations
- National tourist organisations
- Professional conference organisers
- Sporting and gaming venues
- Technology providers
- Travel agencies
- Travel management companies
- Trade associations/media

The same website lists the range of exhibition visitor categories as follows:

- Corporate organisations
- Associations and societies
- Independent meeting planners
- Incentive and venue finding agencies
- Professional conference organisers
- Destination and event management
- Business travel management

- Live events and experiential agencies
- Government organisations

The organisers of many of these events promote the trade show to potential exhibitors by attracting the type of qualified attendees that exhibitors want to meet, through a 'hosted buyer' programme. Details of ibtm china's Hosted Buyer Programme are given in Case Study 4.1.

In their quest to attract exhibitors and visitors, the organisers of these events offer a number of 'added-value' services. Principal among these are seminar programmes, which offer presentations and educational sessions from experts in the field of business events; and networking sessions, during which exhibitors and visitors can meet on a more informal basis.

Exhibiting at trade shows, therefore, can be a key element of a venue or destination's marketing strategy, and part of a planned campaign. Simply being present and exhibiting at such events is a statement in itself. For effective destination marketing, Gartrell (1994:194) maintains that:

> *The fact that staff are present and visible becomes an important factor in a destination attaining recognition and credibility among meetings planners ... There is no question that trade show participation is costly; but it should be looked upon as an investment and a necessary part of any bureau's marketing mix.*

Best practice in the use of trade shows in marketing

The suggestions for effective exhibiting given below draw heavily on ideas presented by Ray Bloom, Chairman of UK-based Regent Exhibitions Ltd and Organiser of 'IMEX' and 'IMEX America', two of the leading conventions and business events exhibitions held annually in Frankfurt and Las Vegas respectively.

Participation in a trade exhibition can often provide the opportunity to launch a new brochure, a new campaign, new products or a new image. The destination or venue's presence and proposed activities at the show should be highlighted, well in advance, nationally or worldwide – in e-mails, social media, news bulletins and advertisements. It is, for example, possible to target the world's leading 100 business events publications and aim for news coverage that appears just before, during or immediately after the exhibition. One interesting approach is to engineer the sense that a special launch is going to take place during the exhibition. The deliberate excitement of this beforehand can be added to by using promotional teasers, promised gifts for buyers who come to the stand and the offer of a fulfilment pack explaining the new product or service in detail.

In addition to ensuring an integrated marketing approach and taking advantage of the exhibition organiser's own promotional activities (such as ensuring a full entry in the exhibition guide and on the show's website, which may well be designed as a year-round 'virtual exhibition'), there are a number of key textbook approaches to exhibition success that should not be by-passed.

1. Set objectives

The first such requirement is to set challenging objectives! These, for example, might be to:

- Confirm current contracts and thank existing clients
- Win new business
- Launch new products
- Raise profile and awareness
- Achieve hundreds of good leads

- Develop new relationships with influential partners
- Undertake market research
- Spot industry trends
- Meet the world's top trade publications' editors
- Observe what competitors are doing
- Spark off some creative thinking
- Seek involvement in wider initiatives within the industry

In other words, through setting clear objectives, the time-honoured justification for exhibition attendance can be realised – namely, to be commercially successful. But there are additional goals that may be achieved through participation in trade shows, such as:

- building databases for the future;
- exploiting brand awareness;
- expressing market leadership;
- positioning or re-positioning the image of the brand; or
- testing reaction to a new product.

In her blog for Praxis Events, *Four Basic Types of Trade Show Objectives*, Shannon Caldwell divides the possible objectives for trade show attendance into four categories, some or all of which may have precedence for a specific marketing campaign:

- Sales
- Product launch or showcasing
- Communication
- Distribution

According to Caldwell:

> *Determining your chief trade show objectives is essential in defining your all-important exhibit objectives. The purpose of your physical exhibit space is to be persuasive and compelling and, hopefully, to have a definite WOW factor. Your purpose here is to move attendees of the show into taking the action necessary to achieve each of your stated objectives. This may be something as simple as taking a brochure or promotional give-away, filling out a form that will provide you with a prospective lead source, or to view a video or presentation describing a new product or service you are offering.*

What follows is her analysis of the four basic trade show objectives. Although some of them may be more appropriate for manufactured goods rather than the services and facilities offered by exhibitors at business events trade shows, the majority of her observations are valid to any industry.

SALES OBJECTIVES

A main reason many companies participate in trade show events is to boost sales. This includes immediate sales right on the trade show floor as well as future sales made possible through obtaining prospect leads from those visiting your exhibit. This is also an ideal venue for meeting face-to-face with current customers and expressing gratitude for their loyalty.

You may also have the objective of attracting new distributors for your product(s) or to add to your current sales force. Having a well-trained staff staffing your exhibit booth is important to capitalise fully on this particular strategy.

PRODUCT OBJECTIVES

Whether you are launching a new product or reintroducing an existing one, trade shows provide a good means of getting in front of potential customers to spread the word. Surveys and focus groups discussing product design and application can be utilised here for effective results. Giving away free samples of a particular product may also prove beneficial, especially for consumables that will be used up and then repurchased if met with user approval.

This is also an opportunity to display products still in the development pipeline. As an example, automobile trade shows that feature new models of vehicles will usually also display a number of 'concept cars' that are still in development phase and for which customer reactions are sought to incorporate in future design considerations.

COMMUNICATION OBJECTIVES

An effective communication objective will be geared toward enhancing company or product visibility, establishing a strong brand, educating and/or establishing your organisation as an expert in the industry or to garner press or media attention.

Doing something specific to make your exhibit presentation newsworthy will help create the buzz you want to surround your exhibit booth, as more people will be drawn to your location if they sense a great deal of activity occurring. News travels fast on a trade show floor and the more people you can attract the better.

DISTRIBUTION OBJECTIVES

Trade shows are a good place to learn about your competition and to form alliances with others in related industries that may prove beneficial. It is also an opportunity to further develop your distributor network or to attract fresh sales recruits if this is in line with your business model.

2. Stand/booth design

Second, the stand (or booth) design will have an impact on success at the exhibition. In such an environment where marketing is at its most direct, exhibitors have the freedom to employ all five senses – sight, sound, taste, touch and smell – as weapons in their armoury. Such a sensual (or experiential) approach could be employed to attract and then keep buyers on the stand. Key points of differentiation might be the colours used, an open and welcoming stand layout, special eye-catching features and presentation techniques, as well as trained professional staff who understand and promote the destination/venue's values and objectives to buyers walking the aisles.

Davidson and Hyde (2014) recommend that, for conference venues exhibiting at trade shows (and these points are equally relevant for conference destinations):

> *The graphics on the stand should be visually striking and strictly in line with the venue's brand. The wording and graphics should make it immediately clear to the visitor: that the exhibitor is a venue for meetings and events: where it is located; and what its key characteristics are (size, style of building, unique selling points). All of this, however, must be achieved with the minimum number of actual words – and judicious use of carefully-selected images*
>
> *The design of the stand should be sufficiently flexible to enable it to be used year after year. One way of ensuring this is to make certain that the graphics can be changed in order to reflect any change in the messages to be transmitted by the stand's graphics at future exhibitions*

The layout of the stand should be open and inviting, regardless of its size. There should be no form of barrier or obstruction (for example, a counter) that prevents visitors from walking on to the stand or discourages them from approaching the people working on it

Modern stand layout often includes a dedicated space where exhibitors can sit down and have a meeting or even negotiate with prospects, away from distractions and other visitors to the stand. In the case of the more elaborate 'double-decker' exhibitions stands, this private space may be on the upper level

Putting material such as brochures at the back of the stand encourages visitors to enter the stand space, giving venue staff the opportunity to engage with them

Adding some kind of eye-catching 'attractor' to the stand can give the casual passer-by a reason to pause and spend time there – which in turn gives those working on the stand the opportunity to engage with them. It could be something as simple as a prize draw that visitors can enter by leaving their business cards in a bowl. Movement of any kind tends to attract the attention of passers-by, and for that reason many venues have a video tour of their facility running on a loop on one or more screens on their stand.

3. Interacting with visitors

Thirdly, it is important to adopt different approaches to different kinds of visitors to the stand. Mark Saunders, brand experience account director for event management consultancy George P Johnson, expressed this as follows in *Exhibiting* magazine:

A warm prospect that you know by name and who has interacted with you well in advance of an event needs to be treated very differently from someone coming to your stand cold. For example, a warm prospect who knows and rates your product, but who hasn't yet become a customer, may benefit from having a high-level pre-booked meeting on the stand with your CEO. This will communicate the personal attention they will receive if they become a customer. To underscore this, you might then invite them to a customer reception where they can mix with satisfied customers. In contrast, a browser, someone who hasn't yet proved their value to you as a prospect, and who possibly doesn't know your organisation, will need to get a clear 'at a glance' feel for your company and offer. They may need theatre presentations and hands-on demonstrations. All of this will have implications for the layout, architecture and signage on your stand.

4. Measuring return on investment

Exhibitors are now in a position actually to measure the anticipated revenue outcome of their exhibition investment. For example, this could be done by computing the potential value of the follow-up quotations that are submitted; the actual level of business that has been booked; the volume of brochures distributed; the degree of response to the stand competitions that were organised; and the total number of centimetres of editorial coverage that was subsequently achieved. More sophisticated approaches could involve the use of market research – by telephone or using focus groups, perhaps – in order to track changing perceptions towards a particular destination. Destinations will be keen to monitor the resulting improvement in positive attitudes amongst decision-makers and, therefore, their growing willingness to book and buy. Such measurement may take place over months and years in order to evaluate fully the results from a show's attendance.

5. Follow-up

This same disciplined and professional approach must, of course, apply also to follow-ups after the event. The exhibition sales team should be de-briefed, their achievements related to the original goals and the subsequent week-by-week progress checked. It is especially important to exploit that immediate exhibition 'afterglow' during which the potential clients can still easily recall their conversation on a particular stand.

Case Study 4.3 describes the best stand winners at the ibtm world exhibition and Case Study 4.4 describes a virtual trade show organised by the Tourist Office of Spain for the US market.

Workshops and roadshows

The use of workshops and roadshows in marketing

In the same way in which exhibitions do, workshops (occasionally known as forums or showcases) offer suppliers the opportunity to have one-to-one interactions with possible customers in a specific marketplace, for a limited period of time. However, workshops are a much more structured and focused type of event.

Typically, workshops last for a few hours rather than for several days, and, rather than involving fully-fledged exhibition stands, may simply involve a table-top setting with some literature by the exhibitors. Workshops are appointment-driven, in the sense that buyers and suppliers usually know in advance of the event the people they will be meeting there for scheduled appointments. In addition to the opportunities for those one-to-one meetings between suppliers and visitors, workshops may also include the following elements:

- Formal audio-visual presentations of the products, to those visiting the event
- Informal networking sessions
- Educational sessions, with expert speakers
- Discussion groups

As they are on a much smaller scale than exhibitions, workshops can therefore be held in a hotel or conference centre or in an unusual or unique venue in order to provide added appeal to visitors.

In the context of the meetings industry, workshops bring together suppliers, such as destinations, venues and DMCs, with those buyers who may be persuaded to use the facilities and services offered by the buyers. As in the case of hosted buyers at exhibitions, the buyers who are invited to participate in such workshops are usually pre-qualified by the organisers to ensure that only those with an authentic interest in planning a meeting in the destination or destinations represented may participate.

Workshops for the meetings industry may be organised by a single convention bureau or venue (see the Adelaide Convention Centre example below) or by an agency specialising in the running of such events.

One such agency is the UK-based company, The Meetings Space (www.themeetingsspace.com), which ran its inaugural workshop in Berlin in 2013. It has since then organised two workshops each year, described by the agency itself as 'seriously good one-on-one meeting forums for influential buyers and inspirational suppliers'. In 2015, the 2.5-day Spring Forum was held at the Grand Hyatt Martinez, Cannes, France, bringing together approximately 100 suppliers from 25 European countries with 200 primarily UK and German buyers. The Meetings Space Autumn Forum was held in Cascais, Portugal, bringing together European buyers and European suppliers.

The 2.5 day programme offers participants a combination of one-to-one meetings, networking events and educational presentations, as seen in the following programme:

Thursday

- Delegates arrive throughout the day
- First official function: 19:30 drinks and networking supper

Friday

- Appointments through to mid-afternoon
- Afternoon networking programme
- The Meetings Space party evening

Saturday

- Ideas exchange session
- Appointments through to lunch
- Final official function: farewell networking lunch 13:00 to 14:15
- Delegates depart from 14:15

Strict criteria are applied in order to ensure that the hosted buyers are of the appropriate quality, for instance:

1. They must be a meeting or incentive planner in one of the following categories:
   - Professional conference organiser
   - Event agency
   - A corporate company
   - An association
   - An independent planner
2. They must organise a minimum of five business events in Europe outside their home country each year – meetings, incentives, conferences, congresses, seminars or roadshows.
3. They must be a decision-maker or major influencer on venue selection for these events

Workshops organised by a convention bureau or venue can be held on home territory, with event organisers/buyers being invited to visit the destination/venue and experience what it can offer, perhaps as part of a familiarisation trip or educational (see the next section of this chapter). Alternatively, they can be staged in a location identified as an important potential source market, in other words, taking the destination or venue to the potential buyers and meeting them on their home ground. The latter approach has the advantage of convenience for buyers – they can perhaps visit the workshop in late afternoon/early evening, allowing them to do a full day in the office and combine this with participation in the workshop. The disadvantage is that they do not actually experience the destinations/venues at first hand, although being invited to participate in a familiarisation trip may well be one of the outcomes from a workshop held in the buyers' own area.

Case Study 4.2 describes innovative approaches to workshop organisation adopted by Adelaide Convention Centre (Australia).

When workshops move around from one location to another during the course of an intensive few days, they are known as roadshows. Such roadshows are often organised by national tourist boards/national convention bureaux, who invite a limited number of suppliers to join them for a trip of up to a week to an overseas destination identified as an important potential market, during which, workshops are organised in several leading cities. For example, in 2013, the Dubai Convention and Events Bureau visited Amsterdam, Zurich and Geneva on a 'Discover Dubai European Roadshow' to discuss the latest developments in business events facilities and services in Dubai with buyers and event planners. Around 100 registered event planners from agencies, corporations and associations attended 'Dubai Meets The Netherlands' and the two 'Dubai Meets Switzerland' events, networking with ten suppliers from Dubai including representatives from DMCs, hotels, venues and airlines.

Best practice in the use of workshops and roadshows

To be successful, those planning workshops and roadshows must ensure that:

- Thorough research is done into the target market (i.e. the buyers) to identify those whom it will be appropriate to invite. One of the major causes of dissatisfaction with such events on the part of destinations and venues (i.e. the suppliers) is attendance by inappropriate visitors (some of whom may be 'timewasters' or 'freeloaders' with little or no business to place). Carrying out in-depth research on potential attendees should obviate or, at least, minimise this risk.

- The timing and duration of the workshop/roadshow are suitable and convenient for visitors and avoid clashes with other industry events.

- The venue to be used is accessible by public transport and is in keeping with the objectives of the workshop. Holding the event in an unusual venue, for example, may increase its appeal to visitors and encourage higher levels of attendance.

- Promotional activity is planned well in advance and it is supported by a structured marketing campaign. An important consideration is whether to use above-the-line activity to inform the widest possible audience that the event is happening or whether to concentrate on below-the-line, direct marketing in order better to control the number and type of visitors.

- A full evaluation takes place after the event in order to gauge both buyer and supplier reactions and to gain ideas for enhancements to any future workshops or roadshows.

Case Study 4.5 describes a workshop or showcase organised by VisitYork4Meetings in 2013 and it highlights how the planning, promotion and staging of the showcase met all of the objectives and criteria listed above.

Familiarisation trips and educationals

The use of familiarisation trips in marketing

For many industries, trade shows are not only events at which exhibitors can meet potential buyers face-to-face, but also a place where those potential buyers can experience and test the products being promoted. Trade shows for the food and drink industry, for example, can offer visitors the opportunity to taste the products for themselves and consumer electronics shows give visitors the chance of having 'hands-on' contact with the laptop computers, for example, that are on display.

Bringing the product directly to the potential customer in this way is not possible for those with responsibility for the marketing of venues and destinations, which are complex products, composed of a variety of facilities and services, many of which are intangible. One solution to this problem is to bring the potential buyers – meeting planners and conference or incentive organisers – to the destination, on a short (usually from 1 to 4 days) all-expenses-paid trip that gives them a direct experience of all aspects of that destination that are important for the hosting of business events, including, of course, its venues.

Familiarisation trips, often abbreviated to fam trips, and sometimes known as 'educationals', are a key part of any destination or venue's marketing mix. They are an activity that combines marketing and sales, but with a greater emphasis on marketing as conference organisers are invited to join the 'fam trip' on a *speculative basis*. In other words, in the hope that they will have appropriate future meetings and events business to place in the destination or venue, but with nothing specific necessarily in mind at this stage. In the same way as hosted buyers are pre-selected for exhibitions and workshops, participants on fam trips are identified through preliminary research as people that it would be beneficial to inform and educate about the facilities available in the destination or venue hosting the trip. They are generally organisers of events which the destination/venue would like to attract but who may not already have expressed a defi-nite interest in bringing their event to the destination or venue that is the focus of the fam trip.

Familiarisation trips differ in this important sense from site inspections (see chapter 5), where the organ-iser has come to assess a destination and venue(s) with a view to confirming a specific event. Site inspec-tions are very clearly part of the sales process but fam trips represent an example of what is known as 'experiential marketing', which gives customers in-depth experiences or interactions with products in order to provide them with enough information to make the purchase decision. This form of experiential marketing represents the difference between telling buyers about the features or benefits of a product within the confines of a promotional brochure or website and letting them experience it directly for them-selves. This makes fam trips one of the most powerful marketing communications techniques available to suppliers in the business events industry.

Fam trips are not only organised for potential buyers. They may also be provided for journalists from the business events media who will subsequently write a feature article on the destination/venue. Fam trips for journalists (in effect, press trips) are offered on an individual basis or for a group (Figure 4.2 describes the experiences of a journalist, Robin Anderson, in attending press trips organised by conference destina-tions). Fam trips for conference organisers are normally planned as a group activity, with the size of the group ranging from six to eight people upwards.

It has often been suggested that, following the global recession of 2008 onwards, it has become more difficult to persuade conference buyers to participate in fam trips. In part, this may be due to perceptions that such trips are a form of corporate entertaining, widely deemed as being inappropriate in times of recession and redundancy. In the UK, the passing of The Bribery Act in 2010 (with similar legislation enacted in other European countries), reinforced such views and brought legal constraints to activities that could be deemed to create 'inappropriate and undue influence' when clients are invited to enjoy free hospitality.

Another reason, according to John Fisher, writing in an article entitled 'Why fam trips need the kiss of life' (*Meetings & Incentive Travel* magazine, September 2014 – www.meetpie.com):

> . . .*is undoubtedly the mania for austerity: you can't be seen to be 'enjoying yourself' on a fam trip when company costs are being cut and colleagues are losing their jobs. Trying to explain to a finance director that an all-expenses paid site visit to an attractive destination is 'research for a marketing conference' is pushing water uphill.*

In the same article, Fisher suggests that event agencies and destinations need to make it morally and com-mercially acceptable again for corporates to go on fam trips. He proposes:

> *One way to do this is to charge a proper amount for the event to defray reasonable costs. But it needs to go further than a £25 registration fee: £350 for example. This then lifts the activity out of the shady corridors of a perk and into the people-development category of expenditure.*

> *Another method may be to compile a register of professional event buyers for which they pay a membership fee. This would weed out the imposters who plague many fam trips. The £100 administration fee would pay the administration cost of checking up on the applicants to vet them before any trips are offered.*

This latter idea is one that has been developed by GMI Portal, a daily e-zine for the global meetings industry, with the introduction of the GMI Fam Club (www.gmifamclub.com/). Subscribers to the e-zine are invited to join the Fam Club and then to register their interest in participating in fam trips to business event desti-nations around the world, organised by the destinations' convention bureaux. Event organisers are asked to complete a 'professional profile', detailing their job role and event management activity. The GMI Fam Club

Go, inspect, enjoy!

- *I have experienced familiarisation trips from almost all likely angles: hosting event planners as a conference and tourism association chairman and convention centre manager, and undertaking myriad press trips and promotional events, worldwide, as a trade journal editor, writer and professional association media consultant.*

- *As a destination manager, pre-event research and painstaking follow-up were always crucial – to ensure that decision-makers had the power or influence that really mattered and post-event to develop dialogue about all future possibilities. They may have been invited in groups but individual attention always delivered the finest returns.*

- *As a journalist, there is sometimes real benefit in joining a buyer's group, particularly if the destination involved is a new experience. That way, follow-up Q&A sessions with group members can often provide new organisational insights.*

- *However, individual inspection trips will always offer maximum versatility – in being able to add extras into an itinerary, based on new information gained during the trip itself. This arrangement also makes for maximum contact with key suppliers, new hotels, venues and attractions, and eliminates the distractions that can be generated by the involvement, requirements and egos of other media.*

- *And more often than not, enjoying a coffee in the lobby lounge with the general manager will give you a much more accurate picture of a hotel's true class and professional capabilities than trailing round an endless array of guestrooms and meeting suites. If you have to join a super-enthusiastic junior sales manager for one of these adventures, ask to see the property's smallest guestroom.*

- *Many of the world's major convention and incentive destinations would do well to follow the experiences presented by Wonderful Copenhagen and Visit Denmark. Between them, their imaginative and enthusiastic teams can create quite remarkable inspection trips, which combine unique individual and group experiences with oddball events in unusual venues, inviting guests to play active roles within the gatherings' utterly memorable fabrics, all helping to illustrate the Danish capital's capabilities and charisma, to the MAX.*

- *Then, colourful, lively and evocative destination and meetings case studies, compiled by experienced writers for the trade media, and focused around an organiser's experiences before, during and after their events, can deliver informative and enjoyable FAM trips in just a few hundred high-impact words! Enticing enough to make you want to go, inspect, enjoy!*

Robin Anderson, Writer and media consultant

Figure 4.2 Go, inspect, enjoy!

Source: Robin Anderson.

was launched in May 2014 with five participating destinations: Berlin, Copenhagen, Dubai, Prague and Singapore. By January 2015, a further three destinations had joined: Brussels, Durban and London, and 382 buyers from around the world had registered. By this date, seven fam trips had been organised with Fam Club members and further trips were in the pipeline. Convention bureaux can use the database throughout the year to find interesting buyers.

Best practice in the use of familiarisation trips

Figure 4.3 details guidelines for a DMO when planning a destination fam trip. Mike Lyon of Write Style Communications Ltd (www.write-style.co.uk) has published a useful guide on 'Familiarisation Trips – How to Maximise Your Return on Investment', written for convention bureaux, venues and hotels. Copies of the guide as a PDF are available free of charge by contacting mike@write-style.co.uk. He has also published a checklist for meeting planners on how to make the most of their participation in fam trips and site inspections.

1. Plan well in advance

- Detailed planning should begin at least 3 to 4 months before the visit is due to take place, with the first batch of invitations being sent out 8-10 weeks prior to the visit. In part this is to ensure that invitees do not already have commitments on the dates in question, in part to give sufficient time for a second mailshot if there has been insufficient take-up from the first mailing.

- Early planning also gives time to involve suppliers fully in the visit, to clarify how it will be funded or paid for, and to look for assistance from transport providers (airlines and rail companies especially) where appropriate.

- Agree what role should be played by local professional conference organisers (PCOs) or destination management companies (DMCs).

2. Clarify your target group

- Decide which kinds of buyers to aim for (corporate, association, agency, or a mixture of some or all of these), and tailor the programme to meet their needs as far as possible. Would it be practicable, if you are inviting a mixed group, to split the group up in order to visit different kinds of venues in order to cater more effectively for specific interests? Identify the appropriate participating venues/suppliers relevant to the agreed target group. Consider a possible theme for the trip based on the interests of the participants.

- What size of group can you accommodate successfully? Bear in mind the need to transport the group around the destination, and also the practicalities of showing them around venues - it is difficult to get more than 5 to 6 people into a hotel bedroom all at the same time, so residential venues may need to run two show-rounds simultaneously. For buyers, fam visits provide an excellent opportunity for networking, and so group dynamics is another factor to be considered. A recommended balance of host destination/venue personnel to customers is no more than 8:1, and 6:1 if participants are accompanied by partners/spouses.

- What is the best time of the week for your suppliers, as well as for the buyers? Corporate and association buyers are usually fairly flexible, but agencies prefer weekends because they cannot afford time away from the office during the week. If the visit is at a weekend, or partly over a weekend, some buyers may expect to bring partners - decide in advance your policy on partner involvement.

3. Plan a balanced itinerary

- The visit should be enjoyable, memorable, creating a positive and favourable impression of your destination, but not a comprehensive one. It is better to give a taste and whet appetites rather than try to show too much and create venue fatigue! Consider a separate table-top workshop during the fam. trip to give non-participating venues/suppliers a chance to meet the clients.

- The visit should be mainly business (the buyers expect to work) but with a mixture of pleasure built in, ideally based on the USPs for your destination. Helicopter rides over the Grampian Mountains, a 'ferry ride across the Mersey', clay pigeon shooting, professional tennis tournaments, theatre visits are just a few examples of activities that have been laid on by UK destinations to add enjoyment to a fam visit and ensure that it shows off to maximum effect the unique aspects of their destination. If appropriate, link the fam trip with other events happening in the area which could form part of the social programme or be an additional draw to maximise response

- Buyers find it helpful to be given an overview of the destination at the outset, ideally including a short audio-visual presentation as part of a welcome reception. Such a reception would also give them a chance to introduce themselves to each other and outline their buyer credentials by briefly describing the kinds of events they organise.

- Set a maximum length of time for coach transfers from one venue to another.

4. Ensure that the venues/suppliers are trained and prepared

- The professionalism and preparedness of a destination's venues can make (or break) a fam visit. Venue sales managers should be looking to create a 'memory trail' for the buyers as they show them around their venue, selling benefits and not features.

- Aim to ensure that your venues know as much as possible about the group in advance. It is good for the venue manager to be on hand to welcome the buyers, even if (s)he is not the one to show them around.

(Continued)

- Try to ensure that the venues are ready and waiting for the group, and are fully prepared. And that the venues keep to your timetable, as far as possible.
- Build in the desire for competitiveness between the venues but ensure that details of the whole programme are shared with all venues in order to avoid duplications such as repetitive menus.

5. **Sponsorship and/or support in kind**
   - Look for ways of sharing the costs through the support of your suppliers, whether this is support in kind or some other form of sponsorship. At the end of the day, they are the ones who can expect direct benefits from the fam visit.
   - Are there other civic budgets that you can tap into to cover a reception or welcome?
   - Agree what gifts are to be given to delegates/partners and ensure they are presented at the appropriate time.

6. **Plan to follow up and provide feedback**
   - It is crucial to follow up the buyers after the visit, in part to thank them for their participation and in part to get their feedback on what they have experienced. Such feedback should be circulated to your venues/suppliers, so that any necessary improvements can be put in place for future visits. Agree with your venues/suppliers who will maintain contact with the buyers and with what frequency.
   - Follow-up should be an ongoing activity to build on the relationships established with the buyers.
   - Consider a face-to-face evaluation meeting with venues and suppliers.
   - Track bookings received by venues/suppliers as well as those received via the destination marketing organisation.

A fam visit is a significant investment in time and money but, well done, can be a very productive way of promoting your destination and showing your suppliers that you are working with them, in partnership, to generate more business for them.

Figure 4.3 Guidelines for successful destination familiarisation visits

Source: Mike Lyon.

Conference ambassador programmes

The use of conference ambassadors programmes in marketing

Establishing and administering conference ambassador programmes is another technique employed by convention bureaux (and occasionally venues) in their efforts to attract meetings. Often known in North America as 'Local Hero Programs' or even 'Bring Home the Business' (for example, see Spokane Area Convention and Visitors Bureau – http://www.visitspokane.com/industry/bring-home-the-business/), such initiatives involve identifying, recruiting, training and supporting key individuals in the local community who are interested in raising the profile of their own organisations and their cities by bidding for major national or international conferences.

Club Liverpool is the new brand (launched in 2015) for Liverpool's event ambassador programme. The programme had secured more than 120 national and international events over the previous decade. Sara Wilde McKeown, chair of Liverpool city region's Visitor Economy Board, sets out the rationale for Club Liverpool (quoted in 'The PCO' newsletter, issue No. 71, Q1 2015) as follows:

> *Hosting business events and conferences has a huge economic impact on the city, extending right across the hospitality, retail and tourism sectors. To secure these events we have to compete with leading cities around the world – creating valuable connections through a robust ambassador scheme is the strongest way to achieve this. Our influential ambassadors raise the credibility of*

the city as a national and international event destination and help open pathways to attracting different subject matters and sponsors to the city.

A convention bureau's aim, therefore, in establishing an ambassador programme is to work with those individuals who are willing to, and in a position to, influence directly or indirectly the conference destination decisions of the professional institutions to which they belong. Likely candidates for inclusion on ambassador programmes are university academics, hospitals' professional staff, leading industrialists, members of the business community and trade unionists.

Why should busy people such as these invest their time and energy in helping their local convention bureau win conferences for the destination? The benefits for individuals in becoming an ambassador include:

- Raising the profile of their work amongst their peers, nationally and internationally
- Being recognised as a leader in their field of expertise
- Establishing a platform for research projects and international collaboration
- Contributing to an organisation's strategic aims
- Generating economic benefits and profile for their home city

Clearly, the convention bureaux themselves must provide a range of support to motivate their ambassadors and assist them in the task of persuading the institutions and associations to which they belong to bring their conferences to the towns and cities where the ambassadors live and work.

The type of assistance that a convention bureau can offer to its ambassadors is indicated in the following extract from Visit Manchester's Convention Bureau website (http://conferences.visitmanchester.com/), written for its potential ambassadors:

- *Visit Manchester provides one-to-one support including research, bid production and a suite of valuable services to help you through the process (of being a conference ambassador). As a valued conference ambassador, we will help you by:*
- *Researching the viability of hosting a meeting in Manchester*
- *Providing expert support and advice on bidding for and winning conferences*
- *Assist with event delivery through a variety of complimentary services*

The following tools and materials are used by convention bureaux around the world to support their ambassadors, although, of course, very few, if any, offer all of these:

- Ambassador-specific newsletter for information, motivation, and to recognise successes
- Destination training: access to destination expertise
- Presentation and/or media training
- Sponsorship for ambassadors to attend events or present papers/abstracts
- Sponsorship to assist ambassadors to be elected to a position of influence within their association
- Bid document preparation and/or funding
- Assistance in booking venues and suppliers
- Legal advice regarding contracts, VAT and tax, insurance and liability issues
- Assistance in preparing budgets within bids
- Bid marketing support, both material and personnel attendance
- Event marketing support to boost delegate attendance
- Motivation and recognition programme (including awards events)
- Access to low or zero interest pre-event funding

Table 4.1 Principal market sectors targeted by conference ambassador programmes

Answer Options	1	2	3	4	5	6
Corporate	4	9	7	19	4	0
International Association	31	4	4	0	3	1
National Association	5	21	11	5	1	0
Regional Association	1	9	17	13	3	0
Other	1	0	1	0	2	39

1 = most important, 6 = least important.

- Subventions enabling reduced price quotations or cash-back arrangements to associations for strategically important events
- Ambassador-to-ambassador programmes, with successful bidders used to motivate and recruit new ambassadors.

International research into conference ambassador programmes was undertaken by the author (Tony Rogers) in conjunction with a consultant colleague, Sue Beverley, in 2014, generating responses from 34 destinations in 15 countries. Some of the key findings are shown below:

Types of organisations being targeted for events

It is apparent from Table 4.1 that international association congresses are the primary target for ambassador programmes, followed by national association congresses. The responses also indicate a growing interest in attracting corporate events through ambassador programmes.

Ambassador sources/types

On average, ambassadors are drawn from:

- Universities and colleges – 59%
- Hospitals – 29%
- Corporate sector – 17%
- Other – 12%

Numbers of ambassadors and proportions of 'live' ambassadors

The research indicated that a significant proportion of respondents were operating quite small programmes with fewer than 50 ambassadors. In some cases, this was because the programme was new or recently launched, but there was also a noticeable trend among some deliberately to limit their programme to a small number of high quality ambassadors with real potential to secure events and with whom productive relationships could be built.

- Up to 50 ambassadors – 36% of respondents
- 51–100 ambassadors – 9%
- 101–250 ambassadors – 15%
- 251–500 ambassadors – 24%
- Over 500 ambassadors – 15%

Economic impact of ambassador programmes

Respondents were asked to quantify the economic impact of business confirmed (but not necessarily completed) through their Ambassador Programme in 2013 in pounds sterling.

Not all respondents were able to answer this question but the replies received demonstrate that the return on investment from Ambassador Programmes can be considerable. The following estimates were provided: £13 million; £1,089,762; over £25 million; £6 million; £19 million; £8 million; £2 million; £500,000; £30 million; £4.9 million.

Respondents were also asked how many events had been secured (i.e. confirmed but not necessarily completed) as a result of their Ambassador Programme in 2013. The responses are given below:

- 1–10 events × 11
- 11–20 events × 3
- 21–30 events × 2
- 31–40 events × 1
- 41–50 events × 1
- 70 events × 1

The research findings cover many other aspects of conference ambassador programme management including budgets and staffing, activities with ambassadors and networking events, ambassador recruitment strategies and current and future trends. Details of the full report can be accessed at http://tony-rogers.com/research/.

A specific example of the economic benefits of an ambassador programme may be seen in the example of the Palais des Congrès de Montréal (Québec, Canada). In February 2015, this venue marked the 30th anniversary of its Ambassadors Club by inducting 14 new members who were actively involved in securing ten international conventions for Montréal. These major events will generate nearly CA$128 million in economic benefits for the city and the province, attracting 40,000 business visitors.

Best practice in the use of conference ambassadors programmes

The International Congress and Convention Association (ICCA) paper 'Congress Ambassador Programmes' suggests that the key trait that all ambassadors should have in common is a 'positive emotional bond to the destination and/or the aspirations of that destination'. It states that, apart from this, the most successful programmes are very flexible in terms of other requirements and it lists the following types of ambassadors:

Ambassador connections

- Born in the destination
- Lives in the destination
- Studied or studies in the destination
- Created something in the destination (e.g. work of art or a building)
- Long-term family ties to the destination
- Passionate supporter of a historic figure linked to the destination
- Fan of destination or some characteristic of the destination

Ambassador backgrounds

- Business leaders
- Senior medical practitioners
- Senior medical administrators
- Scientists (non-academic)
- Academic leaders (all fields)
- Postgraduates and graduates
- Political and social leaders and opinion formers
- Writers or commentators
- Celebrities

Useful ambassador traits or skills

The ICCA paper describes the types of personality and skills that can make a good ambassador. They include:

- Natural communicator
- Internationalist
- Passionate about destination
- Strong 'presence'
- Leadership skills/influential figure
- Recognised expert
- Groundbreaking researcher
- 'Rising star'
- Strong reputation/ethical

Useful reference and information sources for identifying and recruiting potential ambassadors include:

- University websites
- University staff newsletters
- Universities' own departmental research groups/sessions
- Training and induction packs/programmes produced by universities for new academic staff
- Alumni and university communications with alumni
- University inaugural lectures
- University conference offices
- Research institutes
- Local press and media
- Science festivals/special events
- Referrals and word of mouth
- LinkedIn has an advanced search facility, for example, 'who is the conference manager at. . .?'
- Chambers of Commerce
- City Council inward investment and economic development teams

In summary, it should be emphasised that all conference ambassador programmes are different, with programme managers facing different opportunities, challenges and constraints. As a general rule, it is probably advisable to start small and build up the programme gradually, seeking to retain a focus on the quality of available ambassadors rather than the quantity. Ideally, programme managers should aim to achieve a few 'quick wins' in terms of conferences secured through a local ambassador, as this will add to the credibility of, and support for, the programme. It will also help significantly if influential people (such as university vice-chancellors) can be persuaded to lend their support to the ambassador programme. Strengthening and publicising the links between congresses, research and the knowledge economy, as described in other chapters of this book, will also help to underline the important role that local ambassadors ('heroes' or 'champions') can and do play.

Case Study 4.6 describes the collaboration of conference ambassador programme managers in the UK and Ireland, known as GANG, who work together to share best practices and for education and mutual support.

CASE STUDY 4.1   ibtm china and the Hosted Buyer Programme

Reed Travel Exhibitions

Reed Travel Exhibitions (RTE) is the world's leading travel and tourism exhibition organiser, with a growing portfolio of over 20 international travel and tourism trade events in Europe, the Americas, Asia, the Middle East and Africa. RTE's Leisure Travel Portfolio includes the World Travel Market that is held each year in London.

RTE's exhibitions on the theme of meetings, incentives, conferences, and events are grouped under RTE's IBTM Global Events Portfolio, a series of eight annual trade shows focusing on business events:

- ibtm world: Barcelona, Spain
- ibtm arabia: Abu Dhabi, UAE
- ibtm america: Chicago, USA
- ibtm india: Chennai, India
- ibtm Africa: Cape Town, South Africa
- ibtm china: Beijing, China
- AIME: Melbourne, Australia
- Icomex: Sao Paolo, Brazil

ibtm china

ibtm china was launched in 2006 as CIBTM, and retained that name until 2014, when, as part of the rebranding of the IBTM Global Events Portfolio, it became known as ibtm china.

Held in the China National Convention Centre in Beijing in September each year, ibtm china welcomes hosted buyers, exhibitors and visitors from China and across the globe for 3 days of intensive business meetings, education and networking. By attending ibtm china, participants efficiently and effectively gain immediate competitive advantage for their business and keep abreast with the latest developments in the MICE industry.

The exhibition attracts over 4,000 meetings and events industry professionals to Beijing every year.

The Hosted Buyer Programme

Certain visitors who are high quality buyers and senior decision makers are carefully selected to attend ibtm china on the exhibition's Hosted Buyer Programme. This means that all of the travel and accommodation costs that they incur in attending the exhibition are borne by the organisers. In return, the Hosted Buyers receive a personalised diary with pre-scheduled appointments that allow them to meet the exhibitors of their choice. Pre-scheduled appointments are short one-to-one appointments between the Hosted Buyers and the exhibitors. Over a 3-day period, a maximum of 45 pre-scheduled appointments are scheduled in each Hosted Buyer's diary.

All of ibtm china's Hosted Buyers undergo a strict qualification process, ensuring that only those who initiate, influence, organise or approve final decisions and/or budgets for international conferences and other business events are invited to attend on this basis.

According to RTE's own strict selection criteria, in order to qualify as an ibtm china Hosted Buyer, applicants must:

- Have future business to place (especially in China or the Asia region)
- Give evidence of past business placed outside of their home country
- Be a senior decision maker with the authority to procure MICE products and services
- Indicate the number of events they hold annually
- Indicate the level of annual budget they manage

Those who satisfy the selection criteria enjoy a number of important benefits. In addition to receiving a personalised diary of appointments with their choice of meetings with over 400 exhibitors, and being hosted in Beijing with complimentary flights, transfers and 4/5* accommodation, the benefits are the opportunities to:

- Use the online diary facility for scheduling additional meetings
- Network with industry professionals at numerous exciting events taking place during ibtm china
- Enhance their knowledge and grow in their profession through the sessions taking place as part of the exhibition's Education Programme
- Find new ideas and inspiration on the show floor
- Access the private Hosted Buyer Lounge with complimentary refreshments
- Discover the rich history and culture of Beijing by attending the pre-show tours of the capital

Almost 9,000 appointments take place each year between exhibitors and Hosted Buyers at ibtm china.

CASE STUDY 4.2   The Adelaide Convention Centre workshops

The Adelaide Convention Centre (ACC) organises workshop-type events in Adelaide (especially for Australian meeting planners) but also takes such events 'on the road', adopting a regional approach based on the 'regions' of Asia and Europe. The key focus of these workshops are organisers of international association congresses with the aim of attracting their events to Adelaide.

In recent years, European regional events have been held in Brussels, Geneva, The Hague, London and Paris where many international associations have their administrative headquarters. The workshops themselves often have a strong (and usually innovative) food theme, a key sector of Adelaide's economy (see below), with one such event taking the form of a Cookery School (see Figure 4.4) with a signed cookery book from celebrated TV chef John Torode, featuring Adelaide Convention Centre's logo inside the front cover.

Numbers of invitees are kept small (typically five to ten) because relationship building is recognised as a major objective. Invitees are identified through detailed pre-event research using databases such as those managed by ICCA and the Union of International Associations (UIA) (see chapter 9) combined with online research using Google and Microsoft Scholar in particular. The research identifies organisations which, by rotation, are scheduled to hold their event in Australasia within the next 5 to 10 years but which also have a synergy with Adelaide's own economy and research specialisms. In particular, four sectors are targeted:

- Resources and energy
  - Mining equipment and technology
  - Oil and gas
  - Sustainable energy
- Health
  - Tropical health
  - Healthcare services and technology
  - Senior health
  - Biotechnology research and development

Figure 4.4 Delegates at the Adelaide Convention Centre Cookery School workshop

Source: Adelaide Convention Centre.

- Advanced manufacturing
  - Aviation defence
  - Marine technology
  - Technology and innovation
- Agrobusiness and food
  - Food security – agricultural services
  - Food quality
  - Technology and skills

In some cases, ACC works closely with Australian embassies in key overseas countries with ambassadors inviting up to five international association congress organisers to a reception/workshop at the embassy. ACC may also collaborate with Tourism Australia in the event organisation and promotion. ACC underlines the vital necessity of building good, long-term relationships with such individuals to ensure a successful outcome to the workshops. One example of such success is the annual congress of the International Society of Cardiovascular Pharmacotherapy, which brought some 400 delegates to Adelaide in 2014 after attending an ACC workshop in 2012.

CASE STUDY 4.3   ibtm world Best Stand Award winners

Each year in Barcelona, the Best Stand Awards at the ibtm world exhibition for the meetings and events industry (www.ibtmworld.com) recognise and highlight the best and most effective exhibitors and their stands. Judging takes place on the show floor and is conducted by an independent panel. The winners are announced on the second day of ibtm world and they are presented with a trophy and featured in the *Official Show Daily* magazine.

The 2014 winner of the award for the Best Stand Personnel was the Switzerland Convention and Incentive Bureau (SCIB). The staff of the SCIB and all of those who shared the stand with them outplayed the competition with their hospitality and knowledge and easily recognisable red polo shirts. This was the second time since 2012 that SCIB had been awarded this prize.

Barbra Steuri-Albrecht, Managing Director of the SCIB explains the factors that distinguished her organisation's stand from the others at ibtm world:

> I would say that winning the award also had to do with the consistency and continuity we demonstrate at our booth, meaning that we have already worn the red polo shirts at trade shows for a couple of years and visitors are beginning to recognise and appreciate that. Also, all of our stand partners work together as a very good team even though they are, in reality, competitors. We regularly get positive feedback from clients saying that the SCIB booth is one of the few large national booths where they can leave a business card or a message for someone temporarily absent from the stand and the message will be passed on by whomever takes it, even if that person is a direct competitor. In addition, all of our SCIB Managers who are based in our key source markets are present during the three days of the show, facilitating contacts between clients and the destinations, regions, DMCs and venue representatives.

In 2014, the award for the Best Small Stand was won by the Oberoi Hotel Group. The Oberoi Group, founded in 1934, operates 30 hotels, a Nile cruiser and a motor vessel on the backwaters of Kerala. The Oberoi Group has presence in six countries under the luxury brand 'Oberoi Hotels & Resorts' and five-star brand 'Trident Hotels'. The Group is also engaged in in-flight catering, airport restaurants, travel and tour services, car rentals, project management and corporate air charters.

According to a representative of Elevations Exhibition and Design Ltd, the company that designed the stand:

> The challenge with this design was in achieving a warm atmosphere and strong branding on a thin island stand. Due to the organisers' restrictions on the amount of walling that can be used, we were forced to be extra-inventive and used dramatically lit arches with slim, staggered walling to re-create the welcoming, cosy feel of a luxury Oberoi hotel lobby.

> The same design was used at IMEX Vegas last month, with the wall panels shipped back to the UK to be used for Oberoi's forthcoming European shows. To keep costs down, we source furniture locally. In Vegas the stand was wider, so we were able to use lounge seating too.

Figure 4.5 shows the SCIB winning stand team.

Figure 4.5 The Switzerland Convention and Incentive Bureau winning stand team at the ibtm world exhibition 2014

Source: Switzerland Convention and & Incentive Bureau.

CASE STUDY 4.4   The Tourist Office of Spain (Turespaña) virtual trade show for the MICE market

Spain as a destination for international meetings

In the global rankings published by ICCA, Spain is often positioned, with the USA and Germany, as one of the world's top three countries, in terms of the number of international meetings it attracts. In respect of the most successful cities, as measured by the number of international meetings they host, Spain is usually the only country with two cities in ICCA's list of the top ten: Madrid and Barcelona.

Turespaña (The Tourist Office of Spain – TOS) is the name of Spain's government tourism promotion authority based in Madrid. Through its network of overseas offices, it promotes Spain worldwide as a destination for business events as well as for leisure tourism.

Turespaña in Chicago (TOS Chicago)

TOS Chicago is responsible for promoting Spain to the travel trade, press and consumers in the Midwest USA market. In addition, the Turespaña US branch office is responsible for marketing Spain's business events product in North America. To that end, TOS Chicago acts as a link between suppliers and intermediaries in Spain and buyers such as meeting planners in the USA. It carries out a range of marketing activities throughout the year, including workshops, familiarisation trips, participation in trade shows such as IMEX Las Vegas and ibtm america in Chicago, networking events in co-operation with MICE industry associations and convention bureaux in Spain, webcasts and e-learning workshops, the publishing of the MICE sector digital magazine, Meet in Spain (www.meetinspainmagazine.com) and active presence in their Spain Meeting and Events Community portal at i-meet.com/spain.

Meet in Spain 2014

Meet in Spain 2014 is the name given to an online platform that provides virtual meetings between US-based MICE buyers (meeting planners, incentive houses, conference planners, associations and event planners) and Spanish suppliers and intermediaries (convention bureaux, hotel chains, destination management companies and venues). The first virtual trade show of this type, www.meetinspain2014.com, opened on 2 June 2014.

Given the geographical distance, time and numerous costs involved in participating in 'real' trade shows and workshops, Meet in Spain 2014 was created as a new, online environment focused solely on the MICE segment. It was designed to enable equally effective meetings between buyers and suppliers, but with an infinitely smaller budget.

The format is as follows: each exhibitor has his/her own stand, from which the US buyers as well as the Spanish suppliers can request virtual, face-to-face meetings through the application manager. Once the appointment is generated, it is carried out via Skype.

For the first Meet in Spain event, over 20 Spain-based suppliers participated: Basquetour, Málaga Convention Bureau, Turismo de Andalucía, Pamplona City Tourist Board, Palladium Hotel Group, Meliá Hotels, Viavinum, AC Hotels, Insider's Madrid, Hotel Hilton Madrid Airport, Abba Hotels, Factor 3 Events, Stop Incentives and Events, GISTC, Murcia Convention Bureau, Barceló

Hotels & Resorts, Madrid Destino, Radisson Blu Hotels and Resorts, El Batel Auditorium and Conference Center – Cartagena (Murcia), Silken Hotels, and Cititravel DMC.

Jorge Rubio, Consul for Tourism Affairs and Director of the TOS in Chicago, described Meet in Spain as:

> The ideal venue for establishing contacts with companies and institutions in the US prior to carrying out commercial interactions. It's a very significant step for Turespaña to be able to facilitate the promotion of Spanish MICE tourism products in this important market, and this virtual trade show perfectly complements the various online marketing projects the TOS Chicago has done in recent years.

Turespaña, together with the platform designer, Madrid-based IMASTE, pursued a strong marketing campaign in the USA in order to encourage buyers to participate in Meet in Spain 2014. Promotional activities included online marketing campaigns geared toward the 9,000 MICE professionals belonging to 'The Events Network' and the 100,000 MICE professionals on the i-Meet.com social network.

To encourage participation, each MICE professional in the United States who held a virtual meeting with a Spanish provider was treated to a beverage in the form of a Starbucks voucher redeemable at any location in the chain.

CASE STUDY 4.5   The York Minster to Westminster showcase

York as a destination

York is one of the United Kingdom's smaller yet most famous cities. Steeped in history, York boasts Roman, Viking and Norman legacies of the highest quality, with the magnificent York Minster still casting its magical spell over the city and surrounding area. Situated in the northern part of England but centrally within the UK, approximately halfway between London and Edinburgh, York is very well located and its historical treasures and architectural delights attract more than 7 million tourists per year.

York is not just important as a leisure tourism destination. Conferences, meetings and incentives also play an important part in the city's visitor mix. The city's business events infrastructure includes historic and modern hotels, two universities and a range of unique venues including the award-winning York Racecourse and the National Railway Museum. In *The British Meetings & Events Industry Survey 2014/15*, York was ranked in 12th position among the top British meetings destinations. Business events are worth some £150 million per annum to the city.

VisitYork4Meetings

The city's conference bureau, VisitYork4Meetings, forms part of Visit York, the DMO for York. The bureau employs one full-time and one part-time member of staff to undertake business events marketing and enquiry handling.

This case study describes a showcase, *York Minster to Westminster*, organised by VisitYork4Meetings to promote the city to conference organisers and meetings planners. The showcase took place in March 2013.

Key objectives of the showcase

York Minster to Westminster was intended to meet a number of objectives:

To increase the profile of York as a destination for business meetings and events. York is a city well equipped to host a range of business events with capacities up to 1,400 delegates. The showcase was meant to heighten awareness of York's business events' potential.

To promote how accessible York is from the south of England. York is less than 2 hours from London Kings Cross station. If delegates are travelling from other areas of the UK, York is a central location with hotels and conference centres easily accessible on foot from York railway station.

To attract a minimum of 50 decision-making event buyers from London and the south of England, including corporate, government, association and incentive organisers. Research undertaken by Visit York in 2011 had highlighted that 40 per cent of York's business visitors come from London and the South. Many of the corporates, associations and charities that book events into York have London-based headquarters.

To generate a minimum of ten new enquiries and leads for York venues with a city value of £100,000. Whilst raising the profile of York was a key objective, the venues participating also needed to see a return on their investment (i.e. through their paying to take part in the showcase). It was agreed to set a minimum target of generating ten new business leads with an economic impact of £100,000 within a year of the showcase. Commission generated on these bookings could also be reinvested in additional destination marketing by VisitYork4Meetings.

'York Minster to Westminster'

In order to attract the best selection of buyers to the showcase, VisitYork4Meetings looked for a London venue with connections to York or an iconic venue that would attract buyers. It was decided that linking York's most iconic building York Minster and The Houses of Parliament in Westminster would make perfect sense and 'York Minster to Westminster' was created.

Hugh Bayley MP and Julian Sturdy MP, both representing York constituencies, agreed to act as hosts at the Houses of Parliament and provided the showcase visitors with access to the invitation-only venue. The Houses of Parliament are only available for a limited period of time during the day and so a hotel close by was booked for the showcase and dinner – the Intercontinental Westminster, as a newly-opened venue, had the modern, fresh vibe needed to support York and was happy to work with VisitYork4Meetings on the event.

The event

The event needed to be informative – providing information on York's location in relation to London as well as on the range of venues and services the city has to offer for events. Based on experience of previous 'meet the buyer' events, it was decided that the buyers would benefit most from an appointment-based exhibition. Appointments would be made with the venues of the buyers' choice prior to the day of the showcase. The event would be free of charge but, in order to reduce cancellations and get a commitment from buyers, it was decided a £200 'non-attendance' fee would be put in place.

The format of the event would include an overview or presentation about York in The Houses of Parliament, a behind-the-scenes tour of the Houses and then the exhibition and dinner at the Intercontinental Westminster. The showcase started in mid-afternoon with afternoon tea and a tour of the Houses of Parliament and concluded at 10 pm after dinner at the Intercontinental Westminster.

The event had to be unique in order to attract the quality buyers specified and its key characteristics were seen as:

- The hook (to attract buyers) was the visit to the Houses of Parliament
- The selling element was the appointment-based showcase
- The 'fun' element was the dinner and informal networking

Marketing and promotion strategy

In order to encourage participation by the most comprehensive range of York venues, VisitYork4Meetings approached its 150 member businesses that have conference facilities and services, specifically targeting the larger venues mixed with conference venues that were unique to York. The final list of 21 exhibitors included a mixture of hotels, unique venues and purpose-built conference venues, which conveyed the overall flavour of York designed to attract buyers.

As well as engaging with its venue partners to achieve its objectives, VisitYork4Meetings contacted East Coast, the main rail carrier between York and London, and asked if they would support the event and help to reinforce the key messages about the proximity of York to London. This partnership with East Coast allowed VisitYork4Meetings to offer buyers complimentary first class rail travel from London Kings Cross, an offer that was included in the promotional literature about the showcase in order to attract more sign-ups.

Promotion of the event

An event-specific logo (see Figure 4.6) was designed and applied to all promotional materials.

Other promotional activities included:

- Direct mail/email using VisitYork4Meetings' 4000-strong database of buyers – specifically targeting those who had enquired but not held events or necessarily visited York
- E-shots linking to www.visityork4meetings.com for sign-up
- Maximisation of pre-event PR working with the trade press, in particular *Conference News*, which sent the invitation to its mailing list
- Social media including using the Visit York B2B Twitter feed
- All prospective buyers were also contacted by telephone to answer additional pre-qualification questions.

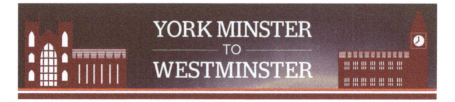

Figure 4.6 Logo designed for the York Minster to Westminster showcase
Source: VisitYork4Meetings.

VisitYork4Meetings worked on the basis of needing approximately 200 registrations of top quality buyers to fill the number of available places (50); 295 buyers pre-registered for the event and 60 buyers plus media representatives attended on the day.

Buyers followed a link where they were asked a series of questions on the volume, location and value of events they booked. At this stage, it was decided to exclude booking agents, as it was felt that the showcase warranted attendance by end-user buyers, not intermediaries. Bookings of events by intermediaries would also have affected negatively the potential revenue generation to VisitYork4Meetings from commissions.

Threats to the showcase included similar events being held at the same time. Research confirmed that the 'International Confex' exhibition was taking place in London the week after the showcase, while other destination showcases would not take place until later in the year.

Action plan and evaluation

VisitYork4Meetings developed a comprehensive marketing and action plan that was kept flexible, adding additional information as and when required. Work on the showcase began 12 months prior to the event.

Buyers registering for the event were reviewed on a weekly basis and declined or accepted based on the questions they had completed and subsequent follow-up telephone calls.

Market segments for VisitYork4Meetings

Visit York4Meetings looked at attracting the following market sectors to attend the showcase:

- National Association conference market (events <700 delegates)
- International Association conference market (events <700 delegates)
- Corporate markets – buyers based in:
  - London and south-east England
  - North-east England
  - Yorkshire

VisitEngland, the national tourism organisation, included *York Minster to Westminster* as part of a familiarisation visit for European buyers including German and Spanish incentive agents.

Key messages describing York's assets and benefits as a business events destination ran through all media and promotional literature.

Use of budget

In 2012/13 Visit York had allocated a core budget of £5,000 for its business events marketing activity. None of this budget was available to the showcase event. The challenge, therefore, was to deliver the showcase without any core budget and so all income generated had to cover costs in full and deliver the best value possible to York venues. Funds were raised through private sector partnerships and by asking venues to contribute, with in-kind support from East Coast through the provision of complimentary tickets.

Great care was taken in the use of funds generated, balancing the 'wow' factor of an iconic central London venue with the associated costs against the quality of the buyers it was intended to attract. The quality of buyers was the greatest priority and a proportion of the budget generated was used to research thoroughly all clients who registered. The second key priority was the on-the-day event management resource and a substantial proportion of the overall budget was devoted to the pre-qualification of the buyers and the on-site event management.

Showcase evaluation and results

York Minster to Westminster was York's first example of the city working together to promote its business events offering. The key ingredients (the venues, the carrier – East Coast – and the buyers) worked together without any core budget to achieve exceptional results.

The return on investment can be summarised in the following areas:

- Advertising value equivalent delivered was approximately £100,000. Journalists attended from all key publications and local (York) media
- Enquiries generated by early Autumn 2013 totalled 11 with a value of £560,000 plus
- Confirmed bookings included an event for 1,000 delegates in 2014
- Site visits for clients using the East Coast Trains tickets were ongoing throughout 2013
- Venues committed to do a repeat event in 2014
- Buyer feedback following the event included the following message: 'Many thanks for putting together a really worthwhile event on Wednesday – it was a marvellous opportunity to focus on one city and all that it can offer. It was also good to see so many suppliers in such a convivial atmosphere. Inspired choice and theme of 'Minster to Minster' – it really worked well. I hope to make use of the train ticket to do a pre-site visit later in the year'. Wendy Holdsworth, American Express

For further information on York visit: www.visityork4meetings.com.

CASE STUDY 4.6   The Great Ambassador Networking Group (GANG)

The Great Ambassador Networking Group (GANG) was established to provide networking opportunities for those involved in running conference ambassador programmes, as well as those considering starting an ambassador programme, from destinations, venues and universities throughout the UK and Ireland. While much of the networking is done electronically by email and via a dedicated LinkedIn group (see below), GANG members also come together once a year for a live one-day meeting. Membership now numbers approximately 50 (as at October 2014) and members are a mix of ambassador programme managers from DMOs, universities and convention centres, with a few PCOs as well.

GANG formation and objectives

The idea to start a networking group for ambassador programme managers came about in 2009 when representatives who were involved in research and ambassador programmes for their destinations met at an ICCA event. This led to the hosting of a meeting in 2010 by Gill Pilkington of NewcastleGateshead Initiative's convention bureau, attended by 20 people.

The first meeting was a fairly informal get-together: a round table discussion took place and everyone was very candid about sharing best practice and offering advice to those in the initial stages of starting an ambassador programme. Those at this initial meeting agreed that a regular get-together would be beneficial and that such meetings would rotate between destinations, with the host destination responsible for organising speakers, catering etc. – the meetings would be free to attend.

Since then, the meeting has been held in Liverpool (2010), where the name GANG came into being, Manchester (2011), Belfast (2012), Edinburgh (2013), Cambridge (2014) and Brighton (2015).

The meeting has grown every year and now around 50 interested individuals are on the mailing list. The growth of the group made it difficult to continue the round table discussion model. Therefore, these days, speakers are invited and interest has been received from convention and visitor bureaux outside the UK and Ireland wanting their staff to attend. The Edinburgh meeting included a delegate from the Calgary convention bureau (Canada). As such, the burden on the host city to pay for increasing delegate numbers and speakers' expenses became too great and a nominal registration fee is now charged to cover the costs of the meeting. Topics and speakers have included:

Cambridge 2014

- 'Engaging and Working with a PCO' – Nicola McGrane, Conference Partners
- 'Big Data' – Marco van Itterzon, ICCA
- 'Conference Ambassador Programme Survey Results' – Tony Rogers, Tony Rogers Conference and Event Services and Sue Beverley, CHS Group
- 'VisitEngland' – a discussion moderated by Simon Gidman, VisitEngland

Edinburgh 2013

- 'Generation Y and the Impact on Ambassador Programmes' – Rob Davidson, University of Greenwich
- 'The Academic Perspective - The Importance of Conferences to the Academic World' – Dr Colin Adams, University of Edinburgh School of Informatics
- 'Ambassador Case Studies and Panel Discussion' – Professor Gary Entrican, Veterinary Immunology, Moredun Research Institute, European Veterinary Immunology Workshop 2012
- 'International Conference on the Biology of Fish (ICBF2014)' – Dr Mark Hartl, Heriot-Watt University
- 'How to Use LinkedIn to Attract and Maintain Dialogue with Ambassadors' – Luan Wise, Independent Marketing Communications Consultant

Belfast 2012

- 'The PCO Factor' – Kerrin Honey, Congrex
- 'Sectoral Research' –Jill Ingham, Visit Manchester
- 'Recruiting New Ambassadors' – Orla Canavan, Failte Ireland
- 'Lead Generation and Sales' – Sarah Gribben, Visit Belfast

The objectives of the GANG meetings are to:

- share best practice;
- facilitate a networking opportunity for those directly involved with running an ambassador programme;
- learn from each other in an open, friendly forum.

As well as the annual meeting, GANG also has an active LinkedIn discussion group where members can contact each other for advice on any burning issues. The group members support each other and advice is always freely given. Topics raised have covered, for example, employing interns for research and mentoring for one ambassador programme manager by another The LinkedIn group can be found here: https://www.linkedin.com/groups?home=&gid=2664866&trk=anet_ug_hm&goback=%2Egmr_2664866.

In an effort to protect the group members from spam, the LinkedIn group is a closed one. However, those genuinely interested in ambassador programmes can send a request to join to the administrator.

Future plans for GANG

GANG now has a steering committee that assists the host destination with sourcing speakers etc. GANG has grown significantly in a very short space of time and, whilst new members are always welcome, there are benefits to keeping the group small, so there are no current plans to grow the group beyond the UK and Ireland.

The growth of the group has led the steering committee to look into options for management of the annual meeting, including the appointment of a PCO. A GANG website is also being considered as part of future plans.

SUMMARY

Destinations and venues experiment with a variety of marketing communications activities and constantly assess their effectiveness in terms of the return on investment that they provide. The latest marketing communications tool to be used by destinations and venues is social media, whose importance as a marketing tool has grown exponentially over recent years, offering many opportunities to establish new client contacts and to strengthen relationships with existing clients.

The number of conference industry exhibitions has increased significantly with events now being staged on all continents, but the budgets and staff resources available to destination and venue marketers have not necessarily increased, and indeed, may have decreased. Therefore, the importance of selecting the right exhibitions to attend becomes ever more crucial. Some destinations and venues are showing a preference for smaller scale, niche events such as workshops and roadshows, but these require substantial investments in research, marketing and creativity if they are to be successful.

For event organisers (or buyers), below-the-line marketing communications demand a greater response from them. They are asked to respond by participating in some form of activity or dialogue which requires time, some expenditure, possibly inconvenience and maybe a commitment of their personal time (for example, to attend a fam trip taking place over a weekend). While the benefits may be greater in the medium to long term, because of the relationships established with suppliers and the direct experience gained of venues and destinations, buyers have to weigh up these benefits against many competing demands on their time and their increasingly busy work schedules.

Conference ambassador programmes provide opportunities to forge one-to-one relationships with locally based clients who can be recruited and supported to bid for major national and international association conventions.

Destinations and venues must constantly assess the returns generated by their above-the-line and below-the-line marketing communications, and adjust the balance of their investments in such activities on a regular basis.

REVIEW AND DISCUSSION QUESTIONS

- 'Attendance at conference industry trade exhibitions will decline in direct proportion to the growing use of the internet by conference organisers'. Is the accuracy of this statement supported by the facts? Substantiate your answers with evidence taken from attendance figures for at least three trade exhibitions, as well as from research among conference organisers on how they source conference destinations and venues.

- Plan a 2-day familiarisation visit to a city destination of your choice. This should include details of the marketing of the event and of the preparations made within the destination in advance of the visit to ensure its success. Provide details of the familiarisation visit itinerary and of the kinds of buyers invited to participate, demonstrating how these buyers would be appropriate for your chosen destination.

- Analyse two discrete destination ambassador programmes, comparing their structures, activities and administrative resources. How successful have they been in meeting the objectives set for them? What recommendations could be made to other destinations looking to establish an ambassador programme?

- 'Rather than companies controlling customers' attitudes, customers themselves are guiding the dialogue by using new media to communicate among themselves about products and companies – often critically'. Undertake research on the internet to find an existing forum where meeting planners can discuss, among themselves, their experiences of using particular destinations and venues for their events. How effective, in your opinion, is the forum? Give reasons for your answer.

BIBLIOGRAPHY

Berthon, P., L. Pitt and C. Campbell (2008) 'Ad lib: when customers create the ad', *California Management Review*, 50(4): 6–30.

Breslauer, B. and T. Smith (2009) *Social Media Trends around the World*, The global Web Index (GWI), Chicago: ESOMAR Research, Online Research.

Caldwell, S. (2012) *Four basic types of trade show objectives, Praxis Events*, published online at http://praxisevents.com/four-basic-types-of-trade-show-objectives/ (accessed 30 July 2015).

Constantinides, E. and S. J. Fountain (2008) 'Web 2.0: Conceptual foundations and marketing issue', *Journal of Direct, Data and Digital Marketing Practice*, 9: 231–244.

Davidson, R. (2011) 'Web 2.0 as a marketing tool for conference centres', *International Journal of Event and Festival Management*, 2(2): 117–38.

Davidson, R. and A. Hyde (2014) *Winning Meetings and Events for your Venue*, Oxford: Goodfellow Publishers.

Davidson, R. and M. Keup (2014) 'The use of Web 2.0 as a marketing tool by European convention bureaux', *Scandinavian Journal of Hospitality and Tourism*, 14(3): 234–54.

Fisher, J. (2014) 'Why fam trips need the kiss of life', *Meetings & Incentive Travel Magazine*, September.

Gartrell, R. B. (1994) *Destination Marketing for Convention and Visitor Bureaux*, Dubuque: Kendall Hunt Publishing.

Gopalakrishna, S. and G. L. Lilien (2012) 'Trade shows in the business marketing communications mix', in G. L. Lilien and R. Grewal (eds.), *Handbook on Business-To-Business Marketing*, Cheltenham: Edward Elgar Publishing, pp. 226–45.

IACC (2012) *A Guide to Social Media*, Southam: International Association of Conference Centres.

Kaplan, A. M. and M. Haenlein (2010) 'Users of the world, unite! The challenges and opportunities of social media', *Business Horizons*, 53(1): 59–68.

Kennedy, G., B. Dalgarno, K. Gray, T. Judd, J. Waycott, S. J. Bennett, K. A. Maton, K. Krause, A. Bishop, R. Chang and A. Churchwood (2007) 'The Net Generation are not big users of Web 2.0 technologies: preliminary findings', in R. Atkinson, C. McBeath, S. Soong and C. Cheers (eds.), *Annual Conference of the Australasian Society for Computers in Learning in Tertiary Education*, Singapore: Nanyang Technology University, pp. 517–25.

Kotler, P., J. Bowen and J. Makens (2003) *Marketing for Hospitality and Tourism*, Upper Saddle River: Prentice Hall.

Leventhal, B. (2015) 'All models are wrong but some are useful: the use of predictive analytics in direct marketing', *Quality Technology and Quantitative Management*, 12(1): 93–104.

Li, C. and J. Bernoff (2008) *Groundswell: Winning in a World Transformed by Social Technologies*, Boston: Harvard Business Press.

Lyon, M. (2004) *Familiarisation Trips – How to Maximise Your Return on Investment*, Newquay: Write Style Communications.

Michaelidou, N., N. T. Siamagka and G. Christodoulides (2011) 'Usage, barriers and measurement of social media marketing: an exploratory investigation of small and medium B2B brands', *Industrial Marketing Management*, 40(7): 1153–9.

Motameni, R. and R. Nordstrom (2014) 'Correlating the social media functionalities to marketing goals and strategies', *Journal of Marketing Management*, 2(3&4): 27–48.

O'Reilly, T. (2005) 'What is web 2.0: design patterns and business models for the next generation of software', *Communications & Strategies*, 1: 17.

Rogers, T. (2003) *Conferences and Conventions: A Global Industry*, Oxford: Elsevier Butterworth-Heinemann.

Rogers, T. (2013) *Conferences and Conventions: A Global Industry*, 3rd edn, London: Routledge.

Saunders, M. (2005) 'Down to Experience', *Exhibiting*, April.

The PCO newsletter (2015), *Freshwater: International Association of Professional Congress Organisers*, Issue No.71, Q1.

Chapter **5**

Sales strategies for destinations and venues

Principles and practice

Chapter overview

This chapter examines the principles and theories underlying the sales strategies employed by venues and destinations and then explores the practical implementation of sales strategies, identifying the skills, knowledge and activities required by destination and venue sales teams. It also suggests ways through which the economic impact of successful bids can be maximised by encouraging leisure extensions to business trips.

This chapter covers:

- The role of personal selling
- Sales promotion and yield management
- The management of a sales force
- Destination and venue selling strategies
- Handling enquiries effectively
- Submitting professional bids and sales proposals
- Managing site inspections and showrounds
- Negotiation skills
- Business retention
- Maximising impact through business extenders

It includes case studies on:

- Singapore's Sales Incentives and Event Support Programmes
- Using a venue representation service: Paje and The Jockey Club
- UniSpace Sunderland's value-added packages
- The International Convention Centre, Birmingham and The Convention Centre Dublin's 'Host Service' and 'Client Associate/Client Host' programmes
- Vancouver Convention Centre's Service Excellence Programme

LEARNING OUTCOMES

On completion of this chapter, you should be able to:

- understand the role of personal selling in generating sales and maintaining long-term relationships with customers;
- understand the different approaches to personal selling;
- discuss the range of personal sales activities undertaken by professional sales representatives;
- analyse the different techniques and roles of sales promotion;
- understand the issues involved in the management of a sales force;
- understand the key factors influencing the selection of destinations and venues;
- appreciate the importance of destination knowledge and expertise in the sales process;
- define the skills needed in professional enquiry handling, bidding for events and negotiating with clients;
- identify appropriate strategies for successful site inspections;
- recognise the benefits in terms of business retention through the provision of excellent customer service; and
- understand the added economic value accruing through maximising extended visits by convention attendees.

Introduction

Advertising and promotion alone are not enough, in themselves, to guarantee a destination or a venue's success. Sales is an essential part of the marketing process and success in the conference and convention industry ultimately depends on the ability to sell effectively.

Many people use the terms 'marketing' and 'selling' interchangeably. However, they are not, in fact, the same activity. It has already been established in earlier chapters of this book that marketing is a broad process involving a number of stages:

1. Discovering what products or services customers want.
2. Producing a product with the appropriate features and quality to meet customers' needs.
3. Pricing the product correctly.
4. Promoting the product – spreading the word about why customers should buy it.

These stages may be considered to have, as their primary aim, the setting up of the sale itself, which is the next, crucial, stage in the marketing process. Selling the product or service to the customer should be the culmination of this entire process if an effective marketing strategy has already created a high degree of customer awareness and a propensity to buy. If conference and convention facilities and services are not actually purchased, then all of the preceding marketing efforts will have been in vain.

Personal selling and sales promotion are key marketing communication activities and they are the primary focus of this chapter, which will begin by analysing the principles and theories underlying the sales process and it will continue with a review of the practical implementation of sales strategies in the context of destination and venue marketing.

The role of personal selling

Personal selling is a vitally important form of interpersonal communication between sales staff and potential buyers. It is a two-way process with great potential for, on the one hand, influencing buyers' preferences and purchasing behaviour, and, on the other hand, for generating useful feedback which, if heeded, can lead to important improvements to what is being sold.

Personal selling may be defined, then, as the element of the communications mix that consists of direct, personal interaction, either face-to-face or by telephone, between sales people and potential customers.

It has two main, and linked, objectives:

* to generate sales; and
* to build and maintain long-term relationships with clients.

Generating sales

The immense power of personal selling to generate sales for an organisation is a common theme in the marketing literature:

> *Personal selling is a powerful element of the promotional mix. Despite the millions of dollars spent on advertising and sales promotion, personal selling is usually superior in converting demand for . . . products and services into actual purchases, because its message can be tailored to individual customers and it allows for immediate feedback and reaction. Person-to-person communication is a potent and persuasive sales technique.*
>
> *(Burke and Resnick, 2000: 226)*

It is clear from this statement that personal selling is an interactive relationship between buyer and seller, involving direct communication and the opportunity for immediate response. Much of the effective nature of personal selling arises from the fact that it allows sales people to adapt their presentation to the individual customer or potential customer with whom they are in discussion, either across the table or on the telephone. Effective sales people use this feature of personal selling to their advantage, by using their communications skills to tailor their sales presentation according to the customer's responses.

Personal selling also offers sales people the opportunity of increasing existing customers' levels of spending by suggesting that they purchase additional products or higher-value products. The marketing literature contains a rich vocabulary to describe these techniques, but those with most relevance for the conference and convention industry are:

* *Upselling*. The technique of suggesting that the buyer purchase higher priced products, rather than those already selected. For example, replacing a conference coffee break consisting of simple coffee and biscuits with one offering coffee, fruit smoothies and Danish pastries.
* *Cross-selling*. The technique of introducing existing customers to additional products that are not necessarily linked with their usual purchases. For example, a hotel might try to sell leisure weekend break

packages to guests staying in the hotel for the purpose of attending a conference. Destinations endeavouring to persuade conference delegates to extend their business trips in order to spend more time enjoying the leisure attractions of the city or resort are engaging in cross-selling. 'Business extenders' will be discussed later in this chapter.

It is, however, important to note that although one objective of upselling and cross-selling is to increase profitability for the seller's organisation, such techniques can only be said to be truly successful if they add real value to the buyer's purchases in such a way that the buyer remains loyal to the organisation and its products. The buyer–seller relationship is the subject of the next section.

Building and maintaining long-term relationships

As personal selling provides organisations with the opportunity to listen directly to their customers' needs, its significance goes beyond the achievement of a single sales transaction. Properly used, this element of the marketing mix can be effective in converting purchasers into regular customers. In this respect, it may be considered a component of customer relationship management, which was discussed in chapter 1. City-centre venues seeking regular, repeat bookings from local businesses, for example, depend on this form of long-term relationship with their clients.

It is important to distinguish, however, between the two basic approaches to personal selling: a sales-oriented approach and a customer-oriented approach. Kotler *et al.* (2003) are among the numerous authors who highlight the contrasting behaviour and tactics used in these two approaches to personal selling:

- A *sales-oriented approach* (using high-pressure sales techniques, exaggerating the product's merits and criticising competitors' products) assumes that customers are only likely to buy under pressure, are influenced by a slick presentation, etc.
- A *customer-oriented approach* (using customer needs analysis, listening and questioning in order to identify customers' needs and proposing appropriate product solutions) assumes that customers have latent needs that present current opportunities and that they will be loyal to sales representatives who have their long-term interests at heart.

These two approaches to selling are almost universally recognised in the literature on selling and sales techniques. Indeed, over 20 years ago, Robert Saxe and Barton Weitz devised a questionnaire to find out which of the two approaches was taken by practising sales people. The statements listed in Table 5.1 make clear the marked contrasts between the two orientations.

It is clear that sales people who use a customer-oriented approach tailor their sales strategies to help customers make purchase decisions that will meet their (the customers') needs. They demonstrate behaviour that is aimed at increasing long-term customer satisfaction and they avoid behaviour that might result in customer dissatisfaction. In this way, they are contributing directly to their company's CRM efforts.

With its emphasis on mutual trust and shared responsibility for the success of any meetings event, the conference and convention industry provides little, if any, scope for the use of selling-oriented techniques.

Who sells?

The characteristics distinguishing conference and convention products have important consequences for the role of staff selling those products.

1. The intangible nature of conference and convention products means that the customers of this industry are highly dependent on the advice and guidance they receive from the professionals who are responsible for selling venues and destinations. The overall experience of holding a convention in a particular

conference centre or in a particular city cannot be tried in advance of the event itself. Consequently, the onus is on sales people to represent their venues and destinations accurately and to fulfil all of the promises they have made, implicitly or explicitly, during the sales process.

2. Being created and supplied by a service industry, the conference product is indivisible from the staff who deliver it. Salesmanship, therefore, forms a part of the consumption of the product itself and it is not limited to the transaction stage before consumption.

It is clear that the word 'selling' may relate to the activities undertaken by a wide range of staff employed by venues and destinations. In a sense, every staff member of a convention bureau or a conference hotel, for example, plays a sales role at one or more stages of the purchasing and consumption process. Although this chapter focuses on the activities of professional sales people, it is important to bear in mind that selling is something that continues long after the sales contract has been signed by the client.

It is useful to think in terms of different levels of sales creativity. Burke and Resnick (2000) are among the many commentators who contend that personal selling ranges from simple order-taking (routine requests from customers) to truly creative selling.

At one end of the sales creativity scale are the order-takers who deal with routine requests from existing customers and who may include front-line staff such as hotel receptionists and waiters. At the other end of

Table 5.1 The selling orientation–customer orientation scale

Selling orientation	Customer orientation
If I am not sure a product is right for a customer, I will still apply pressure to get him to buy	I try to give customers an accurate expectation of what the product will do for them
I imply to a customer that something is beyond my control when it is not	I try to get customers to discuss their needs with me
I try to sell as much as I can, rather than to satisfy a customer	I try to influence a customer by information rather than by pressure
I spend more time trying to persuade a customer to buy than I do trying to discover his needs	I try to help customers achieve their goals
I pretend to agree with customers to please them	I answer a customer's questions about products as correctly as I can
I treat a customer as a rival. It is necessary to stretch the truth in describing a product to a customer	I try to figure out what a customer's needs are. A good salesperson has to have the customer's best interest in mind
I begin the sales talk for a product before exploring a customer's needs with him	I try to bring a customer with a problem together with a product that helps him solve that problem
I try to sell a customer all I can convince him to buy, even if I think it is more than a wise customer would buy	I am willing to disagree with a customer in order to help him make a better decision
I paint too rosy a picture of my products, to make them sound as good as possible	I offer the product of mine that is best suited to the customer's problem
I decide what products to offer on the basis of what I can convince customers to buy, not on the basis of what will satisfy them in the long run	I try to achieve my goals by satisfying customers
I keep alert for weaknesses in a customer's personality so I can use them to put pressure on him to buy	I try to find out what kind of product would be most helpful to a customer

Adapted from Saxe and Weitz (1982).

the scale are the sales professionals employed primarily for the purpose of selling the venue or destination. The activities of these professional sales staff will now be examined. However, before focusing on the more creative sales activities, it is worth emphasising that many order-takers also have the potential to sell and to increase their organisation's profitability while at the same time enhancing the customer's experience. The receptionist who suggests that delegates use the hotel's spa facilities and the waiter who proposes a finer bottle of wine are both engaging in genuine sales activities.

Professional sales activities

The main characteristic that distinguishes the activities of professional sales staff from order-takers is that the former are engaged not only in servicing existing clients but also in demand creation: identifying potential new buyers and motivating them to buy. In this sense, it can be seen that professional sales staff may do much more than simply sell.

Kotler *et al.* (2003) list the possible tasks of sales representatives as follows:

- Prospecting. Finding and cultivating new customers
- Targeting. Deciding how to allocate their scarce time among prospects and customers
- Communicating. Communicating information about the company's products and services
- Selling. Approaching, presenting, answering objections and closing sales.
- Servicing. Consulting on customers' problems, rendering technical assistance. . .
- Information gathering. Conducting market research and intelligence work
- Allocating. Deciding which customers to allocate scarce products to during product shortages (for example, allocating hotel accommodation during a major convention)

(Kotler et al., 2003:667)

Two of these tasks, however, are almost always undertaken by professional sales staff: prospecting and selling.

Prospecting

Burke and Resnick (2000) note that selling to groups and businesses is more complicated and time-consuming than selling to individuals, sometimes requiring additional steps in the personal selling process. This is certainly the case in the business-to-business (B2B) selling that characterises the conference industry, where the selling usually takes place between businesses or between businesses and organisations, and what is being sold is a product designed for consumption by a group, as opposed to an individual.

One of the additional steps required in the conference sector is the preparation of bids and this will be examined in detail later in this chapter. Another is the process of prospecting – conducting research to identify new customers. A common theme in the marketing literature is that one of the main reasons enterprises fail is that people do not spend enough time and resources prospecting for new business.

For many organisations, this is necessarily an ongoing process: a hotel may find that some of the local businesses that hold their meetings there have moved away or have gone out of business or have decided to change to using videoconferencing for their meetings; a destination may find that the political party that held its annual conference there every year has switched to a competitor destination. Associations, as stated in chapter 1, rotate their annual conferences between destinations. For that reason, convention bureaux are obliged to spend considerable resources prospecting for future association events – as their competitors are doing exactly that.

There are two main steps involved in prospecting:

- Identifying 'suspects' or leads – potential customers who may eventually be persuaded to purchase
- Qualifying these – determining which suspects are the most promising (most likely to become 'prospects' of high potential)

Prospecting for conference and convention business can involve professional sales staff researching a range of sources, including computerised databases, business directories and other listings and even internet searches using key words to identify companies, organisations and associations that fit their customer profile.

For the conference and convention industry, Harrill (2005) lists other potential sources of suspects as:

- Leads generated at trade shows
- MINT – the Meeting Information Network database, for members of Destination Marketing Association International (www.destinationmarketing.org)
- Telephone directories
- Chamber of Commerce member lists
- Networking – meeting with people in their environment

He also emphasises the importance of using existing clients as potential sources of new business: 'customers currently doing business with you are the most important group to research. Not only might they buy from you again, they can be excellent sources for referrals. A careful analysis of current customers can yield a profile of the ideal prospect. Customers will respect your enquiry once they understand that you are trying to expand a market and could use their advice on potential customers' (Harrill, 2005:18).

Qualifying prospects involves using professional judgement to decide which of them are most likely to become customers. This judgement may be partly based on the past buying patterns of the prospect. For example, an association that has recently held its annual conference in a particular city is unlikely to return for several years, at least. Consequently, for that city's convention bureau sales staff, that association will have low potential as a customer for the immediate future.

For the more promising prospects, the next task for the sales professional is likely to be arranging an appointment to meet. If that appointment is granted and the prospect and the sales person meet face-to-face, then the actual selling begins. Selling skills will be explored in detail in the second part of this chapter. Before that, three other, related, topics must be examined: sales promotion and yield management and the management of a sales force.

Sales promotion and yield management

Sales promotion

Closely linked to personal selling is the technique of sales promotion, defined by the Institute of Sales Promotion as 'any scheme designed to sell more product'. Burke and Resnick (2000) define sales promotion as specialised activities designed to stimulate demand for a particular product. They emphasise that sales promotion is distinct from the general term 'promotion' and that it has as its specific purpose the boosting of sales, often in a very direct manner. Used effectively, sales promotion can be an extremely powerful device in organisations' efforts to increase sales volume.

In the market for consumer goods, sales promotion has generally been defined as a tactical example of marketing used to generate additional sales at the point-of-sale in retail outlets, through the use of inducements such as money-off vouchers, two-for-the-price-of-one offers and 'free' gifts. However, in recent years, sales promotion has seen increasing respectability as a discipline and it has come to be regarded as more of a strategic tool used across the marketing mix. Sales promotion is now believed by many to be a core part of any integrated marketing programme and it is a technique that is widely used by conference venues.

Middleton describes the use of sales promotion in the context of travel and tourism, but his comments apply equally to the conference industry: 'the "perishability" of tourism products means that marketing managers are constantly preoccupied with the necessity to manipulate demand in response to unforeseen events, as well as the normal daily, weekly or seasonal fluctuations' (Middleton 2001:255). Those responsible for marketing destinations and venues are also faced with the challenge of dealing with unforeseen events (SARS, 9/11, currency devaluations, etc.) and fluctuating levels of demand, such as the lower levels of business in the summer months and at weekends.

Sales promotion techniques are particularly suitable for dealing with such demand adjustments, and as such, may be regarded as vital weapons in the marketing armoury of many conference and convention organisations.

How may sales promotion techniques be applied in the context of the conference industry? It was stated earlier that these techniques are usually used at the point-of-sale. But it is clear that, unlike the case of the distribution of consumer goods, the conference and convention industry has no retail outlets or showrooms. However, if a point-of-sale may be said to be any place at which a purchase transaction takes place, then it is clear that this will include, for the booking of venue services:

- Customers' own places of work: when they make bookings in response to direct mail and telephone calls from venues
- A venue's own website – the primary target for sales promotion
- Trade shows/workshops where venues take bookings

Middleton (2001) highlights three main targets to which sales promotion techniques may be applied in order to stimulate the sale of specific products at particular times:

- Individual buyers
- Distribution networks – in the case of any organisation that achieves a large proportion of its sales through intermediaries, such as hotel booking agencies and venue finding services
- Sales force – in the case of larger organisations, such as international conference centres, any additional effort required on top of routine sales efforts requires some additional form of incentive/reward

The actual sales promotion techniques that may be used are listed in Table 5.2. Although these apply primarily to the use of sales promotion in the travel and tourism sector, many of them are commonly used as direct inducements to boost bookings for conference venues.

Of all the techniques listed, price cuts are generally acknowledged to be the most effective of incentives to purchase (or, in the case of intermediaries and sales forces, to sell). However, most commentators also emphasise the perils associated with price-cutting, a technique that is easily matched by other venues and raises the possibility of 'price wars', if over-used. In addition: 'there is a danger . . . that if sales boosts are achieved through money-off or bargain offers, this can have the effect of demeaning the brand'. (Holloway, 2004:304).

For these reasons, organisations often prefer to use special offers and packages (which, in reality, are disguised price cuts) such as three delegate nights for the price of two or 'free' food and drink during coffee breaks. In this way, the venue is able to maintain its regular price structure while still offering added value to customers and an incentive to buy.

Table 5.2 Sales promotion techniques

Sales promotion techniques		
Individual buyers	Distribution networks	Sales force
• Price cuts/sale offers • Discount vouchers/coupons • Disguised price cuts • Extra product • Additional services • Free gifts • Competitions • Passport schemes for regular customers • Prize draws	• Extra commission and overrides • Prize draws • Competitions • Free gifts • Parties/receptions	• Bonuses and other money/incentives • Gift incentives • Travel incentives • Prize draws

Adapted from Middleton (2001).

It is clear that sales promotion can be an effective device for boosting sagging sales volumes. However, the short-lived, temporary nature of the results they can have means that they must be used with caution. In particular, it is generally agreed that sales promotion techniques are not effective at building long-term brand preferences. There is, therefore, a need for a genuine balance to be struck between short-term sales increases and the longer-term need for organisations to develop a sound reputation and solid brand image. The two are not incompatible, however:

> *Sales promotion techniques should be seen first and foremost as aids in building a relationship between organisations and their customers. They should not be viewed merely as a 'quick fix' to unload surplus stock, even where this may be one of the objectives within a promotional campaign. Behind any such campaign, there should always be the overall aim of building loyalty and adding value to the product, rather than undermining it.*
>
> (Holloway, 2004:303)

Holloway emphasises that sales promotion techniques are complementary to advertising, the main tool used to achieve longer-term strategic objectives, such as building the corporate image of the organisation and its products. Sales promotion and advertising work together most effectively when they are mutually reinforcing.

Case Study 5.1 describes sales promotional campaigns developed by the Singapore Exhibition and Convention Bureau™ to attract more conferences and business events.

Yield management

Yield management programmes also generally reflect fluctuating levels of demand and for that reason they are closely linked with sales promotion campaigns in venues' efforts to maximise revenue by adjusting prices to suit market demand. Yield management is essentially derived from the basic economic theory of supply and demand that dictates that in times of high demand, high prices can be charged, but when demand is low, prices will drop. Similarly, when supply is limited, prices rise (a sellers' market) and when there is an over-supply, prices fall (a buyers' market).

Widely used by the airlines since the 1980s and by hotels since the 1990s, yield management has now been recognised by conference venues as an essential element in the marketing and selling process. Basically, yield management is an inventory management system that allows venue managers and their sales staff to forecast supply and demand and adjust their pricing strategies accordingly – in order to max-imise revenue. It is, therefore, a systematic approach to simultaneously optimising both average rate and occupancy for a venue, the ultimate aim being 100 per cent yield – that is, 100 per cent occupancy at the published rack (non-discounted) rate.

Clearly, a venue's forecasting must be based on what patterns of purchasing behaviour a venue's manage-ment have observed in the past, as well as what they think will happen in the future. Davidson and Hyde (2014:65) underline this point:

> *Historical data from the venue itself also constitute an important factor in the calculation. How much has each meeting/event space earned in the past, on different days of the week, on different weeks of the year? Those rates can be a useful guide to what the venue can real-istically earn from the same spaces in the future. Occupancy rates for each space are also vital statistics that must be taken into account in yield management calculations. Therefore, it is essential that venues create and maintain an efficient system for recording and storing these data.*

The management of a sales force

Any organisation investing in employing a sales force is making a long-term commitment to sales and selling. The salaries and commission of sales staff make personal selling one of the most expensive of the promotional tools available. But, used effectively, the sales force can hold the key to any organisation's sustained growth and profitability. It is vital, therefore, that an organisation's sales force is managed in such a way that it achieves the desired sales objectives. This is one of the principal aims of sales management.

Sales force objectives

A key initial step is to establish clear objectives for the sales force. This is a vitally important task for the sales manager, as everything else that follows rests on effective decisions being made at this stage. Accord-ing to Kotler *et al.* (2003), objectives are typically established for sales staff for two reasons:

- to ensure that corporate goals are met (these may include revenue generation, market share, improving corporate image, etc.); and
- to assist sales staff to plan and execute their personal sales programmes effectively.

Berkowitz *et al.* (2003) also place emphasis on the importance of setting objectives, noting that these are used to give direction and purpose and to act as a standard for evaluation of the sales force's performance. For the members of the sales force, the main objective will always be the converting of customer interest into actual sales. However, other possible features of sales force objectives include:

- A time frame. Sales objectives are generally expected to be accomplished within a certain period of time.
- Objectives may be set for the total sales force as a whole and/or for each individual salesperson.
- They may be measured in terms of revenue earned, units sold or market share achieved for individual salespersons. They may also include results measured in terms of average order size, average number of sales/time period and ratio orders/calls.

Sales objectives must be reviewed regularly and they may be altered in the case of circumstances changing considerably, such as natural or man-made disasters.

Recruiting and training the sales force

Given the importance of direct interpersonal communication to the sales process, it is generally agreed that recruiting and training the sales force are vitally important sales management tasks. Berkowitz *et al.* (2003) recommend that a set of required qualifications be established before beginning to recruit and suggest that preparing a job description that lists specific tasks the salesperson should perform and analysing traits of the successful salespeople within the organisation are additional tasks for the sales manager. They also advise that whether using formal training programmes, or informal on-the-job training, training should focus on:

- the company;
- its products;
- selling techniques.

Furthermore, the same authors contend that training should not be limited to new staff, but should also be made available to experienced personnel. Holloway (2004) makes the additional point that training in sales should not only be reserved for members of the sales force:

> *In any company's marketing strategy, adequate training must be built into the marketing plan to ensure that personal selling, with all its associated social skills, is effectively communicated to all staff who are likely at any time to come into contact with customers.*
>
> *(Holloway 2004:239)*

Structuring the sales force

A useful distinction is often made between the 'inside sales staff' (or 'in-house staff') and the 'outside sales staff' (or 'field staff') who may work for a sales manager.

McCabe *et al.* (2000) define the respective tasks of the two groups as follows:

- Inside sales staff support outside sales activities and coordinate sales direction in relation to the overall marketing plan. They also:
  - Provide timely follow-up on all sales leads and enquiries
  - Maintain customer databases
  - Assist in the planning of sales calls/industry promotional events
  - Develop collateral material
  - Conduct site inspections/familiarisation trips
- Outside sales staff operate in the external environment. They:
  - Obtain market feedback on sales and marketing opportunities, competitive activities and client needs
  - Conduct direct sales calls in order to educate, develop customer relationships and create sales

The inside sales staff category may also include telemarketers who use the phone to find new leads, qualify them and either sell to them or pass their details to outside sales staff. Venue reservations staff and convention bureau/conference desk staff dealing with enquiries are further examples of in-house sales staff with an important selling role.

Outside sales staff may be directly and exclusively employed by the organisation or they may be independent sales representatives normally representing a number of different venues or destinations. Hotel representatives who sell hotel rooms' meetings facilities in a given market area often work independently,

Table 5.3 Structures commonly used in organising sales staff

Structure	Definition	Advantages
Territorial-structured	Each sales representative or sales team is assigned an exclusive territory in which to represent the company's entire offer: for example, Scotland or Western Europe	Results in a clear definition of the salesperson's responsibilities Increases the sales representative's incentive to cultivate local business and personal ties Travel expenses are relatively small, as each sales representative travels within a small geographic area
Market-segment structured	Each sales representative or sales team specialises in selling to a different market segment; for example, the association meetings market or the corporate meetings market	Each member of the sales force can become knowledgeable about their specific market segment
Customer-structured	Each sales representative or sales team serves one or more of the major (or 'key') accounts of specific customers whose business is critical to the success of the organisation; for example, large companies with many divisions operating in many parts of the country, such as General Motors in the US	Follows the trend towards increasing buyer concentration resulting from mergers and acquisitions, meaning that fewer buyers account for a larger share of some companies' sales Follows the trend towards more buyers centralising their purchases instead of leaving them to local units. Sales staff can become familiar with major customers, understand trends that affect them and plan appropriate sales strategies and tactics

Adapted from Kotler *et al.* (2003).

for several chains or properties. Kotler *et al.* (2003) maintain that it is often more effective for a hotel to hire a hotel representative than to use their own sales person. This is true when the market is a distant one where the market potential does not justify employing a salaried salesperson and when cultural differences may make it hard for an outsider to penetrate the market. Case Study 5.2 provides details of a representation service used by The Jockey Club venues in the UK.

Whether inside or outside, and regardless of whether or not they work on an independent basis, when there are several sales staff, they must be organised according to particular criteria. The three most commonly used criteria are shown in Table 5.3. Most sales forces are organised using one or more of these.

Organising the sales staff by territory is certainly the most straightforward of methods. However, it is considered by many to be unsuitable in cases where the products are varied or complex or where deep technical knowledge is required.

Compensating and motivating the sales force

In order to attract, motivate and retain the most effective sales people, it is important to determine the best level of compensation/salary required and the best method of calculating it. The sales manager must decide between a number of possible remuneration packages:

- a straight salary;
- a salary plus benefits (commission, bonus, profit-sharing, etc.);

- straight commission – a simple percentage of the value of the sale or a sliding scale of commission;
- a combination.

Finally, the sales force must be motivated to sell and to keep selling effectively. Berkowitz *et al.* (2003) note that a systematic approach to motivating all sales staff is required, as due to burn out, even the best need motivating. They advise that any motivational scheme must also satisfy the important non-financial needs of the sales force:

- Job security
- Good working conditions
- Opportunities to succeed

A commonly used method of increasing sales is through the use of a competition as a motivational programme, with the reward being cash, travel or symbolic awards, such as a plaque for Sales Agent of the Year, as recognition of the extra effort made.

Destination and venue selling strategies

The first part of this chapter has examined the principles that lie behind personal selling. The rest of the chapter will look in greater detail at the skills and techniques involved in personal selling in the context of the meetings industry.

There are many books that describe the sales skills and techniques generic to the selling of any product or service. Price and Ilvento (1999), for example, suggest that the approaches to be adopted by the twenty-first century salesperson will include:

- An ability to customise the sales presentation in order to answer the question in the customer's mind 'What's in it for me?' The salesperson 'must present a value-laden presentation customised to the exact needs of their prospect' (Price and Ilvento, 1999:35).
- A consultative approach that asks questions (which they describe as 'strategic probing') of the customer and is based on doing one's homework about the customer before any interaction takes place.
- Building trust between the salesperson and the customer: 'decisions will still be made based on facts – price, services, features, benefits, warranties, and guarantees – but more than ever, the decision (to buy) will be based upon perceptions of trust, comfort and credibility of you and your company' (Price and Ilvento, 1999:47).

Such generic sales skills are important no matter what product or service is being sold. Nevertheless, when selling a destination or a venue in the conference and business events sector, additional and specific skills, knowledge, tools, resources and activities are used by sales professionals. These will be explored further in this chapter. However, first, it is important for any member of a venue or destination's sales team to understand how buyers evaluate their products.

Destination and venue selection criteria

An understanding of the factors and criteria influencing buyers when they are selecting destinations and venues is essential. Such an understanding will need to be complemented by knowledge of the specific requirements and selection factors deemed critical by the individual buyer, which might be as quirky as ensuring that the destination has the right kind of facilities to satisfy the tastes and interests of the Chairperson's spouse or partner! This understanding will enable the destination salesperson to focus on selling the benefits of the destination, rather than its features. In other words, not simply informing the client of the total number of bed spaces in the destination but demonstrating that the destination has, for example, ample 4-star hotel bedrooms in the right locations to meet the specific requirements of the client's event. Similarly at a venue level, an understanding of the key venue selection criteria for conference organisers and meeting planners will assist the sales staff in demonstrating how their venue's meeting rooms and other facilities and services can be used and configured to ensure the successful staging of a particular event.

Destination and venue selection criteria may show some variation from year-to-year and from country to country, dependent upon economic, social, political and technological factors. Such factors are examined in more detail in other chapters of this book. Table 5.4 illustrates the key determinants of UK meeting planners' bookings of destinations and venues in 2014 (showing the top 12 factors out of a total of 25 in the published research). The results are based on interviews with more than 500 British event organisers from both the corporate and association sectors, published as the 'British Meetings & Events Industry Survey'. Access, location and price are consistently the top influencing factors, while the importance of free Wi-Fi (a factor not even on the radar when the first edition of this book was published) is clearly shown. The same research also reveals that the lack of free Wi-Fi is the largest cause for dissatisfaction among buyers.

In a personal communication to the authors (January 2015), Scott Taylor, chief executive of Glasgow City Marketing Bureau, comments on other destination selection criteria, stressing the importance of reputation management and professional service delivery by destination marketing organisations:

> *Managing the image and reputation of a destination is essential to ensuring place attractiveness and a strong competitive stance. This involves destination marketing organisations not only ensuring that the destination proposition has saliency with its audience, but also delivering on their promises. This brings its own challenges as destination promises are reliant on the local industry acting cohesively, with a shared focus on quality service delivery at the right price. In Glasgow, we focus not only on customer relationship management but commit as much resource to industry relationship management. This granular approach helps us tailor our proposition and promises with a high level of certainty. Reputation is king. This is a word of mouth industry, and reputations are lost on broken promises.*

An article in International Meetings Review (www.internationalmeetingsreview.com; 3 February 2015) entitled 'The New Model for Destination Marketing Organisations' adds a further criterion. It recommends that destinations that want to be 'relevant beyond the confines of the business events industry (via rankings established by organisations such as ICCA) (see chapter 9) must also make greater strides in building reputations within more mainstream pecking orders, such as rankings provided by The Economist Business Intelligence Unit (www.eiu.com/) and The Reputation Management Institute's 'CityReptrack' (www.reputationinstitute.com/thought-leadership/city-reptrack)'.

Destination and venue selling 'hierarchy'

As shown by the 'British Meetings & Events Industry Survey 2014/15' reported above, location is of crucial importance in the selection process. In selling location, account should always be taken of what might be termed a hierarchy of location. In other words, if selling within the international arena to attract an international event, the first priority is to get one's own country onto the shortlist before putting forward a specific city or destination, and then subsequently highlighting a particular venue or venues and other suppliers. For example, Cardiff, the capital city of Wales, might wish to put forward St David's Hall as the ideal setting for a major international corporate or association conference. A key element of the sales process would be to persuade the client to consider firstly bringing the event to Wales (rather than to France or Thailand or Canada) and then to focus on the city (i.e. Cardiff) and, finally, on the venue itself.

Table 5.4 Key factors influencing venue and destination selection

Ranking	Selection criteria for companies/corporations	% Respondents	Selection criteria for associations	% Respondents
1	Access (road/rail links)	58.7	Access (road/rail links)	74.3
2	Location (area of the country)	58.1	Location (area of the country)	62.4
3	Price/value for money	34.8	Price/value for money	55.0
4	Quality of service	30.3	Capacity of conference facilities	32.6
5	Free Wi-Fi	29.0	Availability	27.1
6	Availability	28.4	Free Wi-Fi	26.1
7	Quality of food	27.1	Quality of conference facilities	22.5
8	Quality of conference facilities	23.2	Parking on site	21.6
9	Capacity of conference facilities	22.6	Previous experience of venue	17.4
10	Parking on site	21.9	Quality of food	16.5
11	Previous experience of venue	16.1	Relationship with venue staff	9.2
12	Quality of bedrooms	11.0	Reputation	8.7

Source: 'The British Meetings & Events Industry Survey 2014/15' – (www.meetpie.com/bmeis) – reproduced with permission of CAT Publications Ltd.

Even when, as with international association conferences, it would normally be the city rather than the country that would be bidding to host the event, the destination and venue sales teams must also promote the benefits and attractions of the country. Clients or buyers have to be convinced that the national context for their event is appropriate (taking account of such things as language, culture, environment, access, political stability, etc.) before they can be persuaded to look in detail at the discrete destination or destinations, and then venues, within that country.

Adding value

While price will always continue to be one of the major factors influencing venue (and destination) selection (as shown in Table 5.4), price can be interpreted as being good value for money rather than simply what is the cheapest.

Davidson and Hyde (2014:68) contend that:

> In the meetings and events market, most buyers tend to be value-oriented, in the sense that they will choose higher value services, if they perceive genuine value, or can be made to understand that, by using a particular venue rather than its competitors, they will be more likely to achieve the objectives for their event. Therefore, in preference to price cutting, a much more effective approach for venue sales managers in negotiations is to demonstrate or add value, thereby shifting the focus from price to questions of value.

They suggest that:

> At a time when a growing number of clients have a fixed budget for their events, with no scope for paying for 'extras', it can be attractive for them if, during the negotiation process, facilities such as audio-visual or cloakroom services can be added to the overall package at no extra cost – in particular if competing venues are charging extra for these. Adding value in this way can often be done at negligible cost to the venue, since such facilities are usually already in place.

The 'British Meetings & Events Industry Survey 2014/15' (www.meetpie.com) asked buyers about their preferred added value items. It found that: 'added value items remain the most popular incentive even with the lower budgeted delegate rates, putting even more pressure on venues to "deliver more for less"'.

The most popular added value items were found to be the provision of extra audio-visual services or the complimentary use of an organiser's office, followed by discounts on multiple bookings.

Case study 5.3 describes a range of creative added value packages developed by UniSpace Sunderland (the commercial arm of the University of Sunderland in north-east England) to enhance its conference and meetings business.

Destination expertise

To be effective in selling any product or service, the salesperson must have in-depth knowledge of that product or service. This principle applies equally to selling a convention or business event destination, whether operating in a destination or venue sales role. This will mean having good first-hand knowledge of the destination through visits to, and experience of, the facilities and infrastructure that make up the destination. It means becoming an expert on the destination to be sold, combining that first-hand knowledge with a database or library of information and intelligence on the destination. For a venue's sales team, such intelligence forms part of the backcloth against which its facilities are to be sold, but also builds a picture of the local competition against which its business must be won.

Such a destination database resource should hold information on venues, local suppliers, transport, communications and accessibility, attractions and events and the local economy and infrastructure.

Venues

- Number, types and location of conference and business events venues.
- Their capacities in terms of number and size of meeting rooms and number of bedrooms.
- The special features and facilities or unique selling propositions (USPs) of the venues (e.g. swimming pool, golf course, Michelin-star restaurant, videoconferencing suite).
- Quality accreditations, including an assessment of the quality, experience and professionalism of the venue staff.
- Prices.
- Accessibility of venues and their ability to handle delegates with disabilities.
- Sustainability and green credentials.
- The venues' client portfolios – this will give an indication of the kind of conference and convention business currently being attracted to individual venues. It does not necessarily mean knowing the names of client companies but it should include details of the kinds of business by industry sector, by organisation type, by size and duration of events, etc.

Local suppliers

Another important aspect of a destination's overall 'product' are the local companies supplying specialist services to incoming conferences and events, such as:

- Audio-visual and production companies: some organisations prefer to work with the same audio-visual companies no matter where their events take place because they have worked with them over a period of time and have confidence in their ability to provide an efficient and cost-effective service. They may not, therefore, have a need to appoint locally based audio-visual companies. Even so, it strengthens the overall image and profile of a destination if it can demonstrate that it has good quality, local audio-visual suppliers and production companies.
- Exhibition contractors: similar to audio-visual companies, exhibition contractors often work on a national rather than local basis, but the destination gains added credibility if it can point to locally based exhibition contractors and suppliers. It demonstrates that the sector's importance is recognised within the local economy.
- Marquee and furniture hire companies.
- Speciality caterers who can be hired for a convention banquet or for a special function that forms part of the convention programme and which will often be held in one of the destination's unique venues.
- Interpreters.
- Activity providers, for example, companies offering flights in hot air balloons, team building activities, off-road driving, etc.
- Transport providers such as coach companies, taxi services, car rental companies, helicopter hire, train chartering, to emphasise the facilities that exist for transporting delegates within the destination and, if appropriate, to nearby attractions.

Transport, communications and accessibility

Here the focus is on showing the range and ease of access to the destination from other areas or from other countries. Intelligence needs to be gathered, stored and regularly updated on:

- Rail services, showing direct services with other major cities/destinations and holding information on the length of journey (in miles/kilometres) and duration (in hours/minutes), frequency of service and price.

- Air connections, with similar information to that collected on rail services above. If the destination does not have its own airport, there should be information on the nearest airports and their services, plus details of transfer times between the airport and the destination.
- Road links/communications with details of average journey times from other major hubs.
- Good quality maps that position the destination on at least two levels: showing the destination (i) within the national context and (ii) within its local/regional context. The latter should ideally show where the major venues and hotels are located within the destination.

Attractions and events

Visitor attractions and major events taking place within a destination can both be important as components of social programmes, partner programmes and pre- and post-convention tours. The database should, therefore, feature details of:

- Visitor attractions: information on local attractions (e.g. country parks, castles or stately homes, museums, zoos, theme parks, etc.), which can be visited during any free time or as part of the convention social programme and/or pre- and post-convention tours.
- Restaurants.
- Shopping.
- Activities (outdoor and indoor): theatres and cinemas, sports facilities and leisure centres, golf courses, etc.
- Major events: conference organisers may want their conference to coincide with a major event taking place in the area because it will be of interest to their delegates, perhaps linking in with the theme of the conference in some way. Conversely, they may prefer to avoid a clash with a major event because of possible transport problems, congested accommodation, price rises or other factors.
- Tourist/visitor information centres: the destination and venue salespersons must know about the range of information and services available through the local tourist and visitor information centres, with full contact/address details and information on their hours of opening.

Local economy and infrastructure

- Business sectors and major companies: it is vital to know about the key businesses and companies operating in the destination. At one level, such businesses will doubtless generate many local conference and meeting bookings in the destination's venues, making them very important clients. On another level, these businesses and the business sectors they represent should give some strong clues about the types of future conference business to be sought. If a destination has a strong financial services sector or engineering industry, it is likely to have more success in winning conferences and business events from the financial services or engineering industries because of the natural synergies and links that will exist (see also chapter 6 for specific examples of this).
- Inward investment successes: the term 'inward investment' is used to describe the relocation of a company or organisation to a particular destination or a decision by such companies to establish a subsidiary operation in another destination. Inward investments are beneficial because they also give indicators about the inherent strengths and potential growth sectors of the local economy. Inward investment success stories provide valuable promotional material ('we have a vibrant local economy which has attracted the following new businesses in the past year. . .') but they are also, in their own right, an important source of future events business.
- New infrastructure developments: the database should hold information on proposed and actual development to the destination's physical infrastructure, for example, new roads or bridges, an extension to the airport, developments to the railway station, new retail parks, new leisure facilities, etc.

- New transport services – information on new or planned air or rail services, for example.
- Road traffic volumes – road congestion and traffic jams are an increasingly common phenomenon in our twenty-first century cities and on our motorways. Local government and central government agencies capture statistics on road traffic volumes – a destination that can demonstrate that, for example, driving is a pleasure because the roads are uncluttered could promote this as one of the benefits and pleasures of holding an event there.

The intelligence held within this database can be used in sales proposals and bids to clients, but also as an invaluable resource in communicating with the trade media, with consultants and with potential investment companies.

Handling enquiries effectively

Destination and venue marketing and sales activity has, as its objective, the generation of leads and enquiries from clients that can be converted into actual business. For a venue, winning business is essential for its survival while, for the destination, success in securing conventions and business events creates increased economic benefits in terms of visitor expenditure, job creation and enhanced destination profile, thus providing key measures for the destination marketing organisation's effectiveness.

Destination level enquiry handling

The destination marketing and sales team will, for the most part, act as a conduit or intermediary organisation between the client/customer and the venue with which the business or event will finally be contracted. The sales team's role is to stimulate and then direct enquiries to those venues within the destination that most closely match the client's requirements. They may also make referrals to professional conference organisers (PCOs) or destination management companies (DMCs) to assist them in securing the business. They act as an honest broker or match-maker, seeking to bring together two parties (buyer and supplier) in the hope and expectation that they will reach agreement, strike up a relationship and work together in partnership to ensure a successful event, with further potential events to follow through repeat business.

The destination sales team may also fulfil a role in reassuring buyers and providing consistency of support, especially in countries where high turnover among venue staff can threaten to undermine buyers' confidence that their event will be delivered successfully. Gartrell (1994) writes:

> *Convention and visitor bureaus have become the stabilizing influence in an industry that has a reputation for high turnover. This continuity of sales and marketing personnel provides a positive image for a city.*

The stimulation of sales enquiries is achieved both proactively and reactively. The proactive approach is based on researching or 'prospecting' for sales leads by identifying potential clients whose event requirements match what the destination can offer. Contact is made with such clients by telephone or email (or through a personal visit) with the aim of building a rapport and clarifying whether there might be forthcoming events for which the destination could tender. These initial contacts or 'cold calls' seek to generate leads for onward referral to appropriate venues within the destination. Gartrell (1994) sets out the proactive approach diagrammatically (Gartrell, 1994:181). The reactive approach entails responding to enquiries received as a result of the types of marketing communications activity outlined in earlier chapters.

Once the introduction between buyer and supplier (venue and/or PCO/DMC) has been effected, the destination team generally pulls back to allow the venue and possibly other service suppliers to deliver the event for and with the client. The client signs a contract with the venue, not with the destination. The destination team are available to offer support and additional services (such as assistance with pre- and post-tours, social programme planning, the provision of a civic reception), if required, and to follow-up after the event to check that the client has been satisfied with the facilities and service experienced from the destination – and clearly also to check on the likelihood of repeat business at some future point.

The process outlined above will certainly apply to the smaller meetings and conferences and to the majority of corporate events. Where, however, the event is of a larger scale, perhaps justifying the description of a 'destination event' involving hundreds or even thousands of delegates, the destination team may also be involved in the whole bidding process, adopting a team approach with the major conference venue, and possibly a PCO, to bid for the event.

Venue level enquiry handling

At a venue level, the sales team seeks to maximise appropriate business for their venue. As with the destination sales team, the venue sales team should also adopt both a proactive and reactive approach to sales leads and enquiries. It may well be that, especially for hotel venues that are part of a large chain, sales activity will be co-ordinated through a regional sales team, with national call centres established to handle initial enquiries and bookings. Chapters 2 and 8 give examples of venue marketing consortia and hotel brands, many of which offer a centralised enquiry or booking service.

The venue sales team seeks to win business that gives the best occupancy but which also provides the highest possible yield or revenue (see the section on yield management earlier in this chapter). There may well be other factors influencing how they handle an enquiry and respond to a client. For example , if they are new clients who have not used the venue before, how flexible does the venue wish to be in meeting the clients' requirements and making an 'offer they can't refuse', sometimes known as 'buying the business'? If the event is from an existing client, a similar weighing of commercial benefits may be needed, balancing the benefits of retaining the client and getting further repeat business against opportunities to win higher-yield business but from just a one-off event, with no further events forthcoming in the future. Do they take the short-term view and fill their rooms now or do they take a medium to longer-term view in order to achieve a sustainable business balance, bearing in mind that client retention is normally less expensive than having constantly to find new clients, and generally, makes good business sense anyway.

Venues are sometimes criticised for taking the short-term perspective rather than investing in longer-term business relationships. This may not be surprising when general managers of hotels (especially), but other venues as well, have to justify and defend their sales figures for the next few months, but not normally for 2 or 3 years in the future. Gary England, at the time Head of Sales for a major non-residential conference centre in London, argued against this short-term approach using the following rationale (*Conference & Exhibition Fact Finder* magazine, December 2004):

> *One of the many buzz words for the moment is relationship management. Let us not forget that this is a volatile market, reactive to international events, so investing in relationships is one sure fire way of managing against disaster. It is sometimes the case that, during the better times, good relationships are forgotten. I have recently experienced a frustrating example of this: a large hotel chain, with which I have a 5-year relationship, put a 45 per cent price increase onto its rooms! For me this is five years of good relationship building down the drain. A reactive decision taken at head office against an upturn in business. Of course, I understand the economies of supply and demand, but for me this does not take into account the economies of the local market place. If, God forbid, another 9/11 or SARS scare should hit the industry, not only has the relationship been lost, but you could bet the subsequent price drop would be equally both dramatic and unhealthy. It is these short-term, reactive strategies that we need to move away from as an*

industry. Not just milking every upturn and struggling against damage limitation when things go bad. A long-term strategy is where business growth leads to business investment. The benefits are that, during the good times, you will gather a budgetary surplus that will help pay for your plans during the not-so-good times.

Another issue with which some venues have to wrestle, particularly those belonging to a chain or consortium, concerns the onward referral of business. If they are unable to handle an enquiry, perhaps because of lack of availability, do they offer to refer the enquiry to another 'competitor' venue in the locality (i.e. keep the business in the destination) or do they pass it on to other venues in their chain (but which may well be in a different part of the country) in order to try to win the business for the chain? Practice varies enormously but the overriding consideration should be: what is best for the client?

How, then, do destinations and venues gain a clear understanding of clients' requirements for their events? What enquiry handling skills and procedures are needed, how is event intelligence to be gathered and how should sales teams seek to empathise with clients to understand the client's priorities for achieving a successful event?

Enquiry handling skills

Destination and venue sales staff must understand, from the outset, that the clients and customers who contact them with an enquiry are, in many cases (possibly as high as 60 to 70 per cent), not full-time conference and event organisers. They may be secretaries or PAs, trainers or human resource managers, marketing or public relations staff, with only limited experience and knowledge of convention and event management. They may well not be the decision-makers: their role is to collect information on a destination and venue options for an event, perhaps make recommendations and attempt to sell a destination or venue, but then leave senior managers or directors, or a selection committee, to make the final choice. It is, therefore, important, when handling an enquiry, to establish at an early stage the status of the enquirer and to clarify the scope they have to influence the final choice of event location.

The limited professional expertise of enquirers, or perhaps their limited ability to influence the choice of destination or venue, can prove frustrating. It can frequently mean that enquirers do not have complete information on the event for which they have been asked to locate a suitable destination and venue. Their 'brief' may lack some of the essential detail required by the destination and venue sales teams to enable them to put forward a full and properly tailored sales proposal. It may also be unclear when a decision will be taken on the choice of destination and venue, complicating the processes for follow-up sales calls once a bid or proposal has been submitted to the enquirer.

Customer frustrations, on the other hand, often centre upon the destination or venue's perceived inability to supply appropriate information within a specified time frame. Comments such as 'they didn't listen to us' or 'they didn't interpret our needs correctly' are sometimes heard. The destination sales team may respond that customers only wanted to know about venue availability and price and that they gave the customers what they wanted. In doing so, the sales team has failed to gain a proper understanding of the customers' real needs and they have missed the opportunity to give a response different from that being submitted by other destinations. Where they do adopt a more customer-focused approach, they enjoy a higher success rate with more enquiries being converted. All customers have different needs and experiences. They organise different types of events with quite different requirements. The destination sales team must understand these differences and then assess and present the destination's unique 'product', or offering, in order to most closely match the customers' unique requirements.

In practical terms, it means not only obtaining the factual information necessary to process an enquiry (such as size, dates, type of event) but also seeking other information to enable the sales team to really understand the objectives for an event and what will be its critical success factors. This means asking the client open questions. Rudyard Kipling's apposite verse is one that should be known to all sales professionals:

> *I kept six honest serving men.*
>
> *They taught me all I knew.*
>
> *Their names are What and Why and When*
>
> *And How and Where and Who*

Table 5.5 illustrates how such open questioning can be used to gather the crucial and distinctive support information in addition to the basic factual event information, which will enable the destination and venue sales teams to get under the customers' skin, understand their priorities, and hence, tailor the destination bid and venue sales proposal in such a way that they will have a much higher chance of success.

As well as asking open questions, it is vital to listen actively and carefully to the answers being given. People speak on average at 125 words per minute but the mind is capable of hearing and receiving up to 500 words a minute. It is very easy to get bored or distracted and to miss some key words unless listening very closely to what the customer is actually saying.

In an article entitled 'Going the extra mile' (*Meetings & Incentive Travel* magazine, June 2014), the results of research into enquiry handling undertaken by specialist research consultancy BDRC Continental (www.bdrc-continental.com) were published, as part of the company's VenueVerdict programme. They were

Table 5.5 Enquiry support information (Who? What? Where? Why? When? How?)

Date	How flexible can you be with your chosen date? If we were able to offer you a better deal on an alternative date, would you be interested?
The event	What is its purpose? How confidential is it? How frequently is it held? Who are the delegates? How much free time will they have?
Destination knowledge	When did the client last visit the destination? How many times have they been previously? What is their source of knowledge about the destination?
Location	How will the delegates be travelling to the destination? Where will they be travelling from? How important is location in the overall decision?
Other venues and destinations	Which other venues/destinations have you used previously? What was your experience like? Which other venues/destinations are you considering for this event? Why have you decided not to return to last year's venue/destination?
Decision	When will the decision be taken on the choice of destination? (This question will often also elicit information on who will be making the decision.) Who is the main organiser? When do you expect delegates to book?
Budget	What is the budget for the event? How will payment be made? To what extent is the price important to you in your choice of venue/destination?
Site visit	When can you visit us? How long can you stay? What are you looking to achieve from your visit? Who will be visiting?
Client's priorities	What is important to you about the destination/venue you select? How will the success of the event be judged?
Extra services	To what extent do your delegates appreciate a welcome pack or a gift from the area? Do any of your delegates have special needs? What other services can we offer you to support the success of your event?

based on an analysis of 4,145 sales enquiries made to 681 UK-based venues between April 2013 and March 2014. Sales performance was assessed on the percentage of venues that:

- made the package seem attractive;
- proposed a provisional booking;
- outlined the benefits of the venue;
- mentioned a specific request in the proposal;
- asked what the decision-influencer was; and
- followed up with a call.

The best-rated venues in the research were specialist conference centres, with 70 per cent rated as excellent for 'continued interest in enquiry'. High-end hotels did not fare so well, with only 42 per cent rated as excellent. Commenting on the findings, James Bland, client services director at BDRC Continental, said:

> There is a very real difference between a consultative event salesperson and someone who is an 'order taker'. Selling skills tend to be the measures that really discriminate between good and excellent performance. The true test of a salesperson's interest in your particular enquiry is not the first reaction they give, it's how well they maintain their level of interest throughout the call.

The advent of the internet and email has meant that customers increasingly supply their enquiry details in electronic form and do not necessarily have any direct interaction with another human being (see also chapter 3 – section on websites). There may not be the telephone conversation between the destination/venue sales team and the customer, which often signals the first steps in building a relationship between both parties. It is, therefore, crucial to design the electronic enquiry questionnaire (which, when completed by the customer, is then submitted to the destination/venue as a document known as an 'RFP' or 'request for proposal'; sometimes RFPs are preceded by 'RFIs', 'requests for information') in a way that adheres to the principles outlined above and elicits the maximum amount of information from the customer.

In order to increase their own efficiency and to respond to customer demands for information in an electronic format, many destination sales teams have invested in dedicated enquiry handling software which, to a large extent, automates enquiry handling systems while still enabling them to provide a personalised and tailored response to the client. One example of such software in the UK is known as 'Gratis', developed by venuedirectory.com. 'Gratis' was designed and developed specifically for UK conference agencies and convention bureaux and it has the following features:

- It is designed as the complete solution for conference enquiry management, automating time-consuming processes associated with enquiry handling, report generation and financial administration.
- It integrates information on a destination's venues, attractions and suppliers into the enquiry response process.
- It maintains entire client profiles including venue preferences and a history of their past events.
- It publishes venues on destinations' websites and provides a client portal for online enquiry submission and management.
- It is central to the national venue-finding service operated by the Meetings Industry Association (MIA). The web-based system distributes enquiries to venues and destinations, collates destination responses and aggregates information on the economic impact of enquiries for inclusion in national business tourism/business event statistics.

Submitting professional bids and sales proposals

Submitting a professional bid for a high-profile national or international convention can be a lengthy and costly undertaking and it may involve the bid team travelling to another country in order to present its bid to a selection panel or committee. It also requires considerable sensitivity to the situation of the bid's recipients, appreciating that it is possible to oversell or 'over-egg' a destination and provoke a negative response from those whom it was intended to impress. For example, it might not be appropriate to stress the luxuriousness of the facilities to be found in a bidding city from a developed country if many of the expected delegate attendees will be travelling from developing countries. A sensitivity to different cultural, political and economic situations when bidding for international conventions, in particular, is a vital requirement.

Destination level bids

Once the enquiry or RFP has been received, the destination sales team has to decide whether it can match the event requirements and, if so, what scale and type of response will be suitable. Some events are, of course, very large and have complex requirements but also detailed stipulations about the format and content of the bids to be submitted by those destinations interested in securing them. If the event is simply a small meeting with relatively straightforward needs, the destination may establish systems that direct the enquiry to appropriate venues in the destination for them to respond to the client, with minimal involvement by the destination sales team. For example, Convention Edinburgh, the business tourism arm of Marketing Edinburgh, implemented such a system following considerable research and a decision to benchmark their system against Boston's (USA) successful www.meetingpath.com. For enquiries below 150 delegates, the Edinburgh sales team, in the first instance, direct meeting planners and conference organisers to the web-based system (www.meetingedinburgh.com) to access information on all the members of Convention Edinburgh, as well as developing a shopping list of members selected, emailing RFPs directly to suppliers and maintaining a record of RFPs sent to suppliers. The website cost some £10,000 to develop and it came into operation in March 2004. By January 2015, it had generated enquiries with an economic value to the city in excess of £80 million.

Once it has been established that the enquiry is an appropriate one for the destination, the sales team begins the process of assembling its response or bid document. Computerised and web-based systems do allow bids to be compiled very speedily (i.e. within hours). Vienna Convention Bureau (www.vienna.convention.at) in Austria has the proud boast that it will respond to any enquiry, from any part of the world, within 24 hours, and the city's success in the international congress and conventions market in recent years is testimony to the Bureau's ability to respond quickly, effectively and professionally.

Yukon Convention Bureau (YCB) in Canada (www.ycb.ca) has developed a 'bid package' that has proved highly successful in its bids to host meetings in the territory. The package includes a customised written bid, either in hard copy (CD-ROM or printed) or e-file format, including a PowerPoint presentation of the proposal. YCB is also happy to provide Yukon products such as teas, smoked salmon, CDs and cosmetics and locally made art – all donated by YCB members. The package also contains personalised letters of invitation from the Premier and the Minister of Tourism, as well as photos and stories that reflect the nature of the recipient group.

Formal bid documents for major conferences and congresses are likely to include sections on:

- Letters of invitation (e.g. from the Mayor or other civic or government dignitary inviting and welcoming the convention)
- Letter/information from the host organisation (involved in co-ordinating the bid and in organising the event) – to cover also the rationale for the bid
- Details of convention bureau services and support

- Information on the host city covering location/climate/geography/culture/history/economy; its expertise and reputation as a conference destination; visitors' impressions of the city ideally including testimonials from satisfied conference organisers; entertainment/cuisine/arts and culture/recreation and shopping; useful information sources
- Access and transportation: how to reach the destination by air, road and rail
- Venues and accommodation: photos and data on the main congress centre; details of major hotels; a map showing the location of main venue(s) and hotels
- PCOs and references: details of professional conference organiser services
- Preliminary programme
- Sustainability and the environment, corporate social responsibility issues and event legacies
- Budget: quotations for the costs of different elements of the convention, to include details of financial support or subvention, as appropriate
- Tours and excursions: city tours and excursions; ideas for pre- and post-event activities

Rogers (2013) cites the factors and topics/issues to be covered by destinations in their proposals when bidding to host the annual conference of the International Congress and Convention Association (ICCA). These include:

- *Value for money* – ICCA perspective: how low is the 'package' price? What is the level of local sponsorship and reduced prices? This section should also state clearly any tax implications facing ICCA if the Congress is held in this country and recommendations for the efficient handling of such matters.
- *Value for money* – delegate perspective: what are the cost implications for delegates in addition to the package price, for example, airfare deals? Hotel rates? This section should include information regarding any visa costs facing delegates.
- *Accessibility* - international and local: provide objective data on access from worldwide, case studies of other large events hosted recently and transfer times on site and distance between key locations in host destination.
- *Capacity to attract delegates/destination appeal*: what is unique or new about the destination? Why is '2015' a suitable year to hold the event in your destination? Marketing ideas?
- *Level of support/evidence of teamwork (ICCA members, local industry, political)*: vital that the bid is not reliant on one individual or organisation and that there is strong support from ICCA members throughout the country. Successful bids inevitably have strong bidding teams.
- *Suitability/capacity/quality of meeting and exhibition venue(s)*: floor plans, capacities, track record, etc.
- *Quality and attractiveness of the social event venues*: give options and creative ideas that demonstrate the unique appeal of your destination.
- *Networking opportunities*: suitability of hotel(s) for this purpose, short transfer times and networking space available in venue.
- *ICCA development opportunities*: opportunities to recruit members in country/region, ideas for educating local meetings industry, whether ICCA has met in the country before and strategic changes that have occurred if proposing to return to a country where the Congress has been held previously.
- *Creativity*: each ICCA Congress is unique, with a strong local flavour. Creative ideas are needed each year to continuously improve the delegate experience and can relate to any aspect of the Congress including marketing, formats and networking.
- *Environmental and corporate social responsibility*: each destination should highlight the key environmental and/or CSR factors that they wish the ICCA Board of Directors to take into account. This could include any 'green venues' included in the programme, local initiatives that will help to make the Congress more sustainable, suggestions for including local CSR speakers in the educational programme, etc.

The ICCA Board has subsequently added two separate considerations:

- Priority should be given to three 'dimensions': financial viability, a match-up with ICCA's development objectives and support for delegates' business opportunities.
- All five regions of the world (Europe, North America, Latin America, Asia-Pacific and Africa/Middle East) should host the Congress in each 7-year time frame.

The use of conference ambassadors to assist with lobbying and bid presentation can enhance significantly the chances of a bid's success. In January 2015, Dubai recognised the efforts of 28 individuals and organisations to reinforce Dubai's position as a global hub for knowledge exchange. Its Al Safeer Congress Ambassadors Programme brought 10,000 delegates and over a dozen major international conferences to Dubai in 2014. In a similar vein, Meetings + Conventions Calgary (Canada) hosted its inaugural 'Calgary Champion' recognition event in January 2015, connecting over 35 leaders from a diverse array of key Calgary associations and industries. Further information on conference ambassadors is given in chapter 4.

Sarawak Convention Bureau (Malaysia) reported (GMI Portal, 17 February 2015) that, in 2014, it had surpassed its targeted bid wins with an 86 per cent bid success rate. With an average of 1.2 bid wins per week, it secured 60 conferences to be held between 2015 and 2017, recording an estimated 34 million Malaysian Ringgit (approximately US$8 million) in direct delegate expenditure. Among the major conventions secured in 2014 were:

- Asia for Animals International Conference (2015)
- Sixth International Research Symposium on Service Management (2015)
- 29th World Congress of the International Association for Suicide Prevention (2017)

Venue sales proposals or bids

A sales proposal or bid from a venue must 'sell' the reason why clients should choose this venue for their event. It is *not* purely an acknowledgement that the venue is available, giving details of costs.

The bid document is likely to be submitted by email with a link to the venue's website for additional information including a 'virtual' tour of the venue. The bid or sales proposal should include (inter alia):

- A short covering letter (accuracy of the client's contact details is crucial) to include:
  - Thanks and personal comment (if appropriate)
  - Summary of initial event requirements
  - Clarification of status of booking
  - Invitation to visit
  - Reassurance of venue's experience/flexibility/enthusiasm for the booking
  - Name of contact for further information/assistance
- The sales proposal (set out in an attractive, easy-to-read format):
  - Full client contact details
  - Event dates (arrival and departure)
  - Numbers of delegates (minimum and maximum numbers, with agreed timescales for notification)
  - General introduction personalised to the client and emphasising 'you' and 'your'
  - Benefits of the venue's location (with details of travel and communications, parking, special deals and the situation (i.e. rural/city centre) selling the style of the venue, with map
  - Event requirements in chronological order with an outline programme

- Meeting rooms/exhibition space, selling the benefits of individual facilities and giving an internal location plan and photo(s)
- Accommodation, with details of the venue's strengths and any special access requirements
- Catering requirements, with specific benefits and names of room(s)/restaurant(s) to be used
- Terms and conditions, including deposit requirements
- Draft contract/booking form
- Prices, tailored specifically to the event and giving rates 'up to' a specified maximum: listing items included before stating the price, clarifying whether inclusive of any applicable taxes
- Testimonials from previous clients
- Timetable for handling the event
- Experience of similar events over a period of 'x' years
- Any accreditations such as 'AIM' or ISO 9001
- A copy of the venue's promotional brochure
- Key reason why the client should choose this particular venue.

ACC Liverpool, Liverpool's major conference and exhibition centre, has launched (February 2015) an online toolkit aimed at assisting conference agencies and professional conference organisers during the pitch or bid process. Entitled 'Pitch Perfect', the toolkit contains essential venue and destination information useful for a broad range of scenarios: from a detailed high-level pitch to an internal briefing for management. The range of documents, which can be accessed through a secure login system via ACC Liverpool's client extranet, include venue layouts, access to an image library, CAD drawings and digital versions of destination information including hotels and supporting venues.

In an attempt to differentiate their bids and event support services from their competitors, The International Convention Centre (Birmingham, UK) and The Convention Centre Dublin (Ireland) have developed enhanced packages for their clients, branded as Host Service and Client Associate/Client Host respectively. These packages are detailed in Case Study 5.4.

Once the destination and/or venue sales team has submitted its bid or proposal, this is normally followed up after a few days, preferably by telephone, to check that the client has received the information safely and to clarify that it provides all the information needed. There may also be questions that arise from the contents of the bid and this follow-up sales call gives the client the chance to raise such questions.

Perhaps the key to remember in submitting bids and proposals is the need for such proposals to be tailored to the specific requirements of the client. It is less and less acceptable for a venue simply to offer a standard, off-the-shelf day delegate or residential conference 'package'. Offerings need to be customised and tailored to the specific needs of the client, a point strongly affirmed in research published in the 'UK Events Market Trends Survey 2014' where 92 per cent of UK meetings venues confirmed that their clients now expected customised meetings packages.

Managing site inspections and showrounds

The sales team will be hoping that their bid has convinced the client to shortlist their destination/venue for further consideration, which will often take the form of a site visit by the client to view the destination/venue at first hand and to assess how well it matches the requirements for their event.

Site visits are different from the familiarisation visits and 'educationals' described in chapter 4. Familiarisation visits and 'educationals' take place at an earlier stage in the promotional process. They are designed to stimulate an interest in the destination or venue, to develop an understanding and experience of what it can offer and to create a predisposition on the part of the client to consider the destination or venue seriously when placing future business. The site visit, on the other hand, takes place with a specific event in mind, the requirements and success criteria for which will be known. Therefore, the destination and venue sales teams can focus their efforts on converting the enquiry by giving the client the confidence and assurance that his event will be even more successful with them than with any of the other destinations/ venues on his shortlist.

One of the keys to a successful destination site visit (as opposed to venue site visit – see below) is cross-destination communications. All of the destination's suppliers (venues, hotels, attractions, transport providers, civic or municipality representatives, etc.) to whom the client will be introduced during the inspection visit must be properly briefed on the characteristics of the client's event and on its critical success factors. This will enable them to prepare their information accordingly and to sell their product or service in a way that is customised to the client's needs. It will also demonstrate to the client a cohesive and united approach by the destination, giving confidence that the destination will indeed deliver on the day. For major events, the briefing should take the form of a get-together of all the main supplier contacts in order to run through the detailed arrangements of the site inspection, to ensure that the appropriate co-ordination takes place and to minimise unnecessary duplication.

Other important aspects in the staging of good site inspections are:

- Good timekeeping in adhering to the schedule of the visit programme – this conveys a sense of professionalism.
- A welcome to the client from the general manager or senior representative of the facilities being visited, underlining the prestige of the event and the importance attached to winning his event for the destination. This senior representative will not necessarily be the one to undertake the showround for the client (this should be left to the sales staff who are more likely to have at their fingertips the answers to questions raised by the client), but their involvement at the outset of the visit is crucial in setting the right tone.
- A programme schedule that allows some flexibility. It may become apparent during the visit that the client has concerns or questions that need to be addressed by showing him some aspect of the destination that was not originally planned. Such flexibility will also show that the destination is listening actively to the client and is not making false assumptions about what his requirements are.

For venues, a site inspection and showround is the best opportunity to win new business, but it needs to be planned and prepared for with great attention to detail. Davidson and Hyde describe venue site visits as:

> *...the ultimate form of experiential marketing for venues. Experiential marketing tries to immerse consumers within the product by engaging as many other human sensations as possible.*

They suggest that:

> *The venue manager's prime objective should be not simply to show the venue to the visitor, but to attempt to get them to visualise how their event will work very well in the venue.*

In planning site visits with great attention to detail, venue sales managers must assess:

- The length of the visit and the appropriate level of hospitality to be offered, and whether this should include an overnight stay
- Which of the venue's staff should be introduced to the client and how will they be briefed for this
- How the meeting rooms should be laid out and best brought to life and how the client can be introduced to any rooms that may be in use for another event

- What is the most logical order for the showround, showing those parts of the venue relevant to the client's needs, with an appropriate layout plan
- Where is there a quiet area in which to sit down with the client, check and overcome any concerns, clarify the next steps and ask for the business!

In an article entitled 'Site inspections: what hotel sales managers wish event planners knew' (*International Meetings Review*, 8 September 2014), Dave Walsh, director of sales at the Omni Shoreham Hotel, Washington, DC, gave a number of tips for meeting planners to get the most from venue site visits. These tips also offer some useful insights for the venue sales team in how to assist their clients:

- *Take pictures. We have official photography but it won't look like the room when it's set up for a meeting. Just don't take pictures of the guests*
- *Ask to see more*
- *Dine with us. Spend more time and get to know us and try the hotel's cuisine*
- *Tell us it won't work sooner rather than later. We can either work through it or help you find another place*
- *Come back for a second inspection and re-walk the space.*

Dealing with objections

Davidson and Hyde offer some practical tips on dealing with objections raised by clients during a site visit. They recommend:

> *At regular intervals throughout the site inspection, it is advisable to solicit feedback from the visitor on what they think of the venue so far. It is also good policy to invite the visitor to openly express any objections they may have. This lowers the possibility of the prospect leaving with unexpressed concerns or mistaken impressions. By proactively soliciting feedback as the site inspection proceeds, the venue representative gets the opportunity to answer any points raised.*
>
> *Objections should be anticipated and dealt with convincingly. For example, if the visitor comments that there is a long walk from the entrance to the meeting room, or that attendees may experience problems of orientation between meeting rooms, this can be countered by a description of how the venue will strive to provide solutions . . . it can be suggested that the venue will provide extra directional signage or human signage, and that the event organiser's logo can be displayed on signage, to help boost their branding, for example.*

Once the site inspection is over, a follow-up sales call should be made to deal with any further queries, unless the client has made clear that the onus is now on him or her to make contact with the destination/venue sales team. Even if no sales call is to be made, a letter should be sent to the client thanking them for their time in visiting the destination/venue, expressing the hope that he/she has been impressed by what they have seen and reminding the client that the destination/venue is available to answer any further questions that might have arisen. By this time, a rapport and relationship should have been established with the client, one that has given the client a sense of trust and comfort in the destination and venue's ability to deliver a successful event for the client.

Negotiation skills

The principles of yield management (see earlier in this chapter) provide the context for a venue's sales activity and, especially, for its approach to negotiating with clients. A successful site visit will have persuaded the client that the destination and venue are suitable for his event but he may still wish to negotiate further to secure the best possible deal before he signs a contract with the chosen venue. From a venue perspective, there are a number of factors to be considered as part of this negotiation process, all of which link with the objectives of maximising occupancy and yield, and help in determining whether the venue wants the piece of business and, if so, at what rate. Such factors include:

- Decisions on the correct business mix for the venue, identifying the most appropriate conference market segments (see chapter 1) as well as other types of business if, for example, the venue is a hotel also seeking individual business travellers, leisure tourists, coach groups, etc.
- Dates – accepting business that allows the venue to maximise bookings on 365 days a year, including considerations such as whether the event is weekday or weekend or a combination of the two
- Timings of a meeting or conference – if, for example, the event does not start until the afternoon or evening, is there an opportunity to sell the meeting room(s) to another client for the first part of this day?
- Duration and seasonality
- Numbers of delegates, bedroom occupancy and overall value of the piece of business
- Numbers of meeting rooms required and any implications this may have for other potential business that might have to be refused
- Future opportunities for business from this client.

The venue sales team should not begin negotiating with a client without a detailed knowledge of the market. This market knowledge should include:

- Knowing the main sources of business for the venue
- Understanding market segmentation and the different types of conference clients with different types of events, objectives and budgets. What is the market position of the client?
- Keeping abreast of the current state of the conference market (strengths and weaknesses, trends) and of the general economy (local/national and increasingly international)
- Being aware of the venue's principal competitors
- Being fully informed of major events in the locality (sporting, cultural and business) that will have an impact on demand for bedrooms and possibly function rooms.

The venue needs to decide, prior to negotiation, what the ideal outcome would be. In addition, what a realistic outcome would be and, finally, what its fallback position should be.

Once negotiations start, it is important to establish at an early stage what the important criteria (i.e. critical factors in determining the success of an event) are for the client. What alternatives are available (both other venues being considered but also alternative dates and formats for the event to allow maximum flexibility) and whether the client has any concessions to offer and, if so, what he might be expecting in return. Furthermore, what concessions the venue can bring to the negotiating table that will cost little but will be perceived as valuable by the client.

Successful negotiation is about achieving a 'win/win' situation for both the client and the venue. This requires both parties to be willing to give in order to gain. A win/win situation is achieved by joint decision-making and discussion, and therefore:

- Meets the needs of both parties
- Leads to a decision that is not unacceptable to anyone
- Requires two-way communication
- Has an emphasis on flexibility
- Concentrates on objectives
- Maintains a long-term relationship

Critical mistakes leading to unsuccessful negotiations include:

- Inadequate preparation
- Ignoring the give/get principle
- Use of intimidating behaviour
- Impatience and loss of temper
- Talking too much and listening too little
- Arguing instead of influencing
- Ignoring conflict

Business retention

An important element of sales activity is the generation of further orders from a client. In the context of conferences and business events, it may not always be possible to bring a client's event back to your destination/venue because of circumstances beyond your control. For example, it may be the policy of the organisation to rotate its event around different locations and not to re-use the same destination/venue in subsequent years.

However, it is generally accepted that business retention (i.e. keeping existing clients) is much more cost-effective than constantly having to find and attract new customers. In this competitive age, it is crucial that destinations and venues devote resources to retaining their customers and encouraging them to return time after time.

One of the well-known, but nonetheless apposite, clichés within business is that 'you never get a second chance to make a first impression'. Destination and venue visitors and guests must be made to feel welcome from the moment of their arrival – indeed, with the wide availability of social media, such welcomes can extend to well before the guests' physical arrival and continue well after their departure (see examples of such social media applications in chapter 4). The warmth of this welcome and the professionalism of service delivery must be maintained to a high standard throughout an event.

An assessment of venue service factors was made as part of the 'British Meetings & Events Industry Survey 2014/15' research, based on interviews with over 500 buyers. The results are shown separately for associations and corporates in Figures 5.1 and 5.2. While there is a substantial element of consistency in the findings for both types of buyer, and clearly both share concerns about the (lack of) availability of free Wi-Fi in venues, it is noticeable that associations are more critical of the quality of bedrooms. This is perhaps indicative of the fact that association delegates/attendees are more likely to book their own accommodation than attendees at corporate events and they may be more likely to opt for accommodation at the budget end of the spectrum, especially if paying their own expenses to attend the event.

Vancouver Convention Centre, Canada, has taken its service delivery to clients very seriously and it has invested accordingly. Its achievements have won awards and its policies and practices are described in Case Study 5.5.

Another tool used to retain clients, especially by hotel groups, is what are known as loyalty programmes. These programmes provide incentives in the form of points or awards that can be saved and redeemed to pay, for example, for an upgraded bedroom on a future stay, a free overnight stay or VIP access to sporting events, as well as a range of other benefits. The principle is similar to that offered by airlines via their frequent flier programmes or by retailers and supermarkets through their reward cards.

An example of such a loyalty programme is that run by Starwood Hotels and Resorts Worldwide, known as SPG (Starwood Preferred Guest). Guests earn 'Starpoints' and can achieve 'elite' status by signing up to

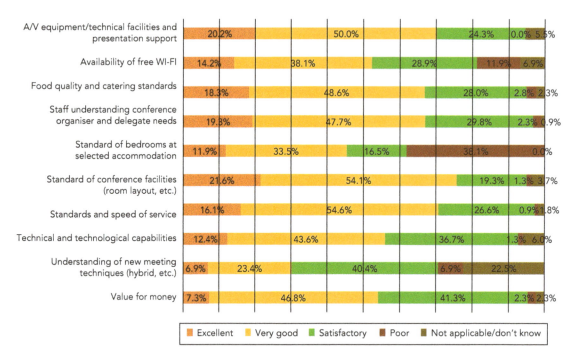

Figure 5.1 Ratings of venue service factors by association buyers

Source: 'The British Meetings & Events Industry Survey 2014/15' – www.meetpie.com/bmeis – reproduced with permission of CAT Publications Ltd.

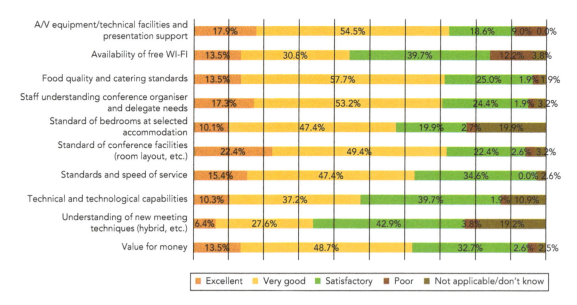

Figure 5.2 Ratings of venue service factors by corporate buyers

Source: 'The British Meetings & Events Industry Survey 2014/15' – www.meetpie.com/bmeis – reproduced with permission of CAT Publications Ltd.

SPG Pro, launched at the end of 2014. SPG Pro is designed to strengthen the original SPG programme. It offers meeting and travel professionals SPG elite status, upgrades and Starpoints for booking B2B events, but also weddings and family reunions, at Starwood's 1,100 hotels and resorts worldwide. It also allows any SPG member who books a group stay, event or corporate business meeting to earn Starpoints and elite status for the business they influence, whether or not they are a travel professional. Further information at www.spg.com/pro. Other examples of hotel loyalty programmes include the Hyatt Gold Passport, Hilton Honors and Marriott Rewards.

Maximising impact through business extenders

While launching successful bids for events is, of course, the principal *raison d'être* of the destination and venue sales team, it is not the only one. It is now recognised that it is also of paramount importance to maximise the economic benefits of the event for the destination, and revenue for the venue, by ensuring the highest possible number of delegates (and, where appropriate, accompanying individuals) and by encouraging the delegates to extend their stay through pre- or post-convention tours.

It can be very difficult for business visitors to change their return travel dates or organise extra time off work at the last minute, therefore, leisure extensions to business trips need to be planned in advance. This means that information on available options needs to be available well before the event is due to take place and actively circulated to the delegates.

Understandably, the priority for conference organisers and hosts is for the event to be successful, so their main concern is with the logistics of the conference itself. Nevertheless, most organisers also realise that selling the attractions of the destination can be an effective way of boosting attendance figures, particularly in the association conference market. Making conference organisers fully aware of the destination's attractions and leisure opportunities is, therefore, essential.

Davidson (2003) suggests that actions to be taken by destination sales teams to encourage business extenders and to maximise delegate attendance can include:

- The incorporation of information on local tours, attractions and events in familiarisation trips, bid documents and presentations to organising committees.
- Attendance at an association conference in the year prior to its being held in their destination to showcase the leisure opportunities on offer in the destination and the surrounding area. This usually entails having a stand with tourist literature in the reception area of the conference and/or being given the opportunity to sponsor a reception at the conference and say a few words of welcome on behalf of the destination for the following year's event.
- Offering conference and trade show organisers photographic material and tourism information to be included in their printed publicity material and on their websites.
- Providing bulk supplies of tourist literature to be sent out to delegates by the event organiser.
- Encouraging destination management companies to tailor tours, guest programmes and excursions to the interests of the particular delegate group.
- Suggesting to the conference organisers and meeting planners that they time their event to begin just after, or end just before, key cultural/sports events in the destination.
- Setting up discount schemes for business visitors by involving local suppliers such as restaurants, shops, car hire companies and attractions. For example, NYC & Company (the DMO for New York www.nycgo.com) – launched, in January 2015, its latest New York City Delegate Discount Pass, offering exclusive savings throughout the year at more than 70 restaurants, walking and bus tours, attractions and retailers. The Delegate Discount Pass, which is available to all attendees, meeting planners

and event staff, offers delegates the opportunity to experience all the city has to offer during their stay at an affordable price. To redeem offers, visitors must show a printed or mobile version of the Delegate Discount Pass. Marketing Edinburgh's Delegate Reward Card, launched in June 2014, provides discounts and 'value-adds' at over 90 of Edinburgh's popular bars, restaurants and retail outlets – within its first 6 months, the card had been used by 44 conferences and some 25,000 delegates (www.conventionedinburgh.com).

Davidson recommends that residential conference venues can drive leisure business through their corporate base and increase occupancy rates at weekends by:

- Offering business visitors, at the time of booking, weekend extensions at a special discount, lower than the conference rate, if attending an event as a delegate
- Offering business extenders complimentary 'add-ons' such as dinner
- Offering special discounts on leisure breaks for the employees of key corporate customers booking meetings in the venue, as an incentive
- Teaming up with local attractions to offer business guests special themed packages

Maximising the impact of a major event can also involve collaboration with adjacent destinations in order to provide the necessary bed stock and to give visitors knowledge of, and access to, attractions and experiences within the wider region, thus further increasing the enjoyment of their visit and encouraging them to extend their stay.

It is vital, therefore, that all stakeholders are made aware of the full value of this type of incremental spending by business visitors. That means taking care to measure the benefits of business visitors who extend their trip, return or bring guests, or any combination of these. Only when these indirect benefits are demonstrated will the significant contribution made by conventions and business events to national and local economies be fully recognised.

CASE STUDY 5.1   Singapore's Sales Incentives and Event Support Programmes

The first edition of this book included a case study on the 'Make It Singapore PLUS!' sales promotion campaign, developed and administered by the Singapore Exhibition and Convention Bureau™ (SECB), a division of the Singapore Tourist Board (STB). 'Make It Singapore PLUS!' was an extension of an earlier campaign, 'Make It Singapore', a S$15 million initiative from 2003 to 2004 designed to reinforce Singapore's reputation as a business hub and to attract more Meetings, Incentive Travel, Conventions and Exhibitions (MICE) events to Singapore.

'Make It Singapore PLUS' has subsequently been superseded by two complementary schemes:

- Business Events in Singapore (BEiS)
- Singapore MICE Advantage Programme (SMAP)

The aim of both schemes is to strengthen Singapore's business events global market share by providing additional leverage for those tasked with procuring more MICE events for the city-state.

Business Events in Singapore

The BEiS scheme, launched in 2012, seeks to 'encourage the business events industry to anchor and grow quality events as well as catalyse the innovation of new content' (STB website). BEiS provides customised support ranging from the selection of venues, introductions to leading government agencies and business partners, as well as publicity support. Funding support is also available upon the fulfilment of deliverables (see below). BEiS is open to all businesses/companies or associations in the MICE sector and proposed events should fall under one of the following categories:

- Meetings
- Incentive travel
- Corporate activities
- Association conventions
- Trade conferences
- Exhibitions

Successful applicants will receive funding support of up to 70 per cent of qualifying costs, subject to the scope of the project and the SECB's evaluation of the merits of the project. Qualifying costs include costs related to third party professionals (e.g. professional conference organisers, event management agencies), content development, marketing and bidding activities. The evaluation of proposed events will be based on the following factors:

- Content – for example, the extent to which the event brings in key content relevant to Singapore's strategic industry clusters
- Brand – for example, the extent to which the event has the potential to make an impact in Singapore
- Delegate profile (i.e. numbers of foreign visitors/delegates)

Applicants (i.e. event organisers from MICE companies, businesses and associations) are advised to discuss the proposed project with the officer-in-charge at the SECB prior to making a formal application – formal applications must be made on prescribed application forms and submitted to the SECB.

Singapore MICE Advantage Programme

Launched in October 2013, SMAP is a new partnership jointly developed by the Changi Airport Group, Singapore Airlines and Singapore Exhibition and Convention Bureau™. SMAP offers enhanced event management services for event organisers and overseas MICE visitors and it is intended to complement the BEiS incentive scheme.

SMAP can help event organisers, through a variety of services and benefits, to achieve cost savings and to smooth the event planning processes and operations. MICE delegates travelling to Singapore to attend SMAP-supported events can also enjoy exclusive airline and airport benefits. Table 5.6 sets out the eligibility criteria and benefits.

Additional benefits

In addition, all groups that fulfil the minimum number of foreign trade visitors will enjoy the following benefits:

- Changi Dollar Value vouchers for shopping and dining at Singapore Changi Airport for participants or discounts on advertising spaces across all terminals at Singapore Changi Airport
- A selection of exceptional value fares to Singapore on Singapore Airlines for participants, from over 60 destinations around the world

Table 5.6 Singapore MICE Advantage Programme eligibility criteria and benefits

Eligibility criteria	Benefits
Meetings and incentives A minimum of 100 foreign participants	• Financial grants of up to 50 per cent of qualifying costs* • Up to two complimentary Economy Class tickets on Singapore Airlines, subject to minimum expenditure on airfare • Additional check-in baggage of 10 kg across all classes of travel for participants • A warm Singapore Airlines welcome with a special on-board announcement, exclusively for groups of more than 50 people
Association-based conventions A minimum of 1,000 foreign participants	• Financial grants of up to 30 per cent of qualifying costs* • Up to five complimentary Economy Class tickets on Singapore Airlines, subject to minimum expenditure on airfare • Exceptional value fares on Singapore Airlines and hotel accommodation in Singapore for site inspections • Preferential rates with Singapore Airlines Cargo for safe delivery of bulky, sensitive or fragile cargo • Additional check-in baggage allowance of 10 kg across all classes of travel
First exhibition in Singapore A minimum of 2,000 foreign trade visitors *Anchored exhibition in Singapore* A minimum of 500 incremental foreign trade visitors from the previous exhibition	• Financial grants of up to 30 per cent of qualifying costs* • Up to five complimentary Economy Class tickets on Singapore Airlines, subject to minimum expenditure on airfare • Exceptional value fares on Singapore Airlines and hotel accommodation in Singapore for site inspections • Complimentary advertising spaces on SilverKris, Singapore Airlines' inflight magazine and/or KrisWorld, Singapore Airlines' inflight entertainment system
First trade conference in Singapore A minimum of 500 foreign trade visitors *Anchored trade conference in Singapore* A minimum of 100 foreign trade visitors	• Financial grants of up to 30 per cent of qualifying costs* • Up to five complimentary Economy Class tickets on Singapore Airlines, subject to minimum expenditure on airfare • Exceptional value fares on Singapore Airlines and hotel accommodation in Singapore for site inspections • Complimentary advertising spaces on SilverKris, Singapore Airlines' inflight magazine and/or KrisWorld, Singapore Airlines' inflight entertainment system

*Qualifying costs include fees relating to content development, marketing, experience development and professional services engaged

- Special rates on Singapore Stopover Business and Singapore Stopover Holiday packages for participants
- Complimentary welcome desk at Singapore Changi Airport for organisers to greet their participants on arrival
- Suggestions on social activities, such as Singapore city tours
- Recommendations on social and MICE venues
- Introductions to relevant agencies and suppliers for event facilitation
- Visa facilities for participants
- Complimentary Singapore maps and brochures.

One event that will benefit from the SMAP programme is the 2017 Pacific Rim International Conference on Lasers and Electro-Optics (CLEO), expected to attract some 900 delegates over a 5-day period. The conference selection committee chose Singapore in preference to several other Asian cities that were bidding for the event, being won over by the SMAP offerings, which address some of the issues commonly faced by meeting attendees.

In the period to March 2015, 64 applications had been received for assistance under SMAP, and 11 events had been staged with SMAP support.

Further information on BEiS and SMAP is available at www.mice.yoursingapore.com. See also section on 'Subvention and bid support practices' in chapter 6.

CASE STUDY 5.2   Using a venue representation service: Paje and The Jockey Club

Paje is a UK-based consultancy specialising in providing sales-related services to venues. Those services include sales training and mystery shopping, but venue representation is also one of Paje's most valuable services. Their slogan, 'Representation – acting as an extension of your sales force. . .' accurately describes how they can add value by bringing extra business to the venues that are their clients.

Paje's expertise in the sales field is based upon the collective years of experience of the team in pre-opening, launching and positioning a vast selection of hotels and venues in the UK and Europe.

An example of the work they do is the 3-year partnership they had with the 15 Jockey Club Venues (www.jockeyclubracecourses.com/jockey-club-venues) in the UK. The Jockey Club Venues are located on famous racecourses, including the highly renowned Cheltenham, Aintree, Sandown Park and Epsom Downs. Altogether, The Jockey Club offers 81 large event spaces and conference rooms plus over 250 small meeting or syndicate spaces.

One of the services offered to The Jockey Club Venues was an entry on Paje's website, as follows:

15 Unique and Iconic Event Spaces - Introducing the Jockey Club Venues

Jockey Club Venues provide the ideal location for your business event, in some of the most beautiful surroundings in the UK.

The venues provide the right space for your training, meetings and conference needs, with an abundance of natural daylight and flexibility of 30,000m2 of inside space. From a Board Room or intimate Training Room to a grand space for a new brand or product launch, they have certainly got all the right spaces in the right places.

With racing only taking place on about 30 days a year at most of the venues - they have lots of opportunity to host your event. Offering a total of 82,000 free car parking spaces and easy access - over three quarters of the UK population live within 30 minutes' drive of one of our racecourse venues. Overnight accommodation at nearby hotels can be easily arranged as part of your package.

The benefits of choosing a Jockey Club Venue for your business event include;

- *14 inspiring and memorable locations across the UK*
- *Venues offer conference rooms for up to 2000 delegates featuring the latest in communications technology and internet access*
- *Reassurance and transparency - no hidden costs*
- *Flexible space - whatever your needs*

Furthermore, the other representation services provided by Paje to The Jockey Club Venues included:

- Regularly visiting over 100 key booking agencies and event management companies
- Completing over 100 telesales calls on average per month
- Attending many of the major UK exhibitions including Confex, The Meetings Show and Square Meal
- Launching Jockey Club Venues to the conference and event market
- Completing bi-monthly e-shots to a qualified agency database of over 700+ key agencies in the UK and completing follow up calls.
- Recommending and assisting with Jockey Club Venues Conference and Events brochures and promotions

As evidence of The Jockey Club Venues' return on investment - Paje tracked £4 million worth of conference and event enquiries for the 15 venues over the 3-year period

(*Source*: Paje Consultancy Ltd).

CASE STUDY 5.3   UniSpace Sunderland's value-added packages

UniSpace Sunderland

UniSpace Sunderland is the commercial events arm of the University of Sunderland, located in north-east England. Launched as a dedicated venue brand in 2012, UniSpace has gone from strength to strength, increasing events bookings and establishing a strong reputation in the events sector for creative packages designed to add value to its core events services. This case study (written by Sharon Olver, Business Development Manager for Events and Commercial at UniSpace Sunderland and Academic Tutor in Hospitality and Events) provides details of UniSpace's sales and marketing strategy of 'Adding Value' and outlines how this has increased business opportunities for the University of Sunderland.

The launch

When UniSpace launched as a dedicated brand to the national conference and events market at the 'International Confex 2012' exhibition, it was a significant departure for the University of Sunderland. We wanted to ensure that we hit the market with a bang and so invested time up front devising a strategy that would help us stand out from the crowd when it comes to venues and academic venues in particular.

With buyers spoilt for choice, we wanted to develop a compelling story for the UniSpace brand. Having evaluated our strengths and differentiators, we realised that the creativity symbolised by our unique National Glass Centre and arts and ceramics departments gave us the spark to develop other creative initiatives for events packages. Our focus was on 'Adding Value', ensuring organisers who brought their events to our venues were offered a range of creative packages for team building, incentives and other initiatives that would offer options to enrich their experience. In the words of a famous retail chain, 'every little helps'.

Strategy

With our overall strategy agreed, we worked closely with the university faculty to explore options to package up creative experiences for delegates and to add new services that would enhance an event experience. We also examined areas of core subject expertise at the university and devised initiatives to target these sectors, working closely with our faculty members to identify appropriate target organisations that might look to bring their event to UniSpace.

Tactics and initiatives

When we first launched, we opted to leverage our presence at 'International Confex 2012' with a PR campaign around the show and our launch to the national market. With our initial launch press release, Twitter launch, media interviews and announcement at the event of contract wins, our first push to the market certainly helped to put UniSpace on the map.

In order to maintain momentum, we continued with a trade media PR programme as a key channel to help build our brand and key positioning. We also leveraged digital marketing techniques and ensured a partnership approach with the regional convention bureau, NewcastleGateshead Initiative (NGI), and co-operated with other suppliers in the Sunderland region to pool resources and market 'Destination Sunderland' within the region at trade shows and at bespoke NGI events such as a London showcase. We developed a vibrancy initiative with seven other key organisations and NGI to collectively develop specific destination management literature for the Sunderland region.

In terms of large-scale events, joint bidding with the NGI convention bureau and other Sunderland venues has been a key aspect of driving conference business for UniSpace. In terms of the association sector, we have also worked closely with the university to develop our ambassador programme, supported by NGI and other regional business partners, which has helped to identify appropriate target conferences that the university would be well positioned to host. We have taken this a step further, linking the university core areas of expertise with identified inward investment priority sectors, such as pharma, bio-sciences, media, early years and special needs education.

Product development

The National Glass Centre is an iconic building, national visitor attraction and fully equipped hot glass blowing studio. Developing incentive packages for the corporate market around this facility was a logical first step. We looked at seasonal themed activities, such as making your own Christmas bauble, in addition to demonstrations and workshops for corporate groups.

Following the success of these packages, we looked further into added value packages and found that our media school, in particular, provided a great source of inspiration. The university benefits from a fully equipped TV and radio recording studio and cinema, lending itself to a range of team building options. We worked with faculty to develop Archers' style radio show incentive packages, TV production options and more.

In addition to the indoor opportunities for team building packages, UniSpace benefits from a wealth of outdoor space and range of sporting facilities. Again, working with faculty, we looked at options to incorporate more physical activities, such as the indoor climbing wall.

Internal communications

We are an academic institution first and foremost and must not lose sight of this when developing our conference and events business. Ultimately, our aim is to support the university with a commercial arm, but the academic priorities of the university are the first consideration. With this in mind, we developed an internal communications programme to ensure awareness of UniSpace and the benefits it brings to the university as a whole. We developed an internal brochure communicating the purpose of UniSpace and outlining some of the achievements so that we could work more closely with the university in joint activities. This was vital to laying the groundwork for our external strategy as it ensured support for our initiatives and creative ideas.

The team at UniSpace continues to work closely with the university faculty and is looking to develop opportunities for and with our students, leveraging relationships with sponsors, external clients and also looking at ways we may be able to commercialise internal events.

Added value options

In addition to packaged activities, we looked at how we could maximise certain features of our venue to offer a unique aspect to an event. For example, we leveraged the art gallery within the National Glass Centre to offer an inspiring space for drinks receptions. We are even able to access many of the glass and ceramics artists to support an event by talking to delegates about their works on display. Our Moot Court room, effectively a mock courtroom, could also be used either for team building or to lend a more serious setting for events according to what the organiser was looking for. It was all about offering variety and something different.

In terms of offering add-on services, we developed our Conference Crèche in order to enable event organisers to encourage parents to attend events. The crèche is managed by a fully accredited service and set up in conjunction with our on-site nursery to provide peace of mind to parents and carers.

The results

UniSpace is now a well-established brand and our meetings and events business continues to grow. There was a 76 per cent rise in the number of day meetings held in the year up to July 2014, compared with the financial year 2012/13. The increase follows the development of group experience packages.

In 2014, we saw demand for our added value services grow significantly, with the majority of day meetings also booking an additional package. We have expanded our team and seen events business grow significantly, particularly with a regional focus.

The future

In 2013, a £2.3m refurbishment of the National Glass Centre was completed and we are opening an on-site hotel in early 2015 to complement our existing accommodation. We anticipate continued development of our value-added services and a further strengthening of our ties with the university faculty to develop new opportunities. Further information: http://www.unispacesunderland.com.

CASE STUDY 5.4   The International Convention Centre, Birmingham and The Convention Centre Dublin's 'Host Service' and 'Client Associate/ Client Host' programmes

The Convention Centre Dublin (CCD) receives management services from the International Convention Centre, Birmingham (ICC), which operates under the overall control of the NEC Group. Both venues have introduced innovative approaches to welcoming event attendees through their Host service and adding value for their clients via their Client Associate/Client Host. Both services are designed to offer an enhanced experience for clients and delegates and, in part, to create a point of difference with other similar venues.

Host Service

The Host Service was first launched at The Convention Centre Dublin in 2010 and subsequently introduced at the ICC Birmingham. While both venues still have uniformed security staff, the objective of the Host Service is to provide dedicated venue staff for major events whose role is to make delegates and attendees feel genuinely welcome and to ensure that they get the most from their visit. Hosts are recruited for their good social skills and their focus is to meet and greet delegates, while offering information about the venue and the wider destination, so good local knowledge is important too. The ICC Birmingham has a pool of approximately 30 trained hosts and The Convention Centre Dublin approximately 40. The venue management team decides the number of hosts to be allocated to each event, based on the event requirements and delegate numbers: it also takes account of delegate movement around the venues.

Client Associate and Client Host

The ICC Birmingham launched a Client Associate service that was extended to The Convention Centre Dublin in 2012, where it is branded Client Host service. Both services give VIP clients a dedicated personal assistant, who is also a uniformed chauffeur, for the duration of their event. Whether it is collecting VIP delegates from the airport or train station, booking restaurants, photocopying, shopping or running errands, Client Associates/Hosts can take on all of these time-consuming but important tasks, allowing clients (i.e. the event organisers) to focus on the main event. The service has had great feedback and it truly enhances the client experience at both venues. Nicki Bird, NetApp Insight 2012, commented:

> Having a Client Host is not something we've come across before, but it's certainly a great value to The CCD package.

Figure 5.3 shows Client Hosts with limousine outside The Convention Centre Dublin.

Figure 5.3 Client hosts and limousine in Dublin

Source: The Convention Centre Dublin.

CASE STUDY 5.5   Vancouver Convention Centre's Service Excellence Programme

This case study was compiled by Jinny Wu, Communications Manager, Vancouver Convention Centre.

Background

The Vancouver Convention Centre opened its West building expansion – an architectural masterpiece located on the downtown waterfront – in April 2009, tripling its original capacity. With a new state-of-the-art facility, Vancouver moved on to the global stage as a major convention destination.

Launching a new, unique expansion that effectively re-defined the facility's brand comes with new opportunities and challenges from a service perspective. In particular, the Vancouver Convention Centre needed to ensure that service levels do not decline amidst massive growth and change. The organisation saw this as the ideal opportunity to elevate and re-define its service reputation by creating a service programme that would be embraced by all staff and differentiate the organisation from other venues.

The Convention Centre's Service Excellence Programme was first launched in April 2009 to coincide with the unveiling of the West building, with an aim to ensure that every guest is inspired by the visual experience of the brick and mortar and the human experience of exceptional service.

The Programme is a unique platform that encompasses the organisation's Purpose, Values and Guest Service Promises and it is characterised by distinctive service practices and standards. The consistent execution of these service practices is intended to strengthen the trust guests have in the Vancouver Convention Centre, enhance the organisation's image and reputation as a leading convention venue in the world and enable clients to have more successful events.

Essentially, it is a framework that enables the Convention Centre to deliver its service difference – unparalleled, seamless service for guests at every touch point. The Programme encompasses every area of operation at the Convention Centre, every department, partner supplier and employee.

The Service Excellence Programme

The Service Excellence Programme is multi-faceted and cross-functional ensuring that all employees at the Vancouver Convention Centre are prepared to provide outstanding service to clients, guests and visitors. Key components of the Programme include:

1. *Service excellence training.* All staff undergo service excellence training delivered by the manager of guest experience. All employees of the Convention Centre's official and exclusive suppliers also undergo this training to ensure seamless service for guests.

2. *Daily service line-up meetings.* To maintain the momentum and to embed the Service Excellence Programme in organisational culture, daily service line-up meetings are conducted by every department and supplier group, facility-wide.

3. *Guest service ambassador team.* A dedicated team of guest service ambassadors is the first point of contact for any guest visiting the facility. They provide a warm greeting to all guests, as well as assistance, direction and information about the Centre. They are also destination ambassadors, providing direction and general information about Vancouver, local attractions, hotels and restaurants.

Each member takes a proactive service approach, identifying and addressing guests' needs immediately, and also resolving issues quickly and liaising with other departments when necessary.

Public tour programme

The Vancouver Convention Centre offers a popular tour programme for visitors and guests, launched when the West building first opened. By engaging the public in the story of our facility and the purpose and nature of the events we host, we are demonstrating to a broader audience the significant value of meetings and the important role they play in our local economy.

Outcomes

Since launching the Service Excellence Programme in 2009, the initiative has shown great success.

The Service Excellence Programme has made a significant impact on client satisfaction and the Vancouver Convention Centre's reputation in the global marketplace. The most notable measurement of the Programme's success is based on the results of its online Client Feedback Survey. Results for the Customer Loyalty Index have consistently been very high since launching the Programme. The Convention Centre's strong service reputation has also played a role in successfully attracting repeat business. Many significant conventions hosted in the first few years since opening the West building have already re-booked for future years.

In addition to delivering a great level of satisfaction to clients and delegates, the Service Excellence Programme has been instrumental in building organisational culture and employee engagement. An Employee Engagement Survey showed that employees are overwhelmingly supportive of the Vancouver Convention Centre's commitment to its purpose and goals, and identify with its reputation for customer service – which is a key driver of employee engagement.

The Service Excellence Programme was recognised with the International Association of Convention Centres' Innovation Award in 2011. To ensure the continued success and relevance of the Programme, the Vancouver Convention Centre evaluated and revitalised the programme in 2013 and rebranded it as 'Be the Difference'. Further information: www.vancouverconvention centre.com.

SUMMARY

This chapter has examined the key elements that must be taken into account when a sales strategy is being devised. Designing an effective sales strategy demands an understanding of the complex set of variables that constitutes any organisation's approach to selling its products. If undertaken successfully, the sales strategy can be the blueprint for the organisation's sustainability and growth.

As stated at the beginning of this chapter, sales should be the culmination of the entire marketing process. To be successful, it must be fully integrated within the overall marketing communications mix, in such a way that it is supported by advertising and public relations that create awareness of the product and the desire to buy it; and it must be fully co-ordinated with sales promotions that motivate customers to purchase.

Above all, the selling function must be undertaken by men and women who are motivated by a genuine desire to serve the customer and provide them with real value for the money they are spending. The conference and convention marketplace is crowded and competitive, and sales people who can deliver high levels of service and value-for-money to customers have the potential to bring a distinct advantage to the venues and destinations that employ them.

Destination selling is a challenging but exciting and stimulating occupation. It demands skills that are generic to the selling of any product or service; nevertheless, it requires additional skills, expertise and information resources, commensurate with the task of selling and promoting a living, changing and constantly evolving entity: a place. Destination selling is a crucial component in place marketing activity, essential for the conversion of a convention organiser's interest in a destination into confirmed business for the destination. Similarly, venue sales activity calls for a high level of skill and a broad knowledge base. Destination and venue selling both require a planned, strategic approach, one that will be implemented by marketing and sales teams whose professionalism should infuse their enquiry handling, event bidding and overall customer relationship management in order to be successful in an extremely competitive marketplace. It will follow through into their strategies for maximising the economic benefits and revenue generation of conventions, meetings and other business events.

REVIEW AND DISCUSSION QUESTIONS

• You have been asked to develop a destination database of the kind outlined in the section on 'Destination expertise'. Describe the steps you would take, the information sources you would use (i.e. how and where you will find the information needed) and the data access and retrieval systems required in order to store the requisite information and data on: (i) venues; (ii) transport, communications and accessibility; and (iii) local economy and infrastructure.

• 'Destination selling is very different from selling a car or a washing machine'. Discuss the merits and accuracy of this statement, giving full reasons for the conclusions you draw.

• Your destination has been shortlisted for consideration as the host destination of the 2020 congress of the International Association of Chiropodists and Podiatrists (fictitious as far as is known). The congress is held every 2 years and typically attracts around 1,000 delegates from around the world, half of whom bring with them partners/accompanying individuals. How would you approach the compilation, content and presentation of your bid? One of the underlying objectives of the bid is to maximise the economic impact of the event for your destination – outline separately how your bid, if successful, will meet this objective.

• Compare and contrast the sales team structures for

  - a major purpose-built convention centre; and

  - a hotel venue which is part of a national or international chain.

• What are the key target markets for each? What kind of performance measures and incentives are in place? How effective are they?

REFERENCES

Berkowitz, E., F. Crane, R. Kerin, S. Hartley and W. Rudelius (2003) *Marketing*, New York: McGraw-Hill.

Burke, J. and B. Resnick (2000) *Marketing and Selling the Travel Product*, Independence: Delmar Thomson Learning.

Davidson, R. (2003) *Making the Most of our Business Visitors*, London: Business Tourism Partnership, published online at www.businesstourismpartnership.com (accessed 31 July 2015).

Davidson, R. and A. Hyde (2014) *Winning Meetings and Events for your Venue*, Oxford: Goodfellow Publishers.

Gartrell, R. B. (1994) *Destination Marketing for Convention and Visitor Bureaux*, Dubuque: Kendall Hunt Publishing.

Harrill, R. (2005) *Fundamentals of Destination Management and Marketing*, Educational Institute of the American Hotel and Motel Association.

Holloway, J. C. (2004) *Marketing for Tourism*, Upper Saddle River: Prentice Hall.

Kotler, P., J. Bowen and J. Makens (2003) *Marketing for Hospitality and Tourism*, Upper Saddle River: Prentice Hall.

McCabe, V., B. Poole, P. Weeks and N. Leiper (2000) *The Business and Management of Conventions*, Chichester: Wiley.

Middleton, V. (2001) *Marketing in Travel and Tourism*, Oxford: Butterworth-Heinemann.

Price, D. and J. Ilvento (1999) *License to Sell*, West Springfield: Applied Business Communications, Inc.

Rogers, T. (2013) *Conferences and Conventions: A Global Industry*, 3rd edn, London: Routledge.

Saxe, R. and B. A. Weitz (1982), 'The SOCO scale: a measure of the customer orientation of salespeople', *Journal of Marketing Research*, 19(3): 343–51.

Chapter **6**

The marketing environment for destination marketing organisations

Chapter overview

This chapter looks at a number of key issues and current trends affecting the marketing of conference and convention destinations.

The chapter covers:

- Destination marketing or destination management?
- Content marketing for destinations
- Alignment of destination event bidding strategies with local economy strengths
- Subvention and bid support practices
- Product development and investment
- Sustainability and the environment for destinations

It includes case studies on:

- Destination management in Glasgow, Scotland
- *'Germany. Expertise.'* brochure
- Sustainable destination best practice: Tampere, Finland

On completion of this chapter, you should be able to:

- discuss the evolving role of destination marketing organisations and their responsibilities for destination marketing and destination management;
- understand the new opportunities for destination marketing using the principles and practice of content marketing;
- discuss the changing approaches to event bidding, especially the need to align bidding strategies with the core strengths and characteristics of a destination's own economy, coupled with the important role played by subvention in supporting event bids;
- appreciate the need for, and the strategies and issues associated with, investments in a destination's conference and convention 'product'; and
- describe the sustainable policies and practices being adopted by destinations which are seeking to enhance their 'green' credentials.

Introduction

While it may be true to say that the broad principles of marketing remain more or less constant, apart from fine-tuning and some changes given to the priorities attached to them, it is certainly the case that their practical application is extremely dynamic. It has to take account of the impacts of new legislation; for example, those affecting customer relationship management and client database development. It must be sensitive and respond effectively to a plethora of political, social, environmental and technological developments. And, of course, it must highlight innovations and enhancements to the product or service which is the focus of the marketing activity.

Some of these factors may be less critical if the 'product' to be marketed is a washing machine, a retail outlet or the latest home insurance package, for example, where the product is clearly defined and relatively static. Yet they are all extremely pertinent when it comes to the marketing of a destination, a living and continuously changing entity. There are many issues, challenges and opportunities confronting those tasked with the promotion of a destination in the conference and business events sector, most of which have a universal resonance. No matter whether the destination is in the northern or southern hemisphere, or in a developed or newly developing country, the same types of issues apply and must be understood and addressed.

Furthermore, there is a sense in which such issues gain further importance simply because of the growing number of conference destinations joining the market. There are now approximately 200 countries worldwide competing for their share of conventions and business events and new destinations are forcing their way up the rankings of the most successful countries and cities. Statistics published by the Union of International Associations and the International Congress and Convention Association (ICCA) (see chapter 9) clearly reveal the emergence of successful new destinations, such as Busan, Shanghai and São Paulo, a trend that seems likely to continue for some years to come.

This chapter, therefore, examines a number of the most important contemporary issues and trends confronting destinations that are marketing themselves to attract conferences, as well as issues and trends that affect them no matter whether they are established destinations or one of the more recent arrivals on the destination scene. Chapter 7 will then analyse the current marketing environment for conference venues.

Destination marketing or destination management?

One of the growing roles for convention bureaux and destination marketing organisations (DMOs) is an increased responsibility for destination development and management. While there is still an important focus on destination promotion and on selling the destination product, this in itself is no longer sufficient. DMOs need to take a role in defining what the product is and what it will become, a role not only in marketing but also in managing the destination and in helping to develop new destination products and features to ensure that the destination is offering what the consumer needs. The DMO has to take to the marketplace what the client will want to buy, taking the destination's personality and products on to the national or world stage.

In the UK during the 1960s, 1970s and 1980s, many of the leading conference destinations were seaside resorts, often with convention halls and facilities built during the heyday of the Victorian era in the nineteenth century. During the 1990s and the early years of the twenty-first century, a number of these destinations had to withdraw from the conference market because they had failed to attract investment in their destination's hotels, attractions and general infrastructure to make sure that it kept pace with trends in the market and the changing demands and higher expectations of the consumer. They had lost substantial market share because of a failure to manage their destination and keep abreast of the market. Their destination product was no longer what the customer wanted to buy.

Destination management is not so much about managing the physical product (i.e. the venues, hotels, transport systems, visitor attractions, etc.). In fact, managing these is rarely the responsibility of the DMO. However, destination management is very much to do with building collaboration and partnerships across the destination (see also chapter 8). It can include developing the education and training of the destination's workforce and equipping them with the skills and knowledge needed to service the business events visitor effectively and professionally. Destination management also has an important part to play in creating understanding and recognition across the community for the economic importance of the convention and business events sector. It can entail looking at local planning regulations to ensure that they facilitate rather than hinder appropriate product investment, as well as proactively approaching potential investors in order to stimulate and attract new investments.

Management of the destination also means protecting the product and developing sustainable policies that balance visitor experiences with the need to minimise damage to the environment. Such policies often focus on transport issues; for example, the promotion of 'park and ride' schemes that encourage visitors and local residents to park in specially designated car parks on the outskirts of cities and use public transport to transfer into the city centre. Nevertheless, this could equally embrace policies to encourage major event venues to introduce waste management and recycling initiatives (see also the section on 'Sustainability and the environment for destinations' later in this chapter).

In Case Study 6.1, Scott Taylor, Chief Executive of Glasgow City Marketing Bureau, explains why destination management is an important part of his organisation's role and outlines several practical ways in which destination management has been implemented in Glasgow.

The role of a DMO can no longer solely be in the specific field of sales and marketing. That role now needs to be, more than ever before, in ensuring that the product is relevant, that new products are coming on-line, that the destination is being managed and anything that visitors say has spoiled their visitor experience is addressed and remedied. The initials DMO increasingly stand for 'destination management organisation' as much as 'destination marketing organisation'.

Content marketing for destinations

Content marketing is defined by the Content Marketing Institute as 'the marketing and business process for creating and distributing relevant and valuable content to attract, acquire and engage a clearly defined and understood target audience – with the objective of driving profitable customer action'. It suggests that a content marketing strategy 'can leverage all story channels (print, online, in-person, mobile, social, etc.), be employed at any and all stages of the buying process, from attention-oriented strategies to retention and loyalty strategies, and including multiple buying groups'. The Institute adds: 'Content marketing is comparable to what media companies do as their core business, except that in place of paid content or sponsorship as a measure of success, brands define success as ultimately selling more products or services'.

The Institute also provides some less formal definitions, viz.:

> *Content marketing is owning, as opposed to renting, media. It's a marketing process to attract and retain customers by consistently creating or curating content in order to change or enhance customer behaviour*

> *Content marketing is the process of developing and sharing relevant, valuable and engaging content to target audiences with the goal of acquiring new customers or increasing business from existing customers*

> *Your customers don't care about you, your products, your services . . . they care about themselves, their wants and their needs. Content marketing is about creating interesting information your customers are passionate about so they actually pay attention to you.*

In other words, content marketing is thinking about the target audience's needs first. More than anything, marketers want to engage with customers. One of the disadvantages of traditional advertising is the one-way aspect of the conversation: sales are almost your only measurement to see if engagement is really happening. With content marketing, you can have a two-way conversation with your customers and use varied tools to measure engagement. If you are not getting the results you want, you can quickly change tack without a major investment in printing, advertising and production costs.

Through the use of content marketing, an organisation can set itself apart from its competitors, developing trust and credibility with its online communities. It enables the company to deliver relevant content and build intimate relationships with customers before they even make contact and long after they buy.

Content marketing is pertinent to the marketing of business events destinations and the ways in which it is now being used by destinations was the subject of research undertaken by Marketing Challenges International, Inc. (MCintl). Findings from the research were published (September 2014) in a report entitled '*The Business of Storytelling*' and extracts are reproduced below with permission. While the report is especially pertinent to the corporate meetings market of North America, the principles and practices it outlines would seem to be applicable worldwide.

Although content marketing has become a buzzword in recent times, the concept itself is not new, harking back to the days when in-flight magazines first appeared in airlines. When the airline Pan Am introduced the world's first in-flight magazine, *Clipper*, it provided passengers with useful, entertaining content on destinations that encouraged more air travel without having to advertise Pan Am explicitly. The goals remain the same today: to produce content that resonates with your customer in order to build consumer trust, create community, and cultivate brand loyalty. But the means by which to produce, distribute and consume content in today's digital age have vastly expanded.

DMOs for the leisure travel industry have found much success in digital content marketing, but convention bureaux responsible for marketing destinations for meetings and events have been slow to utilise this marketing strategy, the report argues. It is also suggests that the convention bureau's role in conference and event planning is changing, however, particularly in the fragmented and fast-paced corporate meetings market of North America. The influx of digitally savvy, socially connected Millennials (Generation Y) into the workforce and the growth of the international knowledge economy have changed the way corporate meeting planners evaluate destinations. Convention bureaux can no longer rely solely on traditional marketing tactics to influence destination selection.

Content marketing provides an opportunity to reach this market, as many corporate planners seek ways to become more strategic in their professional roles. However, many convention bureaux continue to use digital only as a broadcasting and sales tool rather than an engagement tool.

One particular bureau, Tourisme Montréal (www.tourisme-montreal.org/), has set a leading example in content marketing with a dedicated meetings and conventions blog. The blog not only features prominent content about Montréal, but also provides planners with helpful tips, downloadable guides and thoughtful interviews and articles about the meetings industry in general. The investment in the blog has paid off in helping to position the city as an innovative destination with a dynamic community and it has enabled Montréal's sales team to start meaningful conversations with potential leads. See also the Tourisme Montréal case study in chapter 1 that provides more detailed information on the Montréal blog.

The most important element to remember about content marketing is that it is not about advertising or promotion, but rather about providing useful and relevant information that positions a brand or organisation as a credible resource. Over the long-term, good content can build authority, cultivate trust and brand loyalty. It provides a unique opportunity for convention bureaux to evolve their relationship with meeting planners from simply being a seller to that of a trusted partner.

The report provides strategies and tips on content creation and distribution to convention bureaux looking to build a successful content marketing strategy for meetings and events. It recommends:

* Keep content short, digestible and useful – consider content that does not require much time or energy from the reader. Things like how-to guides and tip sheets are great for planners to bookmark and revisit later when they need the information.

* Use visual media to create an impact – planners like visual content because it can be shared. High-resolution pictures or quick video clips (one to two minutes maximum) are great because they can be embedded in presentations to clients. It is also helpful to create and organise content by theme: culture, activities, nightlife, dining and so on.

* Showcase the destination's intellectual resources – identify pockets of industry expertise in the destination and then feature local business leaders and influencers to include their perspective on the city. The 'Big Influence' microsite and video series produced by Dallas Convention and Visitors Bureau (www.visitdallas.com) is quoted as an example of good practice.

* Become a thought leader in your industry – convention bureaux should use content to help promote their brand and reputation goals. For example, Montréal, in its efforts to be seen as a forward-thinking hub of creativity and innovation, frequently interviews meeting professionals and industry influencers on topics ranging from interactive meeting technology and mobile app platforms to managing Wi-Fi needs at events.

Content has little effect without a proper distribution strategy. The big difference between the content marketing of early inflight magazines and now is the means by which content is created and distributed. In today's digital age, content comes in a multitude of forms (blogs, video, podcasts, webinars, ebooks, etc.) and it is distributed through a variety of new channels, including social media, search engine optimisation (SEO), sponsored content, guest contributing, email newsletters and more. Furthermore, the speed at which we can now create and disseminate content is equally matched by how fast we consume and share it, to the point where a piece of content's 'virality' is now an important measure of its success.

When it comes to the corporate meetings market (and the principle could apply equally to national and international associations), good content marketing can position convention bureaux as part of the trusted 'experts' that planners turn to for advice. Corporate planners have indicated that it is often a challenge to be seen as a strategic member of their organisations by their own leadership – they are seen more as fulfilling an administrative or logistics function rather than as someone who can achieve the strategic goals of a company and show a return on investment. Destinations can build a trusted relationship with these planners with quality content that helps them to be better at their jobs. The goal is not just to sell your destination but also to position yourself as a thought leader. By using content to position themselves as helpful experts and thought leaders, convention bureaux can build a trusted, long-term relationship with these planners.

The Business of Storytelling report also includes case studies and practical tips and advice. To view the report or for additional information visit: www.mcintl.com or contact Michel Couturier at: mc@mcintl.com.

Alignment of destination event bidding strategies with local economy strengths

One of the emerging trends in recent years, and one almost certain to grow in the future, is the strategy being adopted by many cities to align their bidding for events with the strengths of their particular local economy. This is not just local industry and commerce (i.e. manufacturing and service sector businesses) but also the local 'knowledge economy', encompassing universities, research centres and institutes and so forth. Such an alignment strategy makes sense when destinations' marketing budgets are finite (and may be reducing). It is appropriate to target not only those events that they have the most chance of winning but also those that have synergies with their destination's own economy.

For example, London & Partners (London's destination marketing organisation) has now set its sights on growing events in four specific industries: technology, life sciences, the creative industries and financial/banking/business services. Through inward investment, it hopes to make London a world leader in these sectors – and an integral part of its strategy includes attracting high profile international events. London & Partners believes that, by focusing on the four sectors in which London is already strong, it will gain more support from the city to attract congresses and events from these sectors. It maintains that meetings and events can support foreign direct investment and growth in these sectors, have a take-up effect on study and create and support new jobs.

The Australian city of Melbourne is globally renowned as a knowledge, research and innovation capital, excelling in medicine, science and health research and development. A flourishing innovation community, Melbourne is home to 263 biotechnology companies, 13 major medical research institutions and ten teaching hospitals (as at 2014). The Biomedical Precinct is one of few such concentrations of research excellence worldwide. The city's standing as a leader in science and medicine – Melbourne has yielded four Nobel Prize winners in medicine and physiology – is one of the major factors in attracting scientific conferences and medical conventions. For associations seeking to attract delegates to these events, access to Melbourne's research institutes and academics provides exceptional keynote speakers, a strong education programme and knowledge exchange that leads to far-reaching legacies. In February 2012, Melbourne Convention Bureau launched a new positioning campaign: 'Melbourne IQ: The Intelligent Choice for Conventions', designed to highlight the intellectual capital within the destination and the city's strengths as a centre of excellence for research and development in the medical, science, technology, engineering and education industries. 'Melbourne IQ' continues to evolve to deliver a 'unique and compelling position' for Melbourne as a business events destination and it has contributed to Melbourne securing a number of major international congresses, including the World Congress of Cardiology 2014, the 20th International AIDS Conference 2014 and the World Cancer Congress (2014).

In north-east England, the NewcastleGateshead Initiative's Convention Bureau is aligning its business tourism strategy with its inward investment strategy and proactively seeking events that are in line with the destination's inward investment sector strengths: health and life sciences, creative and digital and marine and offshore technologies. Paul Szomoru, Head of Business Tourism for the NewcastleGateshead Initiative (NGI – www.NewcastleGateshead.com/Meet), comments (in a personal communication to the authors):

> *Driving this approach forward requires a lot of new, uncharted collaboration and partnership: inward investment teams in local authorities and in NGI, UK Trade & Investment (UKTI - a central government agency), the universities, Chamber of Commerce, Confederation of British Industry (CBI), the Federation of Small Businesses (FSB), often people and organisations who may never have been aware of (why would they be?) the economic benefits of business tourism and the work of NewcastleGateshead Convention Bureau to attract MICE business to the region. The key is to demonstrate how business tourism benefits their own agendas and goals.*

Embracing the challenges and opportunities of a move into a knowledge-based economy, Dubai claims to be the first city in the Gulf region to establish knowledge clusters, including Dubai Internet City, Dubai Media City and Knowledge Village. Dubai Internet City is the Middle East and North Africa's largest ICT hub and is one of the forerunners of Dubai's vision of transitioning into a knowledge-based economy. Dubai Knowledge Village is dedicated to human resource management and learning excellence, built with the aim of developing regional talent and establishing Dubai as a knowledge-based economy, while Dubai Media City is a thriving business community offering global and regional media companies a pro-business environment. This commitment to the knowledge economy, plus significant knowledge capital already accumulated, has been instrumental in Dubai winning the bid for Expo 2020, which is expected to attract 25 million visitors from around the world over 6 months, making Expo 2020 the biggest international event in World Expo history. Dubai Business Events, the city's convention bureau, is focusing its marketing on knowledge clusters and the knowledge economy, as evidenced by its publication of a special supplement entitled 'Dubai – A Global Knowledge Hub' in association with Intellectual Capitals (see below) and *Association Meetings International* magazine (November 2014).

The above examples show how individual cities, destinations and regions have adopted this new focus for their marketing and bidding strategies. However, it is also possible to detect similar approaches being developed at a national level. For example, South Africa has recognised the potential of business events to improve the country's knowledge economy, and by hosting international events where South Africa is a global leader, the country gets an opportunity to highlight its expertise to a high-level audience from across the world. This provides exceptional networking opportunities that could lead to further investment and growth in the field or industry in question. An illustration of this is the construction of the Square Kilometre Array Radio Telescope (SKA), which will be the biggest telescope in the world and one of the biggest scientific projects in history. The project, which is attracting the best scientists and engineers in the world to South Africa, is already giving rise to a number of workshops and conferences.

A special supplement on New Zealand, published by *Association Meetings International* magazine (www.meetpie.com) on behalf of Business Events New Zealand (www.businessevents.newzealand.com) (October 2014) suggests that 'holding a convention in New Zealand not only taps into trade and investment opportunities, but builds relationships with thought leaders for the transfer of knowledge and ongoing education. New Zealand's areas of expertise are helping to attract events business from these key sectors:

- Agribusiness
- Aviation
- Earth science
- Marine

- Health science
- High value foods
- Tourism

'Intellectual Capitals'

The 2014 IMEX America exhibition (October 2014, Las Vegas) saw the launch of a new online initiative for conference destinations known as 'Intellectual Capitals' (www.intellectualcapitals.com). Intellectual Capitals claims to be the 'definitive information resource highlighting the world's knowledge hubs . . . using digital, rich and print media to introduce meeting planners, institutions, investors, professionals and businesses to leading scientific and professional communities'. It has been established by the media company, CAT Publications, to enable destinations to attract inward investment, conferences, business events and talent by promoting their capacity and capability in scientific and business sectors. It is also designed to provide 'ammunition and assistance to existing ambassador programmes'.

Intellectual Capitals aims to supply all of the information needed to persuade the user to choose the destination for relocation, work, business event or investment, using online video and digital print modules on all iOS and Android platforms.

Comments from several international associations on the usefulness of Intellectual Capitals illustrate the new focus for associations and their key selection criteria when deciding upon the locations for their future congresses:

> *As we are an international association of innovation professionals, when it comes to deciding on a destination for our events, we are primarily concerned with identifying cities that are considered to be innovative, and where we can engage with the local innovation community, rather than being good event cities or cities that are popular with tourists.*
>
> *Ian Bitran, Executive Director, International Society for Professional Innovation Management*

> *For our team who researches and evaluates future destinations for our annual Urology Congress, focused information on the destination's scientific/academic/medical strengths and capabilities would constitute a definite advantage; one that could make a difference in the final shortlist and selection. In addition, looking at attendee benefits, strategic clusters could facilitate the organisation of technical visits, to hospitals for example, and incubate international exchanges of knowledge and research.*
>
> *Martine Coutu, Executive Director, Société Internationale d'Urologie*

(Reproduced with permission: Copyright www.IntellectualCapitals.com – CAT Publications Ltd.)

Case Study 6.2 summarises the German Convention Bureau publication, *Germany. Expertise*. The document describes the core scientific, industrial and commercial strengths of all the German regions, and thus, the congresses and meetings for which they are particularly suited.

Subvention and bid support practices

Subvention (defined by the Oxford Dictionary of English as a 'grant of money, especially from a government'), seems increasingly to be a requisite component in bids to secure international (and often national) conference and events business. It can take a variety of forms of monetary and in-kind support (such as the provision of civic receptions). It has been suggested that 'subvention is recognised nationally and internationally as the single most important factor for attracting many types of conferences, in particular those affiliated to international associations' (Business Visits and Events Partnership report, 2011).

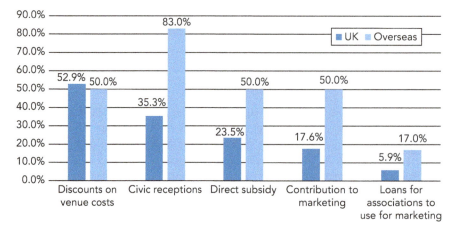

Figure 6.1 Forms of subvention available

Source: 'Subvention and Bid Support Practices for International Conferences and Events in Britain' – published by the Business Visits and Events Partnership.

The key objectives and uses for subvention include the following:

1. To attract high yield, high spend international conferences linked to a country's areas of expertise in industry, commerce or science and medicine and to boost the economy and benefit inward investment
2. To enable a country's cities and destinations to be competitive within the international conference market
3. To attract additional international conferences that may not be attracted without subvention

Figure 6.1 shows the different forms and levels of subvention available, comparing the UK with overseas destinations/countries.

In comparison to their UK counterparts, international destinations are more frequently providing welcome receptions at the town hall, banners in the town, welcome desks at airports/rail stations and public transport for delegates, all free to the conference. Loans to associations or funding of the association's marketing activity prior to registration funds being received by associations are increasingly popular. These enable funding allocations to be recouped by the city and help both parties – association and city – to attract more attendees through increased marketing.

Subvention, and the need for it, are not showing any signs of decline, despite many in the industry disliking it as a practice (particularly because it is seen as 'buying the business', almost a form of bribery, and destinations would prefer to invest their money in developing infrastructure and enhancing their marketing). In fact, the opposite seems to be the case: 86 per cent of international destinations and 41 per cent of UK destinations contributing to the BVEP report said that subvention requests from international associations are on the increase. The average annual subvention budget in 2011 among international destinations was found to be €358,109, all provided by individual cities or municipal governments' budgets.

Destinations that provide subvention evaluate the qualification of associations applying through analysis of the economic benefits generated by the conference. This can include the room nights, total spend value and other values such as PR, marketing or profile gained as a result of the conference taking place. Many require accommodation for attending delegates to be booked through the DMO's own booking services in order to quantify and justify the subvention provided. Other evaluation criteria include the synergy of the conference content with the specific strengths of the local destination economy and with the ambassadors recruited to assist in the bidding process. Some destinations link subvention to the booking of their destination for more than one year by the association. The return on investment of subvention funding averages in the region of 12.5 to 1, according to the BVEP research. The full BVEP subvention report can be downloaded free of charge from www.businessvisitsandeventspartnership.com.

Some examples of subvention funding include:

1. Malaysia's annual US$7.5 million subvention budget is being used to increase its business events arrivals from 1.2 million (in 2012) to 2.9 million by 2020. Totally funded by central government, the Malaysia Convention and Exhibition Bureau (MyCEB) operates with a budget of US$15 million, of which 50 per cent is devoted to the subvention programme. To receive subvention funding, clients are required to sign a memorandum of understanding that ensures certain economic impact targets are achieved – otherwise, the subventions can be withdrawn. Further information: www.myceb.com.my.

2. In 2013, the Dutch city of Utrecht was offering congress organisers up to €10,000 if they committed to holding a 'knowledge-based' event in the city. It aimed to attract conferences in areas such as life sciences, creative industries, care and sustainability. Utrecht developed a €100,000 'congress fund' for 2013, unusual in that it was restricted to 1-year only. The fund was a collaboration between the city and the province, designed to highlight the Utrecht region to more knowledge institutions. Further information: www.utrechtconventionbureau.nl.

3. In November 2013, the Czech capital of Prague announced incentive support for large international conventions. Grants are available to non-profit organisation congresses with 1,500 or more delegates, at least 50 per cent of these being from abroad. Organisations can receive US$12 per participant, up to an estimated US$50,000 per event. This subvention can be used towards the cost of the venue rental or a welcome reception. Previous subvention support took the form of free public transport for congresses with more than 500 participants. Further information: www.praha.eu in the section Subsidies and Grants/Urban Grants/Tourism.

4. In 2012, it was announced that five conferences had won subsidies from Chiba Prefecture (near Tokyo) to hold their events in Japan. They were the first events to benefit from a new subsidy system and included the International Forge Masters Meeting and the World Congress on Dance Research (both taking place in 2014). Under the subsidy scheme, international conferences with over 1,200 participants can receive up to 10 million yen (nearly €95,000), while those with fewer than 1,200 participants can receive up to 7.5 million yen.

5. Also in 2012, Scotland established a Conference Bid Fund of £2 million to bring almost 50 international association conferences – and more than £100 million – to the country. Two years later, VisitScotland confirmed that 46 international association conferences had been secured before 2021. It was anticipated that these congresses, covering topics as diverse as life sciences and education to food and drink and renewable energy, would attract around 62,000 delegates and generate revenue of almost £106 million, a return on investment of more than 50:1. Scotland's four biggest cities – Aberdeen, Dundee, Edinburgh and Glasgow – have all made use of the funding, with other conferences taking place in Perth, St Andrews, Stornoway and Shetland.

6. According to an article entitled 'Show Us the Money', published in the January-February 2015 edition of *Association Meetings International* magazine, Lisbon has established an International Congress Fund offering €50,000 to any international event attracting 3,600 or more delegates. Funding starts at €7,500 for events of 600-plus delegates and rises in stages. As with most subvention funds, no cash actually changes hands. Instead, the money must be used for space rental, room hire, social programmes, transfer services and accommodation. A further condition means that the grant must be applied for at the bidding stage and not retrospectively. Applications for Lisbon's International Congress Fund must be made before the end of 2015.

Case Study 5.1 in chapter 5 provides a more in-depth description of Singapore's Sales Incentives and Event Support Programmes, a form of subvention for attracting business events.

It is also interesting to note that national governments are increasingly lending their support to city/regional convention bureaux in the process of bidding for, and delivering, major events. For example, it was reported in December 2014 (*International Meetings Review*, 2 December 2014) that, in Australia, the Minister for Trade and Investment, the Hon. Andrew Robb AO MP, had announced a historic new framework for collaboration: *Attracting Business Events to Australia: Role of Government Agencies*. The framework delivers on a Government commitment to support key international business events and strategically aligns the Federal Government, through Austrade and Tourism Australia, to work with Australian convention bureaux and the business events sector to attract world-class events to Australia. Lyn Lewis-Smith, President of the Australian Association of Convention Bureaux, is quoted in the same article as saying:

> *Letters of support from key government departments and ministers are vital (to the bidding process), especially given the growth potential of key Asian markets. This support will ensure that Australian convention bureaux are in the best-possible position to identify, bid for and win business events that align with national priority areas and better connect industry, academia, government and the private sector.*

A new development in the use of subvention, one that will be disturbing for many in the industry, is the potential extension of subvention to corporate meetings and events. For example, Abu Dhabi Convention Bureau announced, in March 2013, the introduction of an incentive scheme for corporate meetings. The scheme provides 13 structured offerings as part of its Advantage Abu Dhabi initiative aimed at the corporate meetings and incentive travel industry. Such offerings include:

- welcome dinners at host hotels;
- city tours;
- evening functions Emirati-style;
- 'Speedster Specials' at Ferrari World; and
- Abu Dhabi desert safaris and dune dinners.

To qualify for any selection of these incentive offerings, organisers had to hold an event in Abu Dhabi that had a minimum of 50 paid room nights during 2013 or 2014. The number of incentives on offer for a single event was on a sliding scale based on the number of paid room nights booked (e.g. 1,001 to 1,500 room nights qualified for three incentives).

An article in the October 2014 issue of *Meetings & Incentive Travel* magazine (www.meetpie.com) entitled 'Just say no to the carrots' describes the provision of subvention support by Fáilte Ireland (the Irish Tourist Board) to an unnamed major US insurance company in order to attract the company's salesforce meeting to Ireland. Fáilte Ireland operates a Corporate Meeting Fund, set up to offer 'a suite of financial . . . supports to attract corporate meetings and events to Ireland'. The magazine article criticises this form of subvention as follows:

> *Now, I know it's commonplace to offer sweeteners to associations. Arguably, the prestige, affiliation with the subject and the fact that associations are chiefly not-for-profit, can outweigh the costs. So a subvention has been the norm. But even for associations, the issue of accepting a payment to go to a certain city raises eyebrows. And for corporate business it should raise more.*

The article goes on to explain that the Irish destinations of Dublin and Killarney beat competition from London and Edinburgh to win the 2015 salesforce meeting – where the insurance company will receive financial support towards transport, receptions and entertainment. The article concludes:

> *And this is my plea to buyers and influencers: ignore such sweeteners. Choose the destination and venue that are the right fit for your event, for your clients and for your company. If you want to*

be influenced by price, hold your event in a village hall or a scout hut. They are invariably cheap. To the unnamed, and in my view shamed, US insurance company, I say: if Dublin and Killarney are so great then you don't need their financial support. Give the money to charity.

It is certainly true that, while it may be possible to justify subvention-type support to not-for-profit organisations and such national and international associations, it is much harder to do so in respect of for-profit entities such as major corporations, especially at a time when public sector funding for DMOs is under huge pressure in many countries. This is a very slippery slope that the managers of subvention budgets would do well to avoid.

Product development and investment

Earlier in this chapter, reference was made to the importance of ongoing investment in a destination's physical product and infrastructure in order to keep pace with changing market trends and to retain and, hopefully, increase market share. For all destinations, this poses a constant challenge, in both attracting appropriate investment and then in meeting the increased expectations from investors for a return on their investment.

Investment patterns and trends differ from country to country. For example, in the UK over the past 20 years or so, much of the investment in the conventions and business events sector has gone to cities as they have worked to diversify their economies away from manufacturing and into the service sector.

Birmingham is now well established as one of the UK's top conference and business events destinations. The city's first major steps into the conference and business events market were taken in 1976 with the opening of the National Exhibition Centre adjacent to Birmingham's 'Elmdon Airport', now re-named 'Birmingham International Airport'. The change of airport name itself epitomises the transformation and diversification of the city's economy, fully embracing the service sector, with business events or meetings, incentives, conferences and exhibitions or events (MICE) acting as the catalyst for much of the investment in new hotels, visitor attractions, restaurants, retail, transport infrastructure and other regeneration projects.

There is a delicate balancing act for all destinations in attracting the right kind of investment, in the right location, investment that is not only suitable for contemporary needs but which will also anticipate future market trends. Few countries, if any, have in place a national investment plan for the conventions sector to provide intelligence and direction for future investment projects. It is still left to individual destinations and the investment community to determine where money is spent and new facilities are developed. This can mean, and often does mean, that new venues are constructed that are not appropriate, or which compete with existing local facilities in ways that create difficulties for both, displacing business rather than creating additional new business for the destination [on displacement see also Rogers (2013:256)]. Tress and Sacks (2004), referring to convention facilities built in a number of smaller US cities, state:

These smaller cities are spending millions of dollars on new and expanded convention centres in a bid to reap the economic benefit from the national meetings market, but they are not meeting attendance targets. This is mostly because they have developed the centres in the belief that they will be an economic panacea rather than just a piece in the city's overall visitor package. They have often failed to consider that meeting planners don't merely want a large hall in which to hold their event; they also prefer that the host city offers desirable hotels, accessible restaurants and cultural facilities, plentiful transportation to and within the city, and even good weather. In short, a convention centre should be part of a city that is a legitimate destination for both business and leisure travellers, and one that will attract people because there are things to do there in addition to attending a meeting. Cities that build convention centres in the belief that they will be the foundation of economic prosperity are likely to be disappointed unless those facilities are part of a broader system to draw people to the city.

Destinations need to develop a balanced convention product, in line with the market segments being targeted for their main business. If the destination has a major purpose-built convention centre, say with a capacity of 2,500 theatre-style seating in its main auditorium, it is likely to need a bed stock (assuming an average occupancy rate of 70 per cent year-round) of around 8,000 rooms as a minimum to provide sufficient availability for those events which will fill the centre. However, the quality and standard of accommodation also needs to be considered because some conventions will need budget-style accommodation (guesthouses, 2-star hotels, for example) whereas others will demand higher quality 3-star, 4-star and perhaps even 5-star hotels. Location of bed stock is also a factor, with proximity to the centre being advantageous from a delegate and organiser perspective, minimising the time and costs of transfers between hotels and the centre itself.

While there is undoubtedly an increasing trend for the private sector to be involved with the planning, financing, development and management of major convention and exhibition facilities, historically, they have usually been funded by public monies, often through local municipalities and city councils. An interesting and innovative private/public sector approach to meetings infrastructure development was reported in *Association Meetings International* magazine (November 2014 – www.meetpie.com), describing subsidies available from the Indian state of Madhya Pradesh for developers to build convention centres. The article states that Madhya Pradesh Tourism Development Corporation (MPTDC) has recognised the potential of the meetings industry and decided to boost its infrastructure in order to enable it to target the MICE sector for growth. It quotes Raghwendra Kumar Singh, managing director of MPTDC, as saying:

> *We have, in our tourism policy, identified the MICE sector as an area where development can be done. We have put in place an attractive incentive scheme for potential investors. There are huge land banks with us. If a developer plans to build a convention centre, we have decided to give capital subsidy to the tune of around 10 crore rupees (€12 million) (crore is a unit in the South Asian numbering system equal to ten million) or 25 per cent of the total capital cost, whichever is less.*

MPTDC has land banks at Sanchi, Orchha and Khajuraho, as well as various urban centres where it is keen to attract developers to invest in tourism projects including convention and exhibition centres.

To ensure success, the developers and planning authorities, whether in India or elsewhere, will need to ensure that any proposals cover a fully integrated and balanced business events product, embracing hotels, restaurants, transport infrastructure, cultural and entertainment attractions and communications networks – all of which need to be developed in tandem with the convention and exhibition centres themselves.

The case study in chapter 2 on the Seoul Master Plan gives details of the long-term planning in infrastructure development being undertaken by one of the world's leading convention cities, setting a benchmark for other destinations to follow.

Sustainability and the environment for destinations

Few news broadcasts today are completed without some reference to environmental issues such as global warming, carbon emissions and the very sustainability of our planet. These same issues have also become mainstream concerns and challenges within the conference and conventions industry. Barbara Maple, at the time President of the International Association of Convention Centres (AIPC), President of the

Vancouver Convention and Exhibition Centre, President of the Joint Meetings Industry Council and Chairman of the World Council for Venue Management, listed four reasons for this in an article entitled 'Green Meetings: does anyone really care?' (*Conference & Meetings World* magazine, January 2007):

1. *Our communities will increasingly expect it of us. We and our activities are highly visible wherever we operate, and attract a lot of attention from the local community: this means people expect that we will take a leadership role in implementing more programmes where the good of the community is at stake. At the same time, we are often government-owned and operated, which means we are under pressure to set an example in this regard.*

2. *The second reason is that our clients will increasingly want it because their own members will want it. Environmental concern has gone from being a 'cause' to simply an expectation; people today just assume that environmental concerns are being addressed because they have become a fact of life in most parts of the world. For this reason, the people who make up the membership of the organizations whose events we host will be applying more pressure on organizers to address the role environmental and sustainability considerations can play in their events. This, in turn, will make sustainability issues and the record of a centre in this regard more of a decision factor for meeting planners.*

3. *The third reason sustainability will become a bigger factor is that it will contribute to cost-effective oper-ations, particularly in key areas like energy. One of the big points of the sustainability concept is that industries must manage long term costs if they are to be successful in an ongoing way, and the costs of energy and waste management are among the largest and least predictable we face as facility managers. Like so many other aspects of environmental management, it is often only when there are significant cost implications that action gets taken.*

4. *Finally, this whole area will increasingly be a matter of law, as communities and governments in many parts of the world strengthen their regulations around how businesses manage their environmental and social impacts. Just as issues like smoking have moved from the encouragement stage to outright prohibition, so we can expect that what are today seen as being good practices will likely become legal requirements as community expectations evolve.*

She concluded that:

The results of all this will affect many different areas of facility management: everything from building operations and environmental control measures to how new facilities are designed and constructed, and even how we market and sell our facilities. We will, for example, likely have to get more involved with our clients to make sure that they comply with community sustainability expectations when they hold their events in our cities. This is now simply a 'good thing to do', but will increasingly be a requirement for being allowed to operate at all.

Barbara Maple's comments are pertinent to both event destinations and venues – venue impacts and issues are explored more fully in chapter 7. From a destination perspective, different challenges are posed when cities seek to develop innovative sustainability and environmental credentials and position themselves as leading players in this area. Some examples of initiatives adopted by cities to enhance their sustainability credentials are described below and in Case Study 6.3 on Tampere, Finland.

European Green Capital is an annual award granted by the European Commission to a city in recognition of its efforts to lead the way in environmentally friendly urban living. Winning cities to date are Stockholm (2010), Hamburg (2011), Vitoria-Gastiez (2012), Nantes (2013), Copenhagen (2014), Bristol (2015) and Ljubljana (2016). Characteristics and activities that have helped Bristol to achieve the status of European Green Capital 2015 include:

- It is the proud home to leading environmental and ethical organisations such as the Soil Association, Triodos Bank and Sustrans

- For a major urban city, Bristol has a vast amount of outdoor space, with over 450 parks and green spaces, proportionally more than any other UK city
- Food and drink is also extremely important and many venues pride themselves on being able to offer a specific locally sourced menu
- Many Bristol venues are accredited through the Green Business Tourism Scheme, which recognises business excellence in sustainable management and environmental impact
- Bristol is widely recognised as the leading Fair Trade City in the UK with annual events celebrating fair trade across the city, including hosting the first ever Fair Trade Business Awards in 2012, the first regional Fair Trade Business Awards in 2013 and the International Fair Trade Towns Conference in 2015
- 'Bristol Big Green Week' is an annual world-class festival of sustainability, bringing together leading global experts and thinkers to share ideas and inspiration on developing a green future
- Bristol is home to the world-renowned BBC Natural History Unit and to the Wildscreen festival, the world's largest and most prestigious international wildlife and environmental film festival
- One of the most cycle-friendly cities in the world and England's first ever cycling city, with more cyclists than any other major UK city (despite the hills!), Bristol has more 16 to 74 year olds cycling or walking to work than any other municipality in England and Wales – 17.6 per cent (2011 Census). A 3-year Action Plan (2012 to 2015) is being implemented aiming to increase further cycling by 42 per cent, bus use by 15 per cent and Rail use by 15 per cent
- At-Bristol is the city's award-winning sustainable venue, featuring the UK's only phase-change tank which, along with air source heat pumps, thermal wheels, green roofs and photovoltaic array, is part of At-Bristol's environmentally friendly design
- Bristol's low carbon economy employs around 9,000 people
- Bristol has one of the highest recycling rates of the UK's largest cities
- Bristol demonstrated 4.7 per cent growth in the green economy in 2012 and it has the ambition of becoming a European hub for low-carbon industry with a target of 17,000 new jobs in creative, digital and low-carbon sectors by 2030.

Bristol developed three strategic objectives for 2015, its year as European Green Capital:

1. *Local empowerment*: working with communities in the Bristol area to ensure the value of sustainable living is delivered across neighbourhoods, businesses and the voluntary sector and result in attitude and behaviour change
2. *Sustainable leadership*: becoming the leading forum for UK, European and Global exchange of sustainability expertise in the lead-up to the 2015 Global Climate Summit
3. *International profile*: building Bristol's global profile as the UK's most pioneering, sustainable city region to drive exports, inward investment, tourism and economic growth.

For more information on Bristol 2015 visit www.bristol2015.co.uk and for details of the European Green Capital award visit http://ec.europa.eu/environment/europeangreencapital/about-the-award/index.html.

Rogers (2013) describes a number of the main international environmental and sustainability standards currently applicable to the conference and meetings sector.

While it is likely to be the green credentials of the meetings venue that will prove to be a major influencing factor for event organisers, the sustainable and environmentally friendly policies and practices implemented by host destinations (cities) are also likely to play an increasingly significant role.

The case study on Tampere later in this chapter examines how a city has sought to develop its sustainable credentials with specific reference to the meetings and conference industry.

CASE STUDY 6.1   Destination management in Glasgow, Scotland

DMOs also need to be destination management organisations for the specific reason that cities need to be able to live up to their marketing promise. If the city's infrastructure and supply chain fail to deliver on the marketing promise, then the city's reputation is at risk. In an age when reputation marketing is key to successful destination positioning, DMOs are inevitably going to be involved in destination management.

In Glasgow, for instance, by way of preparing the city to welcome more than 1 million ticket holders attending Commonwealth Games events in the city, 10,000 service delivery personnel were trained in the 'Glasgow Welcomes' initiative. More than 500 courses and training events were delivered to 49,000 individuals across Glasgow, including 15,000 Clydesider Games Volunteers and 1,500 City Hosts in the lead-up to the Glasgow 2014 Commonwealth Games.

To support the training, nearly 20,000 pocket training guides were distributed in the build-up to the Games, ensuring not just a warm welcome to the city but also bringing the new city brand, PEOPLE MAKE GLASGOW, to reality.

As a destination marketing organisation, it is essential to understand the strategic objectives of both the event and conference organisers. For many conference organisers, their conference is their primary organisation tool to speak to their members and a wider audience. Glasgow City Marketing Bureau (GCMB) helps organisations by bringing city infrastructure and supply chains together to help deliver these objectives for the organiser.

An example of this in action was the Healthy Heart Roadshow that took place in a city centre shopping mall with more than 80,000 visitors. The event was linked to the 500-delegate European Cardiac Nurses Conference that took place in 2013 at the Scottish Exhibition and Conference Centre. GCMB brought together a variety of stakeholders, such as the British Heart Foundation, Scottish Ambulance Service and the European Heart House, to educate and inform the public about a healthy heart and healthy lifestyle. Visitors to the booth learned how to do CPR and used bike power to make fruit smoothies.

GCMB developed another community initiative called the Coffee Shop Conference. The inaugural Coffee Shop Conference took place at a local coffee shop during the 3,000-delegate Europaediatrics conference at the Scottish Exhibition and Conference Centre in 2013. One of the keynote speakers left the conference to meet 30 local parents and toddlers to discuss issues around early year education and development.

GCMB supported the Diabetes UK Annual Meeting in 2012 with a Diabetes UK Roadshow where a testing site for the public was located on the city's busiest thoroughfare. GCMB worked with NHS Greater Glasgow and Clyde Health Board to inform the city's 3,000 GPs that this testing was taking place; therefore, referrals from members of the public to their doctor were expected. A total of 31 type 2 diabetes referrals were made from this public health exercise.

CASE STUDY 6.2   *'Germany. Expertise.'* brochure

Traditionally, good infrastructure and accessibility, value for money and, of course, the attractiveness of a country are all key criteria for selecting a destination for international, as well as national, meetings or incentives.

However, the German Convention Bureau's (GCB) research shows that it is now increasingly important for event organisers to select a destination based on local knowledge and expertise, which can be linked to the content of the meeting.

In 2013, the GCB launched its promotional brochure, *Germany. Expertise.*, in response to growing demand from event organisers for conference venues in destinations that are linked to a particular industry. The brochure was developed in conjunction with experts and focused on the country's key sectors. This search tool enables event planners to research destinations that have links to a particular area of expertise in order to maximise the synergies with their event.

Objectives for the *Germany. Expertise.* brochure

The brochure has been published by the GCB to provide an overview of key industry sectors in Germany in order to enable meeting planners to find regional clusters of those sectors. In addition, it highlights examples of those key industry sectors and important events that are of particular interest. Figure 6.2 is taken directly from the brochure and illustrates the range of information it contains.

The objective is to help meeting planners identify destinations that are relevant to their meeting based on local industry expertise, enabling this expertise to be a source of added value for events.

Tapping into local expertise brings a number of benefits for event organisers. For example, they can:

- develop appropriate topical themes around the meeting;
- arrange tours and talks at local facilities;
- organise networking opportunities with local experts;
- invite high profile speakers from local research institutions or businesses; and
- deliver added value for attendees.

Development and production processes for the brochure

Initially, German key industries were mapped against core industries in important source markets to identify potential overlaps. This was carried out by TNS Infratest, a specialist global business analysis and market research company, for five source markets: UK, USA, China, Brazil and Russia in 2011/2012.

The GCB also worked very closely with its partners across Germany for additional information on the regional key sectors, such as important companies, research institutes, universities/ educational institutions and programmes, personalities/opinion leaders, associations, local initiatives, relevant conferences, fairs or events and corporate/factory tours and other site visits. This extensive input from partners was compiled in 2012/2013.

The country has six main areas of expertise:

- Medicine and healthcare (including fields such as medical technology and the healthcare industry)
- Transport and logistics (including automotive engineering, transport system engineering and aerospace)
- Chemicals and pharmaceuticals (including disciplines such as life sciences and biotechnology)

- Technology and innovation (from mechanical engineering and IT to microelectronics and nanotechnology)
- Energy and the environment
- Financial services

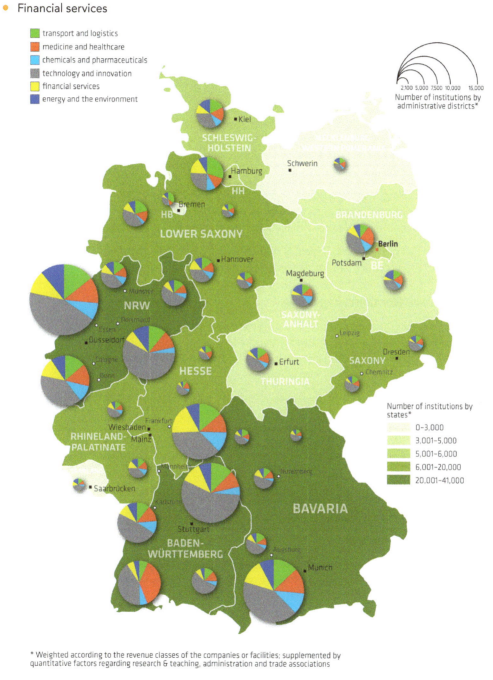

Figure 6.2 Page illustration from the *Germany. Expertise.* brochure

Source: German Convention Bureau.

This level of expertise, coupled with the availability of relevant cultural and leisure facilities, activities and services, makes it easy for meeting planners to make the most of local resources to maximise the impact and effectiveness of their meetings and conventions.

The development of the study took around 2 years, with research workshops with GCB partners taking place in November 2012.

Germany. Expertise. was published in German, English and Chinese, with German and English publications launched in May 2013 at IMEX Frankfurt and the Chinese publication in 2014.

Usage of *Germany. Expertise.*

The brochure *Germany. Expertise.* forms part of a wealth of marketing material focusing on industry expertise/intellectual capital that the GCB employs to market Germany. This material helps to deliver a competitive advantage for Germany as an event destination and provides a source of added value for events.

The brochure is being used to support and provide content for educational trips (fam trips), customer events and the GCB presence at trade shows. For example, it forms part of press packs and is used in media material and press briefings during media visits and exhibitions.

GCB's website (http://www.gcb.de/en) is regularly updated with information on German industry expertise and the brochure can be downloaded online.

Next steps for *Germany. Expertise.*

There will be further updates to the GCB's website as a valuable source of information. The GCB is also looking to develop case studies around events that have used local expertise. The GCB is now linking its main marketing themes closely to the results of the brochure. Its main areas of focus are expertise, sustainability and innovation.

To view a copy of the *Germany. Expertise.* brochure, visit http://www.gcb.de/en/key-industries/key-industries-in-germany.

CASE STUDY 6.3   Sustainable destination best practice: Tampere, Finland

Tampere the destination

Tampere is Finland's second largest urban region after Helsinki and it has established itself as a major Nordic congress destination. It is a beautiful, lively but quite small university city with a population of 220,000 inhabitants, situated between two lakes. Tampere offers leisure activities in nature; examples of these are Nordic walking, lake cruises, skating on natural ice and swimming in fresh water lakes. Figure 6.3 shows an aerial view of Tampere and its two lakes.

The city centre is compact with all major hotels, restaurants and shops located within walking distance of each other. Tampere Hall lays claim to being the leading conference facility in Finland and one of the major conference and concert centres in Scandinavia, hosting over 20 international conferences every year.

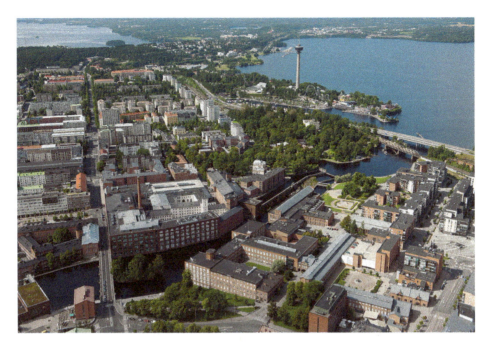

Figure 6.3 Tampere and its two lakes

Source: Tampere Convention Bureau.

A sustainable conference destination and the ICCA Scandinavian Destinations Sustainability Index

Tampere aims to be a reliable choice when organisers are seeking a sustainable conference destination. Its natural surroundings provide the city with an ideal setting for sustainable events. It offers fresh air and not too much traffic. The atmosphere is calm and relaxed.

Tampere Convention Bureau is strongly committed to environmental sustainability and stewardship. Its decisions are taken in line with the Scandinavian Sustainable Meetings Accord, which is a declaration of the ICCA Scandinavian Chapter member organisations. To measure the results of sustainable development, the ICCA Scandinavian Destinations Sustainability Index was created in compliance with the above-mentioned accord. The Index is a tool developed by the Scandinavian ICCA members and MCI Sustainability Services to measure and drive progress on the industry-transforming Sustainable Scandinavian Meetings Region collaboration. In 2014, the Index received the 'Most Innovative Project Award' at the second United Nations World Tourism Organisation's (UNWTO) Knowledge Network Global Forum.

Since 2010, visionary leaders from Denmark, Finland, Iceland, Norway and Sweden (the five countries that form the ICCA Scandinavian Chapter) have been working with MCI Sustainability Services to transform Scandinavia into the world's first sustainable meetings region. The ICCA Scandinavian Destination Sustainability Index measures and compares the social and environmental sustainability commitment and performance of over 20 capital and regional cities in the five participating countries. The purpose is to benchmark and share the cities' sustainability performances, driving a significant shift in the development and implementation of each destination's sustainability strategies, communication campaigns and certification initiatives. Improvements have been recorded regularly, including a 7 per cent overall increase in destination performance in 2013 compared to 2012. The Index has a number of indicators such as recycling, use of renewable energy, climate change commitment and percentage of hotels with eco-certification.

Tampere is one of these cities and recognises that aiming for good performance in sustainability is an ongoing learning and development process. Through policy and operational practices, Tampere Convention Bureau is dedicated to continuous improvement in:

- The incorporation of environmentally responsible initiatives in decision-making
- Everyday work practices that promote sustainability, including energy-saving measures, increasing the use of renewable resources and decreasing the production of waste materials
- Providing educational programmes and encouraging environmental awareness and practices among staff, partners, conference and event organisers, delegates and the local community
- The establishment of sustainability indicators to enable monitoring, reporting and improvement measures

Principal stakeholders

Key stakeholders in Tampere's sustainability strategy include Tampere Hall, where sustainability initiatives began 25 years ago and many goals have already been achieved; Scandic Hotels and Sokos Hotels, both of which have gained the Nordic eco label; the ICCA Scandinavian Chapter, an important source of inspiration and motivation, as well as benchmarking; and the City of Tampere, with whose officials Tampere Convention Bureau maintains an ongoing dialogue.

Fair Trade City

The City of Tampere was the first in Finland to be awarded the status of Fair Trade City in 2008. Congress caterers at the university venues, as well as Tampere Hall, serve fair trade tea and coffee during coffee breaks. Fair Trade wines are available for dinners.

Covenant of Mayors

The Covenant of Mayors is the mainstream European movement involving local and regional authorities in the fight against climate change. It is based on a voluntary commitment by signatories to meet and exceed the European Union 20 per cent CO^2 reduction objective through increased energy efficiency and the development of renewable energy sources. Tampere is one of the signatories, and thus, it has documented its Sustainable Energy Action Plan.

ECO2 (Eco-efficient Tampere 2020)

The ECO2 is a project related to the European Union's climate commitments. It continues until 2020, which is the target year for the European Union's climate commitments. The project aims to develop co-operation in eco-efficient and low-carbon business within the city municipality's many departments, researchers and company partners, such as Tampere Hall and Särkänniemi Amusement Park. In addition, it aims to promote co-operation between major players contributing to the city's development and to generate low-carbon and eco-efficient tools and policies to support marketing and public relations of eco-efficient urban development projects. For example, the co-Zed-Constructing zero-energy districts is a project that aims to design and construct a near zero-energy housing area in Tampere.

EcoFellows Ltd

The City of Tampere has also established a unique co-operation, called EcoFellows Ltd. It was launched in 2003, when the City of Tampere, together with Tampere City Transport and Tampere Regional Solid Waste Management Ltd, established EcoFellows Ltd. Tampere Power Utility Ltd has been the third owner of the company since the beginning of 2009. EcoFellows Ltd produces information, guidance, educational and expert services in the field of sustainability. The company is committed to promoting sustainable ways of living in all of its actions.

Tampere Hall achievements

Tampere Hall was the first conference centre in the world to launch a sustainability programme in 1992. The pioneering work covered reduction and recycling of waste, energy-saving measures and training for its employees. Some of the most significant steps taken since then include:

- *Carbon dioxide production is monitored.* One of the steps towards a greener Tampere Hall is the deployment of a carbon footprint calculator. With the help of this calculator, Tampere Hall has now calculated its carbon footprint to be 4.8kg/visitor. The total amount of carbon dioxide produced by all the visitors during a year is the equivalent of 240 small cars. This is a relatively low amount for a building the age of Tampere Hall (25 years old). With the aid of the carbon footprint calculator, the staff are better able to plan for the future, constantly trying to minimise the venue's carbon footprint.
- *New roofing that cleans the air.* One way of compensating for the carbon footprint has been to install Noxite roofing, which uses a sustainable construction technology that helps to depollute the air. An area covering 650m² of roofing was installed in 2012 and a further 730m² in 2013.
- *Ecological catering.* The catering at Tampere Hall is done using the latest in ecological table-ware. The supplier of the new products, Steelite International, has won multiple awards for its environmentally friendly production methods. The Tampere Hall restaurant also uses local and ecologically grown foods as widely as possible.
- *Nordic Eco Label.* Tampere Hall was a pilot centre in the testing and development of the criteria for the Nordic Eco Label. In May 2014, Tampere Hall became the first congress centre in the Nordic countries to obtain this eminent label. One of the main strengths of Tampere Hall is its energy efficiency and waste management. As much as 99 per cent of all accumulated waste is either recycled or turned into heat energy. Strong emphasis is also given to using ecologically grown foods in the Tampere Hall restaurant. Tampere Hall sorts landfill and burnable waste, recyclable paper, white office paper, brown cardboard, small metal waste, recyclable glass, e-waste, hazardous waste and furniture. Unrecyclable but burnable waste is collected for incineration that generates heat and electricity.
- *Procurement.* Tampere Hall strives to observe sustainable development principles in its procurement practices. For instance, all photocopying and tissue paper used are environmentally labelled products. Tampere Hall restaurants favour fresh local seasonal ingredients. The cleaning service provider, SOL, is committed to following the venue's sustainable development policy. The environmental impact of detergents and cleaning equipment is considered. Cleaning methods have been developed that minimise the need for cleaning agents.
- *Renewable energy.* In 2010, Tampere Hall and the Tampere power utility (Tampereen Sähkölaitos Oy) concluded an agreement on the use of hydroelectric power. Tampere Hall runs its lighting and all equipment and machinery on hydropower. Tampere power utility also invested in a district

cooling system in Tampere in 2014. Affordable, energy-efficient and silent district cooling means that Tampere Hall, among other properties in the vicinity, is cooled with the water from nearby Lake Näsijärvi.

Figure 6.4 shows Tampere Hall.

Challenges and issues

One of the main sustainability challenges identified by Tampere Convention Bureau relates to its effectiveness in communicating information on its actions towards becoming a more sustainable congress destination. Its partners require more consistent and proactive communication about the different actions in which they could be involved. As an example, by late 2014 only 30 per cent of Tampere's hotel capacity was eco-certified by the Nordic eco label. The Convention Bureau could be more persuasive in seeking to promote the benefits of different eco labels to hotel chains and venues.

Future plans

In terms of destination infrastructure, Tampere is planning some major developments, including enhancements to the city's transportation that will see a fast tram system added to the existing bus network, plus the introduction of new biking routes and pedestrian areas – all of which will help to reduce pollution and improve the environment.

As a convention destination, Tampere will focus on building a stronger and better-known image as a safe, peaceful city, where everything works when it comes to general infrastructure and congress services and facilities. Tampere wants to strengthen its reputation as a city with an easy-going and no-stress atmosphere, yet with well-functioning and state-of-the-art facilities. It already enjoys a

Figure 6.4 Tampere Hall

Source: Tampere Convention Bureau.

high quality of life and education for all. Tampere sees sustainability as being not only about the environment but also about quality, equality and reliability.

Useful websites

- Tampere Hall (http://www.tamperehall.com/ecological-footprint)
- Tampere Convention Bureau: (http://www.tampereconventionbureau.fi/contact_us/sustainability-policy/)
- City of Tampere: (http://www.tampere.fi/material/attachments/e/6G5lrE7uX/Environmental_Policy_2020_English.pdf)

SUMMARY

It is clear that, over recent years, the marketing environment for destinations has undergone radical change. Coping effectively with rapid and constant change seems likely to be one of the major challenges facing convention bureaux and DMOs in the years to come. No longer do they simply carry out the relatively straightforward task of destination promotion but increasingly their role is one of managing the overall development of their destination to ensure that its product offering is one that is appropriate to the present and future needs of conference and convention organisers.

DMOs need a highly developed understanding of the particular strengths of their local economy and they must facilitate partnerships with other organisations, such as universities, inward investment agencies and chambers of commerce, to focus their bidding on events that match the core strengths of their economies. This can entail developing subvention policies and funding to support professional event bids. DMOs must keep abreast of new marketing channels and opportunities such as those provided by content marketing. In addition, they must maintain an awareness and understanding of the wider issues affecting society, such as the need to operate sustainably and to demonstrate genuine green credentials, not only as a good thing to do but also as a practice that may give them a competitive edge in the increasingly competitive, global industry of business events.

REVIEW AND DISCUSSION QUESTIONS

- Critically assess the knowledge and skill sets required by today's conference destination marketing organisation. Illustrate your answer by comparing and contrasting the staffing structures of two DMOs, one from your home country and one from overseas.
- Discuss the rationale for the alignment of a destination's event bidding strategy with its economic and academic/research strengths. Is it best left to cities and destinations to identify their priority industries and sectors or does there need to be a national strategy (as developed in Germany) to inform and educate conference organisers about the particular opportunities presented by individual countries and which city or cities would be most appropriate for their events?
- 'Subvention is a necessary evil in the business events sector'. Critically review this statement assessing the benefits and disadvantages of subvention, from both a supplier (i.e. destination/venue) and buyer (conference organiser) perspective.
- Conference destinations that fail to develop effective sustainability policies and practices will lose market share to those that do. Discuss this claim and assess the relative importance of sustainability policies and practices against the other selection criteria used by event organisers (e.g. location, price, accessibility, destination infrastructure, quality of facilities, etc.).

BIBLIOGRAPHY

AMI (2014) 'Indian state offers 25 per cent subsidy to venue developers', *Association Meetings International*, November 2014, published online at www.meetpie.com.

AMI (2015) 'Show Us The Money', *Association Meetings International*, February 2015, published online at www.meetpie.com.

Association Meetings International Special Supplement (2014) 'New Zealand – Naturally Beyond Convention', *Association Meetings International*, October, published online at http://www.meetpie.com/documents/archives/AMI_243449_NEW%20ZEALAND%20SUPPLEMENT.pdf (accessed 5 August 2015).

Business Visits and Events Partnership (2011) 'Subvention and bid support practices for international conferences and events in Britain', published online at www.businessvisitsandeventspartnership.com (accessed 5 August 2015).

IMR (2014) 'Australia Launches Federal Framework to Attract International Events', *International Meetings Review*, 2 December 2014, published online at www.internationalmeetingsreview.com.

Maple, B. (2007) 'Green meetings: does anyone really care?' *Conference & Meetings World magazine*, January.

MCintl (2014) *The Business of Storytelling*, New York: Marketing Challenges International Inc.

MIT (2014) 'Just say no to the carrots', *Meetings & Incentive Travel*, October, published online at www.meetpie.com.

Rogers, T. (2013) *Conferences and Conventions: A Global Industry*, 3rd edn, London: Routledge.

Tress, B. and A. Sacks (2004) *Convention Centers Alone Not An Economic Panacea*, London: Ernst & Young LLP (SCORE Retrieval File No. AL0055).

Chapter **7**

The marketing environment for venues

Chapter overview

This chapter looks at a number of key issues and current trends affecting the marketing of conference venues.

The chapter covers:

- The growing diversity of conference venues
- Brand alignment as a criterion in selecting venues
- Venues' growing use of technology
- Changing trends in venue design
- Venues and sustainability
- Venue security and accessibility

It includes case studies on:

- SnapEvent
- A technologically advanced venue: the Cleveland Convention Center (USA)
- Venue marketing using social media: Central Hall Westminster, London, UK
- Iconic architecture: the ICE, Kraków, Poland
- A sustainable venue: the Hong Kong Convention and Exhibition Centre

LEARNING OUTCOMES

On completion of this chapter, you should be able to:

- appreciate the growing diversity in the supply of conference venues;
- understand the importance of brand alignment in the selection of venues;
- understand the range of technological innovations that venues are adopting;
- appreciate how changing trends in venue design are producing venues that are more iconic, flexible and integrated with their destinations;
- understand the measures that may be taken by venues to minimise their negative impacts on the environment; and
- understand the growing need for venues to ensure security for visitors as well as accessibility for the disabled.

Introduction

Just as those responsible for marketing destinations must understand and respond to important changes in the marketing environment over which they have little or no control, so too must the marketing staff of individual conference venues be aware of the various opportunities and threats created by changes in the wider context within which they operate. Some of these changes are slow and gradual, reflecting subtle variations in society as a whole; others, such as new laws and technological innovations, are more rapid in their impacts. Nevertheless, the fact remains that businesses and organisations that are slow to understand and respond to changed conditions can quickly lose their competitive advantage in the market.

This chapter reviews some of the key elements that are currently influencing the market environment for conference venues.

The growing diversity of conference venues

The twenty-first century has seen a rapid increase in the supply of new types of venues entering the global marketplace. In addition to the ongoing worldwide expansion in the construction of conference centres and hotel-based meetings facilities, a wide range of new categories of venues have added considerably to the diversity of the market for meetings and events. In addition to conference centres and hotel meeting rooms, planners can now choose to hold their events in universities, management training centres or even resorts. But the principal contribution to the diversity of venue supply has been the dramatic rise in the number and variety of 'unusual' or 'unique' or 'non-traditional' venues such as castles, boats, museums, amusement parks, holiday camps, zoos, sports stadia, theatres, cinemas and even lighthouses. For most of these facilities, their role as venues for meetings and events is secondary to their main activity, which is to operate as leisure or visitor attractions.

Authors, such as Marr (2011), have highlighted that for many such attractions, it is the growing pressure to create additional revenue streams that has led to a situation whereby the hosting of meetings and events now represents an increasingly important aspect of their business development plans. The prospects of enjoying an additional revenue stream, as well as the opportunity to more effectively manage fluctuations in demand resulting from the effects of tourist seasonality, mean that more and more visitor attractions are entering the conference business and adding to the diversity of venues available.

An important demand-side factor contributing to the growth in the use of unusual venues has been the widespread trend towards smaller and shorter meetings. A number of respondents to the survey underpinning the White Paper produced by Maritz Research entitled *The Future of Meeting Venues* made this

Table 7.1 Advantages and disadvantages of using unusual venues

Advantages	Disadvantages
Novelty value – good for jaded delegates who need to be motivated to attend	Venues that are open to the public may only be available during the evenings
A rich, built-in ambience can make the event itself more atmospheric and memorable.	Most types of unusual venue do not offer overnight accommodation
Interesting recreational opportunities for participants – things to do and things to see, as part of the social programme.	Because of their original function and age, some unusual venues may present access problems for the disabled
The venue itself can be a topic of conversation – useful in networking sessions	May not have in-house catering and security services or parking facilities
There may be some creative backdrops for photographs taken during the event – a useful source of images for use in marketing strategies, etc.	There may be restrictions in terms of licensing and use
The venue may have a link with the theme of the conference, for example, using a meeting space in an aquarium venue for a conference on marine biology	

connection, leading the authors to conclude that 'the rise in smaller meetings, as well as shorter meetings, is causing the market to increasingly consider the idea of booking non-traditional venues'. It may be assumed that the move towards single day events (not requiring overnight accommodation) and the growth in the type of smaller events that unusual venues are well suited to hosting have accelerated this increase in such venues. Respondents to the survey added a number of motivations for using non-traditional venues, including: 'meetings are looking for options other than "cookie-cutter" type of venues' and 'attendance increases at unique venues and delegates are more engaged, interested and therefore more apt to learn, gain from the experience'.

From the demand-side of the market, unusual venues clearly offer a range of benefits to those who plan and participate in meetings of all kinds. Nevertheless, there can be disadvantages associated with the use of facilities that have a double function, with their role as meetings venues as the secondary one. Table 7.1 lists the pros and cons, as expressed by meetings planners, of unusual venues as places in which to hold a business event.

From the perspective of the meeting planner, perhaps the greatest advantage of using unusual venues is that they have the potential to increase attendance levels by attracting delegates who may otherwise have declined the invitation. This is particularly important in the case of events for which there is no obligation to attend on the part of those invited – such as press conferences, product launches and product presentations, for example.

Nevertheless, as always in meeting planning, the chosen venue must be matched to the objectives, tone and intended message of the event and unusual venues are not always an appropriate choice. For example, an outdoor butterfly farm would be a stunning setting for many types of business events, but it could be less of a good fit for a corporate sales conference.

However, the contribution of unusual venues to the overall diversity of the supply of meetings facilities continues to grow in importance and they are emerging as formidable competitors for the more traditional types of meetings facilities. For example, research shows that around 20 per cent of all UK meetings and conferences are now held in unusual venues (UKCAMS, 2015). In order to compete with their more established rivals in this market, many unique and unusual spaces now offer dedicated in-house event teams as well as technical AV suppliers and preferred caterers. One particular challenge for unusual venues, widely acknowledged by their sales and marketing managers, is the difficulty faced when attempting to secure repeat business from clients. Clearly, the first time a client uses an unusual venue for an event, the novelty factor is a major benefit. Nevertheless, the law of diminishing returns means that the novelty factor would be all but absent from any subsequent event held in the same unusual venue. Therefore, the quest to constantly identify and convince new sources of events business can be more of a preoccupation for unusual venues than for other types of venues that can more realistically rely upon clients' loyalty and repeat business for their revenue.

Case Study 7.1 describes the latest exploitation of unusual venues by SnapEvents.

Brand alignment as a criterion in selecting venues

A related market development – and one that is fuelling the demand for unusual venues – is the fast-growing trend towards meeting planners seeking 'brand fit' or 'brand alignment' as an important criterion in their selection of venues.

Corporate brands, in particular, are precious commodities in establishing and maintaining a company's unique and distinct identity that is easily recognised and appreciated by their customers and other stakeholders. Such brands – often linked to a company's Mission Statement – are a useful way of companies differentiating themselves in crowded and confusing markets.

Companies attempt to project their brands in as many of their activities as possible, from the style of their advertising and customer service to their corporate social responsibility activities. Increasingly, therefore, corporate meeting planners, as well as taking into account the usual selection criteria, such as dates, rates and space, are assessing potential venues in terms of the extent to which they can help reinforce their company's brand. For example, a planner choosing a venue for a meeting of a bank's shareholders may opt to hold it in a castle, to reflect and reinforce the bank's brand, if that includes values such as tradition, strength and the unassailable protection of their customers' assets. By way of contrast, a young video games start-up company, whose values are more closely associated with modernity, informality, creativity and fun may find it appropriate to hold their meetings in an amusement park.

The rise in importance of brand alignment was noted by Grass Roots' Events and Communications Global Supply Chain Director, Alan Newton:

> More and more companies, particularly media and fashion houses, are very brand-led. They want to use venues that reflect or complement their own brand values and definitely gravitate to unusual venues. Even if a hotel is being used it tends to be one of the more unconventional, quirky or boutique hotels. Even the more traditional corporates, such as professional services firms, are now looking for venues that reflect that brand image and have moved away from conventional venues. However, that said, there are a plethora of hotels that have individuality within their venues, such as ornate or quirky banqueting rooms and facilities that could equally be classified as unique and unusual.

Isabelle Mills-Tannenbaum, who offers advice to meeting planners, concurs with the above contention, arguing in her blog, '3 reasons to consider a non-traditional venue for your next meeting':

> The venue where you hold your event says a lot about your ideas, brand and/or product. Guests will see the venue as a reflection of your business's goals and values and thus the selection shouldn't be taken lightly. When you visit the venue, make sure to not only check on amenities and costs but also how the venue feels to you. Does it have the 'it factor' you're looking for?

Does it match the thought leadership, mission and image of the company or organization you work for?

This rise in importance of brand alignment means that venues of all kinds must ensure that their own brand is entirely clear and distinctive to potential clients. The venue's own values and 'personality' should be evident not only to those visiting the facility but in every aspect of its marketing, from its website to the tone, style and content of the messages it sends in direct mail.

Venues' growing use of technology

It was once believed that the unprecedented advances in information and communications technology seen towards the end of the twentieth century heralded the certain decline of the conference industry, as these allowed people to easily communicate their ideas and messages without actually travelling to business events. However, rather than killing the industry, as was once feared, these technological advances are now helping venues attract more business by providing tools that make all types of meetings more engaging and more productive for those who attend them. From videoconferencing facilities that enable speakers to make their presentations without physically travelling to the conference venue, to sophisticated new audio-visual services, venues large and small have readily embraced the fruits of technological progress in order to enhance their clients' experience while using the facility. In fact, such is the pace of technological change and the rate at which hardware and software become obsolete that a major challenge for venues is knowing when to invest in the purchase of new technology and when it may be advisable to simply hire it from specialist suppliers.

Web-based technology has given venues a range of indispensable tools for marketing themselves, such as websites, social media and other applications of Web 2.0. In chapter 3, we reviewed the essential characteristics of an effective website. Table 7.2 gives the results of a 2014 survey of meeting planners conducted by the Market Dynamics Research Group to determine which tools and resources they use to compare and select hotel venues. The results clearly show that meeting planners are frequently using online resources to identify venues with, for example, 90 per cent of those surveyed using hotel venues' websites as a source of information.

But it is worthy of note that, in the same survey, one in five planners reported that they were making use of social media as a tool to help them compare and select hotel venues. The harnessing of social

Table 7.2 Tools and resources used by meeting planners to compare and select hotel venues

90%	Go to hotel website
80%	Contact hotel sales department directly
79%	Conduct online research
77%	Use online reviews and ratings
68%	Contact CVB sales reps
60%	Go to convention facility websites
53%	Contact hotel Global Sales Office
50%	Use a list of places given by meeting sponsor
24%	Trade journal advertising
22%	Use social media

Source: Market Dynamics Research Group, for Destination Marketing Association International.

media as a marketing tool by another type of venue, conference centres, was highlighted in the research undertaken by Davidson (2011). UK conference centres were found to be already making significant use of social media in their marketing strategies, and this was set to grow even more in the near future. LinkedIn and Twitter were found to be the most popular social media applications, followed by Facebook and YouTube. As the use of social media for professional, as well as personal, purposes continues to expand, it can be expected that more venues of all types will take advantage of these tools in order to reach potential clients.

It is widely predicted that another advance in technology, radio frequency identification (RFID), will also have a significant impact on the meetings industry in general, and on venues in particular, in the next few years.

RFID tags are small computer chips that contain a string of identifying digits similar to a bar code. When the tag comes within range of a reader device, the information on the tag is captured via radio frequency waves. RF tags are faster and more reliable than bar code technology. RFID eliminates the need for line-of-sight reading that bar coding requires. An entire palate of product, for example, can be scanned automatically in a second compared to what would take minutes or hours to do manually with today's barcode scanners.

As the applications of RFID technology to the meetings industry are numerous – including the insertion of RFID tags into delegates' name badges – venues equipped with RFID scanners are now able to offer a range of additional services to conference planners and delegates. Ball (2005) lists these as:

- Access control. Scanners at the entrances to venues will be able to verify instantly that the person wearing the RFID-enabled badge has legitimate access to a specific room or rooms.
- Access to cyber cafes will open by sensing delegates' identity from their badges. It will not be necessary for delegates to type in their names.
- Collection of registration materials will be more easily tracked.
- VIPs could be tracked and be given special service, for example, by notifying staff when they have come 'within range'.

However, Manis (2012) has identified an additional innovative use of RFID in business events venues – its application to the tracking of the location of furniture and equipment within the venue. As he explains:

> *Equipment is tagged such that a sensor positioned near the room entry can track which rooms contain which pieces of equipment (and the quantity of each). This feature comes in handy for knowing how many chairs are already set up in a conference room and where additional chairs are stored.*

Case Study 7.2 describes the technological advances introduced by Cleveland Convention Center in Ohio (USA). Case Study 7.3 describes the successful use of social media marketing by the Central Hall, Westminster.

Changing trends in venue design

Convention centres built in the 1980s tended to be utilitarian boxes designed to accommodate a large number of people. Aesthetics and amenities were more of an afterthought than a necessity at that time. Nevertheless, with attendees being more discriminating in the events they choose and with meeting planners eager to choose venues that their delegates actually enjoy meeting in, the design of convention centres has changed considerably in the twenty-first century.

More aesthetic, iconic design

Writing in *Collaborate Meetings* magazine on the theme of 'Convention centres of the future, designed today', Craig Guillot quotes Todd Voth, senior principal at Populous, an architecture firm in Kansas City:

> *Today's successful convention centres need five critical attributes: beauty, functional efficiency, urban integration, a spirit of place and sustainability. From the front entrance and lobby to the bathroom facilities and large meeting rooms, beauty and aesthetics are as important as functionality.*

Populous is an example of a new generation of architects with a deep understanding of what makes a convention centre successful in its design. According to Voth, 'no-one wants boring old meeting space anymore. They want a space that is exciting and interesting, where people want to stay for a while. We're breaking all the rules that no one broke years ago'.

One venue that demonstrates just how radically convention centre design has changed in recent years is the Qatar National Convention Centre, in the design of which Populous played a key role. Opened in 2011, it has a striking entrance designed to mimic Sidrat al-Muntaha, a tree Muslims believe symbolises the end of the seventh heaven.

The Qatar National Convention Centre is a glowing example of a new generation of beautiful, iconic venues whose imaginative and striking architecture makes them a source of considerable civic pride for the local population and important attractions for visitors. In the same way that, for instance, the Gaudi Cathedral in Barcelona, the Coliseum in Rome and the Houses of Parliament in London are outstanding examples of buildings that have a timeless appeal and close associations with the cities in which they are situated, a growing number of conference centres have become the symbols of the cities in which they stand. Indeed, part of the motivation for many local municipalities commissioning the construction of a new conference centre is the desire to create a prestigious and magnificent 'signature' building for their city, rather than the somewhat unimaginative 'empty boxes' of yesteryear. Some shining examples of iconic venues of renown are the Colorado Convention Center, which has a 125-foot-high roof blade rising into the air above it, significantly altering the Denver skyline, the award-winning Hong Kong Convention and Exhibition Centre and the ICE in Kraków (Case Study 7.4).

More integration of venues with their destinations

Another trend to emerge in architectural design in recent years is the constructing of buildings that integrate into the communities around them. Interviewed by Craig Guillot for his article in *Collaborate Meetings* magazine, Brian Tennyson, principal of convention centres at LMN Architects in Seattle, recalled that many centres built 20 to 30 years ago were placed on the outskirts of town. Not only was space at a premium in many cities, but some meeting planners wanted a captive audience. The idea was to keep them in the facility and avoid the temptation for them to wander off the premises. Today, according to Tennyson, meeting planners use their destinations as selling points, and delegates expect to experience the flavour of the city:

> *When meeting planners look at destinations, they're looking for a city that attracts people. People want to experience the city and not be stuck in a windowless room. People who are attending conferences today are a lot more discriminating, so planners need a space where they can connect people with their surroundings. No one wants to sit in a box for 8 hours anymore.*

Today's conference centres tend to have a more open design that includes large windows and glass facades that offer panoramic views of the destination. Event organisers' original fear that delegates would go off-site, in the case of events held in centrally located venues, has been alleviated to some extent by the fact that, when the venue's design incorporates some actual experience of the city, they are less likely to wander off during important conference programming.

Indeed, when a venue is located within walking distance to hotels and entertainment facilities, this can add to its appeal for delegates who often have to squeeze in entertainment into a short period of free time. Successful business events destinations such as Cannes and New Orleans, for example, are known for their 'walkability', with most of their primary attractions being located within a one-mile radius of their conference centres.

More flexibility

Large amounts of space are one of the selling points of today's conference centres. Nevertheless, in order for that space to be used effectively by giving meeting planners more options, it needs to be flexible and customisable for a meeting of 50 delegates or for one of 5,000. Contiguous space – or the total area of a building that can be configured for one single event – is critical for many event planners, especially those with very large groups.

Many large, modern conference centres have 500,000 square feet of contiguous space or more. A number of those are to be found in the US, where, for example, the Ernest N. Morial Convention Centre in New Orleans has one of the largest contiguous spaces at 1.1 million square feet. The Kay Bailey Hutchinson Convention Center in Dallas has contiguous space of more than 700,000 square feet. To be able to use such space more flexibly, architects are increasingly designing venues with fewer columns and more air walls that can be easily and quickly deployed to divide meeting rooms and exhibition halls into smaller spaces.

In her blog, 'How convention centers are becoming more flexible', Adele Chapin notes that venue operators are increasingly looking for input from meeting planners when designing spaces and a recurring theme is the importance of flexible space. As an example of meeting planners' input in action, she describes how, prior to the design of the US$299 million, multiphase renovation at Detroit's Cobo Center, the venue management and the Detroit Metro Convention and Visitors Bureau established a Customer Advisory Board of national and international event and meeting planners. They meet twice a year to review progress, provide input to design and construction decisions and express their opinion on topics including food and beverage choices, rebranding, marketing and current and future trends in the industry.

Chapin quotes Thom Connors, regional vice president and general manager of SMG/Cobo Center, as saying 'specific input from this group created more flexible space in the final design scheme. They were very vocal about providing access to both work space and unprogrammed exterior space'. Components of the renovation included adapting the former Cobo Arena into the Grand River Ballroom and adding a new 30,000-square-foot atrium lobby with an 80-foot ceiling that has been used for registration, receptions, meal functions, exhibits, networking and concerts. The atrium connects the new ballroom and meeting rooms and makes a less-used exhibit space more connected to the natural pedestrian flow of the facility. Other flexible spaces at the Cobo Center include a 20,000-square-foot annex to the 600,000-square-foot main exhibition space that can be separated by moveable partitions to be used independently or in conjunction with activities in the adjacent halls.

In the same blog, Chapin reports on the example of the 600,000-square-foot Puerto Rico Convention Center in San Juan, which was completed in 2005 with both iconic architecture and flexibility in mind. The venue has the largest ballroom in the Caribbean at 39,500 square feet and a 152,700-square-foot exhibition hall that seats 15,576 people theatre-style. Its layout allows for the seamless flow of different groups and the sound level is controlled between different events. According to Milton Segarra, president and

CEO of Meet Puerto Rico, the tourism and convention authority, 'there have been days at the convention centre where in the exhibition hall, you have a volleyball tournament. In the second floor, where you have a lot of meeting space and breakout space, you have seven meetings. And at the top you have a conference in the ballroom with a huge lunch or dinner'.

Advances in technology make the reconfiguration of venue space even more effortless. For example, the Swiss Tech Convention Centre in Lausanne, Switzerland, opened in 2014, has been designed with Skyfold walls – a Gala Venue technology that automatically transforms stage platforms and detachable seating rows to accommodate a variety of events. With an innovative system of swivels attached to each seat, a computer system can automatically configure the building with the required seating. When not in use, seats swivel underneath the floor. This cutting-edge technology means that it is likely to be installed in more conference centres in the future. The Swiss Tech Convention Centre technology can be seen in action in this YouTube video: https://www.youtube.com/watch?v=uKjStZBldz4.

At the LEED Gold-certified Ottawa Convention Centre in Canada, state-of-the-art technology includes projection screens that are configured to work when rooms are divided or combined. Meeting planners have access to Crestron screens, which are installed in meeting rooms and allow for full control of the room's temperature and background music, as well as the ability to contact the venue's service staff, use the building's page system and make emergency calls. For future building upgrades to keep pace with changing technology, the convention centre was built to provide easy access and accommodation for future polls, ports, cabling and chases.

Venues and sustainability

The need to observe high environmental standards in every aspect of human activity is now widely acknowledged. As was discussed in chapter 1, the conference industry as a whole can have a range of impacts on the built and the natural environment and stakeholders are increasingly acknowledging their responsibility for minimising the negative effects of conference activity wherever it takes place.

Those who design and operate conference venues can also contribute to environmental protection. Purpose-built conference centres, in particular, have the potential to make a significant detrimental impact on the locality in which they are situated through their use of resources such as energy and fresh water and the substantial amounts of waste they can generate.

Interviewed by Craig Guillot for his article in *Collaborate Meetings* magazine, Brian Tennyson, principal of convention centres at LMN Architects in Seattle stated his opinion that when it comes to sustainable building design, 'the honeymoon period is over. Recycling programmes, energy-efficient features and water-conservation systems are no longer distinguishers—they're expectations'.

As an indication of the sustainability of their design and operations, a growing number of venues now hold some level of LEED certification – Leadership in Energy and Environmental Design. Manis (2012) describes LEED as an excellent roadmap for engineers and architects, allowing them to weigh the benefits of different sustainable concepts as they develop designs. For example, skylights or large glazed areas can both accentuate architectural features and effectively provide light without the need for power consumption during daytime hours. Natural lighting also provides a connection to the outside world and improves the overall appeal of the interior space. Designing for building efficiency might also include a grey water system to conserve water. Grey water — wastewater collected from sources such as dishwashing and laundry activities — can be collected, stored, treated and reused on site as a non-potable water supply. A venue's grey water system can provide it with multiple LEED credits by reducing wastewater outflows and potable water demand.

Vancouver Convention Centre, which in 2009 became the first LEED Platinum certified convention centre in the world, features a six-acre 'living roof', extensive use of controlled daylighting, natural ventilation and radiant floor cooling and heating. Other LEED-certified facilities include the gold-certified Austin (Texas) Convention Center and the silver-certified Raleigh (NC) Convention Center.

Nevertheless, sustainability and environmentally friendly design are about more than recycling or saving on heating and cooling. Returning to Guillot's interview of Tennyson, the latter notes that, as venues have moved back into city centres and have grown to accommodate larger meetings, the focus has shifted to 'smart' transportation considerations.

> *The addition of bicycle lanes and racks, greater use of public transportation and more walk-ability means cumulative savings for conventioneers and meeting planners as well as a more enjoyable and less cluttered convention district with traffic and cars. At some facilities, such as the Anaheim Convention Center, visitors can even find bicycle-sharing services that allow rentals by the day or hour.*

As a final point, Tennyson contends that 'what is getting more and more traction in the green movement is now all about cost savings. Green design equals energy savings and that equals cost savings. Green design initiatives have moved directly to the realm of cost savings as facility managers see that upfront invest-ments can produce substantial savings down the line and pay off in relatively little time'.

Case Study 7.5 gives details of the sustainability initiatives of the Hong Kong Convention and Exhibition Centre.

Venue security and accessibility

More emphasis on security

- In 2008, 174 people were killed in attacks on two hotels in Mumbai
- In 2013, a terrorist attack in the Westgate shopping centre in Nairobi left 67 people dead
- In 2014, a gunman shot dead two men and a woman at the Jewish Museum in Brussels

Fatal attacks such as these, on semi-public buildings, mean that security has become an over-riding concern of those planning conferences and those attending them. It is therefore incumbent on all venues to ensure that risks incurred by delegates and other visitors are reduced to a minimum. Some venues attract many sensitive events – such as political summits or arms fairs – which, by their very nature, demand security on several levels, dependent on the threat assessment.

These threats can be summed up as shown in Table 7.3.

Venue designers, by taking account of the potential risk situations at the design stage, will help facilitate the task of the venue's managers when a high-risk event is due to take place. This is not merely altruistic – it is a positive contribution to the marketability and profitability of the venue.

Eric Rymer, a venue security specialist for the UK-based consultancy The Right Solution Limited, makes the following observations about building in safety and security at the venue design stage:

> *Operating a conference centre safely and securely can be made much easier if the initial design and construction of the building is done with these aspects in mind. It costs no more to design in safety and security. Furthermore, the venue operator will be grateful for a design which allows him to secure the building in as short a time as possible. If a high security conference requires an 'island site', the shortest time possible to achieve a secure perimeter means more time available for selling the space, as the centre will be closed down for a shorter period.*

Table 7.3 Potential threats faced by venues

Threat	Duty of the venue	Example
Petty crime	To combat casual vandalism and petty crime	Pickpockets infiltrating the event
Industrial security	To protect against industrial espionage during corporate conferences	Theft of delegates' laptops containing confidential company files
Public disorder	To protect delegates against demonstrations and similar during sensitive events	Protests against high-profile summits, for example, the 2012 NATO summit in Chicago.
Terrorism	To protect the building and delegates during events that are attended by high-profile terrorist targets	Personal attacks on scientists using animals for research

Naturally, there are building regulations, which cover the statutory requirements, particularly for fire safety. These regulations vary from country to country – and some countries do not have regulations at all. The UK regulations are among the strictest in the world and, consequently, they make a good minimum basis for design.

Over and above the statutory requirements, the interior design and finishes can enhance delegate safety and security. For example, floor finishes that become slippery when wet should not be used, particularly by entrance doors. The designer should avoid dark corridors, or small corners hidden away from sight. Clear and airy foyers and circulation spaces not only make for a more pleasant environment, but for a safer one also. Even the simplest elements of design should be considered with security in mind. It is hard to believe, but some conference centres have been designed with meeting room doors that do not lock!

Circulation routes are particularly important in the design. Linear routes, with clear signposting, help to avoid confusion, especially in emergency situations. At the same time, natural control points should be built in to the routes. For example, stairs and escalators become control points, easily policed by one steward, to ensure only authorised delegates can go into a particular area.

VIP circulation routes should be carefully considered during design. A VIP may want to arrive or exit the building secretly, via a back-of-house route. There should also be a route from the main presentation area (typically an auditorium stage) to the exit, or a press interview room, without having to go through front of house areas.

In front of house areas, places of safety should be considered. For example, a concrete planter strategically placed can be used to shelter from bullets, should the need arise.

Early consideration of electronic security measures is beneficial. Intruder alarms, door entry indicators, electronic locking systems and CCTV (with both overt and covert cameras) all help towards a secure environment. Some electronic systems may not be required at all times, such as X-ray equipment or metal detectors. However, these will be needed for some events and consequently the building should have the ability to install such equipment on a temporary basis. This often just means the simplest of provision, such as power sockets by the entrance doors. If such measures are incorporated into the design at an early stage, it will avoid considerable disruption later on.

More emphasis on accessibility

Making sure that conferences are accessible for disabled people should be a key design consideration for any venue. In many countries, by law, buildings must be designed to be accessible by disabled people.

For example, in the UK, the 1995 Disability Discrimination Act gave disabled people equal rights to attend, participate in and enjoy events. In the US, the Americans with Disabilities Act guarantees that disabled travellers receive equal treatment under the law. This means that venues in many countries are required to make reasonable adjustments to their facilities and services to make them accessible to people with disabilities. Moreover, it is not only conference delegates who are affected by the accessibility (or lack of it) of venues. Speakers, exhibitors, and even some of the people employed by the venue can be disabled. There is, therefore, a compelling case for designing venues of all kinds for maximum accessibility.

A simple example of the type of problem disabled delegates can face – and a solution to the problem – is provided in the following example:

A hotel conference suite has a policy of only providing a self-service buffet at lunchtime for delegates, who eat while standing, resting their drinks on small tables at waist height. But some disabled people with mobility impairments or visual impairments may find it difficult or impossible to help themselves to food from a buffet selection and to eat it without placing their plate on a table. It would be a reasonable adjustment for the venue to provide staff to serve people at the buffet and to carry food to a few tables provided for seated delegates. It would be good practice to reserve some places at these tables for disabled people who need this service.

Ultimately, the choice of which venue is used for their events is made by the events organisers. Aware of their own responsibilities under disability legislation, a growing number of meetings planners will only consider fully accessible venues: those that allow people to enter, exit and to move around the building with ease, that offer adapted toilet facilities and where, ideally, the event can take place on one floor only.

One of the most effective ways of establishing the impact that any building has on disabled people is to undertake an access audit, a technique being increasingly used by meeting planners when they are considering potential venues for their events. Increasingly, these audits are undertaken by independent, professional consultants, who inspect the venue and produce a report outlining existing access provision and recommending improvements. However, for those meetings planners who wish to carry out their own access audit, a number of checklists are available.

Such checklists include the assessment of car parks, toilets, corridors, lifts, catering areas, plenary rooms, breakout rooms, and entrance foyers. For example, if there are going to be exhibition stands and display cases, will there be ample room for safe and easy manoeuvring between the stands for everybody, including people using wheelchairs or guide dogs? The access audit will usually recommend changes such as installing accessible toilets, door opening mechanisms or simpler measures such as changing door handles and painting door and window surrounds in contrasting colours to assist people with visual impairments.

One example of a venue that is well adapted for disabled access is the QEII Centre in London, which describes its disabled-friendly features as follows:

QEII CENTRE: DISABLED ACCESS

- Getting to the Centre
  - *Driving*. If you have a disabled badge for your vehicle you will be allowed to park on the forecourt of the QEII Centre. Taxis and other vehicles carrying disabled passengers are also allowed onto the forecourt so that their passengers can disembark.
  - *Public transport*. Our nearest step-free tube station is Westminster. It allows anyone who needs to get from the platform to street level to do so using lifts and ramps. Details for Westminster Underground Station.

- Getting around the Centre
  - There is a ramp from the forecourt which leads to the front doors and is wide enough for easy wheelchair access. Inside, all of our rooms have step-free access via corridors wide enough to easily manoeuvre a wheelchair. We have nine passenger lifts, all of which can accommodate a wheelchair and have audio announcements. One of these is a fireman's lift that can be used in the event of an evacuation.
  - There is no fixed seating at the QEII Centre, therefore wheelchair spaces can be positioned anywhere in the meeting rooms. We can fit a wheelchair ramp to the stage in larger meeting areas, or arrange a portable wheelchair lift to provide access to the stage in smaller meeting areas.
- Induction loops
  - Many of our rooms have permanent induction loops, and in all of our rooms induction loops can be fitted by arrangement with Interface, our in-house audio-visual team. You can contact Interface on 00 44 (0)20 7798 4118 or use our enquiry form.
- Toilet facilities
  - There are eight accessible toilet facilities throughout the QEII Centre. These are equipped with emergency alarms and can be accessed from all of our rooms by using lifts where necessary.
- Assistance and guide dogs
  - You are welcome to bring your guide dog, hearing dog or other assistance dog into the QEII Centre.
- Personal evacuation plans
  - We must ensure that everyone can be safely evacuated in the unlikely event of an emergency. If you feel that your disability could delay evacuation of yourself or others via the fire escape stairs, please contact the QEII Centre's Fire Officer prior to your event, to agree a mutually convenient personal evacuation plan.

For new venues wishing to ensure that they are completely accessible to disabled people, or for established venues wishing to adapt their facilities for this market, there are many sources of advice and guidance. Venues should need no external pressure to compel them to undertake these measures. Making changes to the design of the physical environment not only makes venues more attractive to event organisers, it also makes them more accessible for people who are not disabled. Clearer signposting within the venue, for example, helps all delegates, not only the visually impaired.

CASE STUDY 7.1   SnapEvent

The 'sharing economy'

The 'sharing economy' and 'collaborative consumption' are the names that are most often given to the trading system in which individuals turn their physical assets (their house, their car, their pet and so on) into a source of income by logging on to online peer-to-peer rental schemes that connect owners of underused assets with others willing to pay to use them.

Among the best-known examples are Airbnb (www.airbnb.com), which allows people to temporarily turn their home into a hotel by renting out all or part of it to visitors to their hometown; Park On My Drive (www.parkonmydrive.com) allows householders to rent out their empty driveway or garage to motorists looking for convenient parking facilities. There are over a hundred online companies that have been created in recent years (many of them between 2008 and 2010, in the aftermath of the global financial crisis), connecting people with something to rent out with people interested in hiring that something: anything from a pet to a wedding dress.

SnapEvent

Since 2014, it has been possible for householders in one major meetings destination, Paris, to participate in the sharing economy by renting out part of or their entire home as venues for meetings and events. The intermediary that makes this possible is SnapEvent (www.snapevent.fr), a start-up business that puts events planners in touch with people who have a home, a roof terrace, a garden, or workshop, etc. that they want to rent out as venues in order to earn some additional income.

SnapEvent's slogan is 'Organise your event in three clicks', which is precisely what the website enables meeting planners to do. They enter the number of attendees (up to 50), the type of event and the date – the website then brings up all the options available. A selection of caterers is proposed through the same website, as well as companies hiring equipment for events. Quality is assured by the two founders of SnapEvent, who visit every place that applies to be on their books.

Prices are competitive, but the main source of these venues' appeal is that they are well aligned to the trend towards today's event planners seeking more non-traditional, unusual venues with individual character. The list of clients that have already used SnapEvent's services suggests that in the first 2 years of its operations, the company is already making a huge impact on the Parisian meetings and events scene. Household names in France such as the mobile phone company, SFR; the cosmetics firm, Sephora; the energy conglomerate, Total; the bank, Société Générale; and M6, the television company, have all held meetings and events in venues that they found through SnapEvent.

In 2015, the two founders of SnapEvent announced their intention to establish their company in London.

CASE STUDY 7.2   A technologically advanced venue: the Cleveland Convention Center (USA)

A convention centre that has been remodelled taking into account many innovative principles in venue design is the Cleveland Convention Center (CCC), in the US state of Ohio. Located on the shores of Lake Erie in the heart of the city, the city's new venue – designed by LMN Architects – opened in June 2014 and features 225,000 square feet of exhibit space that is dividable into three halls. There is also a 32,000-square foot, column-free ballroom that offers spectacular views of the lakefront. According to Brian Tennyson, principal of convention centres at LMN, the remodel and expansion was not simply about improving the space, it was about better integrating it with the local community and becoming more competitive as a destination.

As a result of the remodelling, CCC now features updated technology, higher ceilings, fewer columns and an updated design. It also has more energy-efficient elements such as natural-light features. Much of the building is underground, reducing the need for expensive air conditioning and heating by making efficient use of Earth's geothermal and insulating properties to help naturally reduce heat loss and more efficiently maintain steady temperatures. All departments and partners of the CCC use green products whenever possible. For example, the CCC's housekeeping staff use products that are environmentally safe and non-toxic. The venue's restaurants source products that are locally grown, in season and organic. In addition, the digital signage located throughout the facility is a very effective way of cutting back on the use of paper signage and posters, etc. The CCC also has bicycle racks and a highly walkable location and it is connected to the airport via a rapid transit service that can transport visitors between the two locations in 20 minutes.

According to Anthony Prusak, Director of Convention Sales of the CCC, 'we're perfectly situated between New York and Chicago, and we now have a facility that will just wow visitors. The new centre better integrates with [the rest of downtown]'.

In terms of technology, the facility was designed with 250 utility boxes, allowing cabling to deliver technical services to every square foot of the building. It also has 500 Cisco Wi-Fi access points to ensure that no one is left without a high-speed signal for their smart devices.

All technology related to audio, visual, data delivery, electricity, cooling and heating merges into one main control room at the venue. Another implementation of useful technology in the venue is LED lighting that can change colours on demand. Therefore, if a client organisation's colours are green, all of the lighting and signage in the venue can easily be changed to reflect that.

CASE STUDY 7.3   Venue marketing using social media: Central Hall Westminster, London, UK

The venue

Central Hall Westminster (CHW – www.c-h-w.com) is central London's largest conference venue, located opposite Westminster Abbey and adjacent to the Houses of Parliament and Big Ben. Built in 1912, Central Hall Westminster offers a wide range of flexible event spaces with natural light and blackout facilities, for corporate, public and private events.

This unique, historic venue, which boasts Europe's largest domed ceiling, is a well-known London landmark, with its elegant theatre entrance, marble flooring, spacious foyer areas and Grand Staircase. The 22 meeting rooms offer large windows, high ceilings and state-of-the-art technology and all rooms are easily accessible. In terms of capacity, the meeting spaces range from meeting rooms for five to 450 delegates, while the main auditorium is capable of holding 2,160 delegates.

CHW's target markets

The types of events targeted by CHW, and examples of events hosted, are as follows:

- Large conferences such as annual general meetings, congresses and week-long conferences – all requiring multiple breakout rooms (for example: LE WEB - Europe's largest Technology Conference, World Nuclear Symposium, Tesco AGM)

- Award ceremonies, fashion shows and graduation ceremonies (for example: London Fashion Week, Laureus World Sports Awards, Chinese International Film Festival)
- Media events (for example: the announcement of Higgs Boson, Royal Wedding media, BBC Election debate 2015)
- Entertainment events (for example: Channel 4 'Stand up for Cancer', BBC New Year's Concert with Gary Barlow, Queen, Classic FM and the London Philharmonic Orchestra).

CHW's use of social media in their marketing: the Meet The Future campaign

In 2013, CHW was seeking to re-position itself based on the combination of its rich cultural heritage with its ultra-modern technology offering and the super-fast broadband it had just installed to enable interactive events. The venue was looking for a creative digital marketing campaign to inspire professional event organisers and re-position the venue as technologically superior to its main competitors.

The concept of 'Meet The Future' (MTF) was developed – a campaign designed to explore event technologies. The objectives of the campaign were:

- To position CHW as a technologically capable venue
- To drive more traffic to the CHW website
- To increase social media followers across multiple channels
- To encourage engagement and dialogue with buyers
- To increase enquiries from potential clients.

The target audience was senior-level event planners from agencies, corporates and associations. A two-phase approach was used.

Phase one – audit, strategy and follower building:

- Mexia's Foresight for social media process was undertaken to evaluate current profile against competitors and devise appropriate content and a follower-building strategy. Mexia's Foresight is a powerful communications planning tool devised by Mexia Communications (www.mexiacommunications.com), a UK-based full service PR and communications consultancy that has worked with many venue and convention bureau clients, both in the UK and overseas. Mexia's Foresight audit enables an organisation to work through its business objectives and marketing strategy to develop a powerful plan of action that will maximise opportunities and augment the organisation's messages.
- Research identified the Twitter handles of buyers and collated them into target VIP lists to monitor and engage with, and to be used in follower-building.
- The hashtag #FutureCHW was created.
- Content in phase 1 focused on event technology in order to build CHW's reputation in the technology sector.
- A technology blog was set up on CHW's website to create a portal for campaign content and to drive traffic to the website.
- A hybrid event on 'Wi-Fi woes' was organised, which attracted an online audience of 100 planners. All content was used to drive social media engagement.

Phase two – thought leadership:

- The second phase significantly increased the content related to event technology of the future, leveraging the blog, sharing relevant third-party content and stakeholder engagement through the use of competitions and polls, for example.
- The big finale of the campaign was an 'un-conference' live event featuring new technology, experience pods and keynotes to attract senior-level planners.

Digital content was a critical element of the campaign. The guest blog was used to explore technologies with input from various suppliers and experts and to help to build interest in the campaign. This portal was used to fuel the social media content programme and assist with driving traffic to the CHW website. In addition to guest blogs, a series of videos and a unique futuristic graphic was created to support campaign branding.

Return on investment from the Meet The Future campaign

The Meet The Future campaign resulted in:

- 122% increase in Twitter followers
- 42% increase in Facebook likes
- 58% increase in LinkedIn followers
- Estimated Twitter reach of over 119,000 for #FutureCHW
- 57% increase in web traffic compared to the same period during 2012/13
- 5,475 page hits on the MTF portal
- 41% increase in direct venue enquiries
- Over 600 registrations for the MTF conference
- 48 press clippings with a potential reach of 1,275,198

According to CHW, the social media effort was a key aspect of the campaign and it would have been difficult to achieve such outstanding results without it. The role of Mexia Communications in the campaign was essential to the campaign's success. The PR consultancy devised the initial Meet The Future framework in the PR and social media proposal that they submitted to CHW. They played an integral part in the development of the campaign and managed all social media channels. They also curated and created content for social media.

CASE STUDY 7.4   Iconic architecture: the ICE, Kraków, Poland

In May 2007, the Municipality of the City of Kraków, Poland's second largest city, launched an open international architecture competition for the design of a new conference centre to be located on a 1.14-hectare plot of land in the area of the Grunwaldzkie Roundabout (Rondo Grunwaldzkie) in Kraków. The objective of the competition was to identify the best possible architectural, functional and operational concept for the building of the conference centre. Some of the specifications mentioned in the rules of the competition are given below.

Due to the prominent location and significance on the city scale, the building of the Congress Centre should be adapted to the present spatial context and harmoniously inscribed into the outlines and viewpoint connections. The location of the Congress Centre ensures a unique view of the city panorama across the Vistula River: from Wawel all the way to the Church on the Rock (Kościół na Skałce.) Its location is key in relation to the walking trails connecting the Vistula River Boulevard with the Twardowski Rocks (Skałki Twardowskiego) and open spaces, the so-called 'Vistula River salon'.

The unique location, the rank and significance of the Centre imposes a requirement to ensure the highest architectural and planning standard. The Contracting Authority wishes for the Congress Centre to become yet another symbol, icon of the city of Kraków, representing its modern face.

The role of the designed centre will be twofold: on the one hand, it will enable the organisation of conventions and congresses; on the other hand, it will enable the hosting of cultural undertakings: music concerts, cultural and social events. The main functional element of the centre will consist of an auditorium hall with 1,800 places. The second important functional element will consist of the chamber hall for 600 people.

In November 2007, the winners of the competition were announced: Ingarden and Ewý Architects in co-operation with the Japanese architect Arata Isozaki and Associates.

ICE Kraków Congress Centre was inaugurated in October 2014. The building, dedicated to the hosting of conferences and cultural events, comprises three main halls with 1,800, 600 and 300 seats. A multi-functional conference area with a floor space of 550 square metres benefits from a system of mobile partitions allowing the free arrangement of this space, plus ancillary rooms and areas including offices, artists' dressing rooms and a commercial area.

ICE Kraków Congress Centre was designed in conformity with the highest functional and acoustic standards and equipped with state-of-the-art stage technology systems – the responsibility of experts from Arup Acoustic (London), Arup Theatre Consulting (Winchester) and Ramboll Acoustics (Cambridge). Taking into account the extensive range of events to be held in this venue, ranging from symphony concerts, rock and jazz music, theatre performances to major international conferences, the architects decided to design the main hall to allow various configurations of both audience and stage, thus ensuring the best acoustic setting for every purpose.

Besides the need to cope with functional and technological requirements, the architects designing the building had to take account of its exquisite and unique urban environment. ICE Kraków stands in one of the most prestigious locations in Poland: on the banks of the River Vistula opposite Wawel Castle, one of the most historically and culturally important sites in Poland. Therefore, the attractiveness of the Congress Centre results not only from the merits of its architecture and functionality but also from its location and the spectacular panoramic view that this offers. To maximise the benefits of its location, the building boasts a spectacular glass façade facing the embankment of the River Vistula, with the multi-storey foyer offering a panoramic view of the ancient City of Kraków situated immediately opposite. This enables those attending conferences and concerts to admire the city from an excellent perspective. Suspended in the foyer area is an elaborate staircase leading visitors to the many levels of the centre, opening before them successive levels of a panorama over the city, with Wawel Castle located in centre view. The height of the building is reduced on the Vistula side so that the scale of the development blends smoothly into the surrounding boulevards.

The primary materials used in the elevation of the venue are glass and titanium-zinc sheet, rounded off with individually designed ceramic and stone tiles made from granite, lime and sandstone. The materials for the tiles were chosen to allude to the building materials that were originally used to construct the castle on Wawel Hill. The colours of the external ceramic wall tiles reflect the colour range applied inside the building: the red of the Auditorium Hall, the graphite of the Theatre Hall, the white of the foyer and the silvery aluminium used for the roof finishing. The architects intended the multi-element composition of the façades to reflect motion and life: the dynamics of a modern developing city.

Through its scale and spectacular form, the building provides a new architectural point of reference for the ancient city of Kraków, a spatially dominant feature symbolising the gate to the city and its modern strategy of development.

CASE STUDY 7.5   A sustainable venue: the Hong Kong Convention and Exhibition Centre

The Hong Kong Convention and Exhibition Centre (HKCEC) opened in 1988, after which Hong Kong's business events industry experienced a period of rapid growth, enabling Hong Kong to establish its position as a premier international convention and meeting location.

The HKCEC, located on Victoria Harbour, is owned by the Hong Kong Trade Development Council (TDC) and the Hong Kong Special Administrative Region Government. The TDC is entrusted by the Government to be responsible for the centre's development, design and management. The TDC has contracted with Hong Kong Convention and Exhibition Centre (Management) Limited (HML) for management and operation of the Centre. HML is a wholly owned subsidiary of NWS Holdings Ltd.

The mission of HML, with a staff team of over 850, is 'to position the HKCEC as the best exhibition and convention centre in Asia, internationally renowned for excellence and hosting the world's greatest events, supported by innovative and creative operating techniques'.

Having experienced escalating demand from its time of opening, the HKCEC was expanded in 1997, doubling its prime function space. The expanded venue further strengthened Hong Kong's leading position as Asia's trade fair hub and ensured that Hong Kong could successfully meet the growing demand for space into the twenty-first century.

With the continuous growing demand of exhibition space from HKCEC's current and potential new clients, the HKCEC began its second expansion project in 2006 and completed it in 2009. That project brought 19,400 square metres of additional exhibition space to the HKCEC.

The cost of the HKCEC when it first opened in 1988 was approximately HK$2.5 billion (US$322 million), including two hotels, an office tower and a service apartment tower. The first expansion cost HK$4.8 billion (US$620 million), including site reclamation that began in June 1994 and the second expansion cost HK$1.4 billion (US$180 million). The HKCEC presently provides 66,000 square metres of purpose-built exhibition space, 20,000 square metres of multi-functional venues and 5,500 square metres of event support space.

It was reported in November 2014 (www.asiatoday.com) that the HKCEC had successfully achieved Level One certification of the ASTM Standard for the Evaluation and Selection of Venues for Environmentally Sustainable Meetings, Events, Trade Shows and Conferences. Since its launch in 2012, this stringent standard has only been achieved by a small number of major venues in the world.

ASTM International, or the American Society for Testing and Materials (ASTM), was established in 1898. It is a world renowned organisation that specialises in developing standards for a broad range of professions and industries. The ASTM Standard defines the considerations for venue selection by environmentally conscious event organisers. It requires the venue management to demonstrate commitment to sustainability in nine areas such as waste management, energy and water conservation and air quality.

Ms Monica Lee-Müller, Managing Director of Hong Kong Convention and Exhibition Centre (Management) Limited (HML), commented, 'we are proud that the HKCEC is recognised by the ASTM Standard. It is a strong evidence of the HML's ongoing commitment to reducing our environmental footprint and acting in a socially responsible manner. This achievement resulted from concerted effort of the entire HML team. I am also pleased that, as indicated in a company-wide staff survey conducted earlier this year, a vast majority of our staff have shown favourable support to the company's sustainability strategies'.

The development of the ASTM Standard was led by the Green Meeting and Industry Council (GMIC). GMIC is a professional organisation with over 600 members and it provides educational resources to event organisers, suppliers and venues seeking to meet the ever-rising expectations for sustainable events. Ms Connie Bergeron, President of the GMIC added, 'Responsible environmental and social practices in the event and meeting industry is a global concern. Congratulations to the HKCEC for joining the league of pioneering world class venues that have been certified to the ASTM Standard'.

During the last 2 years, with investment in technology upgrade and process enhancement, HML has successfully reduced its electricity and water consumption by almost 10 per cent. A remarkable achievement considering its extensive portfolio of over 1,000 events and close to 6 million visitors a year. HML has a full-time managerial executive dedicated to driving the company's sustainability initiatives.

SUMMARY

The number of new venues, and types of venues, opening their doors to conference delegates appears to be escalating in many parts of the world. Venues are not only changing in quantity, but also in their quality, as a greater variety of meetings facilities – many of them classified as unusual venues – are now competing for conference business. Venues are becoming more integrated with the destinations in which they are located to enhance the delegates' experience.

Information and communications technology is rapidly changing the ways venues host their events and market themselves, with social media being increasingly used as marketing tools.

The design of new and converted venues is increasingly taking into account issues such as flexibility, security and accessibility for disabled visitors. Meeting planners themselves are being invited to contribute their ideas when venues are at the design stage in order to ensure that they are not only attractive but also functional.

Nevertheless, perhaps the most over-riding concern is that venues should be constructed and operated in such a way that their negative impacts on the natural environment are minimal. New standards in venue design, construction and operations are increasingly being observed – and promoted in venues' marketing messages.

REVIEW AND DISCUSSION QUESTIONS

- Identify a local tourist attraction that, in your opinion, could also operate as a venue for meetings. What reasons can you give for believing that it could be used in this way? Are there any features of the attraction that would make it attractive in terms of brand alignment for some potential clients?

- Visit the website of a conference centre that is located in your vicinity. What use is the venue making of web-based marketing tools such as its website and social media? Can you suggest any improvements to the use it is making of these tools?

- 'Traditional media gives the control of message to the marketer whereas social media shifts the balance to the consumer'. In the context of conference venue marketing, where the consumers are the meeting planners, can you see any challenges for venues if the balance of power moves towards the meeting planners?

- You have been hired as a consultant to advise on the re-design and refurbishment of a venue built in the 1970s. How would you proceed with this project?

BIBLIOGRAPHY

Ball, C. (2005) 'RFID: what's in it for me?' published online at http://www.corbinball.com/articles_technology/index.cfm?fuseaction=cor_av&artID=1887 (accessed 5 August 2015).

Chapin, A. (2014) 'How convention centers are becoming more flexible', 22 October, published online at http://www.bizbash.com/how-convention-centers-are-becoming-more-flexible/atlanta/story/29442#.VS0DtcpFDIU (accessed 5 August 2015).

Davidson, R. (2011) 'Web 2.0 as a marketing tool for conference centres', *International Journal of Event and Festival Management*, 2(2): 117–38.

Grass Roots (2011) *Creating and Using Unusual Venues*, London: Grass Roots Meeting Industry Report.

Guillot, C. (2015) 'Convention centres of the future, designed today', *Collaborate Meetings*, February/March.

HKCEC (2014) 'HKCEC receives international recognition for sustainability', 17 November, published online at http://www.hkcec.com/about-hkcec/media-centre/2014/hkcec-receives-international-recognition-sustainability (accessed 5 August 2015).

Manis, P. (2012) 'Emerging trends for comprehensive convention center design: maximizing user experience, facility flexibility and building efficiency', *TechBriefs*, 1: 6–8.

Maritz (2012) *The Future of Meeting Venues White Paper*, Fenton: Maritz Research.

Market Dynamics Research Group (2014) *Understanding the Role of Digital Resources for Planning Meetings*, New Orleans: Market Dynamics Research Group.

Marr, S. (2011) 'Applying "work process knowledge" to visitor attractions venues', *International Journal of Event and Festival Management*, 2(2): 151–69.

Mills-Tannenbaum, I. (2014) '3 reasons to consider a non-traditional venue for your next meeting', published online at http://www.helenmills.com/our-blog/3-reasons-consider-non-traditional-venues-next-meeting (accessed 5 August 2015).

UK CAMS (2015) *The UK Conference and Meeting Survey 2015*, published online at http://www.ukcams.org.uk/.

Chapter **8**

Building effective marketing partnerships

Chapter overview

The marketing of conference destinations and venues requires substantial financial and human resources, as well as expertise. Greater success can often be achieved by destinations and venues through working, not in isolation, but in partnership with other organisations that may be similar in type or geographically close together.

This chapter covers:

- The role of destination marketing organisations in forging partnerships at the destination level
- Membership recruitment and retention for destination marketing organisations
- Working with marketing consortia
- Maximising the benefits of membership of trade associations
- Harnessing political support through effective lobbying

It includes case studies on:

- The Three City Alliance
- The IMEX Politicians Forum

On completion of this chapter, you should be able to:

- describe the ways in which a destination marketing organisation (DMO) or convention bureau provides leadership to a destination;
- understand how a DMO or convention bureau stimulates collaboration, team working and partnerships across a destination;
- appreciate the importance of a team culture in the successful operation of a conference venue;
- understand the different types of membership structures for DMOs and convention bureaux;
- identify strategies used by DMOs and convention bureaux to recruit and retain members;
- describe the different kinds of marketing consortia available to venues and destinations and the potential benefits from joining such consortia;
- understand the role played by industry trade associations and the membership benefits they offer; and
- appreciate the important need for industry lobbying and representational activity and give examples of how such activity is carried out.

Introduction

Success as a business event destination or venue is often achieved through partnership and collaboration with other organisations and with key players in the local community. Positioning and profiling a brand, creating recognition and trust and generating a predisposition to book on the part of conference clients are the result of developing appropriate strategies and campaigns as outlined in earlier chapters. They demand huge investments of time and resources in a world which, today, is often described as a 'global village'. Competition is intense and increases by the day.

At the same time, marketing budgets, especially those deriving from public sector bodies, may be reducing rather than expanding. Yet there is still the challenge and requirement to produce ever greater returns on the investments in marketing that are being made.

It is in this context that the benefits of working with key strategic partners become a major consideration for destination and venue marketers. This chapter will look at how such collaboration works in practical terms and will illustrate the kinds of advantages to be gained.

The role of destination marketing organisations in forging partnerships at the destination level

A fundamental requirement for the successful implementation of a destination marketing strategy is ongoing collaboration by skilled, flexible and committed people who develop a strong team culture. A strong team culture is built upon mutual trust and respect, complementary strengths and abilities and an understanding of, and commitment to, goals that are larger than individual goals, with everyone pulling together to achieve extraordinary results. Success can be achieved when all partners are motivated, inspired and encouraged, working together with a commitment to clear and focused goals and shared values.

In destination terms, this means identifying where there is a need to co-operate but understanding where there is still a need to compete – and the balance required between the two. When managed effectively, working together and developing a real team culture can also become a learning experience, enabling partners to discover what they are already doing well but also, importantly, what they could do better.

The development of a high-performing team can be said to go through the following evolutionary process:

- *Forming*: as the team comes together, tasks, rules and methods are established
- *Storming*: conflict starts to emerge as people test the task, each other and the leader
- *Norming*: co-operation begins to develop with some cohesion and unity of purpose; agreed canons of behaviour emerge
- *Performing*: constructive work surges ahead; energy is focused

Successful team building could be summarised as follows:

- *Caring*: of each other; being respectful of different views; and being mutually encouraging
- *Daring*: being innovative and adventurous
- *Sharing*: of objectives, responsibility, and one another's roles

However, it is vital that the team is supported by appropriate training, development and education. This needs formal education, a commitment to ongoing training and development and, finally, organisational learning; that is, organisations that will truly excel in the future will be those that discover how to tap people's commitment and capacity to learn at all levels within an organisation and do not simply rely on a grand strategy being handed down from the top. Teams must learn how to harness and nurture leadership at all levels, both bottom-up and top-down, empowering individuals and the whole team to take responsibility for the achievement of the team's goals, both in principle and in practice.

A convention bureau or DMO needs to offer leadership to the destination and create a sense of cohesion within that destination. In doing so, clients will feel that they are dealing with a single, united entity where the various suppliers are seen to be co-operating fully with one another to ensure the success of clients' events. In practical terms, this could mean, for example, that the convention bureau will discuss accommodation rates being offered by a number of hotels and seek their commitment to a set of rates that can then be guaranteed to the client as part of the event bidding process, even though the event itself may be several years ahead. It might be that the convention bureau or DMO will put in place a destination training programme to drive up standards and enhance the overall quality of the destination product (see, for example, Glasgow's training programme in the lead-up to the 2014 Commonwealth Games referenced in chapter 6).

Interestingly, in the context of destination team building, the word 'team' is now being used among DMOs to underline this cohesive cross-destination approach. Team Aberdeen Ambassadors, for example, is a collaboration between VisitAberdeen, the University of Aberdeen, Robert Gordon University and Aberdeen Exhibition and Conference Centre to increase the level of national and international association conferences being held in Aberdeen City and Shire (for more details visit: http://www.visitaberdeen.com/conferences/ambassadors/). Team Adelaide, South Australia is the brand used by Adelaide Convention Bureau and Adelaide Convention Centre when they exhibit jointly at trade shows or submit joint bids for events.

Team building is also essential, of course, in the management and operation of a conference venue. In an article entitled 'Building a culture' (*Conference & Meetings World* magazine, Issue 79), Geoff Donaghy, CEO of the new International Convention Centre Sydney, an AU$1.1 billion business events venue due to open in 2016, describes the need for a strong team culture if the venue is to be successful. He says:

> *There are a number of factors that need to occur in order to build a strong culture and it must start at the very top of an organisation. If the head of the organisation doesn't believe, you are*

doomed from the start. How can you build a unified team that lives and breathes a culture if they can't see those same values being acted upon every day by the captain of the ship. It's simple. You can't.

He continues:

Finding the right people isn't just about who is the most qualified on paper, especially if you want to build a strong service culture. It's a 50/50 split between CV and chemistry.

Geoff Donaghy believes that, once you have handpicked your executive team, the next step is to unify them behind the desired culture so that they, in turn, can build departments of people who share those values. The journey to a strong culture is much easier to get right early on in developing a new team. He values trust as core to a successful team and says that a strong driver of that trust and in developing a solid culture is clear and consistent communication. He concludes the article:

There is so much excitement and adrenaline involved in bringing a venue of this scale to market on an international stage (when it opens in December 2016, ICC Sydney will employ over 1,000 people), it is important to harness and maintain that excitement and passion once the venue hits its strides and becomes fully operational. This is the point where strong management and leadership really come into play. This is the critical period to be watching for cues, support-ing managers, testing goals and continuing to gauge employee engagement, all ingredients of a strong culture.

The essence of DMOs and convention bureaux is that they bring together, under a common umbrella, a variety of venues and other suppliers for collaborative marketing activity – venues and suppliers that, at another level, might see themselves in direct competition with one another. DMOs and convention bureaux can unite the public and private sectors in partnerships across a city or community, often to a degree that is rarely replicated in other business sectors. The most successful partnerships are those that develop a real team ethos but also continue to recognise and respect the strengths and needs of the indi-vidual team members, reflecting the unique features of each while, at the same time, portraying them as components of a greater whole: the destination itself.

The DMO fulfils an important communications role in ensuring that venues, visitor attractions, restau-rants, retail outlets, transport operators, the local municipality and the wider business community are all aware that a major convention is coming to town. Each of these can then prepare their products and services accordingly, maximising the economic opportunities afforded by the event but also tailoring these in a way that is personalised to the client and to the event participants. These latter will, in turn, be given the feeling that the whole destination is aware of their event and is working together to make them feel welcome and at home. For convention delegates and attendees, anticipation of an enjoyable and worthwhile event will be increased if they arrive in a city and see welcome banners profiling the event. In addition, they will experience taxi rides with drivers who are informed and able to initiate friendly conversations and make specific reference to the convention and meet hotel reception staff who have been briefed on the importance of the convention and, as a consequence, treat the delegates as VIPs.

The DMO or convention bureau is probably the only destination body able to fulfil this vital co-ordinat-ing role, combining its strengths as a neutral, impartial body with its detailed knowledge of the network of destination suppliers to create a true destination partnership and an image of a properly co-ordinated destination. Where the DMO fails to achieve such collaboration, client perceptions are of a weakened or non-existent destination brand, on the one hand, while on the other, clients may feel that their task of organising a successful event will be made so much harder because there is no-one pulling everything together on behalf of the destination for the benefit of the client.

Scott Taylor, chief executive of Glasgow City Marketing Bureau (http://conventions.peoplemakeglasgow.com), describes how destination partnership opportunities can deliver gross value added benefits over time, but require a different set of measures to understand. Commenting specifically for this book, he expressed his views in the following terms:

> Conventions and conferences deliver a direct economic expenditure that provides a level of return on investment. It is this measure that tends to inform the key performance indicators (KPIs) of the destination. However, what is more difficult to quantify, though equally important, is the resulting gross value added (GVA) that bringing together the world's best minds in one place can deliver. It is these presenting opportunities that are rarely exploited because they are difficult to measure, dependent on partnership working and span a longer period of time. As a result, they rarely feature on any organisation's KPIs.
>
> It is clear that conventions can support the ambitions of an inward investment strategy with a platform that adds relevance and credibility to a ready-made and receptive audience. Conferences can be measured on their indirect longitudinal GVA – the non-direct expenditure spin-off over time, such as a 5-year period. This non-direct GVA comes from making much more of the opportunities that arise from a range of bespoke activities such as convention study visits with a defined and measured purpose, understanding and reinforcing convention research profile, creating the network platforms and events to help secure research contracts, enhancing the media package around the conference, monitoring local and central governmental policy changes and so on. As an example, Glasgow hosted a scientific conference, which was worth £850,000 in economic benefit to the city, but £1.2 million in new research contracts for delegate companies. Conventions have impact far beyond the daily delegate spend but it takes a different set of measures to understand it.

In north-west England, the cities of Liverpool and Manchester are approximately 30 miles apart. In 2014, they began a form of high-level strategic partnership and collaboration which, it is anticipated, will extend into conference and tourism marketing activity in subsequent years. Chris Brown, Chief Executive of Marketing Liverpool, describes the objectives and practical outworking of this co-operation and suggests how it might evolve further in the future:

> There is no formal nature to our arrangements, more of an inherent set of principles, but this way of working has developed from our inward investment promotional work, although we are now moving towards incorporating the same methodology for the Visitor Economy.
>
> The origination of the joint working arrangements started around discussions relating to the international property (or real estate) expo, 'MIPIM', held in Cannes (France) each year. Manchester's presence at the exhibition is organised by Marketing Manchester, and Liverpool's by Marketing Liverpool. Both cities had previously organised their own separate programmes but, for 2014, jointly arranged a business breakfast themed around a concept called 'Atlantic Gateway' – the breakfast was attended by over 100 delegates.
>
> Building on this initial piece of joint working, we developed a similar yet more detailed joint partnership for the inaugural Festival of Business held in Liverpool in June and July 2014. This partnership approach was crafted between the two organisations but strategically supported by the Mayor of Liverpool and the Chief Executive of Manchester City Council. This arrangement encapsulated the following:
> - A launch event in Manchester with the Mayor of Liverpool
> - Six events in Liverpool at which Sir Howard Bernstein (Chief Executive of Manchester City Council) was a speaker

- *Support for four conferences to be held in Manchester as part of the International Festival for Business overall programme*
- *Joint marketing and PR*

All these arrangements worked very well and strengthened our partnership significantly, and so this collaboration was continued into 'MIPIM UK' in October 2014 when, for the first time, Manchester and Liverpool had a joint stand which again worked very well.

We have now established this joint working in relation to investment marketing opportunities and this has provided the catalyst for us to develop a similar way of working for Tourism and Conference marketing and we envisage this taking significant shape in 2015.

There is no doubt that the reducing public sector finances are driving a more collaborative rather than competitive mindset. Accordingly, we would envisage our arrangements with Manchester being extended to include other cities.

Membership recruitment and retention for destination marketing organisations

The majority of convention bureaux and DMOs operate as membership bodies, although in some cases the term 'industry partners' instead of 'members' is in vogue, usually describing an even closer relationship between the convention bureau/DMO and the partner organisation. With some destinations, membership is defined in relatively narrow terms and will just encompass a destination's conference/convention venues, hotels and, perhaps, audio-visual suppliers. In other instances, membership is extended to a much broader section of the business community, including transport companies, retailers, visitor attractions, restaurants, professional conference organisers and even banks and utility companies.

Whichever type of membership structure is adopted, the challenge is always to recruit and retain the members because they provide a key income stream for the DMO, which is sometimes the largest single income stream. Managing and satisfying a potentially diverse membership is never easy, as each member will come with different needs and expectations. It is certainly the case that membership of a DMO must demonstrate 'bottom line' business or commercial benefits (i.e. generate new business and revenue for members), rather than simply offer networking, education or accreditation benefits to members. However, as stated by Walters (2005:163):

> *Most convention bureaux don't want members unless they can help the member to secure business. No-one wants to damage the convention bureau's reputation in the community by signing on companies that will not be helped by bureau membership and that might disparage the bureau at renewal time if they thought they did not receive the services promised.*

Effective recruitment strategies demand good quality promotional materials or 'collateral', which set out clearly the services to be provided by the DMO and quantify the costs and benefits of membership. Such materials should not over-state the benefits because a member who has joined with unrealistic expectations will almost certainly be disappointed and will not renew membership – nonetheless, promotional materials need to be positive and upbeat. It is always worth including quotations from existing members or peers on what they have gained from being a member. There may be opportunities to invite potential members as guests to DMO events and activities, using these as appetisers to give these likely recruits an insight into, and experience of, membership. Special receptions or presentations can be organised where potential recruits meet the DMO's board members and executive team. Most DMOs have a dedicated 'membership services team' with both a sales role (to sell membership to new members) and a servicing role (ensuring effective communications with, and care for, all members).

Retention of members is, in part, about delivering good commercial benefits to members. But it is also about making them feel valued and important and this, in turn, links back to the development and maintenance of accurate member databases. It is vital that members receive regular and appropriate communications from the DMO. Furthermore, it is crucial that the data held on members is comprehensive and up-to-date – misspelling a member's name, holding a wrong email address and omitting them from distribution lists may all be relatively small mistakes in themselves but they invariably give a member the impression that he is not valued and that the DMO is not run professionally.

Membership retention is a 12-months-of-the-year task. It is hard work. It requires attention to detail. It needs a listening ear. Walters (2005:165) suggests:

> *A membership services person should make six to ten calls a day, especially to members who do not seem to be participating. This person should ask questions such as whether they are getting the convention bureau's mail and leads, whether their brochures are at the local visitor centre, and whether they plan to attend an upcoming mixer or other event. At renewal time, convention bureaux should send a letter with the invoice, stress that renewal is optional, and offer to meet with the contact person if they have any doubts about renewing. This is especially important if the contact person has changed and the new person receiving the mail is not sure what the bureau is or why the firm is even a member.*

Working with marketing consortia

It is difficult, and certainly very expensive, for an individual conference venue to market itself effectively by operating on its own. Venues seeking to establish a market presence must contend with factors such as the scale of the competition, the substantial costs of marketing and the predisposition of event organisers or buyers to buy 'location' first.

It is for these reasons that most venues work in partnership with the destination in which they are located to create awareness and to stimulate enquiries from potential clients. The venues build links with the appropriate DMO, be this a convention bureau or conference office, an area or regional tourist board or a national tourism organisation. Many venues are also members of marketing consortia (groupings of similar properties interested in the same types of clients and events business) that give them a higher market profile and through which they engage in collaborative marketing activities. Consortia can also provide tangible business benefits such as bulk purchasing discounts, networking, benchmarking and training. Belonging to a consortium can also give a venue credibility in the eyes of the buyer. Examples of major consortia operating in the conference industry include:

- *Hotel groups* such as Hilton, Accor, Marriott, Starwood Hotels and Resorts, Sol Meliá, Intercontinental and Radisson. These are not strictly consortia as they are groups of hotels under common ownership and management systems. Most, if not all, have central reservations and marketing departments that undertake national and international marketing campaigns and which control the promotional activities of the individual properties to a greater or lesser degree. Even so, the majority of hotels within these chains are also allowed some discretion and budget to engage in their own marketing campaigns, for which the broad strategy and promotional materials are determined by head office. Some of the large chains have developed their own branded conference and meeting products (see chapter 2).

- *Unique Venues* is a grouping of several thousand non-traditional meeting facilities and function rooms in the USA, Canada and the UK: colleges, universities, museums, mansions, cinemas or movie theatres, conference centres, entertainment venues, cruise ships, restaurants, business centres and others. In this case, the common theme is the individuality or uniqueness of the venues involved, with a particular focus on their ambiance, memorability, flexibility, technology and affordability. Unique Venues has administrative offices in Colorado, Pennsylvania and South Carolina (USA), and British Columbia (Canada). Further details can be accessed via www.uniquevenues.com.

- *Conference Centres of Excellence (CCE)* aims 'to be the membership body of choice for the marketing of high quality, innovative, customer-led conference venues in the UK' and it is the UK's largest consortium of dedicated, specialist conference and training venues. It was formed in 1992 with the objective of sharing information, expertise and marketing resources to promote independent venues in the UK, and now (January 2015) has 30 such venues nationwide in membership, with a geographical footprint from the south coast of England to Scotland. Through networking, benchmarking and sharing best practice within the membership, CCE works with its members, who are mostly independent providers, to support the concept that specialist venues are the optimum solution for conferences, training and meetings, offering completely focussed support and a distraction-free environment. Member venues are required to meet stringent quality criteria in terms of facilities, accommodation and customer care, which is monitored on an ongoing assessment basis to ensure customers enjoy the highest quality standards when using one of the group's venues. The group now has a sales and marketing function and offers a free venue-finding service to clients, providing all-inclusive rates in bespoke event package proposals. Further information: www.cceonline.co.uk.

- *Historic Conference Centres of Europe (HCCE)* is a unique network of conference centres located in historic buildings, spanning the length and breadth of Europe. Founded in 1996, by 2015, 26 centres in 13 countries were members of the network, which has administrative offices in Amsterdam. HCCE's promotional material claims that 'there is nothing standardised about these conference centres. Each facility has a unique architectural heritage, an attractive location and a management approach based on personal service'. Further information: www.hcce.com.

Other examples of venue marketing consortia include Leading Hotels of the World (www.lhw.com) and The Westminster Collection (www.thewestminstercollection.co.uk).

However, it is not just venues that form such consortia. Conference destinations and DMOs have increasingly, in recent years, forged alliances for marketing purposes. Examples of these alliances include:

- *BestCities Global Alliance* is a global collaboration comprising the convention bureaux of 12 cities: Berlin, Bogotá, Cape Town, Chicago, Copenhagen, Dubai, Edinburgh, Houston, Melbourne, Singapore, Tokyo and Vancouver. The Alliance was launched in 2000 on the basis of strength in numbers and the optimisation of collective resources to pursue common goals. The Alliance believes in the unique benefits it can offer to its clients that no single bureau can offer. BestCities is also the first global alliance to put in place an alliance-wide quality management system that ensures a consistent level of convention bureau service excellence from all partner bureaux. Each of the partners demonstrates the same qualities, efficiencies and high standards expected as membership criteria. However, as highly regarded and individual cities in their own right, each partner brings its own unique strengths, knowledge and experience to the Alliance which has helped BestCities to become one of the world's most recognised and influential global alliances of convention bureaux. In 2014, the Alliance refreshed its Vision and simplified it with a clearer focus: 'The leading alliance of global destinations and convention bureaux for international association meetings'. A new strapline – 'When the world wants to meet, we set the standard' – was conceived as a positioning statement for BestCities that is reflective of the alliance's Vision and Values. It communicates the Alliance's essence: global gateway, destinations delivery and trusted partnerships. In January 2015, BestCities and the Professional Convention Management Association embarked on a landmark strategic partnership agreement with both organisations levering and supplementing each other's resources. Further information: www.bestcities.net.

- *The Energy Cities Alliance* is an alternative model of global destination partnership and branding. It was formed in 2007 and it comprises four member destinations: Aberdeen, Abu Dhabi, Calgary and

Stavanger. It is a partnership of organisations with a common focus on ensuring conferences and exhibitions held in their destinations are successful. The common factor is, of course, 'energy', which describes the oil and gas industries that thrive in these destinations. However, according to the Alliance website, energy 'also portrays the images of light, life and excitement that are the heart and soul of the cities'. The Alliance is a partnership of some of the world's most dynamic and economically booming cities in the oil and gas and mining resources industries. The Alliance is aimed at supporting meeting planners who are looking to host successful world class conferences. Recognising that these cities are global leaders in trade and investment, the Energy Cities Alliance is about sharing this success with associations and corporations involved with meetings and conventions. Further information: www.energycitiesalliance.com.

- *European National Convention Bureaux Alliance*: in October 2014, 17 European national convention bureaux formed a new alliance to promote the continent's strengths as a business events destination. The objective was to have a constructive and active collaboration on issues to make each member stronger as Europe, without compromising each country's unique identity. The partnership approach is designed to unite the individual and unique offerings of each member country in order to simplify and strengthen the approach to key markets, such as China and the USA. Members include the Austrian Convention Bureau, Czech Convention Bureau, Estonian Convention Bureau, Finland Convention Bureau, German Convention Bureau, Hungarian Convention Bureau, Meet in Reykjavik, Montenegro National Tourist Board/National Convention Bureau, Holland Marketing, Norway Convention Bureau, Poland Convention Bureau, Serbia Convention Bureau, Slovak Convention Bureau, Slovenian Convention Bureau, Switzerland Convention Bureau and VisitDenmark. A further five national convention bureaux, representing Italy, Ireland, France, Portugal and Latvia, joined the alliance in January 2015, taking the total membership to 22.

Other examples of global destination partnerships include:

- Future Convention Cities Initiative (Abu Dhabi, Durban Kwazulu, London, San Francisco, Seoul, Sydney and Toronto) – launched in 2011 (www.fccinitiative.org)
- The Global Science and Convention Alliance (Adelaide, Daejeon, Hyderabad, Prague and Toulouse) – launched in 2012

Case Study 8.1 describes the Three City Alliance, which covers the collaborative activity of three US cities' DMOs: Milwaukee, Pittsburgh and Portland.

Maximising the benefits of membership of trade associations

There are a number of trade associations in the conference industry, some operating at a national level, others at a continental or truly international level. Many cater for a particular niche in the market: Destination Marketing Association International (DMAI), International Association of Conference Centres (IACC), European Cities Marketing, for example, while a few aim to attract a wide variety of members, such as the International Congress and Convention Association (ICCA) or the UK's Meetings Industry Association (mia).

Boléat (2003) defines trade associations in the following terms:

> *Trade associations provide representative and other collective services to businesses, generally in a specific sector, with common interests. There are a number of different types of association. At the margin, trade associations overlap with other industry bodies.*

He describes their role as a representative body in:

> *Putting forward the collective position of members, generally to government departments and agencies and regulators, but also to the media and to other opinion formers.*

He adds that 'many associations also provide other services such as industry statistics, general market information, training, conferences and exhibitions'.

It can be seen from this description that trade associations are not primarily marketing entities, although it is often the case that members join specifically in the expectation of gaining new business through their membership. However, some associations do provide direct sales and marketing opportunities to their members through the organisation of stands at exhibitions (and may even organise the exhibitions themselves), by forwarding business leads and by maintaining databases of clients or buyers that can be accessed by their members as a unique membership benefit. Many associations produce newsletters and issue press releases to highlight the activities and services of their members, thus giving members good PR exposure.

Trade associations can also provide indirect marketing benefits to their members, as membership can confer a sense of accreditation on members, particularly if a rigorous new member recruitment policy is in force requiring potential members to meet certain quality or commercial criteria before being granted membership. Members are then entitled to display the association's logo on their stationery and promotional material and it is anticipated that this will give buyers confidence that they are dealing with a reputable organisation that will perform to certain minimum standards.

Individuals who get fully involved with the running of a trade association may progress to becoming one of its officers, serving as chair or president or treasurer, for example. While this can give invaluable experience to the individual and enhance their own career prospects, the venue or destination that they represent can also benefit through 'association' – one of their employees becomes a recognised figure in the trade association and in the wider conference industry and the exposure that they receive can also reflect positively on their employing organisation.

Successful associations focus clearly on delivering good business networking opportunities, a relevant education programme and up-to-date industry news and best practice guidance. Members are also likely to demand that they demonstrate sound strategic planning, well delivered services and professional management.

Hendrie (2005)) suggests that people join trade associations for leadership, innovation, representation and 'bang for our buck'. He goes on to outline some of the challenges facing trade associations, as well as the recipe for success:

> we recognise what trade associations face: competition for member dues (fees), sensitive community, regional and national issues, a tight economy, internal and external politics, restrictive practices, unenlightened management and directors, and perhaps the worst enemy . . . ennui. But it all comes back to worth! The successful organisations are not static. They continually assess their resources, realign the process, people, products and services to maximise value. Regularly, they survey their constituency, evaluating satisfaction and seeking input. This also includes their allied members and the organisation's staff. Communication is constant, reliable and germane. They are always connected, imaginative and decisive, recognising that flexibility and adaptability make for progress. But it all starts with knowing their stakeholders . . . their needs, their aspirations and their expectations. Then they deliver like crazy.

While it would be a mistake for a venue or a DMO to join a trade association solely for the purpose of business generation, it is undoubtedly the case that many trade associations can, and do, offer a range of direct and indirect commercial development benefits. To take full advantage of these, trade association members need to participate actively in the opportunities on offer, and work hard to maximise the benefits of their membership. Members who sit passively at their own workstations expecting business to fall into their laps simply because they have joined a trade association are likely to be severely disappointed.

Harnessing political support through effective lobbying

The kinds of local, national and international partnerships and consortia outlined in this chapter offer a range of examples and models for emulation or adaptation. However, none of these replaces the complementary need for activity that will raise overall understanding of, and support for, the conference and business events sector. Ours is still, as we have seen in chapter 1, a young industry, one that is all too frequently misunderstood and under-recognised by the political and business communities. It is vital that this situation is addressed urgently in order to ensure that support structures, educational and career frameworks, product investment, funding for marketing and political support in bidding for major international events, for example, are provided at levels commensurate with those given to other industry sectors. Changes and improvements will only be achieved through professional lobbying and representational activity by the industry itself and these need to be undertaken at both international and national levels.

There is still a lack of understanding and recognition of the value that conferences and meetings generate in terms of professional development, knowledge transfer, investment generation, technical progress and all the other areas that define why these events happen in the first place. In reality, meetings, conventions and exhibitions are, in the words of a paper published by the Joint Meetings Industry Council (JMIC) in 2008:

> *Primary engines of both economic and professional development, key vehicles for not just sharing information – something that, in many cases, can be done just as effectively on the Internet – but building the kind of understanding, relationships and confidence that can only be achieved on a face-to-face basis.*

The JMIC paper describes 'three critical areas of interface which the meetings industry has with the broader economy, whether that be at a global level or in the context of an individual community'. The first of these is the economic role. The second is the business development role:

> *Which reaches far beyond the immediate effects of event-related spending. For a start, meetings, conventions and exhibitions attract business audiences that wouldn't necessarily otherwise visit a particular destination, and who are more likely to be investors and decision-makers than other types of visitors. In this way, events serve to expose the host city and its investment opportunities to a whole new audience – a process that can rival even the most highly evolved economic and investment development programmes mounted by the business community. At the same time, they provide a vehicle for local business and professional groups to host colleagues and create a showcase for local products and services, all key elements in the economic development process.*

But, the paper suggests:

> *Above all, there are the benefits associated with the community enhancement role – because these are the ones that most directly impact the largest number of people in a community. For a start, meetings and conventions create access to a wide range of professional development opportunities for local residents by making these more accessible to those in the community. Major, or even regional, gatherings bring what is often world-class knowledge and expertise within the grasp of local businesses and professionals, improving overall knowledge in ways that would not otherwise be possible. When such gains are made in areas such as the medical or research fields, the benefits to the rest of the community can be very profound in terms of how they improve the overall quality of life.*

> *But even without this effect there are ways that the community benefits in a very tangible way from the meetings, conventions and exhibitions taking place there. For a start, it justifies and in large part finances the development of facilities that can then be used for the community's own events and celebrations. But, best of all, the arrival of non-resident delegates means a lot of new*

tax revenues from outside of the usual local tax base which can and will be applied to supporting ongoing community services.

The paper concludes, however, by describing an even more important role, one which goes to the heart of what meetings are all about, which is:

The importance they have in bringing together diverse interests and cultures to address common challenges. Meetings, conventions and exhibitions not only support professional, research, technology and academic development – the pivotal activities that underpin global progress – but they also help build networks and bridge cultural differences that threaten world order and advancement. The simple fact is, meetings are vehicles for finding solutions to global issues – and that is something we will have no shortage of in the years ahead!

The challenge, therefore, is how to communicate all of these benefits through positive messages to a myriad of audiences: political (local, national and international), business, academic, community and others? It is encouraging to note a number of initiatives taking place around the world. One such is the creation of 'National Meetings Weeks' being run on an annual basis in several countries. First begun in the UK at the beginning of the new millennium, these 'Weeks' have enjoyed some success in raising the profile and understanding of the sector. In the UK, 'National Meetings Week' has evolved into a 6-month campaign entitled 'Britain for Events' (www.britainforevents.co.uk), and this campaign has been instrumental in the creation of an All-Party Parliamentary Group for Events, the first time that a group of national politicians has come together to lobby for and support the Events sector. The campaign was also successful in gaining endorsement from the British Prime Minister, David Cameron. The 'Britain for Events' campaign is overseen by the Business Visits and Events Partnership, an umbrella body that brings together over 20 representative bodies and trade associations from the sector (www.businessvisitsan deventspartnership.com).

The trade show, IMEX-Frankfurt, includes, as part of the proceedings, an annual Politicians Forum, designed to bring together both local and national politicians from a number of countries to debate key issues in support of the business events sector. The activities, objectives and achievements of the IMEX Politicians Forum are described in more detail in Case Study 8.2.

In Australia, the Business Events Council (BECA) (www.businesseventscouncil.org.au) was created in 1994 to bring the business events industry and community together and to speak with one voice. Its purpose was, and is, to foster the development of the industry as a united entity and to raise the profile of business events to government and to the business community. Perhaps inevitably this is still a 'work in progress', as acknowledged by the Executive Manager of BECA, Inge Garofani, who was quoted (Conworld.net – 3 March 2012) as saying:

Business and association meetings and events are an undervalued contributor to the economy and community in Australia. They provide not only the tangible benefits of room nights and delegate spend but a far greater contribution to the nation. They have a ripple effect like a stone in a pond where the initial impact is small and defined but the real impact is in the ripples flowing outwards. These ripples are where we provide the greatest benefit to Australia. We bring international experts to Australia to share knowledge, educate our community and this leads to great legacies and benefits, both financial and non-financial.

A BECA paper published in 2010 emphasises the important role that business events can play in fostering innovation. Entitled 'Delivering innovation, knowledge and performance: the role of business events', the paper recommends:

- As fostering innovation is such an important national building endeavour and business events have a key role to play in this activity, strategies need to be identified that can best leverage the role of business events, particularly in key industry sectors targeted for growth by government.

- Given the view that the impacts of business events are largely synonymous with tourism, there needs to be greater efforts made to raise awareness within key government portfolios and industry sectors as to the broader value and potential of business events.
- At a time when Australian universities are under substantial pressure to cut costs, a campaign should be launched to highlight the important role that business events play in helping researchers create and disseminate innovation. The benefits to individual universities hosting international research conferences should also be highlighted.
- More effort should be made to encourage associations and companies to assess the return on investment of the business events they stage so that the outcomes from these events are captured and there is a wider recognition of the benefits that can be derived.

A meeting convened by JMIC in London in May 2011 agreed on five steps to broaden understanding of the benefits to accrue from meetings and conventions. These are:

1. To carry out inventory/comparative analysis of existing valuation models and develop a means for achieving greater consistency among these
2. To encourage the development of local applications for economic impact models in order to generate better data for use in individual communities
3. To create a protocol for assembling value-added 'output' values with emphasis on the use of case studies and examples to illustrate major areas of benefit
4. To identify key audiences along with their priority information requirements and develop a communications 'tool kit' to assist in this process
5. To encourage event owners to assume a more active role in measuring and communicating value

However, there is also a need to re-position the sector, aligning it more closely with business and economic development and downplaying its associations with tourism and leisure. In an article entitled 'How far have we really come?', published in *Conference & Meetings World* magazine (Issue 78 – January 2015), Rod Cameron, Executive Director of the International Association of Convention Centres (AIPC) and of the JMIC, describes this important requirement in the following terms:

> *Ten years ago in an article entitled 'Ten Things We Need to Explain about Our Industry' we said: 'We're not tourism – we really have relatively little to do with the leisure sector that makes up the bulk of the tourism product in most parts of the world. In fact, we're much more connected to the areas of business and economic development'.*
>
> *At the time, many saw this as heresy – even within the industry itself. Today, it is almost universally accepted, driven by a growing awareness that the greatest value of meetings, conventions and other business events is the role they play in supporting economic, academic and professional advancement. In achieving this transition we've managed to better align ourselves with the reasons organisers actually hold events – and at the same time, with what are today the number one priorities of governments and communities everywhere on earth.*

He goes on to argue, however, that this distinction is still far from recognised among the same communities and governments that comprise our most important audiences. He contends that there is still a lot of work to do, not least in changing perceptions that our events *are seen as simply providing an excuse for a paid holiday at someone else's expense,* which is what can happen when there is too much focus on the leisure side of a conference or convention programme.

He concludes:

> *Such a perception problem won't be solved overnight – but as an industry, there's a lot we can do to start moving things in the right direction. At the top of the list is the way we characterise our*

destination products: more emphasis on their business, professional, institutional and intellectu-al qualities and less on golf courses and nightlife would go a long way toward convincing dubious audiences of the serious intent of meetings and conventions. So would putting more focus on what these events achieve in terms of business and professional outcomes rather than just how much spending they generate in the host community.

It was true then (ten years ago) and it's still true now: we're all about economic, professional and academic advancement – but while we may have come to believe it ourselves, we still have a long way to go in convincing others!

CASE STUDY 8.1   The Three City Alliance

This case study is based on an article entitled 'A tale of three cities: driving business with destina-tion partnerships' written by Joy Lin, Content Manager for DMAI, in April 2014.

An alliance is born

At first glance, the US cities of Milwaukee (Wisconsin), Pittsburgh (Pennsylvania) and Portland (Oregon) may not seem to have a lot in common. They are not even located near each other. Nevertheless, senior sales executives in the DMOs of the three cities formed an alliance in 2004 that provides meeting planners with significant financial and logistical benefits if their organisa-tions are booking events into any combination of the three cities.

The motivation behind the so-called 'Three City Alliance' lay in the realisation that all three destina-tions actually face very similar challenges in attracting meetings and conventions. They were, and continue to be, cities of a similar size (with populations ranging between 300,000 and 600,000), with comparable hotel packages and meeting facilities and typically attract similar organisations and groups but not necessarily for the same years.

Consequently, DMO sales leaders decided to capitalise on the opportunity to work together and do more through a partnership than could be done individually.

Meeting planner benefits

Meeting planners and organisations derive three major benefits from participating in the Three City Alliance programme.

Financial incentives

Depending on which combination of the three cities is booked for their meetings, meeting plan-ners can gain significant cost savings for their organisation based on the number of cities selected together and the size of their group(s). The alliance offers incentives of up to US$3.00 per room night booked, which can then be used to offset other expenses.

Logistical efficiency

The sales teams from VISIT Milwaukee, VisitPittsburgh and Travel Portland share valuable infor-mation about the groups and their event needs to ensure that the transition from year to year is seamless and smooth for the customer. Meeting planners take advantage of the benefit of having two or three destination staff teams that know their programmes intimately.

Customer confidence

Groups also benefit from the assurance that they can expect a consistently high-quality experience in all three cities and that each destination will be similar in their approach to serving them. Staff at the various cities share significant insights and information about the groups and their programme needs, making for a seamless transition from location to location each year.

Karl Pietrzak, Vice President of Convention Sales at VisitPittsburgh, said:

> The word has spread that we've got a strong partnership that benefits our clients, and that word of mouth is evidence of the strength of our partnership. I'm looking forward to even more success going forward as we continue to find new ways to market our three cities together, align our appearances at trade shows, and refer clients to each other.

Reasons for success

It is apparent from communications with all three cities that, even after 10 years, the alliance is alive and well. Factors contributing to its success, according to Kark Pietrzak, include the following.

Trust

Each city knows the others well enough to trust each other to make decisions for the partnership. If Pittsburgh sees a good opportunity, it can generally speak for Milwaukee and Portland and vice versa. More than just partners in a business arrangement, the destinations view each other's sales professionals as friends who have each other's best interests at heart.

Flexibility

The cities defined parameters for how they would work together and offer the right incentives to groups planning to meet in their destinations. However, they have also been flexible in stretching these parameters, when needed, to book a piece of business, or even help a partner city.

Quality

Lastly, there is simply a confidence in each other. Pittsburgh knows that, if a group has met recently in Milwaukee or Portland, it should have had a good experience there. It then uses that knowledge to help bring the group to Pittsburgh. The more organisations that have good experiences in each of the cities, the easier it is to pass the business along to the next Alliance destination.

Karl Pietrzak explains:

> We keep open lines of communication on groups using multiple cities the whole way through the process. We will share histories and meeting specs with each other after a group has completed a meeting in one of our cities. More than a set of formal procedures, it's just the ability to pick up the phone or send an email to our counterparts at any time to get vital information about the needs of our shared clients.

I believe (our success) is because our partnership started from a foundation of friendship and trust, and built from there, rather than forming just to take advantage of some business opportunities.

The biggest lesson, therefore, is that an industry-wide alliance has to start from a place of trust between destinations. Can DMOs count on each other to deliver a quality experience for their clients, to share relevant information about their groups to ease the customer's transition from one place to the next, to refer business and make decisions in each other's best interest? Further information on the Three City Alliance can be accessed at http://www.visitmilwaukee.org/meeting-planners/3-city-alliance.

CASE STUDY 8.2   The IMEX Politicians Forum

In 2003, the organisers of the IMEX tradeshow (one of the leading international exhibitions for the business events sector, held annually in Frankfurt, Germany) recognised the need to create a wider awareness of business events or the MICE industry. In addition, there was a need to provide an opportunity for politicians, both national and local, to see the industry at work for themselves and to exchange information and best practices. This led to the staging of the first Politicians Forum.

The IMEX Politicians Forum is held in May each year in Frankfurt, Germany, in conjunction with the IMEX tradeshow. It is organised by IMEX in collaboration with European Cities Marketing (ECM) and the AIPC, under the auspices of the JMIC.

The Forum welcomes over 80 industry leaders and 30 to 40 local and national politicians and government officials from across the globe, who come together to explore ways in which they can benefit from business events, meetings and incentives and use them to achieve their economic and social development objectives.

Politicians Forum objectives and achievements

Initially, the aim of the Forum was to communicate the value of the meetings industry to governments and how this translated into economic activity and the creation of jobs and tax revenues, with the intent of influencing policies favourable to the industry's growth.

The meetings industry is now widely accepted by governments around the world as a major contributor to economic development as well as to tourism. This acceptance and understanding have meant that the focus of the Politicians Forum is now to communicate *how* governments can help to attract more meetings and events to their destination, rather than *why* they should. But it is not only politicians that need educating in this regard: IMEX holds a 'Global Exchange of Best Practice' meeting prior to the Forum where leading cities showcase their models of success to fellow industry leaders, highlighting the crucial importance of good research in promoting the central role the meetings industry plays in economies.

In recent years, the Forum has attracted ministers of tourism from destinations such as South Africa, Egypt and Mexico who are using the meetings industry to drive their nations' knowledge economies.

In 2014, IMEX was instrumental in bringing together the JMIC with the World Travel and Tourism Council and the World Tourism Organization (UNWTO) – the specialised agency of the United Nations. It was believed that the organisations could support each other in discussion with governments and it led to agreement on three major areas of co-operation:

1. *Common messaging.* The meetings and tourism sectors still suffer from a lack of public and political understanding of what each can achieve and of what each really represents and contributes to societies. Therefore, common messaging and common promotion of the respective industries was set as goal number one.

2. *Research and data production.* The industries need facts based on good intelligence. If there is a need to advocate, it needs to be data based advocacy. It needs to be real, it needs to be consistent and what is produced needs to be credible – so it needs to be done together.

3. *Sustainable development.* The meetings and tourism industries need to project themselves to the world as responsible and ethical and promote the principles of sustainability and sustainable development. Their duties and responsibility towards people and the planet must be given priority.

Commenting on this agreement, Rod Cameron, Executive Director, AIPC and the JMIC, said:

> *This statement of collaboration paves the way for a better conversation with governments – it also facilitates a process of starting to contain the amount of leisure messaging in meetings-related marketing, one of the biggest (and largely self-inflicted) challenges we face today in convincing anyone we're really all about economic and professional development.*

Taleb Rifai, Secretary General of the UNWTO, said:

> *In almost every meeting I have with Heads of State, Prime Ministers or Ministers, they say: 'How can we attract more meetings? How can we become more involved and engaged with the meetings industry?' The progress of the meetings industry IS the progress of the travel and tourism industry. The progress of the travel and tourism industry IS the progress of economies and societies and that's exactly why it is at the heart of our mission with the United Nations.*

Declaration of support for the meetings and events industry

In conjunction with the Politicians Forum, IMEX has drafted a 'Declaration of Support for the Meetings and Events Industry', which it urges all those with an interest in the development of the sector to sign. The Declaration states:

> *In a critical period of global economic transition and recovery, I believe that creating jobs and retraining work forces, increasing trade and inward investment, spreading knowledge and improving professional practices, enhancing innovation and creative development, nurturing community awareness and advancement and stimulating business regeneration are all essential factors in sustaining long term economic growth and stability.*
>
> *I further acknowledge the key role that meetings and events play in delivering these important objectives by instigating and facilitating the critical interactions required to exchange information, share knowledge and achieve consensus while at the same time enriching the visitor economy and raising the profile of the host destination.*

The Declaration is supported by a statement that explains that the meetings and events industry is a major driver of economic growth and development in the world economy where it serves to:

- *Create jobs and retrain workforces* by providing skilled employment to a diverse workforce and presenting an opportunity to nurture and develop creative, logistical and marketing talent

- *Increase trade* by promoting international collaboration which encourages and sustains business and professional networks

- *Attract inward investment* by promoting the profile of a city or region. This enables destinations to focus on attracting events to develop their core competencies

- *Spread knowledge* by facilitating academic, technical and professional advancement by encouraging the global development and exchange of research, knowledge, standards and practices

- *Enhance innovation and creative development* by acting as a catalyst for research collaborations that lead to the development of new products and technologies. Out of events come the creativity and innovation that help distinguish world-leading cities from the runners-up

- *Nurture community cohesion* by enhancing professional development that brings regional and international expertise into the community where it is accessible to local professionals. This results in the implementation of new knowledge, techniques or materials that improve outcomes for the wider community

- *Create regeneration* by being a major contributor to infrastructure development on a national, regional and local level from both the public and private sector and providing opportunities for further destination expansion and growth

- *Sustain long term economic growth* by creating forums to facilitate broad networks, innovative and creative advancement

- *Enrich the visitor economy* by creating added value for tourism. A diverse range of annual festivals and promotional events showcase excellence in the creative industries and provide iconic focus for the visitor economy. Not only is the business event visitor the most lucrative visitor but many will extend their stay and return with their families and friends

- *Shape destinations* by hosting international events that showcase a destination's core competencies to the rest of the world

The statement concludes:

> It is critical that national and local governments, whose communities benefit from these positive impacts and whose ongoing support is essential to sustaining the continuing success of this industry, recognise and endorse these values.

The Politicians Forum concept continues to expand around the world through a series of IMEX alliances. Destination-focused Politicians Forums are held in Sweden, Germany and Ukraine. For further information on the IMEX Politicians Forum, visit www.imex-frankfurt.com/events/forums/politicians-forum/.

SUMMARY

This chapter has stressed the importance, for both destinations and venues, of exploring the myriad opportunities for building marketing partnerships with like-minded organisations and with destinations and venues having similar product characteristics. It is undeniably the case that, in a world where over 200 countries are now competing aggressively for their share of the conference and business events 'cake', competition is tough and will only get tougher.

To be successful by working in isolation, 'doing your own thing', is extremely difficult and certainly very expensive. Collaborative marketing ventures should be investigated, not only because they can offer better returns and prove a more cost effective way of spending finite budgets, but also because they frequently bring with them other benefits, such as the creation of information networks and the sharing of best practice.

As an industry there is also a need, at local, regional, national and international levels, to establish a higher profile for, and better understanding of, the many benefits to the world community brought about through meetings, conventions and business events. A cohesive, consistent and business-focused message for the sector is a 'must' if it is to grow and flourish and gain its deserved share of political, economic and social support.

REVIEW AND DISCUSSION QUESTIONS

- 'Conference and event organisers will not place their business in a destination where they perceive the main venues and stakeholders to be disunited and non-collaborative'. Critically review this statement and outline the most effective strategies for creating a joined-up destination brand and effective partnership marketing.

- Are the benefits of participating in a marketing consortium outweighed by the potential loss of brand identity? Illustrate your answer with examples of either conference venues or conference destinations that have (i) joined a marketing consortium and (ii) opted to act independently.

- Rod Cameron (International Association of Convention Centres and Joint Meetings Industry Council) writes: 'we're not tourism – we have relatively little to do with the leisure sector. Meetings and conventions are all about economic, professional and academic advancement'. Critically discuss this statement and evaluate how business event destinations currently profile themselves to their local communities, illustrating your answer with examples from at least two countries.

BIBLIOGRAPHY

BECA (2010) *Delivering Innovation, Knowledge and Performance: The Role of Business Events*, North Sydney: Business Events Council of Australia.

Boléat, M. (2003) *Managing Trade Associations*, Trade Association Forum.

Cameron, R. (2015) 'How far have we really come?' *Conference & Meetings World*, 78: 16.

Donaghy, G. (2015) 'Building a culture', *Conference & Meetings World*, 79: 29–30.

Garofani, I. (2012) 'BECA redefining and refocusing', published online at www.conworld.net/index (www.conworld.net now trades as www.GMIPortal.com).

Hendrie, J. R. (2005) 'The value of membership: what makes a good trade association?' *DMO World e-newsletter*, September.

JMIC (2008) 'Understanding the value of the meetings industry', Brussels: Joint Meetings Industry Council.

Walters, J. (2005), 'Member care', in R. Harrill (ed.) *Fundamentals of Destination Management and Marketing*, Washington, DC: IACVB, pp. 229–44.

Chapter

Current initiatives in the conferences, conventions and business events sector

Chapter overview

As an industry grows and matures, it faces challenges and issues that need to be overcome if it is to progress. The conference, convention and business events industry is no exception. This chapter focuses on some of the current initiatives designed to take the industry forward in a number of fundamental areas.

This chapter covers:

- Research and market intelligence
- Terminology
- Education and training
- Quality standards

It includes case studies on:

- ICCA's Big Data search tool
- IACC/NYU Certificate in International Conference Centre Management
- Accredited in Meetings quality assurance scheme

On completion of this chapter, you should be able to:

- appreciate the need for, and importance of, industry research;
- give examples of best practice research programmes;
- understand the rationale for a clearer and more consistent use of terminology and jargon;
- understand the crucial role of education and training in enhancing the overall professionalism of the conference industry; and
- identify different types of quality assurance schemes now in operation.

Introduction

Many might argue that statistics, terminology, quality standards and even education programmes are all rather dry and somewhat esoteric industry features, of interest only to academics and bearing little relation to the exciting and 'real' world of marketing and events. The reality is that these form the foundations on which a young industry can be built and nurtured into maturity.

Research provides parameters against which an industry's performance and growth can be measured and through which new trends can be identified. The adoption of a standard terminology and a consistent interpretation of both words and statistics are both essential if, at an international level, the industry is to develop data and intelligence that are robust and reliable. Such data are essential to support benchmarking and to enable countries to compare their performance with other countries. How should quality benchmarks for both venues and destinations be brought on stream in ways that will have meaning for clients, the bookers of the venues and destinations?

As regards the human infrastructure of the conferences, conventions and business events sector, the industry's workforce is expanding rapidly, as are education and training programmes to go with this growth. But is there sufficient coherence and standardisation in the provision of such programmes or are they being developed with only passing reference to market demands?

Successful destination marketing depends upon the progress being made in all of the areas covered in this chapter. Nevertheless, convention bureaux operate in a market environment over which they have little or no control. Now more than ever, destination marketing organisations (DMOs) need guidance in the form of practical, clear actions and strategies for sustainable success in a dramatically changing world.

This chapter will examine each of these topics in more detail and highlight a number of best practice initiatives from around the world.

Research and market intelligence

It has been seen that, in comparison with many other industries, the conference industry is still a very young industry, approaching 100 years of age in Europe and North America and still in its infancy in much of the rest of the world. Although it is maturing at a very rapid rate, it is indisputable that one of the legacies of its relative immaturity is a lack of reliable statistics and regular research to provide a base of intelligence and information on trends and the size and value of the industry. Statistics produced annually on international conventions and congresses by the ICCA and the Union of International Associations (UIA) are something of an oasis in what has been, until recent times, a rather barren statistical landscape. This, in turn, has meant that governments have not taken the industry seriously as a major benefactor to national economies because it has been impossible to demonstrate clearly the positive economic impacts that conferences can generate.

It is pleasing to report that, while many gaps still remain, some genuine progress is being made in gathering better market intelligence and there are increasing numbers of best practice examples from around the world, which themselves deserve recognition and emulation. Some of these are summarised on the following pages, but first it will be useful to take note of developments in the system of tourism satellite accounts (TSA) that, in the medium to longer term, could lead to significantly enhanced industry statistics and research at both national and international levels.

Tourism satellite accounts

A TSA provides a means of separating and examining both tourism supply and tourism demand within the general framework of the TSA. The term 'satellite account' was developed by the United Nations to measure the size of economic activities that are not defined either as industries in national accounts or as a cluster of them. Tourism, for example, impacts heavily on industries such as transportation, accommodation, food and beverage services, recreation and entertainment and travel agencies. Jones and James (2005) state that:

> Tourism is a unique phenomenon as it is defined by the consumer or the visitor. Visitors buy goods and services both tourism and non-tourism alike. The key from a measurement standpoint is associating their purchases to the total supply of these goods and services within a country. The TSA:
> - provides credible data on the impact of tourism and the associated employment
> - is a standard framework for organising statistical data on tourism
> - is a new international standard endorsed by the UN Statistical Commission
> - is a powerful instrument for designing economic policies related to tourism development
> - provides data on tourism's impact on a nation's balance of payments
> - provides information on tourism's human resource characteristics

Agreement was reached in 2004 between the World Tourism Organisation (a specialised agency of the United Nations), the ICCA, Meeting Professionals International (MPI) and EIBTM (the international trade exhibition for the conventions and incentives sector – now rebranded as ibtm world) for the TSA to incorporate meeting industry data for the first time. This allowed studies to be made into the relationship between expenditure on meetings and other economic measures such as gross domestic product and job creation.

A standard methodology for measuring the value of the meetings industry based on a TSA was developed and a number of national studies have been undertaken following variations of the same principles. These national studies include Canada (twice), USA, Mexico, Australia, UK and Denmark. The website of the Joint Meetings Industry Council has links to all of these studies, which can be downloaded free of charge from www.themeetingsindustry.org.

The industry has rightly interpreted these developments as a major step forward in gaining recognition for the meetings industry and in enabling industry data and intelligence to be gathered in a more comprehensive and structured way.

Current examples of industry research activity

This section will highlight a number of best practice examples of industry research, at international, national and local/city levels.

International research programmes

ICCA AND UIA

Some of the longest-running industry research programmes are those undertaken by the ICCA (www.iccaworld.com) and the UIA (www.uia.org). Both of these organisations monitor the staging of international congresses and meetings, identifying trends and producing annual rankings of the most successful cities and countries as per the examples shown in Tables 9.1 to 9.5. It is not possible to make direct comparisons between the ICCA and UIA data because they use different criteria when defining which events to include in their surveys [see Rogers (2013: 12–19) for details of the criteria used]. However, they nonetheless provide valuable information on which destinations are maintaining or increasing their market share and which may be losing their position in the international association meetings market. The criteria used by ICCA when monitoring the staging of meetings by international associations are:

- The meetings should take place on a regular basis
- The meetings should rotate between a minimum of three countries
- The meetings should have at least 50 participants

Destinations themselves take the results very seriously and those achieving a high ranking can use such positive and objective data as a key part of their own promotional and PR campaigns. The data held by the UIA and ICCA on international associations and organisations can be purchased for direct marketing and CRM activities. Such data are well used by those destinations active in the international conference and conventions sector. The data can also be used as part of the sales research process (see chapter 5) to identify potential leads, which then become the focus of marketing and sales activity. The ICCA database holds information on some 11,500 international associations.

It should be noted that the rankings in the first column of Tables 9.1 and 9.2 are based on the data for 2013 and *not* on the aggregated totals over the 10-year period. It can be seen that, if the latter ranking option had been chosen, there would be a number of significant changes to the rankings for both countries and cities. Table 9.3 provides a ranking for regions of the world.

The UIA also publishes annual rankings of countries and cities. Its report 'International Meetings Statistics for 2013', published in June 2014, reveals some significant differences from the ICCA research but also substantial common ground. By 2014, there were 408,798 meetings for which details were held in the UIA database (compared with 392,588 in 2013), representing 174 countries and 1,465 cities in the reporting year. Tables 9.4 and 9.5 reveal the top ten countries and cities in 2013.

An ICCA paper entitled 'A Modern History of International Association Meetings 1963–2012' (published 2013) clearly demonstrates the growth in international association meetings over the past 50 years. Figure 9.1, representing 5-year aggregated data of the last 50 years, shows that, since 1963, the number of meetings in the ICCA Association Database has grown exponentially by approximately 10 per cent each year, which means the number of meetings doubled each 10 years. The ICCA Association Database contains 173,432 meetings taking place between 1963 and 2012; 1,795 (1 per cent) of these meetings took place in the period 1963–7, 54,844 (31.6 per cent) in the period 2008–12.

Case study 9.1 describes ICCA's new Big Data search tool (launched in 2014), which seeks to revolutionise the ways in which data on events, especially on potential event or conference ambassadors, are gathered and managed.

From a purely DMO or convention bureau perspective, a valuable insight into the funding, structure, operation and marketing activities of such entities is provided by surveys including the 'ICCA Destination Marketing Category Survey' carried out by Christian Mutschlechner, Director of the Vienna Convention Bureau. This category of ICCA members comprises convention bureaux and national tourist boards and

Table 9.1 Number of meetings per country 2004–13

Rank	Country	2004	2005	2006	2007	2008	2009	2010	2011	2012	2013	Totals
1	USA	669	736	727	786	827	907	903	951	921	829	8,256
2	Germany	419	448	479	561	541	626	664	675	710	722	5,845
3	Spain	379	345	340	400	465	442	567	543	591	562	4,634
4	France	388	367	413	406	485	457	474	516	522	527	4,555
5	UK	330	415	434	429	462	456	539	518	529	525	4,637
6	Italy	362	345	367	421	445	500	485	472	453	447	4,297
7	Japan	230	260	279	314	339	327	362	271	355	342	3,079
8	P. R. China	234	239	289	316	328	360	368	393	351	340	3,218
9	Brazil	173	190	223	227	262	310	295	317	378	315	2,690
10	The Netherlands	229	232	238	230	273	322	262	347	348	302	2,783
11	Canada	219	210	227	267	317	271	294	281	291	290	2,667
12	Republic of Korea	150	144	181	170	236	219	212	236	239	260	2,047
13	Portugal	147	154	157	217	206	222	225	272	234	249	2,083
14	Austria	157	195	233	241	226	266	250	304	292	244	2,408
15	Sweden	157	155	187	171	192	238	236	220	238	238	2,032
16	Australia	186	185	208	218	211	213	264	219	258	231	2,193
17	Argentina	105	103	115	150	163	176	215	206	212	223	1,668
18	Turkey	81	96	108	130	140	164	206	189	201	221	1,536
19	Belgium	118	146	150	166	186	189	249	225	231	214	1,874
20	Switzerland	164	194	191	198	220	236	278	269	260	205	2,215
21	Singapore	94	103	120	128	130	119	168	161	158	175	1,356
22	Finland	120	105	147	140	157	150	172	179	180	171	1,521
23	Poland	100	124	117	130	149	149	134	210	159	170	1,442
24	Denmark	109	108	135	136	152	184	168	165	201	161	1,519
25	Mexico	143	124	149	154	183	164	203	209	178	158	1,665
26	Czech Republic	100	108	122	124	140	139	147	150	141	145	1,316
27	India	69	83	107	132	128	131	136	143	163	142	1,234
28	Colombia	27	57	61	78	73	110	115	130	148	139	938
29=	Ireland	81	89	66	108	108	81	97	119	137	136	1,022
29=	Norway	94	96	96	114	129	149	148	150	170	136	1,282
	Totals	7,513	8,023	8,773	9,638	10,466	11,055	11,727	12,068	12,224	11,685	103,172

Source: International Congress and Convention Association: 'ICCA Statistics Report 1963–2013' (www.iccaworld.com).

Table 9.2 Number of meetings per city 2004–13

Rank	City	2004	2005	2006	2007	2008	2009	2010	2011	2012	2013	Totals
1	Paris	139	121	172	154	173	160	190	210	204	204	1,727
2	Madrid	70	67	74	94	93	88	128	136	171	186	1,107
3	Vienna	106	137	149	171	139	170	184	195	205	182	1,638
4	Barcelona	128	127	98	119	158	154	186	183	168	179	1,500
5	Berlin	117	106	116	142	130	146	174	163	178	178	1,450
6	Singapore	94	103	120	128	130	119	168	161	158	175	1,356
7	London	80	111	105	114	118	121	159	146	171	166	1,291
8	Istanbul	51	59	78	80	97	110	140	137	143	146	1,041
9	Lisbon	80	86	80	107	112	124	115	126	115	125	1,070
10	Seoul	88	85	102	92	132	116	106	117	110	125	1,073
11	Prague	80	89	106	103	116	114	121	121	120	121	1,091
12	Amsterdam	81	99	89	99	113	132	116	137	137	120	1,123
13	Dublin	58	63	47	83	75	51	71	86	98	114	746
14	Buenos Aires	71	60	80	99	102	106	129	105	107	113	972
15	Brussels	53	67	69	82	96	107	128	119	128	111	960
16	Copenhagen	81	78	85	90	101	120	110	110	150	109	1,034
17	Budapest	90	92	96	101	113	98	102	128	113	106	1,039
18	Beijing	113	101	107	121	100	145	131	136	121	105	1,180
19	Rome	71	74	71	86	92	106	109	121	119	99	948
20	Stockholm	68	70	75	70	94	121	102	101	112	93	906
21	Sydney	47	61	59	68	74	67	99	60	83	93	711
22	Bangkok	73	66	80	97	88	97	60	74	112	93	840
23	Hong Kong	87	83	80	91	82	92	102	107	111	89	924
24	Helsinki	53	46	57	54	78	74	75	78	105	85	705
25	Munich	36	54	35	54	54	62	77	58	79	82	591
26	Tokyo	50	74	59	82	101	73	84	59	71	79	732
27	Rio de Janeiro	40	42	51	48	53	66	71	77	87	79	614
28	Taipei	49	52	45	77	65	83	111	92	85	78	737
29	Shanghai	52	59	58	65	72	61	86	83	70	72	678
30	Montreal	47	47	45	65	66	61	64	60	72	71	598
	Totals	7,447	7,945	8,728	9,590	10,422	11,025	11,730	12,070	12,256	11,718	102,931

Source: International Congress and Convention Association: 'ICCA Statistics Report 1963–2013' (www.iccaworld.com).

Table 9.3 Number of meetings per region 2004–13

Rank	Region	2004	2005	2006	2007	2008	2009	2010	2011	2012	2013	Totals
1	Europe	4,124	4,381	4,757	5,166	5,578	5,891	6,265	6,598	6,627	6,313	55,700
2	Asia/Middle East	1,275	1,352	1,594	1,783	1,922	2,022	2,200	2,123	2,240	2,179	18,690
3	North America	1,036	1,075	1,107	1,211	1,336	1,351	1,404	1,448	1,398	1,291	12,657
4	Latin America	638	723	812	911	997	1,113	1,161	1,241	1,294	1,243	10,133
5	Africa	202	266	250	297	364	418	389	385	344	375	3,290
6	Oceania	238	226	253	270	269	260	308	273	321	284	2,702
	Totals	7,513	8,023	8,773	9,638	10,466	11,055	11,727	12,068	12,224	11,685	103,172

Source: International Congress and Convention Association: 'ICCA Statistics Report 1963–2013' (www.iccaworld.com).

Table 9.4 Top international meeting countries 2013

Ranking	Country	Number of meetings	Percentage of all meetings (%)
1	Singapore	994	9.4
2	USA	799	7.5
3	Republic of Korea	635	6.0
4	Japan	588	5.5
5=	Belgium	505	4.8
5=	Spain	505	4.8
7	Germany	428	4.0
8	France	408	3.8
9	Austria	398	3.7
10	UK	349	3.3

Source: Union of International Associations: 'International Meetings Statistics for 2013' – Table 1.2, A+B column (www.uia.org).

Table 9.5 Top international meeting cities 2013

Ranking	City	Number of meetings	Percentage of all meetings (%)
1	Singapore	994	9.4
2	Brussels	436	4.1
3	Vienna	318	3.0
4	Seoul	242	2.3
5	Tokyo	228	2.1
6	Barcelona	195	1.8
7	Paris	180	1.7
8	Madrid	165	1.6
9	Busan	148	1.4
10	London	144	1.4

Source: Union of International Associations: 'International Meetings Statistics for 2013' – Table 1.3, A+B column (www.uia.org).

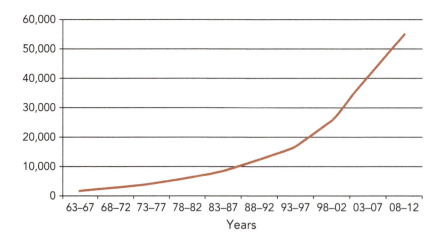

Figure 9.1 Number of international meetings 1963–2012 in the ICCA database (5-year aggregated data)

this survey has been carried out every 3 years since 1994. Further details are available from christian.mutschlechner@vienna.info.

A number of other international trade and professional associations of the meeting industry also view research as a key part of their remit and an important element in the services they provide to their members. Some examples of the most relevant to venue and destination marketing now follow.

DESTINATION MARKETING ASSOCIATION INTERNATIONAL

An outstanding example of an international association research project designed to be of direct use to members at the strategic level is Destination Marketing Association International's (DMAI) Destination-NEXT initiative, of which the results of Phase 1 were published in 2014 (www.destinationmarketing.org/topics/destination-next).

According to the first report, these results are designed to provide 'practical, clear actions and strategies for sustainable success for DMAI's DMO members in a rapidly changing future'. Scott Beck, President and CEO of Visit Salt Lake, and Tammy Blount, President and CEO, Monterey County Convention and Visitors Bureau, Co-Chairs of the DestinationNEXT Advisory Group, explained (July 2014) that:

> DestinationNEXT focuses on the development of a transformational road map to the future for DMO leaders and their stakeholders. Actionable strategies will allow DMO stakeholders to benchmark themselves and their communities against a defined spectrum of destination scenarios, community expectations, and marketplace opportunities. Ultimately, the road map will culminate with a number of co-created DMO prototypes to guide DMO stakeholders toward successful implementation based on their situation.

The project team behind DestinationNEXT circulated a survey questionnaire in March 2014, receiving responses from 327 DMOs from 36 countries. The analysis of the survey responses identified a number of opportunities to exploit. These revolved around the following three areas:

- Playing an expanded role in the community on broader economic development issues
- Improving branding of a destination in leisure and meetings and conventions markets
- Capitalising on social media and smart technology to engage and access residents, industry and markets

Engagement of stakeholders is a key theme of the DestinationNEXT project, which has the overall goal of enabling as many DMOs as possible to become 'Destination Trailblazers', defined as 'DMOs and destinations that realise the benefits of their tourism vision and work to keep the community and marketplace engaged'.

The report of the findings of Phase 1 makes fascinating reading for anyone with an interest in trends in destination marketing, and for practitioners in that field, it lays the foundations of what could be a highly effective roadmap to guide DMOs in their future strategic development. An indication of the direction that their development might take is given in the responses given to the one question in the survey. DMOs were asked to identify their future activity priorities for any increases in their budgets and the results were:

1. Marketing/branding – the number one priority for use of increased budget and the number-one future envisioned primary role for most respondents.
2. Meeting and convention sales – the second highest scoring priority for increased spending. It also scored second highest for future envisioned primary roles.
3. Social media and SEO marketing – the third highest scoring priority for increased investment.

The primary objective for Phase 2 of DestinationNEXT is to identify best practices (i.e. NEXTPractices) around the world to help adjust and effectively deal with the three transformational opportunities listed above.

International association of conference centres

The IACC (www.iacconline.org) regularly commissions research reports on topics that are of direct interest to its members, who are managers/owners of residential and non-residential conference venues worldwide. Recent titles include 'Conference Center Technology', 'A Uniform System of Accounts for Conference Centers' and 'Trends in the Conference Center Industry'. An extract from the third of these, compiled by PKF Hospitality Research on behalf of IACC, demonstrates the level of detail included in the study:

> *This year's trends report provides clear signs that IACC Conference Centres are experiencing recovery and 'outperforming the broader hotel sector in relation to occupancies and profitability.' Demand for conference centres grew along with average rates, with executive-style conference centres performing better than average with an ADR increase of 5% over the previous year. This led to a higher-than-average rise in rates compared with the hotel industry average in 2012.*

International association of exhibitions and events

The International Association of Exhibitions and Events (IAEE – www.iaee.com) is also active in producing valuable research reports for its members. One of the most eagerly anticipated annual research reports is the publication 'Future Trends Impacting the Exhibitions and Events Industry', a white paper produced by the IAEE Future Trends Taskforce that consists of senior exhibitions industry professionals. The IAEE emphasises that this report is not a roadmap to the future in terms of best practices or specific action steps:

> *It is, however, a waypoint to help gain insight as to what is ahead for the exhibition industry as seen by twenty-six senior, experienced professionals representing a broad spectrum of the industry. This report will help to identify and understand the industry challenges ahead in an effort to better prepare to meet those challenges.*

The 2014 Future Trends report presented the results of 14 trends that the Taskforce felt would affect and shape the exhibition industry in the years ahead.

1. Economic outlook
2. Big data
3. On-site data capture
4. Facility data/Wi-Fi infrastructure capabilities and costs
5. New technology
6. Mobile computing
7. Social media marketing
8. Year-round communities; the 24/7 exhibition or event
9. Experiential trade shows
10. Exhibitors stepping up their exhibiting skills
11. Engagement
12. Societal and generational considerations
13. Security
14. Increased industry merger and acquisition activities

Meetings industry exhibitions

The organisers of industry exhibitions such as 'IMEX' and 'ibtm world' also commission research on different aspects of the international conventions industry. The annual 'Trends Watch Report', compiled by a co-author of this book, Rob Davidson, is sponsored by Reed Travel Exhibitions and launched at ibtm world in Barcelona. Such research activity typically has two objectives: first, to supply useful, up-to-date intelligence on hot topics affecting the industry and, second, to position the exhibition itself as being at the cutting edge of all that is happening in the industry, one that will be an important, not-to-be-missed communications event for the industry as a whole. Further details are available from www.imex-frankfurt. com and www.ibtmworld.com.

National research programmes

A growing number of countries are now carrying out regular or one-off studies into their conference and convention sectors. A few examples of such studies are shown below. They fulfil an important role in building the global supply of data and intelligence on the business events sector, although we do still have more work to do to ensure that countries are using consistent methodologies in their approaches to research projects that will enable comparative studies to be undertaken between countries, as well as the aggregation of data by groups of countries and perhaps even continents.

1. The German Meetings Market is measured by the German Convention Bureau through the medium of an annual in-depth study. The 2014 study, for example, entitled 'The Meeting & Event Barometer 2014', showed that 371 million participants attended conferences, meetings and events throughout Germany in 2013. In the previous year, the same study had revealed that conference hotels hosted 66.1 per cent of all such events. In 2014, the German Convention Bureau also published 'Meetings and Conventions 2030: a study of megatrends shaping our industry' – it also announced plans to study further such trends. For more information visit www.gcb.de.

2. The UK conference market is monitored through two separate annual surveys. The 'British Meetings and Events Industry Survey' assesses trends and characteristics from a demand perspective by undertaking in-depth interviews with over 500 conference organisers (further details from www.meetpie. com). The 'UK Conference and Meeting Survey' examines trends and volume and value features from a supply-side perspective, collecting data from conference venues (further details from http://www. ukcams.org.uk).

3. In 2014, Business Events Australia, in conjunction with Tourism Australia, published new research designed to assist the country to reach its 'tourism 2020 potential'. The research, based on interviews with 550 senior company managers and 137 business event agents from Australia's most important source markets, was designed to achieve a better understanding of how corporate decision-makers and business event agents view Australia and the factors that most motivate them to choose the destination in what is an 'increasingly competitive and lucrative sector'. The research will be used to help shape the future marketing of Australia internationally for business events and to identify opportunities to make the country's offering more attractive to the sector. For more details contact bea@tourism.australia. com or www.australia.com/businessevents.

4. Each year since 2000, the Poland Convention Bureau, in co-operation with the principal city-level convention bureaux in that country, has produced its 'Poland Meetings & Events Industry Report', the main purpose of which is to showcase the number and size of meetings and events held in Poland over the previous 12 months and to highlight their economic value to the country. The compilation of this report is conducted in accordance with the Tourism Satellite Account system of which details are given at the beginning of this chapter. The 2014 edition of the Poland Meetings and Events Industry Report included, for the first time, a series of predictions from independent experts in the global meetings industry on the shape and volume of meetings and events in Poland in the year 2020. The report may be downloaded from www.poland-convention.pl/en/download/poland-meetings-events-statistics.

Local/city/venue research programmes

For many, if not all, cities that are active in the conference and conventions market, research is, and should be, an integral part of their day-to-day work. For example, systems should be in place to record the volume and type of business enquiries being handled by the DMO or convention bureau and it will be possible to analyse these enquiries in a variety of ways. visitBerlin's Berlin Convention Office, for instance, was able to report (GMI Portal, 19 February 2015) that 2014 was the capital's most successful year for conferences and meetings, with an average of 360 events and 30,000 participants each day. In total, some 11 million participants attended 131,000 events in the city, an increase of 3 per cent and 4 per cent respectively on the 2013 data. The city's conferences generated more than 7 million hotel stays (an increase of 4.5 per cent on 2013), representing approximately a quarter of all hotel stays in Berlin. The German capital is especially in demand for events related to the sciences and research. The meeting and convention industry generated €2.2 billion in 2014 (9 per cent more than in 2013), sustaining approximately 38,000 full-time jobs. Conference attendees spend an average of €232 per day when visiting the city.

A convention bureau may also undertake client feedback research or 'mystery shopper' surveys (where a research consultant poses as a genuine client in order to test the quality of service provision by the bureau) in order to ascertain how the destination has performed, to identify areas for improvement and to inform future marketing activity. Statistics on website usage offer valuable insights into the source of business leads for the destination and contribute to assessments of e-marketing campaigns. Similar kinds of research information should also be collected by conference venues – much of this will be available to them through their day-to-day work but systems do need to be put in place to make sure that data are captured fully and accurately and interpreted consistently.

The following provide examples of research findings from venue-led economic impact studies:

- ExCeL London (one of the venues used for the 2012 London Olympic Games) generated £2.9 billion of economic impact for the UK and supported 24,258 jobs in 2013, according to an article in *Conference News* (June 2014), based on research undertaken by Grant Thornton. The research also found that:
  - In 2011, there were 3 million visitors to ExCeL London, a figure that was forecast to grow to 6.2 million by 2017
  - Nearly a quarter of these visitors (23 per cent) came from overseas, a proportion that is expected to remain broadly the same (24 per cent) in 2017
  - ExCeL London's net economic contribution to London's economy was estimated at £1 billion for 2013, a 24 per cent increase since 2011. By 2017, this is forecast to have increased to £2 billion, a rise of 144 per cent since 2011
  - The number of jobs supported by ExCeL London is estimated to reach 53,886 by 2017
- Kuala Lumpur Convention Centre hosted 1,442 events in 2012, the highest number recorded since its opening in 2005, serving over 1.6 million delegates and visitors. This resulted in an economic impact contribution of RM590 million (approximately US$190 million). The 2012 figure brought the total number of events held at the Centre between June 2005 and December 2012 to 6,645, with over 13.7 million delegates and visitors, generating a total economic impact contribution to Kuala Lumpur and Malaysia for the period to RM4.2 billion.
- Conferences and meetings had a major bearing on earnings for the Hofburg Vienna venue in 2012, accounting for 55 per cent of the event mix and contributing a total of c.60,000 bed nights for the Austrian capital. The Hofburg Vienna, which also acts as the permanent seat of the Organisation for Security and Co-operation in Europe (OSCE), was responsible for an induced economic impact of €190 million in 2012.

There will also be a need, from time to time, for destinations and venues to commission discrete research programmes, perhaps to assist them in drafting a new business strategy, to assess client demand for new facilities and infrastructure or to undertake economic impact studies for use in lobbying.

Terminology

Non-standardised terminology

One of the reasons for the limited statistics on the size and value of the industry is the lack of an accepted and properly defined terminology. At a macro level, arguments still rage over whether the term 'business tourism' is an accurate or appropriate one to describe the sector encompassing conferences, conventions, exhibitions and incentive travel. The link with 'tourism' is thought by many to be confusing and over-laid with a number of negative perceptions ('candy floss' jobs of a seasonal and poorly paid nature, for example, and dominant associations with holidays and leisure tourism). The phrase 'business events' was adopted originally in Australia some years ago and it is now also widely used in Europe and North America as the accepted generic term to describe the sector's essential focus.

The acronym 'MICE' (for Meetings, Incentives, Conferences, and Exhibitions or Events) is also in wide-spread use around the world, despite its somewhat unfortunate associations! In Canada, this is adjusted to MC&IT: meetings, conventions and incentive travel, although the term 'business events' now seems to be increasingly in vogue in that country.

At the micro level, words such as 'conference', 'congress', 'convention', 'meeting' even, are often used synonymously or indiscriminately. Other words are also used with similar but more specialised connotations, such as 'symposium', 'colloquium', 'assembly', 'conclave' and 'summit', although it is probably only the last of these for which it might be easy to reach a consensus on its precise meaning (namely, a conference of high-level officials, such as heads of government).

There are a number of current initiatives designed to bring some coherence and standardisation to the terminology in use across the global meetings industry. One such initiative is the 'Dictionary of Meeting Industry Terminology', a dictionary with definitions in English for 1,100 terms in use in the industry, including translations of these terms into 14 other languages. The dictionary is now available as a free online resource accessible via the website of the International Association of Professional Congress Organisers (www.iapco.org/dictionary) or may be purchased in book format for €40.

A second initiative comes under the aegis of the Convention Industry Council and has the acronym APEX (Accepted Practices Exchange). The overarching aim of APEX is to bring increased standardisation and consistency to the systems and procedures in operation throughout the conference and business events industry in order to create greater efficiencies and better services for customers. Among several 'accepted practices' now completed is the APEX Industry Glossary, which is an interactive, online tool, intended to be a comprehensive reference for the terminology, jargon and acronyms used industry-wide. The 2011 second edition of the glossary contains more than 1,400 terms, acronyms and abbreviations. It is possible to search by word or by phrase and terms can be listed by major topic areas. The website also invites submissions from browsers who can recommend the inclusion of terms that may be missing or disagree with existing definitions. The APEX Industry Glossary is available free at http://www.conventionindustry.org/StandardsPractices/APEX/glossary.aspx/.

In June 2005, it was announced, following two specialist United Nations meetings, that the profession of meeting and exhibition organising had been recognised by the UN in their 'International Standard Industrial Classification of All Economic Activities (ISIC, Rev 4 provisional draft) as follows:

> *8230   Convention and trade show organisers*
>
> *This class includes the organisation, promotion and management of events such as business and trade shows, conventions, conferences and meetings, whether or not including the management and provision of the staff to operate the facilities in which these events take place.*

7920   Other reservation service activities

This class includes the activities of marketing, promotion and arrangement of accommodation and other services including tours for conventions and visitors, tourist guide services, condominium time-share exchange services and other travel-related reservation services (including for transportation, hotels, restaurants, car rentals, entertainment and sport). Activities of ticket sales, theatrical sports and all other amusement and entertainment are also included.

Further information on ISIC is available at http://unstats.un.org/unsd/publication/seriesM/seriesm_4rev4e.pdf.

To complement the International Standard Industrial Classification, there is also an International Standard Classification of Occupations (ISCO), overseen by the International Labour Office in Geneva, Switzerland. ISCO is a tool for organising jobs into a clearly defined set of groups according to the tasks and duties undertaken in the job. Its main aims are to provide:

- A basis for the international reporting, comparison and exchange of statistical and administrative data about occupations
- A model for the development of national and regional classifications of occupations
- A system that can be used directly in countries that have not developed their own national classifications

Many countries have used one or more versions of ISCO as the model for their own national classifications, whereas others have retained or developed their own national structures. A number of countries are currently adapting their national classification to allow comparability with ISCO-08 (the latest version of ISCO published in 2008), or are developing or updating national classifications based on ISCO-08. Within ISCO, the occupation of 'conference and event planners' is coded as 3332. In the UK's Standard Occupational Classification, for example, 'conference and exhibition managers and organisers' are coded as 3546. Further information on ISCO can be accessed at http://www.ilo.org/public/english/bureau/stat/isco/index.htm.

The ISIC and ISCO initiatives have potential benefits for the conference and business events industry in encouraging greater professional recognition, stimulating better employment data and in supporting the provision of appropriate education and training programmes.

Education and training

Destination marketing is facing increasing competitive pressures with the speed of change, technological advances, shorter product cycles and rising customer expectations. Destination marketing involves three sets of stakeholders whose needs and wants must be satisfied in balance: visitors, suppliers and the host community. The critical success factor in destination marketing will be the ability to create a high-performing team culture – organisations committed to the ongoing education and training of their employees. This will enable the delivery of consistent quality in the successful development and implementation of a conference destination strategy, including turning complex destination information into targeted and integrated communications to potential conference organisers and delegates. The ability to learn faster than one's competitors may be the only sustainable competitive advantage.

The conference and conventions sector is all about high quality and high yield. However, high quality demands high levels of professionalism and productivity on the part of the industry's practitioners and the delivery of customer service that not only meets but regularly exceeds expectations. If clients (conference organisers, meeting planners, delegates and partners) do not enjoy such experiences from a destination or venue, they will certainly not return.

Research has consistently shown that where conference organisers and meeting planners have problems with venues it is not, for the most part, with the facilities and equipment but with staff service, specifically a lack of professionalism and good service. As the physical attributes of conference venues become more standardised and of a generally acceptable level, it is likely to be the quality of the staff that will differentiate one from another. This point was expressed very lucidly in a report published in the UK by the Department of National Heritage (DNH – now known as the Department for Culture, Media and Sport) in 1996. Entitled 'Tourism: competing with the best – people working in tourism and hospitality', the report said that:

> *The quality of personal service is perhaps more important to tourism and hospitality than to any other industry. Consumers who buy one of this industry's products will often have made a significant financial investment, but also an emotional investment and an investment of time. Of course the physical product – the facilities of the holiday village, the distinctiveness of the tourist attraction, the appointments of the hotel, the quality of the restaurant's food – is very important to them. But during the period customers are in the establishment, they will have many interactions with people: some indirect, with the management and chefs and cleaners; and many direct, with the front-line staff. The quality of those interactions is an integral part of the experience and has the potential to delight or disappoint the consumer. We do not believe that this potential is there to the same extent in any other employing sector.*

The DNH report rightly claims that:

> *Excellent service at a competitive price can only be provided by competent, well-managed and well-motivated people. This means recruiting the right people in the first place, equipping them with the skills they need, managing staff well to create motivation, job satisfaction, and high productivity.*

The type of quality standards described above can only be met through the establishment of effective education, training and lifelong learning programmes. Such programmes are necessary at post-school vocational and higher education levels and on a continuous basis through short course provision and flexible distance learning that allows 'students' to combine learning with employment. In order to be fully effective, the programmes must be backed up by an integrated qualifications infrastructure, ideally one that is international in its scope and validity, enabling employees to move between countries and continents and possessing qualifications that are truly portable, which are accepted in many countries around the world.

Some examples of best practice education and training provision are given below.

International courses and qualifications

Certificate in Meetings Management

MPI joined forces in 2014 with the Global Business Travel Association to create an updated Certificate in Meetings Management (CMM) programme, with the aim of delivering a global standard of excellence to bolster business management skills and advance the careers of events and travel sector professionals.

The CMM programme is one of intensive study offering insight and guidance from university professors associated with renowned business schools. These professors will guide CMM 'students' on topics critical for managers to master, including risk mitigation, business analytics and compliance and strategic negotiation, after which, students opt to pursue further learning either about meetings or business travel management.

CMM participants must complete three distinct phases of the programme to achieve CMM designation:

Phase 1. Participate in 3.5 days of rigorous onsite business education sessions administered by university professors. This phase also requires participation in two self-led webinars

Phase 2. Attend a virtual boot camp with either meeting or business travel-focused sessions taught by industry-leading subject matter experts (note: Phase 1 must be completed before starting Phase 2)

Phase 3. Develop an independent business case assessment.

After completing the required training, webinars and boot camp, each CMM participant is required to develop a business case in which they must apply the course materials learned. The business case should reflect real situations, address current challenges that need to be resolved and be actionable (which means that the participant must have responsibility for, and influence over, the challenges' outcome). Each participant's business case is evaluated and scored against a pre-established standard of performance or rubric by CMM programme faculty.

The criteria for participation in the CMM programme align with the Meeting and Business Events Competency Standards (MBECS), which are described separately in this chapter. Each candidate will be evaluated through a comprehensive application process with documented panel review against the following criteria:

- A minimum of 7 to 10 years of professional experience in the meeting and event or business travel industry
- A minimum of 3 to 5 years of management experience with 2 years of profit and loss responsibility
- A personal statement and letter of recommendation from a professional colleague or supervisor

Further details on the CMM are available from: Meeting Professionals International, 3030 LBJ Freeway, Suite 1700, Dallas, TX 75234, USA, Tel.: +1 972 702 3000; e-mail: information@mpiweb.org (www.mpiweb. org/education/cmm) and Global Business Travel Association, 123 North Pitt Street, Alexandria, VA 22314, USA, Te.l: +1 703 684 0836; e-mail: info@gbta.org (www.gbta.org/cmm).

Certified Meeting Professional

The Certified Meeting Professional (CMP) programme recognises individuals who have achieved the industry's highest standard of professionalism. The CMP was established in 1985 and it is administered by the Convention Industry Council. Since its inception, over 14,000 individuals in 46 countries and territories have earned the CMP designation. The CMP credential increases the proficiency of meeting professionals by:

- Identifying a body of knowledge
- Establishing a level of knowledge and performance necessary for certification
- Stimulating the advancement of the art and science of meeting management
- Increasing the value of practitioners to their employers
- Recognising and raising industry standards, practices and ethics
- Maximising the value received from the products and services provided by Certified Meeting Professionals

Through the CMP programme, individuals who are employed in meeting management pursue continuing education, increase their industry involvement and gain industry-wide recognition.

The CMM qualification (described above) does not affect the status of the CMP designation. In fact, the CMM is structured to complement, rather than compete with, the CMP designation: the former is more strategic in approach, the latter more tactical.

To qualify to take the CMP examination, a candidate must demonstrate a minimum number of years in the industry as well as having acquired a minimum number of continuing education hours. From July 2012, the CMP paper-based exam changed to a computer-based model. The electronic advance coincided with the regular update of the CMP exam and the introduction of CMP International Standards (see below), enhancing the global relevance of the certification. The exam is administered four times a year during a 10-day testing window at more than 450 testing centres around the world. There are online courses as well as local study groups that can assist in preparing for the exam.

Certification demonstrates that the certified meeting professional has evolved through self-study and industry-promoted education which, when combined with the individual's experience and practical knowledge, has led to their ability to obtain certification. CMP certification holders:

• are recognised by peers for their professionalism and expertise;
• are able to contribute to the development of industry best practices;
• act as role models to junior meeting professionals; and
• participate in ensuring industry standards.

CMP INTERNATIONAL STANDARDS

The CMP International Standards (CMP-IS) are the body of knowledge for the Certified Meeting Professional programme and examination. The CMP-IS defines and categorises the skills, competencies and abilities an individual needs to be successful in the profession. The CMP-IS, completed in 2011, represents the most significant enhancement to the CMP body of knowledge since the start of the CMP programme in 1985. The CMP-IS is the result of a multi-year project that involved many stakeholders including subject matter experts, educators and CMP designation holders. In developing the CMP-IS, the Convention Industry Council partnered with the Canadian Tourism Human Resource Council (CTHRC), which completed a job analysis in 2009 for their new standard, Event Management – International Competency Standard. The project also utilised MPI's MBECS, which is aligned with CTHRC's competency standards.

The full Standards can be downloaded from the Convention Industry Council website and/or from www.emerit.ca.

Further details on the CMP and CMP-IS are available from Convention Industry Council, 700 N.Fairfax, Suite 510, Alexandria, VA 22314, USA, Tel.:+1 571 527 3116; e-mail: certification@conventionindustry.org (www.conventionindustry.org).

Certified Destination Management Executive and Professional in Destination Management programmes

The Certified Destination Management Executive (CDME) and Professional in Destination Management (PDM) certificate are professional development programmes created by DMAI. Each programme provides destination marketing industry professionals with a flexible approach to targeted professional development. In the case of CDME, this takes the form of a dedicated curriculum. PDM is a self-directed programme to accommodate a more disciplined and focused learning path.

CDME is an advanced educational programme for experienced and career-minded DMO professionals seeking practical skill development and industry recognition. Those who have completed the programme successfully receive their professional certification and are entitled to use the CDME credential. As the CDME programme is in a redesign phase (in 2015), the programme's reinvention will target best practices and professional competencies needed to lead and manage in a changing industry.

The current CDME programme has specific requirements that include three core courses, two elective courses, core research papers and a final exam research project. The core courses are as follows:

- Strategic issues in destination management
- Destination marketing planning
- Destination leadership

Each of the core courses is 2 days in length and the elective courses are a single day. All courses are offered throughout the year in the spring, summer and autumn (fall).

While the CDME is designed for senior staff leaders of a DMO, the PDM is open to both DMO staff and non-DMO staff. The pricing reflects member and non-member status in DMAI.

As referenced earlier, the CDME programme is undergoing a major review and redesign. The assessment and reinvention of the programme is scheduled to take place during 2015 and the first half of 2016. The aim is to strengthen the fundamentals of the programme through business practices and competencies that reflect changing trends of the DMO industry, while aligning the curriculum more closely with NEXTPractices of DestinationNEXT (outlined in more detail in the 'Research' section of this chapter). During the redesign process, all aspects of the programme including framework, curriculum, pricing structure, policies and procedures and partnerships will be assessed.

The PDM programme leads to completion of a certificate and it is designed for DMO professionals seeking the knowledge and skills that will help to ensure successful careers in destination management. The PDM Certificate requires completion of 40 credit hours within a 2-year period. There is one required course – Fundamentals of Destination Management – that equates to five credit hours and it is offered at DMAI's annual convention. The Fundamentals course covers the following subjects:

- Communications in destination management
- Destination marketing
- Destination product development
- Information technology for destination management

The balance of the 40 credits is earned through a variety of educational offerings provided by DMAI and non-DMAI education/conference sessions.

Further details on the CDME and PDM programmes are available via DMAI Education and Professional Development, Destination Marketing Association International, 2025 M Street NW, Suite 500, Washington, DC, 20036, USA, Tel.: +1 202 296 7888; e-mail: info@destinationmarketing.org (www.destinationmarketing.org).

European Cities Marketing Summer School and Educational Programme

European Cities Marketing (ECM) has been running an annual Summer School since 1987, held in a different country each year (traditionally around the last weekend of August). The 2014 and 2015 Summer Schools took place in Genoa (Italy) and Vienna (Austria) respectively.

The primary goal of the ECM Summer School is to provide a solid basic education for those just starting out in the meetings industry. Uniquely, it brings students face-to-face with leading industry practitioners through an event that reflects the latest trends, new technologies and practices. It seeks to maintain the highest standard of course content, retaining and recruiting the best speakers and giving up-to-date examples highlighting the latest trends in the industry.

The format of the course is based on a number of lectures in combination with practical training and interactive group work. Details of the programme can be found at the ECM website (see below). Members of Faculty are renowned experts who are very willing to share their knowledge with the students. Participants have a unique opportunity to receive first-hand information and are encouraged to develop contacts with the speakers in a relaxed atmosphere.

The 2015 Summer School focused on:

- How to create a marketing plan to promote a city or region
- The decision-making processes of corporate and association clients as they relate to meeting and congress planning
- How to find clients: databases, research and trade exhibitions
- How to establish a client database
- To bid or not to bid
- How to bring clients to your city (fam. trips, site inspections)
- The role of intermediaries (PCOs and DMCs)
- Meetings statistics, data collection, mining and interpretation
- How to work with the meetings industry press
- Green meetings, the principle of sustainability for cities and conference centres
- How to go social, mobile and local

The family atmosphere of the ECM Summer School offers participants the chance to establish life-long contacts and friendships. Figure 9.2 shows delegates at the 2013 ECM Summer School held in Istanbul.

In addition to the Summer School, ECM organises two seminars per year with the aim of developing knowledge and expertise in the fields of conventions, city tourism and city marketing. The June 2015 seminar focused on shaping the city and how new events and infrastructure projects can change the image of a destination.

Figure 9.2 Delegates at the 2013 ECM Summer School in Istanbul

Further details are available from European Cities Marketing, 29D Rue de Talant, 21000 Dijon, France, Tel: +33 380 56 02 04; e-mail: headoffice@europeancitiesmarketing.com (www.europeancitiesmarketing.com).

Case study 9.2 describes the International Association of Conference Centres' 'Certificate in International Conference Centre Management', developed in conjunction with New York University.

Competency standards in events management

An important illustration of the growing professionalism and professionalisation of the business events sector has been the development of competency standards for events management. In the UK, for example, competency standards were developed for the National Vocational Qualifications, while similar standards have also been developed in Australia, Canada and South Africa. Bowdin *et al.* (2011:38–9) suggest that:

> *A competency standard for events management gives the industry a benchmark to measure excellence in management. Previously this benchmark was the success of the event; however, stakeholders cannot wait until the event is over to find out whether the event management was competent – by then it is too late.*

Events Management International Competency Standards (EMICS) have been developed by the CTHRC in co-operation with industry participants from 20 countries. The Standards contain a comprehensive summary of the functions, tasks and competencies required to work in event management. They describe in detail the skills, knowledge and attitudes that employers and clients are looking for when obtaining professional services to plan, implement and evaluate different types of events, nationally and internationally.

The International Standards cover a number of 'domains', including:

- Strategic planning
- Project management
- Risk management
- Financial management
- Human resources
- Stakeholder management
- Meeting or event design
- Site management
- Marketing
- Professionalism

Full details of the standards can be downloaded at www.emerit.ca under the 'Free Downloads – Occupational Standards' link (see also the reference under the CMP programme above).

MPI has also developed a comprehensive set of competency standards, known as the MBECS, launched in 2011. A product of several international boards, governmental bodies, task forces and MPI itself, MBECS are designed to provide a detailed catalogue of the skills needed to be a meetings professional.

The Standards cover 12 areas:

1. Strategic Planning
    i. Manage Strategic Plan for Meeting or Event
    ii. Develop Sustainability Plan for Meeting or Event
    iii. Measure Value of Meeting or Business Event

2. Project Management
    i.   Plan Meeting or Event Project
    ii. Manage Meeting or Event Project

3. Risk Management

4. Financial Management
    i.   Develop Financial Resources
    ii. Manage Budget
    iii. Manage Monetary Transactions

5. Administration

6. Human Resources
    i.   Manage Human Resources Plan
    ii. Acquire Staff and Volunteers

The 12 major categories cover 33 individual skills that are, in turn, informed by sub-skills. The full Standards can be downloaded from the MPI website (www.mpiweb.org/mbecs).

University education programmes

A significant number of universities and other higher education institutions now offer undergraduate and postgraduate courses in conference and event management. The University of Nevada, Las Vegas, is one of the leaders in the field both nationally and internationally. Other key players in North America include the Appalachian State University, George Washington University, Georgia State University, Northeastern State University, the University of Houston, the University of New Orleans and the University of Central Florida, all offering specific conference sector-related courses that have close links with, and are supported by, the industry.

Many universities in other continents have initiated and expanded their provision of courses in conference and exhibition management, often building collaborative partnerships with universities in other countries in order to increase the international content and experiences of their programmes. Modules on destination and venue marketing feature in a number of these courses.

As a further sign of progress in the development of an educational infrastructure for the conference industry, academics who teach subjects related to that sector now have a number of annual events during which they meet each other in order to network, share their research and discuss topics connected with the teaching of conference management in higher education. Despite the type of advances described above, in terms of the expansion of higher education provision for the conference industry, academics specialising in this field usually find themselves in the minority in university departments when compared with the number of their colleagues who specialise in leisure tourism or sports and cultural events, for example. Two examples of international annual conferences for business events academics are:

- The ATLAS Business Tourism Special Interest Group conference. ATLAS (www.atlas-euro.org), the Association for Tourism and Leisure Education was established in 1991 to develop transnational educational initiatives in tourism and leisure. It operates through a system of special interest groups (SIGs) whose members specialise in teaching and undertaking research in a specific sub-sector of the tourism industry. The SIG for Business Tourism was launched at the ATLAS conference in Leeuwarden in June 2003. It brings together academics with an interest in business events of all kinds. Each year since its inception, it has held an annual conference for its members.

- PEMES (http://pemes.syskonf.pl/?lang=en), the Polish Event Management Educators Symposium is a conference for researchers, academics and practitioners in the field of tourism and the organisation and management of events and business meetings. The inspiration for the creation of the conference in 2014 was the need to focus on this rapidly developing sector, to stimulate teaching and research in the field, to improve the quality of education and the development of the industry. The language of the annual 2-day conference is Polish on day 1 and English on day 2. The second day attracts significant numbers of academics from all over Europe and beyond.

It is clear that educational provision has improved and expanded exponentially since the first edition of this book was published in 2006. The development of online learning opportunities is also now contributing flexible study possibilities that allow 'students' (employees) to combine short courses with employment or follow distance learning programmes while being employed.

One consequence of the expansion in university educational provision for the meetings industry is that there is a growing body of research being produced by the academics who teach these subjects in higher education institutions. In response to the expansion of research activity in this field, there is now a number of specialist academic journals in which these academics' research papers are published. These include titles such as the *International Journal of Event and Festival Management* (http://www.emerald-grouppublishing.com/products/journals/journals.htm?id=IJEFM) and the *Journal of Convention and Event Tourism* (http://www.tandfonline.com/toc/wcet20/current#).

Such journals are largely written for, and read by, university-based academics. However, much of the material they include takes the form of original and rigorous research into different aspects of the meetings industry that are of direct relevance to practitioners, as shown by these examples of titles of articles from recent editions:

- 'Understanding the role of local food in the meeting industry: an exploratory study of meeting planners' perception of local food in sustainable meeting planning'
- 'The Great Halls of China? Meeting planners' perceptions of Beijing as an international convention destination'
- 'Price competitiveness and government incentives for simulating the meetings industry: a critical look at the case of Macau'
- 'Maximising effectiveness of corporate hospitality programmes at Australian special events'

An ongoing challenge for academia is to get practitioners in the meetings industry to notice the fruits of their research and put them to use in the work they do.

Quality standards

Reference was made earlier in this chapter to the work of the Convention Industry Council, through APEX, in enhancing industry standards and developing 'accepted practices', including the publication of an industry glossary covering the terminology, jargon and acronyms used industry-wide. APEX has also developed a range of other accepted practices:

- Post-Event Report: this provides a format for collecting, storing and sharing accurate and thorough post-event report data on all types of events. It includes best practices as well as a Microsoft Word template for a Post-Event Report.
- Event Specifications Guide: this is a tool for preparing and sharing complete instructions and details for events and provides a Microsoft Word template.
- Housing and Registration: this covers accepted practices for collecting, reporting and retrieving complete housing (accommodation) and registration data for meetings, conventions and other events.

Other accepted practices are being produced and they will cover requests for proposals, meeting and site profiles and contracts. Further details on all the APEX topic areas are available from the Convention Industry Council, 8201 Greensboro Drive, Suite 300, McLean, VA 22102, USA, Tel.: +1 703 610 9000 (www.conventionindustry.org offers free online access to the published practices).

APEX is just one of a number of programmes designed to improve the quality and professionalism of the conference and convention industry worldwide. The rapid growth of the global meetings industry over the past few decades has, perhaps inevitably, meant that quality issues have not always received the attention they deserve. It is an indication of the maturation of our industry that quality standards, consistency of delivery and performance measurement are all beginning to feature strongly in the operations of venue and destination marketers. Certain quality initiatives are particularly appropriate to event venues while others have been developed for application at a destination level. Some examples of quality initiatives are given below:

ISO 9001:2008

ISO is the International Organisation for Standardisation, which is located in Switzerland. It was established in 1947 to facilitate international trade through the provision of a single set of international standards that people everywhere would recognise and respect. Such standards are applicable to all kinds of organisations in all industry sectors. The members of ISO represent over 120 national standards bodies.

ISO 9001:2008 is an international quality management system designed to help both product and service-oriented organisations and replaced the previous ISO 9001:2000 standards. It is being used by an increasing number of business event venues to provide a recognisable and accredited quality foundation leading to enhanced customer satisfaction, better staff motivation and continuous improvement.

An ISO 9001-certified organisation is one that has implemented quality management system requirements in all areas of its business including:

- Facilities
- People
- Training
- Services
- Equipment

Achieving ISO 9001 standards is the first step of a process of continuous improvement that will provide the organisation with the necessary management tools to improve working practices throughout the entire organisation. Benefits to an organisation of gaining ISO 9001 certification are likely to include:

- Providing senior management with an efficient management process
- Setting out areas of responsibility across the organisation
- Communicating a positive message to staff and customers
- Identifying and encouraging more efficient and time-saving processes
- Highlighting deficiencies
- Reducing costs
- Providing continuous assessment and improvement
- Generating marketing opportunities

For customers, the benefits encompass:

- Improved quality and service
- Delivery on time
- The right-first-time attitude
- Fewer complaints

The above are underpinned by an independent audit, demonstrating a commitment to quality.

Standard CVB performance reporting

DMAI has developed a handbook for convention bureaux and DMOs that sets out a series of standards for measuring, evaluating and reporting on their performance. Entitled 'Standard DMO performance reporting: a handbook for DMOs', it provides DMOs with recognised benchmarks for evaluating and communicating their organisation's performance. The handbook is regularly updated and the 2011 edition includes sections on:

- DMO Convention Sales Performance Reporting
- DMO Travel Trade Sales Performance Reporting
- DMO Marketing and Communications Performance Reporting
- DMO Membership Performance Reporting
- DMO Visitor Information Centre Performance Reporting
- DMO Return on Investment

New performance measures to cover online marketing and social media have also been added. The handbook is available for free download from http://www.destinationmarketing.org/performance-reporting-initiative.

BestCities global alliance service standards

Each BestCities (profiled in chapter 8) destination bureau has made a commitment to excellence and to deliver superior destination experiences for its clients. BestCities is the first global alliance to put in place a certification programme – with standards certified by Lloyd's Register Quality Assurance (LRQA) – to ensure a consistent level of convention bureau service excellence from all partner cities. Each bureau conducts an internal audit annually while the LRQA audit takes place every 2 years. Bestcities' Quality Management System monitors the services provided to meeting planners by each of its convention bureau partners. It is designed to ensure that, whichever BestCities bureau is used, meeting planners are guaranteed consistently high service. Appropriate survey data are collected throughout the year to measure the quality of service delivery and customers' satisfaction with the goal of continuous improvement. BestCities' LRQA-certified Service Standards are organised into six key areas of convention planning and event management:

- Destination expertise
- Bid assistance
- Convention planning
- Building attendance
- Onsite event servicing
- Post-event evaluation

Figures 9.3 and 9.4 are taken from the BestCities 2014 Client Surveys that are administered independently; 314 association clients were surveyed, with a 44 per cent response. The surveys were conducted after a bid involving a BestCities bureau and at the conclusion of a meeting or convention held in a BestCities destination.

Case Study 9.3 describes the 'Accredited in Meetings' (AIM) quality initiative developed in the UK to provide a quality standard or benchmark for conference and meeting venues and related suppliers.

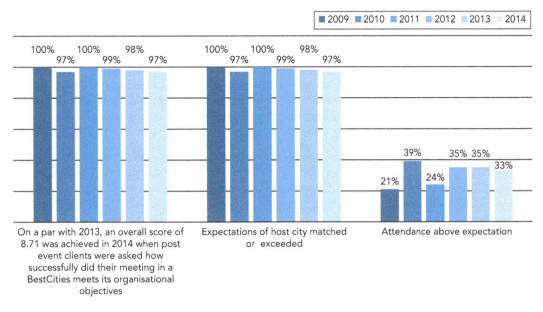

Figure 9.3 BestCities Client Survey 2014 (a)

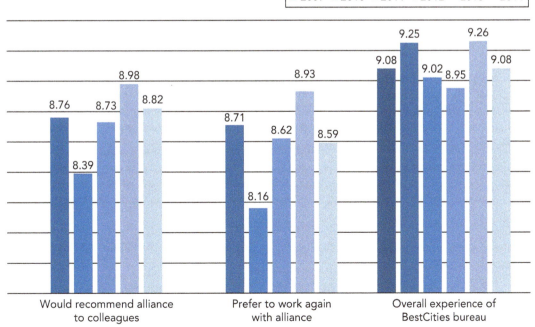

Figure 9.4 BestCities Client Survey 2014 (b). Column figures represent marks out of ten

CASE STUDY 9.1   ICCA's Big Data search tool

The bidding context

The ICCA launched its Big Data search tool to identify local association representatives in May 2014.

Crucial in the bidding process to secure international association conventions and events are local ambassadors or 'key contacts' as ICCA calls them. ICCA's database holds information on approximately 11,500 international associations. The address details of the national member societies (i.e. 'local' entities in this context) are available for some 25 per cent of these international associations through ICCA's database. This implies that, when including the criterion of key contacts being available in any search of the ICCA database, 75 per cent of the potential business is lost by default.

ICCA's Big Data tool addresses this issue by providing its members with the option to look for individuals in a certain location, linked to a specific taxonomy (or classification). The search tool gives ICCA members a unique way to identify local representatives who could help them to bid for an international association meeting.

How does Big Data work?

Big Data is essentially a way to access and utilise both internal and (especially) external data sources in new ways, using tools that enable complex analysis to be undertaken without managing the data directly. Big Data is an all-encompassing term for sets of data that are so large and complex that traditional processing methods are rendered inadequate. Big Data is hard to analyse, as there is no level of control or structure to the data.

The ICCA Big Data project grew out of a single ICCA member's (Tourisme Montréal) initiative, through which Tourisme Montréal had designed a tool to identify quickly and efficiently Montreal-based academic and medical leaders who could potentially be ambassadors for congress bids. ICCA worked with Tourisme Montréal's technical partner, Human Equation, to build a tool that works on a global basis so that ICCA members anywhere can use it for a number of tasks.

Utilising the vast databases of Google Scholar and Microsoft Academic Search, ICCA members can now identify leading academic contacts in specified cities and regions, related to a specific meeting in a specific meeting subject. The involvement of local association representatives is crucial to the success of preparing a bid to host the next edition of an association's international meeting.

In November 2014, an extra sophistication was added to the original ambassador search, identifying whether selected 'ambassadors' in local universities are also featured within the websites of associations and congresses in the selected academic field. This is ICCA's latest step in harnessing the power of Big Data and combining it with its own unique data on associations and their meetings.

Figure 9.5 shows the online 'dashboard' of the Big Data tool.

As an indication of the vast size of the databanks that are accessible, as of March 2015, Big Data provided links to:

- 7.4 million academic authors, 13,446 universities and organisations and 49.8 million scientific publications via Microsoft Academic Search
- 436.2 million articles via Google Scholar

Figure 9.6 illustrates a search for academics in the field of ecology and environment/pollution located within a 10-kilometre range of Cambridge, England.

Figure 9.7 displays the results of this search combining Microsoft Academic Search and the information stored in the ICCA database to indicate if an academic is related to an event or an association.

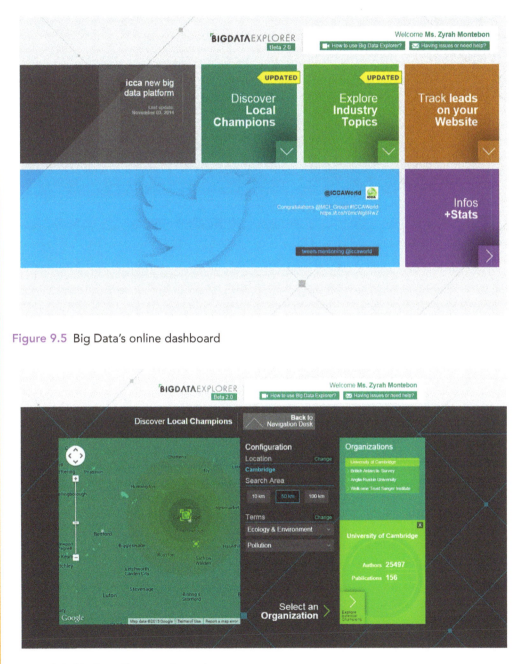

Figure 9.5 Big Data's online dashboard

Figure 9.6 Big Data illustrated search

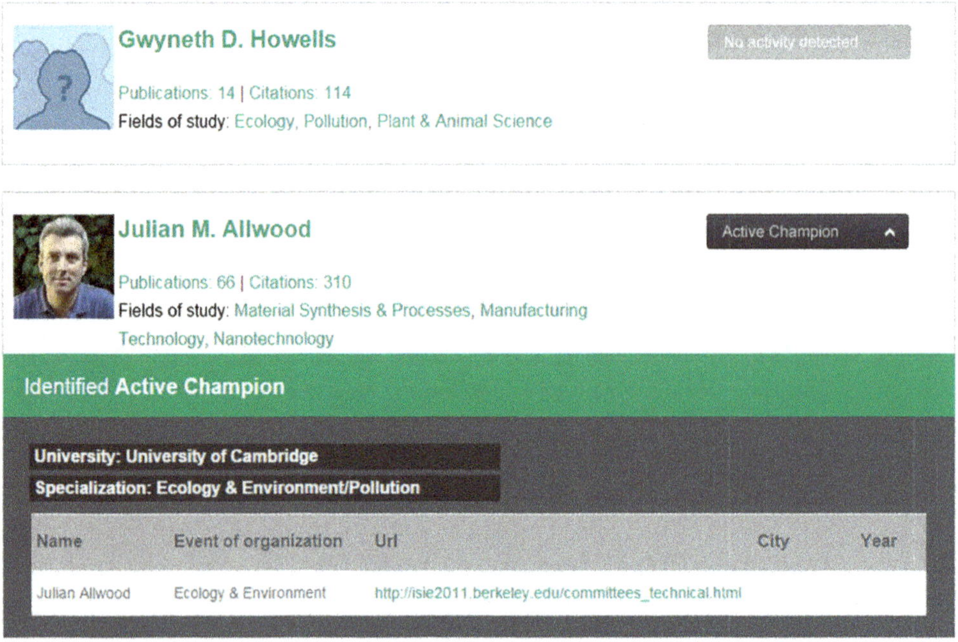

Figure 9.7 Search results

ISIE2011 (International Society for Industrial Ecology) is one of the meetings in the ICCA Database. The event URL is stored whenever possible. Based on this information, the tool can combine the results from Microsoft Academic Search with the data that ICCA holds and it can come up with a match, as with Julian Allwood in this case. Not only is he a much-quoted academic in this field of expertise, he is also connected to an international rotating meeting. To learn exactly in what shape or form his involvement takes, clicking the link provides the answer.

Figure 9.8 displays the relevant webpage where the name of the academic is to be found.

Figure 9.9 provides a view of the information in Microsoft Academic Search.

A publication and citation graph is displayed, together with a link that allows users to search for this individual in Bing and to see his or her contact details.

Relations between authors can be studied and presented graphically, as shown in Figure 9.9. The 'Visual Explorer' of Microsoft Academic Search (free to use) focuses on the relations between people. After selecting a certain author, one can choose 'co-author path' in the left-hand menu. The dynamically generated diagram shows the co-authors of this researcher ('co-author graph'), how the researcher is connected to another researcher ('co-author path') and who cited the researcher ('citation graph').

The relationships shown in Microsoft Academic (as illustrated in Figure 9.10) enable ICCA members to obtain a far more sophisticated understanding of the circles of influence that exist between leading academics, assisting them to identify the best-connected potential ambassadors, not just those with the strongest publishing records. Bidding is becoming so competitive today that every tiny piece of relevant information could potentially provide a critical competitive advantage for the smart-thinking destination. Microsoft Academic, therefore, provides a starting point for ICCA members to identify someone who could be involved in event bidding and/or event organising.

Technical Committee

	Topic	Individual(s)	
1.	Material Flow Analysis	Daniel Muller	Bob Boughton
2.	Life-cycle Methodology	Jeroen Guinee	
3.	Environmentally Extended Input-Output Analysis	Troy Hawkins	Arnold Tukker
4.	Life-cycle Management & Organization of Product Chains	Henrikke Baumann	Frank Boons
5.	Complex Systems and Agent Modeling	Gerard Dijkema	Ruud Kempener
6.	Scenario Development and Analysis	Jim Petrie	Mary Stewart
7.	Eco-Industrial Development and Industrial Symbiosis	Weslynne Ashton	Leenard Baas
8.	Eco-Design: Products and Services for the Future	Julian Allwood	Tim Gutowski
9.	Managing End-of-Life Products	Eric Williams	Kieren Mayers
10.	Footprint Analysis, Reporting and Communication	Sarah McLaren	Matthias Finkbeiner
11.	Eco-Efficiency	Gjalt Huppes	Roland Geyer
12.	Energy Systems	Alissa Kendall	Sabrina Spatari
13.	Sustainable Water Systems	Donna Jefferies	Stephan Pfister
14.	Sustainable Cities and Urban Metabolism	John Femandez / Sangwon Suh	Paulo Ferrao
15.	Industrial Ecology in Developing Countries	Marian Chertow	Megha Shenoy
16.	Sustainable Consumption and Behavior	Angela Druckman	Barbara Kam
17.	Policy Intervention and Planning	Clint Andrews	Edgar Hertwich
18.	Food and Agricultural Systems	Greg Thoma	Deepak Sivaraman
19.	Transportation and Logistics	Mikhail Chester	Heather MacLean
20.	Buildings and Infrastructure Systems	Michael Lepech	Seppo Junnila

Welcome
Committees
  Organizing
  Technical
Program
Venue

Figure 9.8 Relevant web page where relevant academic is to be found

Academic > Authors > Julian M. Allwood

Julian M. Allwood
University of Cambridge
Publications: 66 | Citations: 310
Fields: Material Synthesis & Processes, Manufacturing Technology, Nanotechnology
Collaborated with 80 co-authors from 1997 to 2011 | Cited by 512 authors

Co-authors (80)
A. Erman Tekkaya
Stephen Richard Duncan
Daniel R. Shouler
Ankor Raithathna
N. M. P. Bocken

Co-author Path

Conferences (2)
CACSD-CCA-ISIC
ACC

Journals (26)
J MATER PROCESS TECHNOL
CIRP ANN-MANUF TECHNOL
RESOUR CONSERV RECYCL
J CLEAN PROD
IEEE TRANS CONTROL SYST TECHN

publications citations   Cumulative Annual

Publications (66) Export   Sort by: Year

Material efficiency: A white paper (Citations: 2)
Julian M. Allwood, Michael F. Ashby, Timothy G. Gutowski, Ernst Worrell
Journal: Resources Conservation and Recycling - RESOUR CONSERV RECYCL, vol. 55, no. 3, pp. 362-381, 2011

Phylogenetic analysis of New Zealand earthworms (Oligochaeta: Megascolecidae) reveals ancient clades and cryptic taxonomic diversity (Citations: 3)
Thomas R. Buckley, Sam James, Julia Allwood, Scott Bartlam, Robyn Howitt, Diana Prada
Journal: Molecular Phylogenetics and Evolution - MOL PHYLOGENET EVOL, vol. 58, no. 1, pp. 85-96, 2011

Figure 9.9 A view of the information in Microsoft Academic Search

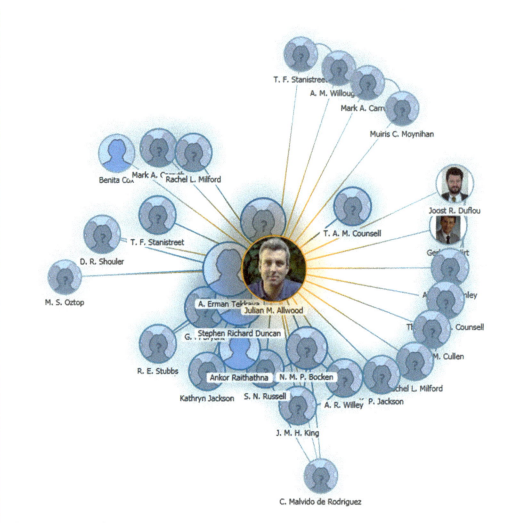

Figure 9.10 Graphic representation of links between authors

Furthermore, the module that identifies the relative academic strength of the local university in a particular field has been upgraded significantly to enable ICCA members to identify new scientific, technological or healthcare fields more easily where they have an academic advantage or to compare their academic strength with that of direct rivals in any competitive bid. Big Data can display the relative academic strength of local universities, as well as show the top institutions globally, as illustrated in Figure 9.11.

The tool has been developed by ICCA member Human Equation, a centre of innovation in digital marketing, specialising in the development of interactive solutions designed to address the business needs of its clients. The initiative presents a revolutionary new way of applying Big Data search techniques in the international association meetings market. It is ICCA's first step in harnessing the power of Big Data and combining it with ICCA's own unique data on associations and their meetings. It is anticipated that new functionality and data sources will be added to the search tool as ICCA receives feedback from users.

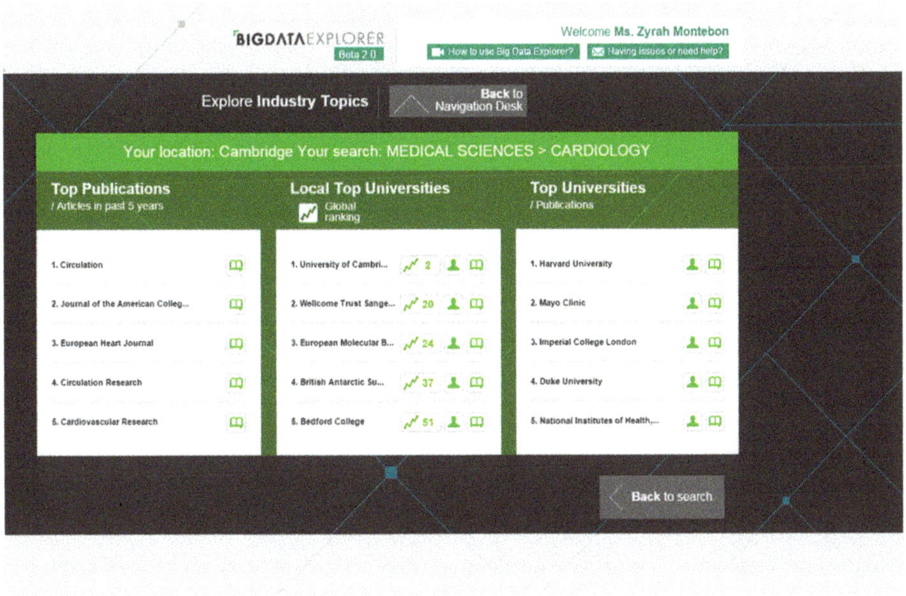

Figure 9.11 The relative academic strength of local universities

ICCA is also offering Human Equation's Lead Analytics tool to its members, which identifies organisation names and tracks the online behaviour of website visitors. The Big Data Search >Find meeting contacts can be accessed via the 'My ICCA' section of the ICCA Association Database Online.

ICCA CEO, Martin Sirk, comments on the importance of Big Data for all associations:

> Long ago in another era, but just a few years in the past, associations could realistically be regarded as the monopoly gatekeepers to their specialist areas of expertise within their traditional geographical territories. If you were based in Europe and wanted to know about liver disease, the only place to go was the European Association for the Study of the Liver. The same principle applied to fusion power generation theory, chicken farming, and even international association meetings (ICCA's own niche area of expertise). The growth of the internet and the global ambitions of many regional associations, particularly over the last decade, had already significantly increased levels of competition, providing association members with more events to choose from and more sources of reliable information. Now, the emergence of Big Data is sure to further accelerate this trend, and the associations which ignore the opportunities and threats risk becoming increasingly irrelevant and outflanked.

> Big Data makes visible what was previously invisible, and makes accessible the previously unaffordable and unimaginable. More and more information is migrating on to gigantic open source databases, driven by public policy, professional peer recognition pressures, and insatiable demand from new audiences for access. More data sources are becoming searchable by ever more sophisticated search tools. And more and more expertly-curated knowledge concepts are being invented (think Wikipedia for general knowledge, or Wolfram Alpha for anything mathematically computable). What this means is that the best global provider of any specialist knowledge will soon be in a position to beat any rival: this could be a European or an Asia-Pacific association, or it could be a commercial company or an association from

a related field. Whoever builds the best search tools and curates the strongest content, both online and at their live events, not just their members' own data and knowledge but everything relevant in their field, will win loyalty and financial success.

In ICCA's case we're in the process of fundamentally changing our strategy, from focusing on gathering data on international association meetings from our members and elsewhere and turning this into a carefully managed database (15 researchers are needed to maintain records on fewer than 20,000 regularly occurring meetings worldwide), to becoming the fastest and most efficient point of access for every possible piece of information about those events, recognising that we won't be able to manage this data ourselves.

For further information, visit www.iccaworld.com.

CASE STUDY 9.2   IACC/NYU Certificate in International Conference Centre Management

Professional development is one of the prime concerns of the IACC (www.iacconline.org) and the IACC Institute within the association offers a series of educational opportunities for members, from conferences to webinars. However, Peter Stewart, IACC's Global President, has highlighted the 'huge void in conference centre-specific educational programmes' that led his association to collaborate with the faculty of New York University (NYU)'s Tisch Center for Professional Development to develop a certificate programme specifically for the conference centre industry.

The partnership between the IACC and NYU

The decision of the IACC to develop the Certificate in International Conference Centre Management (CICCM) in partnership with NYU was logical, given the long history of IACC and NYU working together over the years. For example, in 1997, the IACC joined forces with NYU to fund a scholarship in honour of Doris Sklar, long-time supporter of the conference centre industry and highly recognised leader in the meetings industry. First awarded in 2002, each year the Doris Sklar Award provides a US$5,000 grant-in-aid to a deserving hospitality student at NYU.

The target audience for the CICCM

The result of the IACC/NYU collaboration was the launch, in 2014, of the Certificate in International Conference Centre Management. The decision was made to deliver the programme online, as a means of making it accessible to conference centre managers and staff wherever in the world they are based. The CICCM is open to all entry-level to mid-level managers in venues and it takes a cross-departmental approach, covering topics from sales to operations. However, IACC members are recognised through a discount exclusive to them – the US$100 certificate application fee is waived upon their initial registration on the course.

Course content

This is how NYU describes the Certificate:

Today's conference centre managers face unique challenges and require the appropriate skills and training to succeed in a dynamic and changing business environment. Through this certificate, students employ a global lens to evaluate common business issues, including decisions about ownership structures and day-to-day operations; supervision of a diverse workforce in a service industry; ethical issues and risk assessment; business development, marketing, and positioning; the use of technology to modernize service offerings; and development of a strategic vision to ensure long-term success.

This certificate was developed in consultation with the IACC, which boasts a membership of over 350 venues worldwide. Recognising the significant career opportunities available to both seasoned industry veterans and individuals looking to begin their careers, the NYU School of Professional Studies partnered with IACC to develop a curriculum that would serve the educational and training needs of the global conference centre partner community. This certificate and the Tisch Center's complementary professional development programs provide optimal learning and training opportunities and ensure that the industry cultivates and retains qualified individuals for this growing tourism and hospitality segment.

The certificate is made up of four required and two elective courses:

- Required – Foundations of conference centre management and operations
- Required – HR: practices and techniques
- Required – Current issues in conference centre operations
- Required – Financial and legal frameworks
- Elective – Prospecting and sales strategies for conference centres and event venues
- Elective – Marketing and positioning strategies for meetings, events and conferences
- Elective – New technologies for the meeting and conference industry
- Elective – Global food trends

How the learning is delivered and how students are assessed

All courses are offered in a fully online, asynchronous format (self-paced with weekly milestones and deliverables). However, a high level of engagement among students is ensured through an online community platform that enables them to communicate freely with each other and with faculty members. Those responsible for teaching the course fall into two categories: NYU faculty and guest lecturers, who are distinguished industry experts. In terms of assessment, students are graded in each course and they must earn at least a B+ average to earn their certificate.

For further information visit www.iacconline.org.

CASE STUDY 9.3   Accredited in Meetings quality assurance scheme

AIM is the UK's only nationally recognised quality standard for the meetings, conferences and events industry. It provides organisers, bookers and buyers with the reassurance of venue and supplier excellence in terms of legal compliance, ethical business operations, capability, quality of the facilities and overall fitness for purpose. Figure 9.12 shows the AIM logo.

AIM was developed by the Meetings Industry Association (mia) together with a number of strategic partners (see below). The mia is one of the largest trade associations in the UK meetings

An Assurance of Excellence
Making Meetings Better

Figure 9.12 AIM logo

and events sector and has been connecting people, ideas and best practice for 25 years. Led by a Council of dedicated professionals, the mia seeks to support the industry and see it grow and evolve.

Extensive development process

With the UK venue and hotel landscape so extensively populated, it was felt by the mia chief executive and mia Council in 2004/05 that there was a need for the meetings and events industry to develop a benchmark of quality and ethics for all of those involved in the booking and procurement of meetings and events. The concept was developed and shaped over the following year, with VisitBritain involved in its development and Liverpool and the North West Regional Development Agency piloting and trialling the scheme. AIM was introduced in 2007. The overall development was through a consensus-based process involving: leading MICE organisations, the Best Practice Forum, VisitBritain and purchasing communities, in a collaborative effort that represented the interests of many industry stakeholders. (The Best Practice Forum was a strategic alliance between nine of the UK tourism industry's leading trade associations, led by the British Hospitality Association. The Forum was one of fifteen Industry Forums and a member of the Department of Trade and Industry (DTI) Forum Network. It was launched in 2001 with initial funding and support from the Government through the DTI and Department for Culture, Media and Sport. The Forum was a direct response to the Government's Competitiveness White Paper and set out to disseminate best practice through its 'Profit Through Productivity" programmes of benchmarking and business support. The Forum no longer exists because funding was withdrawn.)

The story of AIM is not one of overnight success: the recent surge in interest in the accreditation, which began in late 2012, is the result of over half a decade's planning and development. Jane Longhurst, the mia chief executive, who spearheaded the accreditation from its earliest stages, explains how AIM's development was a detailed process:

> It had been clear for a long time that meetings venues needed an accreditation that was specific to their needs. The various hotel-related schemes (e.g. star ratings) were not entirely suitable, and were the only alternative, so we set out to create a quality standard that the entire industry could embrace, one that ticked all the procurement boxes. Developing an all-encompassing standard, one that both venues and industry buyers could trust and really see the value of, took time. We spent well over a year developing AIM, working with the Best Practice Forum and calling on experts from all sectors of the industry, such as venue managers and venue finding agents, for advice and input. Finally, when we had all the pieces in place for a robust accreditation scheme, we launched.

The national launch of AIM in spring 2007 was met with mixed feelings because, in what could be considered a bold move, the mia had made AIM accreditation a requirement of membership of the association. All mia members had to achieve AIM entry-level within a year.

Jane Longhurst continued:

> Some people predicted AIM would bring about the end of the mia. They said it was too much too soon, but we kept faith. We knew we had completed extensive research and taken great pains in ensuring AIM was exactly the accreditation the industry was demanding, so we felt confident the majority of our members would quickly see the advantages; thankfully it paid off.

In reality, AIM has had a positive effect on mia's membership, contributing to a steady growth year-on-year since its inception. It is widely agreed that AIM has also benefited the UK meetings industry as a whole, as it has been a key driver of raising quality standards and professionalism.

One of the mia's objectives as a trade association is to raise facility and service standards throughout the meetings, conference and events industry. In order to realise this objective, the mia has made AIM available to all organisations involved in the industry – it does not matter whether these organisations are members of the mia or not, or what their affiliation is – every venue and supplier to the industry can obtain AIM if their standards meet the requirement of the scheme.

As at December 2014, there were approximately 500 AIM-accredited venues and suppliers across the UK. The complete list of organisations upholding the standard is available on http://www.aimaccredited.co.uk/>Venue Directory.

The virtues of AIM

Essentially, AIM helps event organisers quickly find venues they can instantly trust. But what does it mean for prospective buyers and bookers? It means:

- Doing business with venues that care and have integrity
- Staging events and meetings where delegates are well looked after and commitment to service excellence is paramount
- Hosting an event where the facilities and event spaces are fit for purpose and of a high quality standard
- Accountability through an ethical code of conduct
- Knowing every element of the venue's costs in advance
- Industry-approved contracts and terms and conditions
- Doing business with credible, legally compliant venues
- Standardisation of best practice
- Procurement boxes ticked
- Stress-free venue selection
- Total peace of mind

Meetings code

All AIM venues abide by the Meetings CODE (developed prior to AIM and currently being updated). The CODE was written by a mia council working party as a requirement of mia membership many years before AIM. It was reviewed and shaped to take account of differing membership types when AIM was devised. The CODE is a standard that is kept up-to-date and relevant on a consistent basis. The CODE demands:

- Consistency
- Openness
- Decency
- Ethics

AIM venues must achieve 50 grading criteria that include: the location and accessibility of the meeting rooms and facilities; the suitability of the lighting and heating in meeting rooms; the levels of security; the frequency of cleaning and decorating the rooms; the adequacy and suitability of space and furniture; the provision of in-room services such as power sockets; clarity on what is supplied at no extra charge; and how transparent the published prices are.

AIM-accredited venues and suppliers must also comply with a number of Laws, which complement the criteria, including health and safety at work, fire safety, the Bribery Act, licensing laws, data protection and disability discrimination.

The AIM effect on venues and suppliers

For venues and suppliers, achieving AIM means gaining an industry accreditation and receiving recognition for the management of the business. Internally, the accreditation helps to assess and audit current practices and reaffirm excellent levels of service. The process also highlights any weaknesses so they can be addressed quickly and appropriately. AIM has staff benefits, generating a sense of pride and responsibility among employees in what the business is doing and how it is done. In obtaining the accreditation, Nick Milne, conference manager at Robinson College (Cambridge), said:

> The application process was an opportunity for us to assess, review and identify opportunities to improve how we do things. We learnt that much more already happens in the business by way of effective management and customer focus than we realised. The process of preparing for AIM put everything in its place and provided an opportunity for us to 'take stock'. We knew that our customers were already happy with what we do but, by being more formal in recording feedback about specific performance, we have been able to target those areas where we could be even better. Everyone is focused on improving wherever we can, which is a significant and important goal.

AIM Higher

The AIM scheme encourages continual improvement through AIM Higher. Along with the standard entry-level of AIM, there are two 'AIM Higher' levels: AIM Silver and AIM Gold. These demonstrate compliance with a more stringent set of criteria and they are an optional step for venues and suppliers.

Venues that have been awarded AIM Higher have completed a much more rigorous process, covering 50 assessment criteria, including a ten-section self-assessment. They will also have produced a portfolio of evidence in support of their application and been visited by an independent assessor who determines whether the venue is worthy of the accreditation and, if so, whether AIM Silver or AIM Gold should be awarded. For a venue or supplier to achieve AIM Silver or Gold is a significant achievement.

Any venue that achieves AIM Silver/Gold must be re-assessed every 3 years – this is to encourage continuous improvement and it is key to the AIM message of maintaining high standards in the MICE industry.

The challenges

One of the biggest challenges during AIM's launch was gaining the support of the entire conference, meetings and events industry. The route to achieving this began by securing endorsements from other independent organisations concerned with promoting meetings, events and venues in the UK and Ireland. VisitEngland saw the demonstrable advantage of AIM for English venues – AIM's expansion is now a key element of VisitEngland's Business Tourism Action Plan. Visit Wales, VisitScotland and Tourism Ireland also top the list of tourism organisations that have endorsed AIM, along with 29 national and regional DMOs. AIM also has the support of influential UK business tourism-related trade associations MPI UK and ABPCO.

With widespread independent support, the industry has taken note and AIM is now firmly established as the only national standard for meetings venues and suppliers to the industry in the UK and Ireland.

AIM's next challenge is to secure more corporate buying into acceptance of the scheme by convincing all of those involved in the booking and procurement of meetings, events and accommodation to use only AIM-certified companies by including AIM accreditation as a tender or bid pre-requisite.

A recent survey conducted by the mia in association with *The Business Travel Magazine* revealed that 88 per cent of the 500 corporate respondents confirmed that a benchmark of excellence to demonstrate compliance, capability, competence and quality would become a requirement in their decision-making process. The mia's chief executive, Jane Longhurst comments:

> These results show that corporates want an accreditation that tangibly demonstrates overall venue/supplier excellence. There is demonstrable proof that corporates are likely to be influenced by a venue that holds a quality standard, something many of our members are seeing through the financial gains in terms of new and repeat business. We know for a fact that No.11 Cavendish Square has just secured BBC Trust Dinners and the Home Office has chosen the Emmanuel Centre for an event as a direct result of being AIM-accredited. It is great to see British institutions recognising AIM and ultimately placing business with industry suppliers fully committed to meeting and maintaining high standards.

Growing momentum

By 2014, the AIM message had momentum. Venue search portals are including AIM as a search filter and several of the country's leading venue finding agents are requesting that venues have AIM accreditation. AIM is achieving its objectives, driving the industry to become more competitive and accountable, to deliver great value and help clients consistently achieve ROI.

In 2013, the Hotel Booking Agents Association endorsed AIM, recognising that the accreditation supports its core objective of assisting the industry in raising standards and delivering best practice through service and facilities. It also acknowledged that achieving AIM would be a benefit to its members, as it promotes professionalism and gives them a distinct competitive advantage. The endorsement is expected to increase significantly the choice buyers have of venues that offer AIM's reassurance of compliance, capability and competence.

Going global

Once AIM meets its objectives and achieves full uptake in the UK, the mia hopes to introduce the scheme to the international meetings and events industry. The International Standards Certification reports that companies are particularly interested in achieving quality (ISO 9001), environmental impact (ISO 14001) and health and safety (OHSAS 18001) accreditation. This shows that quality is a key concern in the global meeting and event agenda and AIM can help guide planners, buyers, venues and suppliers in their quest for excellence.

For more information on AIM, visit www.aimaccredited.co.uk.

SUMMARY

We live in a world of constant and, it seems, ever faster change. It is encouraging to witness some very positive changes affecting the conference, conventions and business events industry that will enhance the quality, professionalism and stature of the industry. Robust research, consistent use and interpretation of terminology, education and continuing professional development programmes attuned to market needs and the establishment of quality standards and performance measures are all vital building blocks in the creation of a strong and appropriate infrastructure for the sector. Much good work is being done but there is also an important need to ensure that all these developments and innovations are managed in a coherent way and in a way that will minimise duplication of effort and maximise their benefits for venues, destinations and the industry as a whole.

REVIEW AND DISCUSSION QUESTIONS

- Discuss the main challenges to developing research programmes for the business events sector with consistent methodologies and approaches in order to enable more robust comparisons between countries to be made. Suggest ways in which these challenges may be overcome and illustrate your answer with examples of best practice from at least two countries.

- Review the principal issues regarding the terminology in use in the conference and business events sector. How could a more cohesive and standardised use of terminology be best achieved globally?

- Compare and contrast the range of international education programmes and qualifications available within the conference and meetings sector. Assess whether these programmes and qualifications are providing unnecessary duplication and potential confusion or whether they are fulfilling a discrete need and niche. Describe any important gaps in the existing provision and suggest how, and by whom, these might be filled.

- Undertake a survey of conference and meeting venues in a particular destination or region to ascertain and evaluate the quality assurance schemes they have in place. Critically discuss these schemes' particular strengths and weaknesses, with particular reference to the needs of the event organiser and meeting planner.

BIBLIOGRAPHY

BestCities (2014) *Understanding BestCities Service Standards*, published online at http://www.bestcities.net/ (accessed 28 July 2015).
Bowdin, G., J. Allen, W. O'Toole, R. Harris and I. McDonnell (2011) *Events Management*, Oxford: Elsevier.

DNH (1996) *Tourism: Competing with the Best – People Working in Tourism and Hospitality*, Department of National Heritage (now Department for Culture, Media and Sport).

ICCA (2013) *A Modern History of International Association Meetings 1963–2012*, International Congress and Convention Association.

ICCA (2014) *International Meeting Statistics for 2013*, International Congress and Convention Association.

Jones, C. and D. James   (2005) 'The tourism satellite account (TSA): a vision, challenge and reality', *Tourism*, 123, Quarter 2.

Rogers, T. (2013) *Conferences and Conventions: A Global Industry*, 3rd edn, London: Routledge.

Appendix

The main meetings industry exhibitions

Exhibition	Focus	Location	Website
Best of Events	Germany	Dortmund	www.bo-e.de
Conventa	Southeast Europe	Ljubljana	www.conventa.si
EMITT	Turkey	Istanbul	www.emittistanbul.com/en
FITUR	Spain, Southern Europe	Madrid	www.ifema.es/fitur_06
Salon Bedouk	France	Paris	www.salon.bedouk.com
MCE CEE	Central, Eastern Europe	Warsaw	www.europecongress.com
Meeting Planners Russia	Russia	Moscow	www.europecongress.com
Convene	Baltics	Vilnius	www.convene.lt
BIT	Italy	Milan	www.bit.fieramilano.it/en
Meetings Africa	South Africa	Johannesburg	www.meetingsafrica.co.za
AIME	Australia, Southeast Asia	Melbourne	www.aime.com.au
DMAI Destinations Showcase	USA	Washington and Chicago	www.destinationsshowcase.com
International Confex	UK, International	London	www.international-confex.com
ibtm arabia	Gulf	Abu Dhabi	www.ibtmarabia.com

Exhibition	Focus	Location	Website
UITT	Ukraine	Kiev	www.uitt-kiev.com/en
IT&CM China	China	Shanghai	www.itcmchina.com
IMEX	International	Frankfurt	www.imex-frankfurt.com
ibtm america	US, International	Chicago	www.ibtmamerica.com
IT&CM India	India	Delhi	www.itcmindia.com
SuisseEMEX	Switzerland	Zurich	www.suisse-emex.ch
ibtm china	China	Beijing	www.cibtm.com
IT&CMAsia	Asia	Bangkok	www.itcma.com
IMEX America	US, International	Las Vegas	www.imex-america.com
BTC	Italy	Florence	www.btc.it
ibtm world	International	Barcelona	www.ibtmworld.com
MBT Market	Germany	Munich	www.mbt-market.de
The Meetings Show	UK, International	London	www.themeetingsshow.com
Square Meal Venues and Events Live	UK	London	www.venuesandevents.co.uk
ibtm africa	Africa	Cape Town	www.ibtmafrica.com
icomex	Central and South America, Caribbean	Mexico City	www.icomex-mexico.com

Index

Aberdeen 234, 239–40
Abu Dhabi: Abu Dhabi
    Convention Bureau 196,
    239–40; Abu Dhabi National
    Exhibitions Company 105
Accepted Practices Exchange
    (APEX) 263, 272
Accredited in Meetings (AIM)
    283–8
accommodation providers 10
Accor Hotels 238
action plan 47
Adelaide 240; Adelaide
    Convention Centre
    127–8; Team Adelaide 234
advertising 85–90
annual general meeting 5
Antibes 13
association management
    company (AMC) 14
ASTM International/American
    Society for Testing and
    Materials 230
Atlanta 94
ATLAS 271
Austin Convention and
    Visitors Bureau 108; Austin
    Convention Center 220
Australia 253, 261, 270; Tourism
    Australia 105, 196, 261
Austrian Convention Bureau 240

Barcelona 105
Beijing: China National
    Convention Centre 126

Berlin 105, 119, 239, 262
BestCities Global Alliance 239,
    274–5
bidding 164–7, 191–7
Birmingham: Hilton
    Birmingham Metropole 75;
    International Convention
    Centre 181; National
    Exhibition Centre 197
blogs 190
Bogotá 239
Branding 44–6; brand alignment
    214–15
Bristol 199–200
Brussels 119
Buffer 108
Business Events Australia 261
business extenders 173–4
business-to-business (B2B)
    marketing 19, 109
business retention 171–3
Business Events Council of
    Australia (BECA) 243
Business Visits and Events
    Partnership (BVEP) 243
Buyers: association buyers 6;
    corporate buyers 5–7;
    government and public
    sector buyers 7; SMERF
    buyers 7

Calgary 166, 239
Canada 253, 270
Cannes 13, 43, 218
Cape Town 239–40

caterers 10
Certificate in International
    Conference Centre
    Management 282
Certificate in Meetings
    Management (CMM) 265–6
Certified Destination
    Management Executive
    (CDME) 267–8
Certified Meeting Professional
    266–7
Chiba 195
Chicago Convention & Visitor
    Bureau x, 105, 239
Cleveland Convention Center
    224–5
Colorado Convention Center 217
competency standards in event
    management 270
competitor analysis 39
conference ambassador
    programme 121–6, 136–7
Conference Centres of
    Excellence 239
conference production company
    16
content marketing 188–91
convention and visitor bureau
    12, 48
Convention Industry Council
    263, 266, 272–3
Copenhagen 119, 239
cross-selling 143–4
customer relationship
    management (CRM) 19–20, 70

Cvent 74
Czech Convention
    Bureau 240

Daejeon 240
Dallas: Dallas Convention and
    Visitors Bureau 190; Kay
    Bailey Hutchinson Center 218
delegates 8–9
Denmark 253
destination guides 69–71
destination management 188,
    201
destination management
    company (DMC) 15, 159
Destination Marketing
    Association International
    (DMAI) 12, 259, 274;
    Certified Destination
    Management Executive
    (CDME) 267–8; Professional
    in Destination Management
    (PDM) 267–8
destination marketing
    organisation (DMO) 11, 45–8,
    233–9
destination selling strategies
    169–76
Detroit 2; Cobo Center 218;
    Detroit Metro Convention and
    Visitors Bureau 61–4
direct marketing 99–102; direct
    response media advertising
    100; direct mail 100; e-mail
    100; telemarketing 100
Dubai 116, 119, 166, 192, 239
Dublin: The Convention Centre
    Dublin 90–2, 181–2
Durban 119, 240

economic impacts 21–3, 28–31
Edinburgh: Convention
    Edinburgh 70–1, 164, 239;
    delegate reward card 174;
    Edinburgh International
    Conference Centre 24;
    positioning 42
employment generation 22
Energy Cities Alliance 239–40
enquiry handling 159–63
environmental impacts 23–5
Estonian Convention Bureau
    240

European Cities Marketing 268–70
European Green Capital 199
European National Convention
    Bureaux Alliance 240
Eurostar 43
Exhibiting 109–15, 129–30; list
    of the main meetings industry
    exhibitions 290–1; virtual
    exhibition 131–2
Exhibition and Event
    Association of Australia 110

Facebook 102, 104, 105, 108
Fáilte Ireland 196–7
familiarisation trips 117–21,
    133–4
Finland Convention Bureau 12,
    240
Flickr 105, 108
foursquare 105, 108
French Riviera Convention
    Bureau 13
Future Convention Cities
    Initiative 240

German Convention Bureau 12,
    201–4, 240, 261
Glasgow City Marketing Bureau
    69, 154, 201, 236
Global Science and Convention
    Alliance (The) 240
GMI Fam Club 118
Gold Coast Convention and
    Exhibition Centre 27–8
Gold Standard 25
Google+ 105
Gratis software 163
Great Ambassador Networking
    Group (GANG) 136–8
Green Meeting and Industry
    Council 230

Hilton Hotels 238; Hilton
    Birmingham Metropole 75;
    Hilton Honors 173; Hilton
    San Diego 24; Hilton
    Worldwide 45
Historic Conference Centres of
    Europe 239
Holland Marketing 240
Hong Kong Convention and
    Exhibition Centre 229–30
Hootsuite 108

hosted buyer programmes
    126–7
Houston 239
Hungarian Convention Bureau
    240
Hyatt Gold Passport 173
Hyderabad 240

ibtm china 126–7
ibtm world 129–30, 253, 260
IMEX 260; IMEX Politicians
    Forum (The) 247–9
incentive trip 6
independent meeting planner 14
infrastructure costs 22
Instagram 105
Intellectual Capitals 192–93
intermediaries 11–16
Intercontinental Hotels 238
International Association of
    Conference Centres (IACC)
    109, 260, 282–3
International Association of
    Exhibitions and Events
    (IAEE) 260
International Association
    of Professional Congress
    Organisers (IAPCO) 263
International Congress and
    Convention Association
    (ICCA) 40, 124–6, 165, 187,
    252, 254; ICCA's Big Data
    search tool 276–82
International Journal of Event
    and Festival Management 272
ISO 9001:2008 273

Jockey Club venues 177–8
Joint Meetings Industry Council
    242, 253
Journal of Convention and Event
    Tourism 272

Kempinski Group 45
key performance indicators
    (KPIs) 49–50
Klout 108
Kraków 227–9
Kyoto Convention Bureau 93–4

Las Vegas: MGM Grand 9;
    University of Nevada 271
Leading Hotels of the World 239

leakage 23
LEED certification 219
LinkedIn 104–5, 125
Lisbon 195
Liverpool 236–7; ACC Liverpool 167; Club Liverpool 121; Liverpool Convention Bureau 71
Lobbying 77–8, 242–5; IMEX Politicians Forum (The) 247–9
London 119, 191, 240; Central Hall Westminster 225–7; ExCeL London 105, 262; QE11 Conference Centre 70, 222; The Westminster Collection 239; Wembley Conference Centre 3
Luxury Travel Market 43

Madhya Pradesh Tourism Development Corporation 198
Malaysia 105, 195; Kuala Lumpur Convention Centre 262; Sarawak Convention Bureau 166
Malta 7
Manchester 236–7; Visit Manchester 70
market segmentation 41–7
market positioning 41–7
marketing mix 48–9
marketing orientation 17–8
marketing plan 39–42, 47–50
marketing research 39–40
Marriott Hotels 238
Mauritius 41
Meet in Reykjavik 240
Meeting Professionals International (MPI) 253, 270–1
Meetings Industry Association (mia) 163; Accredited in Meetings (AIM) 283–8
Melbourne 191, 239
Mercure Hotels 45
Mexico 43, 253
Milwaukee 245–7
Montenegro National Convention Bureau 240
Montréal: Palais des Congrès de Montréal 124; Tourisme Montréal 59–1, 190
Moscow Convention Bureau 31–4

national tourism authority (NTA) 11
national tourism organisation (NTO) 11
National Meetings Week 243
negotiating 169–71
NewcastleGateshead 78, 191
New Orleans 218
New York 43, 173
New Zealand 192
news releases 82–3
newsletters 70
Niagara Falls Convention Center 24
Nice 13
Norway 89, 240

Oberoi Hotel Group 130
Orlando (Visit Orlando) 106
Ottawa Conference Centre 24, 219

PEMES (Polish Event Management Educators Symposium) 272
personal selling 143–7
PEST/PESTLE analysis 40
Phoenix Convention and Visitor Bureau 105
Pinterest 105, 108
Pittsburgh 245–7
Poland Convention Bureau 240, 261
Portland 245–7
Prague 119, 195, 240
press relations 77
product launch 6
production orientation 17
professional conference organiser (PCO) 14, 159
Professional in Destination Management (PDM) 267–8
prospecting 146–7
public relations 75–85; Atlanta Convention Bureau's I Am ATL campaign 94–5; Kyoto Convention Bureau's PR campaign 93–4
Puerto Rico Convention Center 218

Qatar National Convention Centre 217
quality standards 272–5

Radian 6 108
radio frequency identification (RFID) 216
Radisson Hotels 238
Raleigh Convention Center 220
request for proposal (RFP) 74
research 252–62; marketing research 39–40
retreat 6
roadshows 115–17
Rwanda Convention Bureau 50–6

sales orientation 17
sales meeting 5
sales promotion 147–50
San Diego 24
San Francisco 240
San Sebastian 24
Sarawak Convention Bureau 166
Scotland 195
SCVNGR 105–6
Seattle Convention & Visitor Bureau 105
Seoul 56–9, 240
selling (personal) 143–7; upselling 143; cross-selling 143
Serbia Convention Bureau 240
Simply Measured 108
Singapore 119, 239; Singapore's Sales Incentives and Event Support Programmes 174–7
site inspections/showrounds 167–9
situation analysis 39
Slovak Convention Bureau 240
Slovenian Convention Bureau 240
Snapchat 102
SnapEvent 223–4
social and cultural impacts 25–6
social concierge services 105
social media 102–9, 225–7
societal marketing orientation 18
Sol Meliá Hotels 238
South Africa 192, 270
staff training 6
Starwood Hotels and Resorts 171, 238
Stavanger 239–40
subvention 193–7

Sunderland (Unispace Sunderland) 178–81
suppliers 9–10
sustainability 198–200, 204–9, 219–20, 229–30
Switzerland: Swiss Tech Convention Centre, Lausanne 219; Switzerland Convention and Incentive Bureau 105, 129–30, 240
SWOT analysis 39–40
Sydney 240; Sydney International Convention and Exhibition Centre 105, 234

Tampere 204–9
Taxes: contribution to government revenues 22; US transient tax 13; VAT rate in Mexico 43
technical services 10, 16
technology 215–16, 224–5
terminology 263–4
Three City Alliance (The) 245–7
Tokyo 239
Toronto Convention and Visitors Association 106, 240
Toulouse 240
Tourism Australia 105, 196, 261

tourism satellite account (TSA) 253
Tourisme Montréal 59–61, 190–1
transport providers 10
TrendsWatch report 40
Turespaña (Tourist Office of Spain) 131–2
Twitter 102–8

Union of International Associations (UIA) 40, 252, 254–8
Unique Venues 238
Unispace Sunderland 178–81
United Kingdom 74, 194, 213, 243, 253, 261, 270
upselling 143
USA 3, 13, 28–31, 253
Utrecht 195

Vancouver 239; Vancouver Convention Centre 182–4, 220
venue finding service (VFS) 14
venue representation service 177–8
venue selling strategies 153–9
venues 9, 212–14; trends in venue design 216–19; venues

and sustainability 219–20, 229–30; venue security and accessibility 220–3; venues' use of technology 215–16, 224–5
Vienna 41, 70, 105, 164; Austria Center Vienna 75; The Hofburg Vienna 262
Vine 105
virtual exhibition 131–2
VisitDenmark 240

Web 2.0 73, 103–4
websites 72–5, 90–2
workshops 115–17, 127–9, 132–6
World Tourism Organisation (UNWTO) 248, 253
Wroclaw 43

yield management 149–50
YouTube 104–5, 108
York: The York Minster to Westminster showcase 132–6; VisitYork4Meetings's direct marketing campaign 102
Yukon Convention Bureau 164